Islamophobia in France

Islamophobia in France

The Construction of the "Muslim Problem"

Abdellali Hajjat and
Marwan Mohammed

Translated by Steve Garner

The University of Georgia Press
ATHENS

Sociology of Race and
Ethnicity web page

English translation © 2023 by the University of Georgia Press
Athens, Georgia 30602
www.ugapress.org
All rights reserved
Designed by Kaelin Chappell Broaddus
Set in 10.5/13.5 Garamond Premier Pro Regular
by Classic City Composition

Most University of Georgia Press titles are
available from popular e-book vendors.

Printed digitally

Library of Congress Cataloging-in-Publication Data

Names: Hajjat, Abdellali, author. | Mohammed, Marwan, author. |
    Garner, Steve, translator.
Title: Islamophobia in France : the construction of the "Muslim
    problem" / Abdellali Hajjat and Marwan Mohammed ;
    translated by Steve Garner.
Other titles: Islamophobie, comment les élites françaises fabriquent
    le problème musulman. English
Description: Athens : The University of Georgia Press, 2023. |
    Series: Sociology of race and ethnicity | Includes bibliographical
    references.
Identifiers: LCCN 2022034821 | ISBN 9780820363240 (hardback)
    | ISBN 9780820363257 (paperback) | ISBN 9780820363264
    (ebook)
Subjects: LCSH: Islamophobia—France—History. | Islam—
    Study and teaching—France. | Islam and politics—France. |
    Muslims—France—Social conditions. | France—Ethnic
    relations.
Classification: LCC DC34.5.M87 H34613 2023 |
    DDC 305.6/970944—dc23/eng/20220728
LC record available at https://lccn.loc.gov/2022034821

Originally published in French as *Islamophobie: Comment les élites
françaises fabriquent le «problème musulman»*.
© Editions La Découverte, Paris, 2013, 2016

CONTENTS

ACKNOWLEDGMENTS

We would like to thank Valérie Amiraux, Thomas Deltombe, and AbdoolKarim Vakil for their careful proofreading of all or part of the manuscript and the relevance of their comments, as well as Steve Garner who made this translation into English possible. We are also indebted to Zahra Ali, Marielle Debos, Imen El Bakkali, Nawal El Yadari, Alain Gresh, Mohamed Kaf, Paul Pasquali, Patrick Simon, and Dominique Vidal, who provided comments on individual chapters. We are grateful to the speakers and participants of the Islamophobia seminar at the École des hautes études en sciences sociales (2011–2014), in which we presented and discussed our hypotheses. Finally, we thank Robin Virgin, Adam and Sheïma Merbouche, Sarah and Abdallah Hacène, Naëla Likovic and the families Aitouchen, Bella, Chakir, El Bakkali, El Bastaki, Mohammed, and Hajjat.

This book is dedicated to the memory of Ali Hajjat (1938–2021).

Islamophobia in France

INTRODUCTION

At the end of September 2019, while this new version of the introduction was being written, three stories, varying in importance, received media coverage in France. Chronologically, the first involved Laurent Bouvet, professor of political science at the University of Versailles-Saint-Quentin-en-Yvelines; member of the Conseil national de la laïcité (National Council on Secularism) appointed by the minister of education; and founder and leader of the Printemps républicain (Republican Spring), an organization identifying itself as part of the French Left. Bouvet had mocked up a modified version of a poster produced by the Fédération des conseils de parents d'élèves (FCPE; Federations of Parents' Councils) and posted it online. The original image showed a Muslim woman wearing a headscarf, smiling with her child, and the slogan: "Yes I'm going on a school trip, so what? *Laïcité* is about including all parents in the school, with no exceptions." Bouvet felt this statement was an affront to the principle of secularism or *laïcité*, which refers to the French version of the official separation between church and state. Along with activists from his movement and others from the Far Right, Bouvet published a photomontage (based on the original image from the poster) in which the woman wearing a headscarf and her daughter were replaced with two bearded Isis fighters wearing combat fatigues and holding Kalashnikovs. Muslim women wearing headscarves were thus treated as a visual synonym for a terrorist threat and symbolic of enemies to be fought. On 24 September 2019 the FCPE lodged a case of "incitement to hatred" against Bouvet, a figure embodying the middle-class, neorepublican left in France whose ideas resonate far beyond the confines of that political orientation.[1] Indeed, far from being confined to the Left, his opinions are often communicated by the far-right press, in which he pens articles and answers readers' questions. This headscarf affair, one of so many that it is no longer worth keeping count, re-ignited a recurring debate in France on laïcité, its moral economy, and its legal parameters.

The death of former president Jacques Chirac, on 26 September 2019, immediately stifled this controversy. Chirac was a high-profile personality in the Fifth Republic, and numerous articles and debates engaged with his work and legacy. Alongside the race to eulogize him that featured in editorial opinion pieces, many critical assessments underlined his more negative contribution to the fate of France and its minorities. Among the many things for which he was blamed was the Act of 15 March 2004, which banned conspicuous religious symbols (including headscarves) in state schools. This act became law under his presidency, and it was his initiative to establish a commission—chaired by his appointee Bernard Stasi—that laid the foundations for the ban. It was the first piece of legislation to extend the duty of religious neutrality to public-service users rather than just civil servants, as had been the case since the early twentieth century. This legal loophole has been steadily widening to the point that it has now become the norm. Indeed, since this act was passed, political forces have continuously sought to extend this duty of religious neutrality to the users of other public services—and even to services provided by the private sector. The right of mothers wearing headscarves to accompany their children on school trips had become a battleground for religious freedom and equality—for those supporting them—and a struggle against Islamism and fundamentalism for those seeking to neutralize this form of visible Muslim identification. The FCPE poster was also criticized by the then-minister of education, Jean-Michel Blanquer, as well as the Right and the Far Right but also by two far-left organizations: Lutte ouvrière (Workers' Struggle) and the Parti de gauche (Party of the Left).

In Paris, on 28 September 2019, two days after President Chirac's death, a convention of the Right took place. It was organized by the far-right activist Marion Maréchal Le Pen, the granddaughter of Jean-Marie Le Pen, founder of the Front National. Now known as the Rassemblement national and led by Marine Le Pen (Jean-Marie's daughter and Marion Maréchal Le Pen's aunt), the party is the leading far-right xenophobic and nationalist party in France. The 2019 convention attracted more than a thousand people to debate "the alternative to progressivism." It comprised a succession of speakers from various strands of the Far Right, talking primarily about immigration and Islam. The star guest was Éric Zemmour, a successful journalist and essay writer, labeled a "hero of his generation" by a member of Les Républicains (the largest right-wing party in France). Zemmour repeatedly referred to Muslims as dangerous fifth columnists and "colonizers," comparing djellabas and Islamic headgear to instruments of "de facto propaganda. The islamization of the street, like the uniforms of an army of occupation, remind the vanquished of their subjection."

This rhetoric is drawn directly from the far-right "great replacement" theory, whose architect is writer Renaud Camus, whom Zemmour congratulated several times during his speech. Camus was a significant source of inspiration for the white supremacist terrorist who carried out an attack on two mosques in Christchurch, New Zealand, which claimed the lives of fifty-one Muslims on 15 March 2019. Zemmour's speech, delivered a few days after he had been sentenced by the courts for "incitement to religious hatred," was broadcast live by the twenty-four-hour news channel LCI (owned by the Bouygues group). The LCI journalists' association quickly moved to "distance itself" from this decision by the channel's management, which later glibly acknowledged that the "format" was indeed not "appropriate": as if the "format" was the problem.

Apart from the death of Jacques Chirac, the week's news was not unusual. Islam has been a "problem" in France for decades. This idea is widely held, judging by the copious quantity of negative images and discourses about the Muslim presence in France (and more broadly in Europe). It can be considered a piece of social "evidence" along the lines of philosopher Fernando Gil's definition, that is, not an irrefutable argument, but rather a belief so deeply anchored that it requires no proof and exonerates itself from reason.[2] In fact, in the French context, it is striking to note that the regular voluntary updating of the "Muslim problem" rarely unfolds through constructed arguments based on evidence but is instead filtered through "sad" emotions and passions.[3]

It could be argued that Islamophobia is a response to the increasing number of violent acts motivated by some forms of Islamic religious belief that have hit France, from the 1995 Paris attacks to the present day. Changes in the position and forms of expression of Islam in France, such as the increase in the number of places of worship, the emergence and affirmation of discourses and strands of thought advocating self-segregation, and the types of rupture with society advocated by some Muslims, should be taken seriously.

These are tangible concrete facts that can be linked, first, to the profound changes in political violence in a world experiencing upheaval and, second, to the far-reaching shifts in forms of religiosity in Europe, regardless of the religion in question. The bloody terrorist attacks that have cast a shadow over France in recent years have doubtlessly amplified the polarization and antagonism in French society, particularly around the Muslim question. Moreover, the insecurity linked to the terrorist threat actually impacts more heavily on the daily lives of Muslims: they must deal with police surveillance and more extensive administrative control, not to mention large-scale discrimination in the labor market.

To appreciate the scale of this discrimination, it should be noted that according to a 2015 study, the obstacles encountered in the labor market by Muslim men in France vis-à-vis Catholic men are six times greater than those encountered by African American men vis-à-vis white men in the United States.[4]

However, it is essential to account for historical context and the multiple roots of Islamophobia if we are to avoid being sucked into a conjunctural and ahistorical vision of social reality that prevents us thinking through the specifics of French Islamophobia. An anti-Muslim atmosphere, described as "paranoid" by political scientist Raphaël Liogier, cuts right across political lines, with a specific intensity and consequences.[5] If this cross-cutting quality is so significant in France, it is because Islamophobia rests on a plethora of foundations deeply rooted in national history and culture.

These cross-party and obsessional dimensions of the rejection of any Muslim religious visibility in the public sphere constitute two markers of the specifics of Islamophobia in the French context compared with other Western countries. How can we fully grasp the manner by which a poster of a smiling Muslim woman, with a text reflecting the current legal status quo and referring to an event so mundane in most countries of the world—the fact that a mother can participate in her child's school trips—could be the object of such profound rejection by political figures located on a spectrum running from the Far Left, identifying as anti-racist, to the white supremacist Far Right?

How can the Muslim population provoke so many unfavorable opinions across party lines, when the rejection of the Other more generally is a salient political dividing line?[6] In seeking to explain this, we do not argue that "everyone is Islamophobic" or that Islamophobia is based on shared characteristics uniting people across the political spectrum, regardless of gender and age, etc. These are lazy statements. Instead, we have to account for the plurality of mechanisms that make this politically bipartisan hostility toward Islam and Muslims possible. The idea of a "mechanism" here refers to the driving forces, the main ideological frameworks and social dynamics, that enable adherence to all or some of the forms of Islamophobic expression.

Several long-term historical currents of varying significance now facilitate the expression, spread, and transmission of Islamophobia. These currents are dynamic rather than static and must be placed within their contexts. There is no such thing as a one-size-fits-all, age-old Islamophobia intrinsically bound up in European identity and expressed from one period to another by a mechanical and recurring hostility unaltered since the Middle Ages.[7] The Muslim question in Europe, and particularly in France, has a long and far from linear history, even if it has frequently been characterized by conflict in many respects.

Christian "Anti-Mohammedism"

France did not discover Islam either through the development of its colonial empire or the arrival of immigrants as former colonial subjects in the last century, who came for reasons ranging from the military (to join the French armed forces) to the political (to live in a country enjoying the rule of law) or to the economic (to make a more comfortable life for themselves). A specific *anti-Muslim archive* has steadily accumulated over a long historical period of exposure, in which Islam and Muslims have been configured as the dangerous and/or inferior Other, in both theological thinking and Western politics. This archive is the fruit of the ideological and cultural production of a very diverse group of actors (theologians, philosophers, scholars, diplomats, governments, scientists, journalists, etc.) mobilized in particular social and historical arenas. These include a response to the Muslim conquests of Europe, the Crusades, the decline of the Ottoman Empire, opposition to European and U.S. imperialism, immigration to Europe from Muslim-majority countries, post–Cold War geopolitical and warlike reconfigurations, etc. The initial representations of Islam and Muslims in Europe were the outputs of Christian writers living in Christian and Muslim Europe (Spain, the Balkans) or settled somewhere in the Muslim East, between the seventh and twelfth centuries. The main objective of this work was to fight a competing religious dogma and resist conversions in conquered lands, to justify military conquests that enabled head-to-head engagement with a political enemy growing in power, and lastly, to legitimize the various forms of segregation (legal, spatial, etc.) targeting the Muslim subjects of Christian princes. This Muslim enemy was named in a multitude of ways depending on the place and time period, for example, Arabs, Saracens, Moors, Ishmaelites, Hagarites, Turks, etc.

Orientalist Essentialization

The period from the Reformation to the Enlightenment would be characterized by an even greater diversity of European discourses about Islam and Muslims. The traditional prejudices remained widespread, but the unanimous nature of these discourses was disrupted by the internal struggles within Europe (Protestants and philosophers against the Catholic Church), a profound change in the international balance of power due to the growth and decline of the Ottoman empire, and lastly, the progressive willingness (on the part of the West) to acquire knowledge that embodies Orientalism. Negative representations of Islam and Muslims thus became more secular and diverse, even if Christian anti-

Mohammedism overlaps with emergent Orientalist framings. The Christian monopoly of "anti-Mohammedism" was eroded by competition from Orientalism, that is, the construction of a negative Muslim otherness drawn from the arts, literature and, increasingly, science. The role of Orientalist authors turned out to be decisive. They perceived and constructed the Orient as a space comprised of societies to be explored and colonized on the basis of rationales that were both economic (primary goods, workforces, etc.) and political (struggles for influence between Western states). These colonial explorations resulted in a three-way division of the world: into civilized Western Europe; the world of the "savage," devoid of both history and culture; and, between the two, the Orient, made up of once great but now declining civilizations. While producing a body of pioneering knowledge about the societies of the East, Orientalism enabled not only the scientific legitimation of colonial but also active participation in conquest by Orientalists: the desire for knowledge and the desire for power are often bound up in one another. The Orientalist vision has not gone away. Indeed, it is still part and parcel of the legitimization of the idea that Muslim people's behavior is determined more by their religious affiliation than by political, economic, or social rationales.

Assimilationism and Colonialism

This ideological labor of essentializing identity mirrors the theories establishing the existence of races within mankind, where those races reflect hierarchical biological and psychological substrata of populations. The articulation of religion with race in these streams of thought helped racialize religious affiliation. This is one viewpoint that colonial domination used as a basis for developing a racial definition of nationality and citizenship. For instance, in a law of 1830, indigenous Muslims defeated in the wake of the conquest of Algeria became subjects of an Empire that refused them citizenship and subjected them to a distinct, parallel penal code: the *indigénat* regime. This system of legalized discrimination can be explained by the colonial power's desire to retain control, as well as its belief—still alive and kicking—in the racial and civilizational inferiority of Muslims.

Within the realm of political thought, the civil service and public opinion inherited the concept of "assimilation" from this colonial period.[8] This initially polysemic idea circulated between the metropolis and the colonies, acquiring legal status and aiming increasingly to measure the discrepancy and distance between subjects of empire as potential full citizens and foreigners applying for nationality in metropolitan France. In 1927 a French Nationality Act was passed;

its provisions for implementation mentioned a condition called "assimilation," which makes the racialized, and rarely made explicit, vision of the French nation and its Republican institutions visible. An analysis of the rejection of naturalization because of a lack of assimilation between 1927 and 2007 highlights two factors leading to the denial of citizenship applications: a linguistic pretext linked with a cultural one, applied mainly to Muslim women who wear the hijab. More broadly, this concept of assimilation could be considered a wider cultural embargo entailing the requirement to strip oneself of visible cultural or religious markers in order to melt into a vaguely defined national "lifestyle." French assimilationism is one of the driving forces of Islamophobia in France.

Xenophobia's New Progressive Clothes

The nonassimilable nature of Muslim populations and the incompatibility of cultures and civilizations are ideas that permeate white supremacist discourses of rejection of the Other. Contemporary Islamophobia extends, completes, and interlocks with "traditional" racism, which targets minorities deemed undesirable to have within national borders. Islam here is viewed as the extension of the Other's religion, that is, a foreign religion. This form of Islamophobia can be found above all, but not exclusively, on the right of the political landscape. The confusion brought about by the Far Right's appropriation of "progressive" struggles such as the defense of laïcité and feminism should not obscure these racist foundations. From this perspective, Islamophobia has sanctioned a continuation of anti-Arab racism behind the mask of defending both the Republic and women. Indeed, when it comes to criticizing the presence of women wearing hijab, whether that be in a union, a business, at university, on a public beach, or even a television singing competition, the world of politics shows its "feminist" colors: it is in favor of gender equality defined as one of the drivers of a supposed "French" culture, and of republican values whose content is often presented as the opposite of Islam.

Feminism and Islamophobia

Moreover, in France, the fact that the issue of wearing a hijab is the main building block in the construction of the "Muslim" problem is also tied to the way in which the French feminist movement was developed in the second half of the twentieth century. Although it underwent many struggles and had significant successes, this movement, at least in its organized and institutionalized form, i.e., the Collectif national pour le droit des femmes (CNDF, National Collective for Women's Rights) mainly consisted of upper and middle-class white women, whose relationship with working-class and racialized minority women was neglected for a long time, before becoming a focus for criticism. Ironically, French feminism has had to fight for gender equality within French republicanism, and anxieties around the hijab stem from the precarious gains of feminism in the context of French patriarchy. Indeed, the construction of the practice of wearing the hijab as a "public problem" crashed head-on into the feminist movement and its unexamined assumptions, contributing to the movement's fragmentation. The dominant stance within the feminist movement was to consider the hijab as a reactionary religious-political demand, threatening the status of women. Some Muslim women, particularly those who supported the Ni putes ni soumises organization, shared this stance, stating that outlawing the hijab was a way to make Muslim women's inclusion possible. Not taking subjectivity or women's choice into account, this position framed the hijab as a clothing statement to be countered per se, as it was presumed to be both antisecular and anti-Republican, and was a result of women being manipulated from behind the scenes by a retrograde masculinity. A dynamic and minority strand of French feminism did adopt a different interpretation and above all refused to analyze the issue through this "top down" frame, without considering the opinions of the Muslim women targeted in this political discourse.

However, the fact remains that the anti-hijab consensus that rapidly structured the feminist movement's mainstream response sanctioned the legitimization of the idea that the Muslim presence posed serious problems for women, and that some of its visible expressions were to be combated. By deploying the "hijab problem" as their frame, left, right, and far-right movements and politicians were thus able to appropriate feminist topics on the basis of a "femonationalism" that mobilized gender equality to help promote a nationalist agenda advocating the exclusion of Muslim women.

"Laïcité" as a Battleground

Like gender equality, laïcité is a household term in France. Intense struggles surround its definition and the ways in which it is applied through the law. France and the USA are countries whose constitution specifies and organizes the separation of church and state, which makes the latter formally neutral vis-à-vis the former. This principle theoretically establishes the moral equality of its citizens and freedom of conscience.[9] The proportion of people stating they have "no religion" is similar in each country. On both sides of the Atlantic, around two-thirds of people say they are Christians, while those with "no religion" make up

20–25 percent of the population. However, the ways in which the relationship between church and state is structured, and how the recognition of religious groups is organized in daily social life in the USA and in France diverge drastically, despite the longstanding Christian roots of both nations.

In France, several phases were required to properly establish the secularization process. An initial "secularization threshold" dates back to the French Revolution, which set out the principle of freedom of worship and the recognition of the state's civil and secular character.[10] Despite the restoration of the monarchy and the various counterrevolutionary events of the nineteenth century, this trend would be bolstered through the mechanism of state schools between 1879 and 1882 and the passage of the various education acts piloted through the National Assembly by Jules Ferry. These acts banned religiously derived civic education classes and broke the Ministry of Religion's grip on primary education. The law on the separation of church and state of 9 December 1905 established the principle of laïcité for the long haul. It was structured around a balance between "freedom of conscience" and "freedom of worship," as well as the fact that "the Republic does not recognize, pay for or subsidize any religious group." The principles of separation, freedom, equality, and nondiscrimination structured this act, after decades of antagonism and tension between the supporters of the Catholic Church and those backing the principle of the secularization of public authority. The secular principle, first written into the 1905 Act, and for which Aristide Briand and Jean Jaurès advocated strongly, was drafted into the wording of the Constitution of the Fifth Republic in 1958 ("France is an indivisible, secular, democratic, and social Republic").

This overall balance was challenged by the passage of the Act of 15 March 2004, which marked a major legal and political turning point. The origin and the conflictual, antagonistic, and beleaguered foundations of French republican secularism, and the threatening historical period in which it found itself, left deep traces in its culture and political institutions. Overcoming an omnipresent and stifling Catholic Church, the victory of the secularists was won at the cost of a collective "distancing from religious belonging," henceforth considered both an impediment to individual emancipation and a negative reminder of the past, a step backward. In its French conceptual form, laïcité is not just an organizing principle of relations between church and state: it has also been a means of ensuring national cohesion and individual emancipation and is the basis for modern citizenship. This principle is therefore regarded as a value in itself, like a superior normative benchmark. Laïcité has therefore been recently redefined as *néo-laïcité*, that is, the new French hegemonic and authoritarian mode of framing religion. The principle of religious neutrality no longer set its sights solely on public servants but now also on service users and private-sector workers. Ever since 2004, néo-laïcité has become a mechanism for controlling the bodies and minds of those perceived to be Muslims, through a capillary-like process.

The American Mirror

The end of the eighteenth century was also a crucial period in the USA, with the Bill of Rights being passed into law in 1791. The bill stipulates in its First Amendment that it is not the responsibility of Congress to establish or prohibit the existence of a religion, or its practices. Despite the image of a religious society, with ubiquitous references to God on banknotes and in political speeches, the U.S. Constitution makes virtually no reference to religion, apart from Article VI, which bans religious oaths as means of accessing jobs in the federal government civil service. Influenced by the rationalist Enlightenment thinkers, the founders of the nascent republic avoided imposing an official religion on a multifaith society. However, it was only in the mid-twentieth century that a Supreme Court ruling extended this principle to state legislations. The First Amendment of the Bill of Rights, a legal and constitutional keystone of the relationship between faith groups and the State, has primarily been "interpreted by the Courts as guaranteeing the state's neutrality as regards faith groups, as well as between religious and secular spheres."[11] The secularization of American public institutions and political rituals—through the mechanism of court rulings— has, as in France, been played out in the field of education, although the process took place much later in France. Reading the Bible in school, prayers led by a teacher, and the teaching of creationism have been ruled unconstitutional. Yet with more conservative U.S. presidents coming to power at the end of the twentieth century, a certain flexibility in this respect has been observed. However, the First Amendment to the Bill of Rights is still used as a legal foundation for the religious stewardship of public institutions.

The state's neutrality in the American version of secularization has thus traveled in a very different direction to that of France. Although American secularization implies that the state is neutral, this does not entail hostility, defiance, or serious tension in regard to both religious institutions and believers. Neutrality is not guided by the necessity to distance or place limits on religions, or make them invisible. As Barb concisely states, "unlike French laïcité, which must protect the State against the potentially harmful influence of religious institutions, in the U.S. context the separation of church and state aims primarily to protect the churches against the state's authoritarian control."[12] This is a difference illustrative of the relationship with religious visibility in public life, especially in terms of dress. The U.S. sanctification of religious freedom has for instance led to Californian state schools allowing Sikhs to wear the kirpan (a ceremonial dagger), whereas in France, in October 2019, after banning Islamic students from wearing hijab in state schools for fifteen years, Minister of Education Jean-Michel Blanquer went further, stating his strong opposition to mothers wearing hijab being allowed on school trips.

Fighting "the Opium of the People"

The struggles against Catholic power since the French Revolution have generated and developed a strong anticlerical tendency in French society, whose cultural influence is still considerable. A subbranch of the anticlerical family identifies with the Left, via a virulent materialist anticlericalism drawing its potency from a superficial understanding of the works of Marx, Engels, Lenin, and Rosa Luxembourg, addressing the relationship between religion and the people. These ideas, which feed into a number of social and political theories, conceptualize religious beliefs as obstacles to acquiring consciousness of "true" social relations and forms of domination nesting in them. Arguing for the prominence of class relations and social issues, these heterogenous schools of thought and action are sometimes tempted to deprioritize rather than find a way to connect racial and religious belonging with a socioeconomic position. From this vantage point, religion in general and Islam especially—due to its anchoring in the working classes—are suspected of obstructing the pathways to social and revolutionary emancipation and preventing the unification of the working class. Thus stigmatized and labeled as claims for "identity politics," demands for equality and sometimes merely the public existence of various minority groups, particularly Muslims, are rejected in a way that opens the door to the convergence around Islamophobic positions of figures from groups located at opposite ends of the political spectrum.

Islamophobic Media and Political Discourses

The story of the mocked-up poster and the speeches at the convention in the previous section illustrate the emotive, racialized characteristics of political controversies and events involving Muslims and reveals the kind of hostile, defiant reflexes prevailing in media coverage of Islam. Whether it stems from ideological activism or jumping on an ideological bandwagon, this kind of stance is part and parcel of the construction of the "Muslim problem," fueled in large part by the growing power and increasingly frequent Islamophobic discourse with an expanding audience in the media. Indeed, there have been countless comments and speeches by heads of state, cabinet members, professional politicians, journalists, and influential editors and media and academic intellectuals, in which Muslims and Islam are unproblematically stigmatized. These public figures do not all share a single diagnosis of the "Muslim problem" or of its "solution." Indeed, some of them are political or intellectual opponents. This Islamophobic discourse is neither monolithic nor without nuance, but all the protagonists agree that there is such a thing as a "Muslim problem," which the authorities should urgently address. The growing number of Islamophobic comments made, especially during election campaigns and military conflicts, has produced an ideological climate that is particularly hostile to Muslims in France. In the 1990s, then-mayor of Paris Jacques Chirac, also leader of the Rassemblement pour la République (RPR) party, stated that "having Poles, Italians and Portuguese working here poses fewer problems than having Muslims or Blacks."[13] Pierre-André Taguieff, researcher at the Centre de recherches politiques de Sciences Po (Cevipof) commented that "two million Muslims in France means two million potential fundamentalists."[14] In the context of the events of 11 September 2001, well-known author Michel Houellebecq wrote, "Islam is definitely the most stupid religion. When you read the Quran it's devastating."[15] He went on to add, "Islam was born in the middle of the desert, with scorpions, camels and all kinds of ferocious animals around. Do you know what I call Muslims? The losers of the Sahara. That's the only name they deserve [...] Islam could only originate in a stupid desert, in the midst of filthy nomadic tribesmen with nothing to do—excuse my language—but fuck their camels up the ass."[16]

The French translation of Italian journalist Oriana Fallaci's Islamophobic best seller, *The Rage and the Pride*, was quite well received by the media in 2002–2003, despite the violence of her statements. For example, she describes a campaign for identity papers that some Somalis needed "to run around Europe, but didn't let them bring hordes of their relatives into the country." These Somali Muslims, she continues, "disfigured, defiled, and outraged the Piazza del Duomo in Florence [...] A tent [...] furnished like a sloppy flat. Chairs, tables, sofas, mattresses to sleep or to fuck on, cook stoves to prepare food and befoul the square with smoke and stinking smells. And together with all that, the yellow lines of urine that profaned the marbles of the baptistry. Good God! They have big bladders, these sons of Allah."[17] Thus, "the Albanians, Sudanese, Pakistanis, Tunisians, Algerians, Moroccans, Nigerians, and Bangladeshis" are all characterized as "drug traffickers," "bandits," and "savages," "multiplying like rats."[18]

French philosopher Alain Finkielkraut's review states that Fallaci "has the notable merit of not allowing herself to be intimidated by virtuous lies." She "gets stuck right in" and "strives to look reality in the face."[19] Taguieff for his part argues that she is "right on the money, although some might be shocked by how she sometimes expresses herself."[20] *Charlie Hebdo* journalist Robert Misrahi felt that she "demonstrates intellectual courage."[21]

During the 2012 presidential election campaign, influential Gallimard editor Richard Millet, author of a *Literary Eulogy of Anders Breivik* (the Norwegian far-right terrorist),[22] said he had experienced an "absolute nightmare" when he boarded a subway train at Châtelet-les-Halles (a busy station in central Paris) "especially when he was the only white person": "It was painful to have to wonder what country I was in, ethnically, racially, religiously, etc. [...] I can't bear mosques in France."[23] Reacting to the murders carried out by Mohamed Merah in 2012, presidential candidate Nicolas Sarkozy claimed that "generalizations don't make any sense," because "two of our soldiers [murdered by Merah] were, how would you put it [...] Muslim, or looked Muslim, because one was Catholic, but looked Muslim."[24]

A few months later, UMP leader Jean-François Copé popularized the myth of the "pain au chocolat": "My thoughts are with the parents of pupils traumatized because one of their sons, who was eating a snack when he came out of college, had the food snatched out of his hands by a group of youths who thought they were an Iranian Promotion of Virtue brigade. 'Not during Ramadan!' they told him."[25]

The myth of the Islamification of Europe has also been propagated by a number of European and U.S. intellectuals: Oriana Fallaci, Alexandre Del Valle, Gisèle Littman (alias Bat Ye'or), Christopher Caldwell, Timothy M. Savage, Melanie Phillips, etc.[26] Some of them define Islamification, like Renaud Camus (far-right writer and founder of the Innocence Party), as the "great population replacement": the number of Europeans is in decline, whereas the number of immigrants, their descendants, and Muslims, soon to be a majority, is on the up.[27] Others, such as demographer Michèle Tribalat, who claim to use academic standards, define Islamification as the "emergence of a significant and increasingly confident Muslim minority, expressing its needs, which, it is suggested, would change our quality of life and lifestyles, and restrict our freedoms."[28]

The symbolic violence of this Islamophobic media and political discourse reached its climax when actual death threats were issued, with no response from the authorities, despite warnings from anti-racist intellectuals and organizations (see chapter 13). In 2004 Michèle Vianès, a feminist activist based in Lyon, published a book comparing the husbands of women who wear burqas to "guide dogs." "Excuse this ugly but appropriate metaphor," she writes, "the woman is blind, and the husband is the guide dog. Except guide dogs are likeable because they are not responsible for their owner's blindness, and in fact compensate for it. In this case, the opposite is true."[29] Vianès argues that female Muslim doctors lack courage: "What a waste to see these Turkish women get their degrees in medicine and then not go into practice because of pressure exerted on them by their families, which forbid them to treat men! Although they are doctors, it's a shame they don't think of putting cyanide in the family's mint tea!"[30]

In a similar vein, activist Christine Tasin published a virulent article called "What to Do with Muslims Once the Quran Is Banned" on the Boulevard Voltaire website, run by far-right journalists Robert Ménard and Dominique Jamet. In the "dream scenario" that she constructs, "a law has been passed banning the practice of Islam, the sale of the Quran and the act of teaching it in our country, but at the same time of course, guaranteeing the right to believe in God, whether he is referred to as Allah or not." French and foreign Muslims, she goes on to say,

> will have the choice to stay in France, where they will be in a nation where Islam
> has disappeared from sight [. . .]. Those born Muslim will be able to freely give
> up Islam to become apostates or practice their religion in a completely private
> setting [. . .]. If that doesn't suit them, they have the right to go to one of the
> fifty-seven Muslim countries on the planet where there is Sharia law [. . .] Of
> course, there will be challenges to this, riots and even terrorist threats. The au-
> thorities will put a stop to them thanks to their unflagging determination, and
> if a few extremists have to be sacrificed to restore peace and protection to the
> sixty-five million people who live here, it will be made clear that the army, dis-
> patched rapidly to each threat, will not hesitate to meet fire with fire. It's drastic,
> but there is no other way to quieten things down and impose our law.[31]

Islamophobia as a Total Social Fact

This incredibly violent discourse should not detract from the less overtly hostile one, or the more subdued actions of a whole range of social actors who have contributed to the universalization of the "Muslim problem," campaigned for legislation treating Muslims differently, and advocated for the establishment of discriminatory practices toward Muslims. Generalizations and erroneous correlations should, however, be avoided: Jacques Chirac's and Nicolas Sarkozy's discourses, during their periods of presidency, do not follow the same logic as those of Christine Tasin and Renaud Camus, demonstrated when the latter two took part in the International Tribunal against Islamification in 2010 (see chapter 8). As in any definition of a social phenomenon, a number of levels are distinguishable. We have identified three that enable Islamophobia to be analyzed like a form of racism: ideology, prejudices, and practices. If the "media and political discourse" of Islamophobia refers to a form of racist ideology, this is not necessarily true of other forms of Islamophobia which, for example, stem from prejudice.

From this perspective, Islamophobia is no longer split into media and political fields but extends *by a capillary-like process* through other social spaces: state schools, public services, civil service treatment of foreigners, the private sector, and the street.[32] It occurs in state schools, where young girls are banned from wearing "conspicuous" religious emblems (a headscarf or headband, with a long skirt) and mothers who wear hijab are not allowed to accompany children on school trips, and where Muslim children are made to eat nonhalal meat in the school canteen. In public services, women have to take off headgear to get married, receive their naturalization papers, give evidence in court, take exams, or attend work-related training and university. A visible affiliation to a religion can hinder the process of obtaining a residency card or French nationality from the civil service. In the private sector, there is discrimination against both female customers and female employees wearing hijab, and against employees fasting during Ramadan. Finally, there has been a resurgence of Islamophobic actions in the streets, not only from far-right groups but also among ordinary citizens.

So how have we moved from a position where the supporters of banning the headscarf in state schools (who comprised a minority when the first headscarf affair happened in 1989) have become the majority in the 2000s? How have international events such as the conflicts between al-Qaida and NATO played a role in exacerbating issues in the daily lives of the millions of Muslims in France? Through what social processes has a national consensus been arrived at, not only among elites but also partly in popular culture, over the idea that there is a "Muslim problem" that has to be "resolved" by symbolic and physical violence? How has a legal "state of exception" been established, that is, a legal regime departing from common law, in the case of all or some Muslims? In other words, how can we explain sociologically the growth of Islamophobia?

The aim of this book is to provide an answer and suggest areas for reflection in order to comprehend Islamophobia as a "total social fact," that is, as a social phenomenon cutting across "the whole of society and its political, administrative, legal, economic, media and intellectual institutions."[33] Islamophobia "viscerally" engages individuals and social groups, consciously and unconsciously, which mainly explains the "hysterical" and "passionate" dimensions of controversies around the Muslim question.[34] The sociology of Islamophobia therefore enables us to take account of society-wide transformations, in that it informs us about the ways in which the media, political, legal, and intellectual fields function. What can social sciences bring to the table in terms of knowledge about Islamophobia? What are the advances made by, and the limits of, research carried out, for the most part in English-speaking countries?

Although the religious practices of Muslims in France are relatively well known in French social sciences, Islamophobia has not yet been studied widely or in depth, either in the disciplines of history or sociology. The French situation contrasts with that of anglophone academia, where there is a growing corpus of multidisciplinary work on the concept of Islamophobia. For a decade, the term "Islamophobia" has, in the French public sphere, been actively targeted for discrediting, which leaves little space for an even-tempered debate. Some have come out in favor of banning the word from the contemporary lexicon of politics and from the field of anti-racism, based on four semantic and political arguments.

The first is posited by media figures, according to whom the term was invented by Iranian mullahs who aimed to quash all blasphemy. However, as we shall see in chapter 4, the term Islamophobia has no translation into Farsi and was actually invented in 1910 by a group of French Orientalist scholars specializing in the study of West African Islam.

The second argument focuses on the suffix "-phobia," whose use is said to render Islamophobia an irrational fear, evacuating the dimensions of aversion, hatred, and rejection, to justify expressing a pathology. Indeed, why condemn a fear? However, if we consider that the root, "phobos," is not appropriate for naming a rejection or a form of racism, should we not also eliminate other pivotal terms in public discourse such as "xenophobia" and "homophobia"? From an academic point of view, the suffix "-phobia" is not the most suitable, but the social sciences can deploy this term and redefine it by going beyond the "phobic" dimension.

The third argument states that, in the French context, Islamophobia is merely the newest avatar of anti-Arab racism. Yet not all Arabs are Muslim, and not all Muslims are Arabs. Several anglophone sociological studies enable a distinction to be made between discrimination based on racial belonging and discrimination based on religious affiliation and indeed allow links between them to be understood (part 1). Yet if confusion between multiple markers is enough to delegitimize a concept, then we should also bury the word "antisemitism," a term embracing phenotypical, cultural, and religious markers and which even identifies "semitic" people. So, should we thus consign the concept of antisemitism to the trash can? This point should alert us to the fact that there is no perfect concept we can use to identify and analyze necessarily complex social phenomena.

The final argument is that "Islamophobia" can be used as a tool for censorship, restricting freedom of expression, especially criticism of religions. This is a valid comment and highlights a genuine risk, but it is less about the concept and more about how it is used. However, words do sometimes become hostages to political controversies that are bigger than they are. This is also true for the accusation of antisemitism leveled at all criticism of the State of Israel, which fortunately does not discredit the concept of antisemitism.[35] Thus, like all terms describing various forms of "phobia toward Others," the idea of Islamophobia is not perfect but can be applied effectively and is necessary in order to put a name to and examine a phenomenon now measured and explored in the social sciences: one that is fought against by activists and taken seriously by most international organizations and Western governments. Naming a social reality allows its existence to be acknowledged. Not naming it ultimately boils down to socially and politically concealing it.

What is at stake here is therefore to offer a working definition of Islamophobia that, as far as possible, reduces the confusion surrounding it and its problematic uses. As set out in detail in chapter 5, we argue that Islamophobia constitutes a social process of racialization based on signs of belonging (whether actual or assumed) to the Islamic religion and that this process's formats vary by national context and historical period. It is a worldwide, gendered phenomenon, influenced by the international movement of ideas and people and by gender relations. We theorize that Islamophobia is the consequence of the construction of a "Muslim problem," whose "solution" lies in disciplining bodies and even the minds of Muslims and those assumed to be Muslims.

Beyond the construction of a public problem, the roots of Islamophobia can be analyzed as a relationship between "insiders" and "outsiders," as sociologist Norbert Elias suggested we do in regard to European Jews, Black and Hispanic communities in the USA, and Muslims.[36] "Resentment is expressed," explains Elias, "when a socially inferior despised and stigmatized outsider group is *about to demand not only legal but also social equality, when its members begin to access positions which had previously been closed off to them*, i.e., when they begin to come into direct competition with the majority group as socially equal individuals, and perhaps when they hold positions that grant the despised groups a higher status and the chance to wield more power than the insider groups whose social status is lower, and who do not feel secure." In other words, "*a despised, stigmatized and relatively powerless outsider group can be tolerated as long as its members are content with their low standing*, which, according to the insiders, is the proper status for that group, and provided they behave, in compliance with their low status, like subordinate and submissive people."[37]

The emergence of Islamophobia should thus be studied as an *embodiment of the rejection of equality*, which differs, however, from that which other minority groups can experience (women, LGBT, etc.) in that the crucial stake is *the legit-imacy of the Muslim presence on national soil*, just as it was for the antisemitism of the nineteenth and twentieth centuries (see chapter 11). It is indeed no co-incidence that the initial politicization of the Muslim issue in France occurred when immigrant workers were claiming equality with French workers in terms of working conditions and redundancies (see chapter 6). As sociologist Pierre Bourdieu underlines, in relation to the headscarf affair of 1989, "The ostensible question—should wearing the so-called 'Islamic' headscarf be acceptable at school?—conceals the underlying question—which is, should North African immigrants be accepted in France?"[38]

The underlying question of Islamophobia refers to the legitimacy of the presence of postcolonial immigrants and their children: "immigrants for life," despite having French nationality, which according to cost/benefit logics of im-migration in French thought is closely bound up with their status as workers and their positioning in the relations of production.[39] As most Muslims in France are located in the working classes, they find themselves in vulnerable economic positions—due to the restructuring of industrial capitalism—and hit hard by long-term unemployment and precarious employment.[40] While their economic positioning is challenged by the transformations affecting postindustrial capital-ism, their "legitimate right to be in France" has significantly diminished in the eyes of the dominant classes, for whom the costs of their presence now outweigh the benefits.

The denial of Islamophobia as a new form of racism has been added to the de-nial of Muslims' right to be in France. In spite of the acknowledgement by inter-national organizations such as the European Union and the United Nations, and despite the French voluntary sector campaigns against Islamophobia (see chap-ter 13), this practice of denial appears to be securely moored within the French ruling classes. The underlying support for denial should be borne in mind when undertaking a sociological and historical analysis of Islamophobia. Before pre-senting a history of the concept, introducing the theoretical debates around its definition, and finally, suggesting one ourselves (part 2), the day-to-day reality of Islamophobia should first be appreciated by highlighting not only discrimi-nation as experienced by Muslims but also the tools and statistics available for turning Islamophobic actions and discourses into objective facts (part 1). In our view, these manifestations of Islamophobia result from the construction of both the "Muslim problem" and the "immigration problem," the sociological anal-ysis of which proceeds by an understanding of the logics underpinning how the media works, how politics operates, and how the "space of social movements" function (part 3).[41] The public controversies surrounding Islam reveal a struggle around the definition of Islam that activates what we call here "the anti-Muslim archive," that is, the symbolic repertoire of negative representations of Islam and Muslims. To understand the contemporary uses of the anti-Muslim archive, we have to critically examine the construction, circulation, and transformations undergone by these representations from one period to the next (the Middle Ages, the Enlightenment, the colonial and postcolonial periods) as well as the historical comparison between Islamophobia and antisemitism, whose symbolic forms and sociological stakes have often been similar (part 4). Lastly, we shine a light on what is at stake in the campaigns against Islamophobia, by attempting to examine the persistent divisions within the French anti-racist and feminist movements and the logics of engagement used by specific Muslim and non-Muslim intellectuals and organizations aiming to construct what we term here the "Islamophobic problem" (part 5).

PART 1

Realities of Islamophobia

I found out by word of mouth that there were opportunities in telesales, as there's no direct contact with customers. It's one of the areas you can still work in and wear hijab. I applied and this young guy was going to give me three days of training. By 5 o'clock on day one, the guy says, "We can't keep you on, you're not up to the job" [. . .] I realized quickly that it was because of the headscarf [. . .] So I stopped looking for jobs and fell back on the "hijab-friendly options" you can find on the net, like home help, cleaning, and providing childcare.

"HANANE"

CHAPTER 1

Islamophobia as a
Social Ordeal

For those subjected to it, Islamophobia is a genuine social ordeal comprised of multiple actions and words varying in intensity and seriousness. Since 2003 the Collectif contre l'islamophobie en France (Collective against Islamophobia in France, CCIF) has been the only French NGO compiling a list of Islamophobic acts—in an annex to its annual report. These demonstrations of rejection, which increased twelvefold between 2005 and 2019, sometimes target individual Muslims and sometimes Islam as a religion.[1] They thus give us a general overview of Islamophobia that is more representative of the diversity of its modes of expression than of its breadth. Every year, this report flags the increase in, and variety of, Islamophobic practices, confirming the clear overrepresentation of women among its victims (77 percent in 2012, and 70 percent in 2020). Based on these testimonies, it is difficult to separate that which can be attributed to racism, sexism, or classism. Islamophobia, in some of its forms of expression in any case, must be considered as a phenomenon fed by various processes of othering and categorizing people into inferior status. The objective of this section of the book is to scope out the reality of Islamophobia, not only through Muslims' lived experiences but also using the available statistical data, whose strengths and limits we will strive to present.

In an article on discrimination against Muslims, Amiraux posits a distinction that is useful, but barely engaged with in French scholarship,[2] between discrimination against individuals and unequal or discriminatory treatment in regard to institutions.[3] Islamophobic acts assume a variety of forms (fire, vandalism, occupation, profanation, etc.) against mosques, cemeteries, and Muslim-run shops and other places of business. Muslims are not spared even when they are dead: infantrymen commemorated in war memorials are also targets.[4]

These direct attacks on Muslim institutions come in addition to the many legal and bureaucratic obstacles aimed at impeding or even preventing the construction of cultural centers or religious buildings. The example of the Annecy mosque is illuminating. On 26 October 2012, after prayers for Eid in the southeastern city of Annecy, worshippers were threatened by a man armed with a shotgun. This occurred after a verbal altercation between the man—who lived near the premises (made available to the worshippers on this occasion by the city council)—and the organizers, who asked him to slow down his vehicle near the crowd of worshippers for safety reasons. Responding to the press, one of the event organizers explained that a mosque due to be built on the ageing site of the former place of worship (established in 1978) would enable Muslims to observe their faith under the best conditions, and that building permits had been granted. However, "a local (to the mosque) had organized around twenty people to oppose it, and had managed to stall the plan."

Obstacles may also stem from local authorities abusing their bureaucratic prerogatives and political authority, through the right of first refusal, administrative closures, the imposition of leaders and imams, and the disqualification, both of high-profile figures from such roles, and of not-for-profit organizations deemed obstructive or disobedient from accessing resources, etc. On this point, Frégosi notes that "the practical conditions for observing the Muslim faith are reached by navigating around an array of technical, bureaucratic and intellectual obstacles which, depending on the local contexts and configurations, limit the full observance of religious freedom and may [. . .] result in a conditional religious freedom for Muslims."[5] Although it is undeniable that the situation has been improving for decades, and that most obstacles result from internal divisions and negligence, the practice of faith, collective experience, and public freedom are subject to tight political and police control that can impede the exercise of some basic rights.

Experiences and Extent of Islamophobia

Beyond its institutional targets, Islamophobia is aimed at actual or perceived Muslims.[6] It is an individual experience that can take many forms and which in France affects mainly, but not exclusively, women wearing hijab (about eight out of ten, as of 2012). Since 1989 the headscarf in particular has been the target of both a political stigmatization campaign and legal prohibitions. The focus on women who wear hijab reveals the gendered nature of Islamophobia and the general public discrediting of this religious practice, which is actually very costly in social terms. It is hard to know whether men are less likely to report experiencing Islamophobia, or if they are less vulnerable to the most brutal and explicit forms of Islamophobic behavior. After targeting state primary and secondary schools (the Act of 15 March 2004), recent legislation has switched to extending the ban on wearing hijab to employees in "public service missions," beginning with public and private sector nursery education (see chapter 9).[7]

Islamophobic acts often assume the form of relatively violent injunctions to remove headgear, in both legal and extralegal forms, as testimonies published by the CCIF demonstrate. These testimonies reveal the scale of discriminatory acts against individuals in every area of social life, sometimes going beyond the law.[8] In state schools, where young people no longer have the right to wear "conspicuous" religious symbols, mothers who wear headscarves and volunteer to accompany their children's classes on school trips also find themselves excluded.[9] Some head teachers in nursery and primary schools—for example in the town of Bondy (in the eastern suburbs of Paris)—have used the pretext of a "secular" obligation for all children to eat non-Halal meat in the school canteen. Outside school, women are sometimes asked to take their headscarves off in order to get married; give evidence in court; take exams; take professional development and university classes; hire rural holiday homes, etc. Hypervisible expressions of religion may also become bureaucratic obstacles for Muslims (who are consequently deemed "bad") applying for visas to immigrate, settle permanently in France, or acquire French citizenship.[10]

Interactions with civil servants actually seem to be the main scenarios in which Islamophobia is expressed. But there are many similar stories from the world of work. Simply practicing one's faith may constitute an obstacle to getting into some lines of employment deemed "incompatible" for security reasons (e.g., baggage handlers, security staff, etc.). Private employment agencies and the state employment agency carry out active censorship, sometimes in the form of well-meaning "advice" given to applicants about overly religious appearance (beards or headscarves); self-censorship consequently worsens the situation. It is difficult to cite an exact number of Muslims who want to combine faith and work but no longer dare attempt both at the same time. It may also be the case that removing the headscarf or other constraints is the condition set for keeping one's job. In nursery and primary education, observing Ramadan may be presented as a safety concern because it exposes young children to risk due to their weakened, fasting state. Moreover, while women are required to show their hair, men are strongly advised to hide their facial hair, as in the case of one employee urged to wear a mask over his beard at work, or another told to shave so he would "look smart" in the retail industry.

Freedom to engage in business is also hindered when a bank refuses the right to open a business account to someone who wants to sell Islamic products on-line, or when it becomes impossible to sell such goods in a local market due to the "principle of laïcité." Islamophobia also impacts on everyday activities, such as denial of access to particular services (at airports, restaurants, sports halls, driving schools, etc.). The care sector is not immune either, when the possibility of accessing healthcare, being paid benefits, or even being allowed to volunteer in NGOs like the Restos du coeur (a high-profile national network of food-banks) depends upon removing one's hijab.

Islamophobia sometimes manifests more intensely in violent interactions, generally involving people unknown to the victim. According to the CCIF, the frequency of such incidents is increasing. There are many witness statements out-lining verbal attacks, humiliating acts in the street carried out by strangers who insult, spit at, and order women to take off their headscarves, or even just pull them off themselves. The attackers sometimes say they are doing it in the name of the "law" or "laïcité," thus imposing a personal and brutal version of these concepts. Apart from Keyhani et al.'s as yet unpublished survey, there is so far no sociological study of the perpetrators of acts of discrimination that would enable us to gain an understanding of the mechanisms enabling the shift from thoughts to spoken words, and from there, to physical attacks.[11] These are increasingly fre-quent and virulent, like the one on thirty-year-old Nouredine Rachedi, who was heading home in Guyancourt (southwest of Paris, near Versailles) on the night of 24–25 July 2008, at which point he was severely kicked due to his religion, or the attacks carried out by several people on women wearing headscarves as they walked alone in Argenteuil (northwest of Paris) on 20 May and 13 June 2013. One of these women, who was pregnant, consequently lost her child. Being Is-lamic, whether visibly or not, is thus a stigma people have to live with: it risks an actual and potential social penalty. In some cases it constitutes an offence—such as wearing the niqab in public—under the law of 11 October 2010.

The Intimate Ordeal of Rejection

Islamophobia can therefore be likened to a widespread, permanent risk exerting constraints over Muslims. Islamophobia, as it is experienced, is part of a broader context of hostility, in the form of low-intensity actions that are not always in-telligible. The ordeal of Islamophobia produces situations fueled by a climate of suspicion, in which Muslims are viewed as an "illegitimate" presence.[12] This Is-lamophobic hostility in French society has multiple consequences. It introduces tension into social relationships, puts up barriers, and creates obstacles that, for some people, compound other social disadvantages such as being a woman, belonging to a visible minority group, having low socioeconomic status, having few educational qualifications, or living in a disadvantaged area poorly served by transport links. Islamophobia thus adds its weight to the burden of what Robert Castel calls "negative discrimination."[13]

In 2008 Chouder, Latrèche, and Tevanian published "Les filles voilées parlent" (Girls with headscarves speak), thereby opening a space from which the testimonies of women aged fifteen to forty-five and who wear hijab could be heard for the first time after the law of 15 March 2004 had been passed.[14] In spite of the diverse trajectories and backgrounds of the participants, they all share the same intimate experience of rejection in forms of discrimination and hostility that combine racism and sexism. These relentless, energy-sapping experiences show how it is impossible for these women to "only" react with indifference and to escape the broader pattern of Islam being understood and acted upon as if it were a "problem" (see part 3).[15] The stories compiled in this book also illustrate how, behind the collective trauma of rejection, the specifics of the ordeal of Islamophobia are ultimately taking shape, without, as François Dubet et al. argue, a single and identical characteristic model ordeal emerging from the data.[16]

The stories and testimonies of Islamic converts perfectly demonstrate the idea of diversity and similarity in experiences. Islamophobia experienced by white converts, especially women who choose to wear the headscarf, means a very unusual journey through the racialization of the public gaze aimed at them, as conversion to Islam makes them available for discrimination and exposes them to racialized violence.[17] Several female converts have contacted the CCIF emphasizing the xenophobic element (the "go home!") linked to the rejection of their hijab. Another characteristic of converts' lived experience of Islamophobia may be located in the ruptures and hostility their choice generates, both within their family settings and in friendship circles, where witnesses refer to the rhetoric of "betrayal" and falling away from the right path.[18]

The experience of discrimination entails a multiplicity of ways to adapt. This all-encompassing "total" experience—which is invasive, impacts daily life, and affects one's idea of one's own identity and relations with other people and the world—is distinguished by its mundane, if not internalized nature, anticipated and sometimes repressed in the victims' stories. Discrimination materializes as a set of unconnected constraints, rarely explicit or brutal, which lead the victims to develop multiple strategies of "making do," that is, "building an experience that affords them not only the opportunity to live as well as possible but also to never be assigned an identity that invalidates them."[19]

How should these experiences be dealt with? If, as we see, the increasing number of recorded Islamophobic incidents may indicate a correspondingly stronger mobilization of Muslim victims, several studies of victims have shown that the latter scarcely report such incidents or ask organizations (the state or NGOs working in the areas of anti-racism or human rights) to intervene on their behalf.[20] Exactly why people do not take their grievances to official bodies requires further research.[21] One study has identified two main trends among victims of discrimination. The first tactic is to face up to the stigma and the discriminator from a position of struggle based on taking responsibility for it and responding (in a conflictual or humorous way, for example). Or, in a different register, from a pedagogical standpoint, another response involves positing the other person's ignorance and focusing on education and the call for reason. Yet this procedure very quickly turns out to be draining and even counterproductive when it comprises—as it often does—a succession of justification sessions. This is all the more the case when "political rhetoric often discerns ethnically divisive and even segregationist mechanisms in the resistance to discrimination [whereas] those on the receiving end see above all the need to be individuals and absolutely not victims."[22] It is much rarer to see some victims of discrimination adopt a different tactic, turning the tables by forcing the interlocutor to reveal their intentions, make their principles explicit, and provide justifications for their prejudices.

In the majority of cases, the victims do not face up to the issue but muddle through by developing various coping strategies.[23] The most popular of these is conformism, based on the idea that maintaining the status quo allows one to enjoy "polite indifference." If that is deemed insufficient, this strategy may assume the form of a particularly zealous hyperconformism, just as alienating in what it reveals in a different form, that is, the illegitimacy and feelings of insecurity in those who espouse it.[24] In contrast, avoidance is favored by those who reject both hyperconformism and confrontation. Islamophobia may lead some Muslims to hide their expressions of faith to avoid confrontation: "In order to reduce the pressure generated by the stigma, the threatened person opts for isolation: the stigma-generating identity is kept secret, forcing the individual to present themself differently to how they are with their friends and family, to lie and hide in order to not give the game away."[25]

Motivated principally by the desire for self-preservation and making their lives as easy as possible, people who adopt this stance impose a permanent state of alert on themselves: hypercontrol of their interactions, aimed at not letting anything happen in social spaces they deem "risky," that is, outside of family, community, and other places they have chosen to frequent.

Ramadan and mealtimes are thus often noted to be particularly sensitive moments. In terms of Ramadan, people afford fasting a cultural rather than religious reading, to avoid conflict. If they are in a position of sharing a meal, it is better to say they are vegetarian rather than a practicing Muslim to get round potential questioning, judgement, and speculation about religious food rituals.

Mundane or banal life choices are no longer so mundane or banal in a context of overinterpretation, overreactions to the smallest signs of religious identification, and the conflation of practicing Islam with radicalism and terrorism. Taking up an illegitimate identity is a stance that may well turn out to be socially costly. Concealment, which means doing everything to neutralize the indicators of one's own religious belief, may also assume the form of lies, tricks, hacks, and even exile (either "external," that is, leaving the country to go somewhere thought to be more welcoming for Muslims,[26] or "internal," withdrawing exclusively into one's own community or residential neighborhood), to put distance between oneself and uncomfortable or unbearable situations.

Muslim victims of discrimination who thus "muddle through" may also find resources in their faith that enable them to interpret the scorn they experience through a religious framework and therefore to tolerate it. Indeed, "putting oneself in God's hands is an essential resource in terms of developing a proactive indifference [to discrimination] as, from the perspective of faith and God, sensitivity to human judgement is a type of vanity."[27] This spiritually based indifference can be more passive and submissive when it is embedded in a kind of "mektoubism" (the Arabic word *mektoub* means "fate," or "what is written"), in other words the idea of predestination becomes a form of fatalism. This implies acceptance and the capacity to withstand rejection without reacting, by evacuating its social and political dimensions in order to reduce it to a metaphysical diagnosis. Islamophobia is thus summarized as a divine trial, in which those being discriminated against are merely the vessels.

Islamophobia as a lived phenomenon—which disgusts some people to the extent that that they are encouraged to resist, and which crushes and compresses others to the point of "colonizing" their being, effectively "miniaturizing" them, to borrow Amartya Sen's phrase[28]—produces lasting effects. Whatever the mode of adaptation: confrontation, avoidance, or stoicism, the reaction is always a positioning driven by real or perceived discrimination. It is this feeling of alienation from the discriminator that presses down the hardest and sometimes becomes a stifling obsession, especially when individuals are dealing with multiple markers of social stigma without having the power to neutralize them. It is therefore a profound, intimate experience, which recalls the racist categorization of people as inherently inferior explored by Frantz Fanon,[29] demonstrating the extent to which this reveals the flaws of the individual and imposes an unstable and uncertain floating gaze on the racialized group. The risk here is disengagement, from a "trial based on the struggle for identity experienced by individuals who are placed, sometimes brutally, sometimes subtly, sometimes repeatedly and sometimes unexpectedly in situations where they are distanced from themselves."[30]

Forms of discrimination also impact on health, in ways beyond the problem of accessing health care. Several studies show that the ordeal of discrimination generates psychosocial stress that can affect both physical and mental health.[31] In France, little is known about the lasting social, somatic, public, and domestic consequences of this kind of experience that "wounds souls, paralyzes, hamstrings, demolishes, gives you knots in your stomach, and causes feelings of shame and humiliation."[32] Even though anachronistic and false comparisons should be avoided, the analyses of both Fanon, on the psychiatric consequences of colonization, and Memmi, in the book *Portrait du colonisé*,[33] contain avenues to explore and logical approaches to the issue still relevant today.

All these testimonies do not mean that Islamophobic attitudes are completely spread across French society, or experienced by all Muslims. It is actually extremely difficult to assess the exact degree to which Islamophobia impacts on those who, in France and elsewhere, consider themselves Muslims. However, there is much at stake here, because the design of scientific tools for measuring it is part of the social and political acknowledgement of the phenomenon, and therefore of the chance to deploy effective state-led action to address it.

CHAPTER 2

Measuring Islamophobia

The attacks on 11 September 2001 certainly generated quicker reflections on the knowledge about, and the quantification of hostility toward, Muslims in the context of a dearth of reliable information on religious minorities. In Europe, the first post-2001 initiatives can be traced back to the Open Society Institute and the European Monitoring Centre on Racism and Xenophobia (EUMC) in 2002.[1] Anti-Muslim discrimination and manifestations of Islamophobia were steadily incorporated into the European political agenda due to public reports pinpointing all the deficiencies of the existing statistics.[2] In France, the social consequences of the attacks on New York quickly translated into action, particularly in the Commission nationale consultative des droits de l'homme (CNCDH, National Human Rights Consultative Committee), which introduced a section on hostility toward Islam in its opinion poll on racism and xenophobia as early as 2003.

Overall, the recognition and measurement of Islamophobia have encountered two forms of resistance. The first refers to the illegitimacy of visible forms of religiosity in public space and the ideological modes deployed in the construction of the "Muslim problem." The second relates to the methods for recording and categorizing necessary for a description of both the relevant groups and the forms of discrimination to which they are exposed. We see this in the tensions and debates that preceded the establishment of the Trajectoires et origines (TeO) survey carried out by the Institut national d'études démographiques (INED, National Institute of Demography) and the Institut national de la statistique et des études économiques (Insee, National Statistics and Economics Institute). Previously, the major studies produced by state statistics institutions enabled the existence of an "ethnic penalty" to be analyzed, albeit incompletely, by constructing people's "origins" based on parents' nationality or place of birth.[3] Yet these studies did not really afford any understanding of the inequalities in treatment based on religious belonging or appearance, apart from deducing them from "origins," which is highly problematic from a scientific and epistemological point of view: religious belonging is not hereditary. Despite the limits of the measurement tools, statistical knowledge about Islamophobia has developed and is now a kind of puzzle made up of heterogenous, sometimes flawed pieces, but pieces that complement each other sufficiently well to be able to show a relatively clear pattern of how this phenomenon plays out.

Islamophobic "Opinions"

National and international surveys on opinions and their connection to "values" constitute the main statistical resources on hostility toward Islam and Muslims. Since the early 1980s, the study of Islamophobic "opinions" has relied on vast international surveys, such as the various waves of the Pew Global Attitudes Project, Eurobarometer, and the European and World Values Studies.[4] These surveys ask people questions about their relationship with various cultural and religious minorities, and with "Others," in terms of living together and living near one another. However, the quality of the very few existing questionnaires is poor, and they generate answers that are too narrow, which places a serious limit on the degree to which the various facets of Islamophobia noted above can be understood. This deficiency has justified the development of new research protocols and procedures.

For more than a decade, the quantitative measurement of Islamophobia on the international scale has thus been dominated by quite an old approach (i.e., the analysis of "opinions" and "attitudes") reliant on one method (the construction of attitudinal scales) and a single discipline (social psychology).[5] Two underlying assumptions anchor the work that has inspired this approach. The first sees Islamophobia as a holistic phenomenon: a kind of continuum between thoughts and actions, in which opinions constitute the crucial link in the chain, located between discourse analysis and the study of discriminatory behaviors. The second conceptualizes values, prejudices, and other Islamophobic opinions held by individuals as the reflection of coherent social personalities. For example, hostility toward strangers is often linked to a strong desire for social order.

The various studies carried out in Western societies have given rise to numerous publications since 2010. The 2011 volume edited by Mark Helbling compiles some of this research, which is less interested in comparing very large geographical sites and more focused on identifying Islamophobic attitudes in subgroups.[6]

Deriving from social psychology, some of this work views Islamophobia as a "negative attitude toward Islam and Muslims." The idea of "attitude" here is linked with a strong affective dimension, locating it both in a theory of race and group relations and in more traditional theories such as Theodor Adorno's "authoritarian personality."[7]

Most of this work foregrounds the prevalence of negative stereotypes toward Islam, particularly among the younger generations. It also emphasizes the role of family and friendship networks in the construction of the Muslim "Other" and in the transmission of the idea that this "Other" embodies a threat to established values and identities. However, the degree of rigor with which the analytical tools and samples are constructed is open to criticism.

With a few exceptions, we can also highlight the lack of rigor in the distinction between and deconstruction of the categories of origins, nationality, and religion. Out of convenience, nationality, culture, and religiosity are often amalgamated in references to ethnicity. Henk Dekker and Jolanda Van der Noll, who study Islamophobia in Germany, explain this tendency in research by the fact that religion and origin are often conflated in the representations of Muslims.[8]

Observed or Constructed Opinions?

Since 1990 (with a break in 2001), the CNCDH has administered an annual survey on the "state of public opinion on xenophobia, anti-Semitism, racism, and anti-racism." Various polling organizations have shared this market since it was launched (the 2012 survey was carried out by the Institut CSA, a subsidiary of the Bolloré group) and a secondary, more detailed analysis was done by political scientists (Nonna Mayer, Guy Michelat, Vincent Tiberj, and more recently, Tommaso Vitale) based at Sciences Po-Paris. This study claimed to be "barometric," that is, aiming to produce a history of French "opinion" about "Others" in order to analyze the effects of history, current affairs, and the socioeconomic conjuncture on prejudices toward various minority groups. Although these polls were communicated through the press, through political circles, by activists, and via some sections of academia, the CNCDH did receive pushback.[9]

One initial critique identifies the fact that opinion polls often adhere to demands that reflect the political interests of those who commission them, at the risk, first and foremost, of fulfilling a function of legitimization rather than one of questioning.[10] Because the CNCDH is a government-funded agency, and because it contributes to transforming anti-Muslim racism into an object supported by statistics (via its annual opinion poll on racism), it holds an important position in the recognition of this form of racism as a "social fact" in France.

The use of these findings by researchers should not blind us to the fact that this instrument is barely independent of its commissioning body.[11] "The poll is effectively under the guardianship of a commissioning body that de facto runs it, from commissioning through to the interpretation of the responses," explains anthropologist Alain Morice, who adds that "the Service d'information du gouvernement [SIG, Government Intelligence Agency] is invited annually to give its seal of approval to the Commission's report."[12]

Other critiques focus on the questionnaire, specifically its overall design, the categories used, and the value afforded the responses. As Pierre Bourdieu has argued, not everyone necessarily has an opinion about the questions asked; the pollsters disregard the sociocultural inequalities that influence people's propensity and capacity to respond; and not all opinions are equally valid.[13] However, the CNCDH questionnaire is anchored in the twin hypotheses that the respondents actually have an opinion and that it is held at a constant intensity, based on the same resources and awareness.

By submitting numerous identity and political categories without precise definitions, the questionnaire forces the respondents to do the work of defining terms themselves, which thus completely avoids the basic question about people's comprehension and the meaning of the questions, and lastly, the actual meaning of the data gathered.[14] The words used in the questionnaire are not technical terms but rather concepts used and mobilized in different ways on a gigantic scale in public, political, and media debates. This might be seen as an asset, but the unclear degree to which the subsequent statistical aggregates can be considered coherent makes it problematic.

The form assumed by the questionnaire is also open to criticism. Apart from a few introductory questions, most are "closed questions" and the answers are limited in order to minimize the "no response" rate. Although this approach is convenient for the interviewers, it raises similar questions to the criticisms leveled by Nathalie Heinich regarding international surveys on values, that is, are they capable of statistically capturing the subjective relationship between respondents and values and opinions?[15] As it unfolds, the questionnaire's architects have constructed it to steadily address more complex questions by moving from a level of abstraction ("What are your main fears for French society? What does it mean, in your opinion, to be racist? Would you say that at the moment racism in France is very widespread, quite widespread, etc.") to specifics (what is your opinion about the idea that "in France today you don't feel at home as much as used to be the case," or "immigration is the main cause of the lack of safety"). In a similar vein to public discourses, the wording of the questions suggests dichotomous links between the ideas examined ("immigration" and "uncertainty," "Muslim religious practices" and "problem"). Some framings are imposed through the questions and the establishment of tension between ideas, a form of conditioning that inevitably leads respondents to a stance reflecting such tension.

Additionally, the questionnaire puts forward a very contrasting and binary way of envisaging society, presenting "France" or "society" on the one hand and various minority and othered groups on the other. The respondents are not invited to give opinions on this way of slicing the cake but are instead invited to assess their degree of distance from these various preselected groups.

Many specialists in the sociology of opinion polls have identified these "framing" effects of the wording of the questions.[16] The encoding of the questionnaire "locates the Other in the catalogue of serious risks from the outset, and with absolute clarity."[17] There are multiple forms of Otherness selected: the categories provide alternatives, with no transition between phenotypical, racial, religious, national, cultural markers, etc. However, this mixture of identity registers requires that these categories be defined and clarified. One of the questions, for example, refers to the "integration" of people "of foreign origin," while others question the integration of "foreigners." The term "of foreign origin" implies that it means the most publicly visible "foreign born" and is a category that could cover immigrants with French or foreign nationality as well as their mainly French-born and French citizen descendants. The term "integration" is highly polysemic and loses its relevance when asked to do the work of capturing the behavior of "non-native" French people, for whom this concept—synonymous with an order to assimilate—is often meaningless. It thus appears that beyond the problematic choice of statements, the lack of definition and the mixture of types of difference alluded to significantly undermine the findings produced by opinion polls.[18]

The Prevalence of, and Changes in, Islamophobic Opinions over Time

These legitimate critiques of opinion polls must be borne in mind when assessing the relevance of their findings. For those seasoned researchers who use this type of tool, their robustness stems from their coherence and stability over time, as well as the rigor of the ways in which the statistics are used. Although it is difficult to read these findings as an accurate reflection of "opinion," the match between what the CNCDH records and other databases show should be underlined, particularly regarding the forms of hostility, the profiles of the victims, and the forms of unpopularity. Despite the many limits of the survey tool, the picture of "opinions" that it produces does make sense. Like all the other data produced internationally, those in the CNCDH poll provide partial information: partial, but resonant with the observable ways in which the "Muslim problem" is constructed.

The data has been analyzed in two different ways: a barometer-style diachronic description of the opinions gathered through the survey; and the construction of attitudinal "scales" and "longitudinal indices" that allow further development of the analysis, for example by locating respondents both socially and "ideologically." The incremental distribution of individual attitudes into graded clusters is based on the allocation and coherence of the responses, which then help form subgroups for analysis.[19] In order to sketch out the overall variations, Mayer, Michelat, and Tiberj created indices and scales (in the form of "scores") based on the clustering of various questions (the ones that had not been amended over the previous twenty years) in the CNCDH poll. One of these, the "longitudinal tolerance index," brings together around sixty sets of questions asked at least twice.[20] Finally, an overall annual "score" for "tolerance" is compared over time, running from 0 for no "tolerance" up to 100 for the least "intolerant" responses.[21]

Between 1990 and 2010, the overall changes in the opinions polled by the CNCDH appear to reflect a very gradual diminution of prejudices "through generational change, improvements in education, and openness to the world."[22] However, since 2010, this trend seems to have been lastingly reversed. In the 1999–2011 period, the index of "tolerance" never fell for two successive years and even reached its "record" high of 69.5 in 2009. Since then, the index has fallen by six points. Although downward fluctuations explained by external events have already been identified (e.g., after the urban rebellions in fall 2005, and subsequent to changes in the governing party, particularly in 2002, 2007 and 2012), the current reversal does not seem to correspond to any important geopolitical (Arab revolutions) or economic (subprime loan credit crisis) event. Mayer et al. argue that "we should instead seek the explanation in a specific context, an ambiance, and a series of connected events."[23] In other words, this reversal in the trend toward "tolerance" may have resulted from a structural ideological shift, linked to increased media scrutiny and the politicization of several key incidents (urban rebellions, the Grenoble speech,[24] controversies about "prayers in the street" and "halal meat," etc.) against a backdrop of lasting and compounding socioeconomic crisis. However, this decline in "tolerance" is not focused on all minorities but on one particular group. Indeed, the index of "tolerance" is actually only falling in regard to two groups: Muslims (–4 points) and North Africans (–8.5 points), while it has stayed at the same level for Blacks and has gone up for

Jews. Mayer et al. give an explicit commentary on these findings: "If our era is compared to the prewar one, it could be said that currently, on the level of representations, Muslims and North Africans have replaced Jews as scapegoats."[25]

In relation to Islamophobia in particular, the findings of these polls have interesting things to say. Whether disaggregated and inspected separately or understood as a set, the factors aiming to identify opinion toward Islam and Muslims follow the same downward trend seen in a number of European national contexts. What is striking about the analysis of the graphs is as much that the level of Islamophobia remains stable over time as the fact that it does not mirror the trends of other forms of discrimination. In recent years, the rise in the repudiation of the practices and institutions linked to Islam has been remarkable; it is the case even if it is acknowledged that the first surveys, at the turn of the twenty-first century, already revealed high scores. This is especially true of the relationship between visible Muslim-ness and worship. The headscarf, the principal subject of controversies since 1989, has been the focus of a rejection on a large scale ever since the CNCDH first asked this question. Negative opinions about it reached a peak in 2003, during the debates prior to the vote on the Act of 15 March 2004 (82 percent), and have remained at this level. The hijab is still the most repudiated sign of Muslimness, and the CCIF data corroborates this.

Above and beyond the hostility felt toward the hijab, the whole set of Islamic rituals has drawn growing and virtually continuous mistrust since 2008. Islamic constraints on food and drink (pork and alcohol), toward which 13 percent of those polled were unfavorable in 2003, now disturb one in three respondents. "Intolerance" vis-à-vis the observance of Ramadan rose from 21 to 26 percent. These changes are sensitive to media agendas, as demonstrated by the 10 percent increase in negative opinions expressed about prayers in the street between 2009 and 2011, after Marine Le Pen politicized the "issue" of "prayers in the street," a position endorsed by both the government and the opposition.[26] Lastly, while the sacrifice of sheep linked to the festival of Eid was rejected by 25 percent of those polled in 2003, that figure had grown to 37 percent by 2011.

This increase in the negative opinions polled was rapid, reaching a peak in the 2013 and 2014 CNCDH reports (fig. 1). According to some observers, opinions hardened due to a public debate that impacted on them during that period, related to the issue of terrorism, and more widely, to "radical Islamism" in the wake of the terrorist attacks in Toulouse and Montauban, during which the Franco-Algerian Mohammed Merah killed seven people: three soldiers and four civilians (including three children at a Jewish school) and wounded six others. At that time, 79 percent of those polled felt that wearing the headscarf "could cause a problem," and almost half the respondents felt the same way about sacrificing sheep during Eid, the practice of prayer, and the ban on showing images of the Prophet. In regard to Ramadan and the ban on eating pork, 38 percent and 40 percent respectively expressed negative opinions. Every terrorist act carried out by someone claiming they are inspired by Islam generates many debates that extend beyond the crucial issue of political violence. Instead of a deep, targeted examination of the violence, public debate is actually structured by and saturated with scrutiny of the social practices, and therefore, of the very presence of Muslims.

However, the correlation between intolerance of Islam and terrorist acts was not borne out in the opinion polls carried out after 2014, although the country had to deal with the terrible terrorist attacks of 2015 targeting Jews in a kosher supermarket, the *Charlie Hebdo* magazine, and the Bataclan theater and Parisian cafés. Moreover, the years after that witnessed terrorist acts of varying severity, aimed either at civilians or the armed forces and police. Yet in fact, between 2014 and 2019, negative opinions about wearing headscarves fell from 79 percent to 50 percent, while dropping from 49 percent to 32 percent on the topic of sacrificing sheep for Eid. Intolerance toward prayer fell sixteen points; toward Ramadan, by seventeen points; regarding the ban on consuming pork and alcohol, by 14 percent; and there was even a 9 percent decrease in negative attitudes toward the ban on showing pictures of the Prophet. Therefore, as Mayer, Michelat, Tiberj, and Vitale emphasize, in relation to the January 2015 attacks:

> the CNCDH survey carried out in March of that year shows that they were followed by a 3% increase in tolerance, made all the more remarkable because it occurred in less than two months. It is less the events as such that can influence people's opinions, than the way the events are framed by political, social, and media elites. The responsibilities of these elites are thus particularly significant in setting the tone and enforcing a dominant narrative. For example, in 2005 the debate focused on the idea of "Muslim riots," to the detriment of other ways of covering and interpreting these events, as being to do with social inequalities or urban neglect. Using this Muslim-centered prism had serious consequences for the rise in Islamophobia in certain strands of public opinion, and ended up in a 6% drop in the index of tolerance.[27]

It is the whole set of manifestations of Islamic worship—everything comprising the visibility of Muslims in social life—that appears to be increasingly rejected in the "public opinion" captured by the CNCDH poll. This "aversion to Islam," on the rise and intermittent since it was first measured, is expressed by a more diverse group than the one that usually expresses negative opinions about other minority groups. In poll after poll, the repudiation of Islam in the French

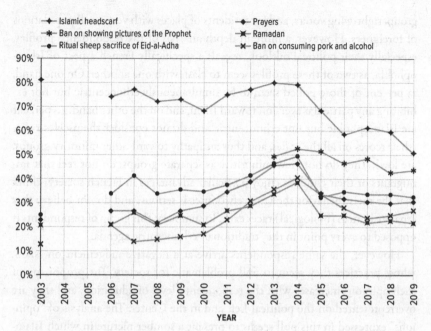

FIGURE I.

Opinions about Muslim religious practices
Source: Annual CNCDH opinion polls on behavior regarding racism,
xenophobia, and anti-Semitism.

context matches the traditional ideological fault lines for rejecting the Other.
In countries where this type of survey has been carried out, the homogeneity of
the profile of respondents that express hostility to Others is often underscored,
as the rejection of one minority generally goes together with a rejection of all
minorities. Therefore, the hostile attitudes toward Muslims seem—in relation
to the people who hold them and their stances—to resemble those attitudes
targeted toward other minorities and are often based on authoritarian, conservative sociopolitical positions.[28] In Swiss polls, it is overall the same groups that
are hostile toward immigrants, foreigners, and Muslims.[29] In the United States,
negative attitudes toward Muslims stem less from the 11 September attacks than
from the idea that they are foreigners or citizens whose values and practices do
not fit the dominant cultural model.[30]

However, in France, two-thirds of respondents in the 2011 CNCDH survey
can be located either in a minority position of overall openness (neither ethnocentric, nor Islamophobic), or in a consistent (majority) pattern of closure
("ethnocentric Islamophobes").[31] The most negative and (fastest rising) opinions regarding the Muslim religion appear to be those of the over-sixty-five age

group, right-wing voters, and/or residents of places with very small populations of foreigners. However, a more in-depth analysis of the respondents' profiles, especially their political outlook, reveals a specifically French aspect of Islamophobia, as two of these profiles seem to clash with one another. On one hand, 13 percent of those polled seem to be simultaneously ethnocentric but not exhibiting any particular aversion toward Islam, and on the other hand, 20 percent are Islamophobic but not ethnocentric and do not consider themselves racist (their scores on all the scales, and thus antipathy toward other minority groups, are low). They do not view minorities as separate groups; do not feel that immigrants or their children enjoy particular advantages in French society; think that the racist behavior the latter encounter is serious; and do not believe that separate human (biological) races exist. In summary, this group of respondents is opposed to every point in the "traditional" ethnocentric agenda.

However, the same respondents arrive at a negative judgement on Islam, whose practices they seem to find problematic for society. The proportion of such opinions increases with the respondent's level of education, and they are overrepresented on the political Left and in the Center. The analysis of "opinions" expressed in this poll seems to present a somber picture in which Islamophobia is rising and spreading through the various spheres of society.

Over recent years, the demarcation between "aversion to Islam" and "ethnocentrism" has solidified over two points, the first of which "is the inversion of the gender effect. In 2009 repudiation of Islam was more frequent among men, but by 2012 it had risen steeply among women (+17 percent), so that they were now 8 percent more reluctant to accept it than men [. . .]. The second difference is the high level of antipathy toward Islam and its practices shown in that year by the most qualified people, who are generally the most tolerant."[32]

CHAPTER 3

From Negative Opinions to Discriminatory Acts

The study of the connection between perceptions, attitudes, and action is one of the main contributions of social psychology.[1] To assess Islamophobia as an act, that is, the social, political, interpersonal, and subjective translation of the repudiation of Islam recorded in statistical data, three main strategies for capturing data are possible: referrals (when the victims campaign themselves), victimization studies (when they are interviewed), and lastly, "situated experiments."

Referrals: Victims Campaigning

Two bodies record referrals from victims of Islamophobia in France: the Ministry of the Interior and the CCIF. The ministry's statistics pull together the cases that have been reported to the various levels of police and gendarmerie and have generated a statement sent to the courts.[2] Criminal statistics occupy a central role in the measurement of racism in France, a position bolstered by the lack of judicial data in civil courts for equivalent types of cases.[3] The police method for recording these incidents distinguishes first between "actions," that is, acts against persons—however long the subsequent time taken off work lasts—and property, with a certain degree of seriousness and, second, "threats," that is, verbal threats and threatening gestures, graffiti, pamphlets, dangerous demonstrations, and other acts of intimidation. In relation to the categories of victim, police recording basically divides incidents into three subgroups: anti-Semitism, anti-North African racism, and most recently, "anti-Muslim racism" (aimed at individuals or institutions).

The CCIF data is essentially based on victim statements (given by phone, over the Internet, or through mail) and less frequently, on reviews of the incidents covered by the press. This database is now a statistical benchmark for part of the French media, but especially for international human rights bodies, which, unlike the French state, have no qualms about acknowledging an independent grassroots movement within the Muslim community (see chapter 12).

Whether for the Ministry of the Interior or the CCIF, recording incidents is subject to several unpredictable factors that play a role in the ultimate construction of the data. The interpretation of the motivation for rejection comes into play the moment when the incident occurs, immediately after, and the moment when an Islamophobic act is recorded. At each step, the incident can be interpreted and deliberated (in different ways). In fact, not all interactions entailing rejection or mistrust are necessarily explicit, and the motivations of the protagonists cannot always be discerned. Recording of cases by police or not-for-profits will therefore depend on the behavior of the victim and the perpetrator when they are known, material elements, usable witness statements, and the sensitivity of the officer or activist to the relevant form of discrimination.

More broadly, in understanding the ways in which the recording role is discharged, the defining elements are the training, subjectivity, and opinion of those doing the recording.

The recording procedures used by the CCIF and the Ministry of the Interior have seen significant changes in collection techniques.[4] Those of the CCIF have been influenced by their increasing staffing levels, their higher public profile due to their website going live in late 2003 with regular updates (particularly in 2011), and a growing public media and communication reach, coupled with international recognition. The Ministry of the Interior has been influenced by the systematization of recording procedures (in 2004) and by the implementation of the Plan national d'enrichissement des procédures (PNE, National Improvement of Procedures Plan) from November 2005 to March 2007, which enabled data-processing to be improved, in particular by establishing a number of priority areas, like violence against the person, cybercrime, racism, and anti-Semitism. From 2010 recording was again impacted by the establishment of a new method piloted by the Sous-direction de l'information générale (SDIG, Office for General Information), in the context of the framework agreement between the ministry and the Conseil français du culte Muslim (French Muslim Worship Council, CFCM), signed on 28 June 2010.[5] Lastly, changes in the law must be added to this list. Statistics came under an extension of criminal law, after the enactment of the Act of 3 February 2003, referred to as the "Lellouche Act"; laws of 9 March and 13 August 2004 that extended the reach of criminal law in terms of racism (particularly the desecration of tombs) and time limits for referral by the courts; the Act of 30 December 2004, which transposed an EU directive on discrimination into French law and enabled the establishment of the Haute Autorité de lutte contre les discriminations et pour l'égalité (HALDE, the High Authority for Fighting Discrimination and Promoting Equality);[6] and the laws of 11 February 2005 and 31 March 2006 on combatting discrimination.

Although it is modest and inseparable from the government's desire to allay Muslim anxieties,[7] the Ministry of the Interior's strategy of improving procedures for recording anti-Muslim racism runs counter to the noticeable prevarications of the Ministry of Justice. The justice system statistics are indeed much less complete and precise. Only criminal law data is included in that ministry's statistical tables; the discriminatory litigation arising from the civil courts and employment tribunals is barely noted, whereas it is probably in that area that it is most obvious. Two categories of data can be identified. The first is the picture of prosecutions based on criminal law offenses as well as racist and discriminatory ones. The second comprise indicators of activity, such as the criminal response rates,[8] and from 2005, prosecution rates. The usefulness of these figures is restricted due to their focus on categories of offense, which makes an interpretation by category of victim impossible, and because of the vagueness of the categories used: "racist," "anti-Semitic," and "anti-religious" violations. In the latter category, apart from a small number of outlying and sporadic studies it is not possible to identify which religion is concerned.[9]

Still, it should be noted that, in the name of more egalitarian treatment of the various religions, the Ministry of Justice decided that the criminal justice system—now in a position to record anti-Semitic acts—should disaggregate incidents aimed at Muslim or Catholic institutions and people.

In March 2006 a working group on the struggle against racism and anti-Semitism approved the establishment of a new nomenclature aimed at replacing the expression "anti-religious acts" with the idea of "anti-Semitic acts," "Islamophobic acts," and others—including "Christianophobia." This strategy was supported by a memorandum from the Directeur des affaires criminelles et des grâces (DACG) dated 4 April 2007, stipulating the categories to report on ("racist offenses"; "anti-Semitic offenses"; "offenses against the Muslim religion"; "offenses against the Christian religion"; and other "offenses against religion"). The memo stipulates that it is the responsibility of *procureurs généraux* (attorney generals' offices) to provide information updating the relevant local tables on a monthly basis, and the DACG's task to produce equivalent tables containing national figures. This willingness to act was not followed up by any impact, for reasons that are still unclear. Hold-ups stemming from issues to do with recording, leadership, and interagency coordination must be distinguished from obstruction resulting from organizational or political pressures.

Such obstruction might be connected to the framework agreements signed by the ministry and the anti-racist organizations Licra and SOS Racisme. While these agreements were supposed to facilitate greater knowledge of racism, these bodies stand out due to their refusal to acknowledge the concept of Islamophobia and engage in activities to combat this form of racism (see chapter 13). In any case, the deployment of the Ministry of Justice's Cassiopée software (initiated in 2008) should enable litigation in cases of discrimination or racism to be more effectively identified and accounted for, by bringing together the police and courts' data using common identifiers. This is above all hypothetical, insofar as, to our knowledge, there are no studies on these recording practices (receipt of complaint, pressing or reviewing charges based on the incidents, processing, etc.).

These reminders are useful for the effort to decode existing charts tracing changes in recorded levels of Islamophobia. Several trends emerge from them. Firstly, the graphs provided by the Ministry of the Interior and the CCIF look similar and turn out to be affected by the media and political agenda of the main public cases connected to the Muslim question. The 2004 peak could be linked to the debates surrounding the vote on the act banning the hijab in state schools; the surge in 2009 (which also has to do with the rejection of North Africans) could be linked to the debates on the ban on the full veil and the launch of the debate on national identity. Moreover, whatever the source of information, the number of Islamophobic incidents recorded has increased steadily since 2008. The CCIF records the largest growth, which consequently increases the gap between its figures and those of the police.[10] In 2011 the CCIF recorded around twice as many Islamophobic acts as the Ministry of the Interior, an unprecedented gap that could be explained by the strong propensity for the CCIF and victims that report to it to criticize what the organization labels "state Islamophobia," which manifests itself at public service reception desks (including those at police stations) and whose presumed protagonists are civil servants and those with similar status and roles. The theory could be floated that beyond the victims' more general relationship with the relevant institutions, particularly those that embody public authority, some of the statistical gaps can be traced to the ways in which the CCIF receives and addresses reports.

The other obvious development concerns the rather contradictory post-2010 trajectories of the trends in anti–North African racism and Islamophobia. From 2010 the CCIF recorded more Islamophobic incidents than the police recorded racist acts against North Africans, which further underscores the argument that these two forms of racism are connected but cannot be reduced to one another; it also supports analyses that highlight ideological and political reconfigurations around the question of Islam (see chapter 8). The similar patterns in the graphs provided by the Ministry of the Interior and the CCIF (fig. 2), despite the differences of quantity and recording, express a trend toward the social deployment of Islamophobia that converges with the changes measured by the CNCDH in opinions about Islam, at least up until recently.

The recurrence of attacks from 2013 and the permanence of virulent media controversies about the place of Muslims in French society have continued to legitimize the enactment of Islamophobic acts, which their victims seem to prefer to report to the CCIF rather than to the Ministry of the Interior. In 2019, for instance, the CCIF recorded five times as many incidents as the state. This ratio had been only 2:1 in 2011. Despite the gaps in numbers, the graphs are similar and correspond to overall changes in anti-Semitism and other forms of racism recorded in France.[11] From 2013 onward, the peaks in the numbers of recorded Islamophobic incidents, particularly physical violence and damage inflicted on Muslim institutions, were recorded amid the terrorist killings of January and November 2015. After a drop in 2016, the figures began to rise again from 2017, showing two new trends. First, the violence targeting worshippers and places of worship (especially the use of firearms and the destruction of places of worship) increased in frequency and seriousness. Second, we see the emergence of discrimination and violent incidents connected to the implementation of antiradicalization or antiterrorism policies.

Despite everything, it is still difficult to separate out exactly what stems from the behavior of victims, recording techniques, the social reality of Islamophobia, and from visibility (i.e., the legitimacy of the CCIF and the ministry). These shortcomings have been partially offset by the progressive development of the measuring instruments, such as the annual victim surveys that measure crime. These tools circumvent the limitations inherent in recording practices that rely either on victims (such as nonreferral) or on institutions (such as denial of recording or recharacterization of facts).

Discrimination Based on Actual or Perceived Muslimness

The main innovations in recent times have occurred in the scientific measurement of discrimination based on religious belonging. As we have underlined in relation to the measurement of crime, the assessment of discrimination against minorities cannot be based solely on referrals, and even less on criminal investigations. It cannot therefore do without the evidential support of statistics. This allows the gaps between various groups that share one or more physical or

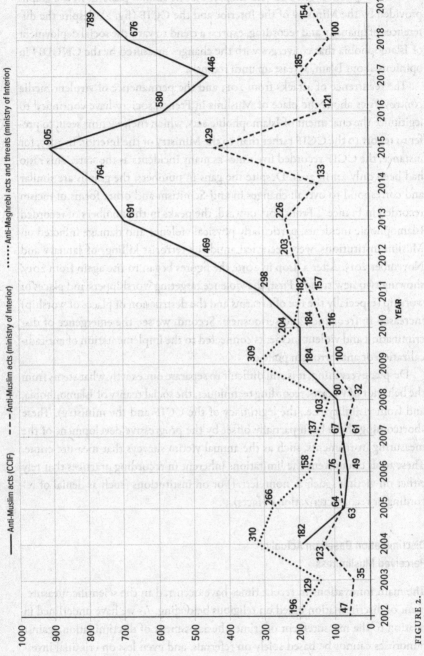

Anti-Muslim acts (CCIF)   **---- Anti-Muslim acts (ministry of Interior)**   **······ Anti-Maghrebi acts and threats (ministry of Interior)**

FIGURE 2.

Increasing number of Islamophobic acts, 2002–2019

Source: CCIF Annual Reports, synthesis of Ministry of the Interior data and CNCDH Annual Reports

identity markers to be measured, while neutralizing the main associated characteristics that could influence the situations analyzed. Although there is still a residual gap, this, by deduction, could be interpreted as discriminatory, even if other parameters are likely to be involved. In a situation of discrimination, the perpetrator's mindset tends to associate an individual with a risk, a negative feeling, or apprehension due to what (s)he is or represents, and is based on a set of deliberations that are not always conscious and are difficult to analyze, even if "the fact that a criterion systematically plays out to the disadvantage of individuals can only be established through the objectivization of its consequences for the opportunities available to these individuals."[12] In other words, the measurement of the discriminatory incident is not necessarily subject to the someone expressing intent. The differential treatment of a group can be observed in its measurable consequences.

In France, this chance to question the existence of a "religious penalty" has been quietly accompanied since the turn of the twenty-first century by the boom in the theme of discrimination.[13] The TeO survey, without being reductive, is the end point of this "invention of discrimination." This survey was a coproduction between the INED and the Insee, carried out between September 2008 and February 2009, with a sample of twenty-one thousand people born in metropolitan France between 1948 and 1990. This survey explored several aspects of people's experiences, particularly in relation to social and ethnoracial origin, migrant trajectories, beliefs, and institutional trajectories (educational, occupational, etc.). Aiming to question the scope and multiple impacts of discrimination over the life course, this study combines several ways of measuring discrimination, some of which stem from self-declared experiences while others refer to perceptions (of the existence of, the extent, and the targets of discrimination). Still other, even less direct, measures were aimed at sketching the contours of a "collective condition."

What Islamophobic Discrimination Feels Like

The experience of discrimination is captured by direct, quite general questions, and other, more concrete ones dealing more precisely with ordeals faced in various situated social spaces ("situational discrimination"). Overall, the survey found that 13 percent of the population aged eighteen to fifty residing in metropolitan France say they have been discriminated against, across all grounds.

These estimates are lower than the measurement of situational discrimination, for which the average rate reached 29 percent.[14] Yet whichever approach is preferred, the descendants of immigrants state that they encounter more inci-

dents of discrimination (44 percent). Within the immigrant populations and
their descendants, respondents from North Africa, sub-Saharan Africa, and
more intensely, Turkey and Southeast Asia, seem most likely to experience such
incidents. These trends are borne out once the main sociodemographic characteristics are controlled for: "Discrimination basically concerns visible minorities."[15] Beyond this general overview,[16] the more specific relationship between
discrimination and religious affiliation can be examined.[17] On a national scale,
religion itself is barely used to explain discrimination (under 1 percent). There
appears to be a link between the use of this motivation for discrimination and
the importance afforded to religion. It is cited as a factor by around 5 percent of
Muslims and almost one out of six Jews,[18] bearing in mind that these two groups
state the most intense attachment to their religion and the practice of worship.[19]
For Muslims, this rate may seem low compared to the extent of discrimination
they explain as stemming from "ethnoracial" grounds. Yet when the proportion
of people of Islamic faith or culture in the overall population (7 percent) is taken
into consideration, it emerges that among those respondents stating that religion
is a motivating factor for discrimination against them, just over half are Muslim.

The analysis of the profile of Muslims stating that religion is the basis for
discrimination against them provides further information.[20] While women —
across all grounds and in the majority population — state they have experienced
more discrimination than men (59 percent and 41 percent respectively), this
ratio is the opposite in the Muslim population (43.5 percent for women and
56.5 percent for men), apart from discrimination based on religious affiliation
(where is it 50.5 percent and 49.5 percent). This 7 percent gap within the Muslim population can be partly explained by the manifestation of signs of religious
faith. In fact, within this 5 percent of Muslims who say they have been discriminated against due to their religion, 38 percent say they wear an identifiable sign
of their religious affiliation, whereas only 21 percent of all Muslims in the survey
say they do so. Moreover, within this 5 percent, women account for more than
90 percent of respondents (who say they "often," and almost two-thirds of those
who "sometimes" wear such signs. In two-thirds of cases this means headgear
[and the rest of the time it is jewellery]).[21]

Factors other than gender and religious visibility also come into play: sensitivity to religious-based discrimination clearly decreases with age. The seventeen to thirty-four cohort is particularly sensitive, probably being more aware
of manifestations of discrimination. Moreover, in proportion to their weight
in the sample, Muslims holding at least a baccalaureate degree report more
religious-based discrimination, whereas socioeconomic status does not seem to
be a determining criterion for facing discrimination. On this point, other studies

show that the intensity of the feeling of suffering discrimination increases along with the level of education, social expectations, and the objective exposure of individuals to discrimination and stigma. In the same vein, it tends to intensify for those who forcefully assert demands for equality.[22] With regard to "origins," the sensitivity of North African minorities is greater than that of those with Turkish or Black African backgrounds, with a distinct overrepresentation of descendants of North African immigrants. The specifics of visible religiosity notwithstanding, these observations converge with the more general profiles of those experiencing discrimination that emerge from the TeO analysis.

Despite the consistent original sample, Muslims who state they have been discriminated against on the basis of their religion make up too small a statistical group (5 percent of the Muslim sample) to give credibility to more detailed statistical analyses. This data, however, provides information on the importance of visible signs in the social construction of a religious penalty in France and fuels the theoretical analysis and discussion of the ways in which origin and religion impact on one another in this regard.

Islamophobia and the "Muslim Condition" in France

Another avenue to explore is to think of Muslims as a social group sharing an experience and common characteristics and to thus set out their "condition."[23] This approach, based on the idea of shared experiences, can be justified by the degree to which Muslims accord importance to their religion, despite the small proportion of Muslims who draw a direct relationship between religion and discrimination. This perspective posits the idea of relative social homogeneity, even if the concept of a "Muslim condition" challenges the configuration of belongings in a context marked by a plurality of social identities, in socioeconomically modest milieux, through the cumulative dimension of social disadvantages. This induces a difficulty in identifying motives and explaining the basis for discriminations. Nevertheless, the TeO survey has provided original information about combinations of social identities. Despite the massive nature of economic precarity and unemployment, as well as the increasing fragmentation of the working classes, this social category still plays a powerful role in social identification, especially among the European-origin populations.

At the same time, "religion (as the basis for identity) is cited specifically by some groups. It can be said to be the case for more than a quarter of those of North African or Turkish origin, and 20 percent of Sub-Sahara Africans, while falling beneath 10 percent for the descendants of immigrants and other groups."[24] It is the basis for identity for only 7 percent of Catholics and 5 percent of Buddhists, but this figure rises to 33 percent for Muslims and 45 percent for Jews. Apart from gender and age, religion, origin, and socioeconomic category combine in what must now surely be completely new ways for some minority people. Although socioeconomic status still acts as one vector of identity among Muslims, their Muslimness and "origins" remain far from secondary factors. We should not dismiss the "collective condition" approach to Muslims, many of whom experience close-knit religious belonging alongside serious social and economic barriers.

This is the approach developed by political scientist Arno Tausch and his team, who show that the socioeconomic disadvantages faced by Muslim communities cannot be entirely explained by the "classic" factors of social and educational exclusion. They indeed suggest that a religious penalty, the weight of Islamophobia, affects individual destinies.[25] The concepts of discrimination and "condition" overlap, through a "minority logic" that can be analyzed via a high degree of identification or an othering process, or by racialization based on religious affiliation.[26] Moreover, "when the importance of religion in the daily lives of respondents is taken into account, it shows that for all faith groups, it is the religious individuals that report higher levels of discrimination, except in the case of Muslims, for whom religious commitment changes practically none of the indicators. In other words, the experience of discrimination in their case is not due to a particular religious practice or commitment but to a dimension to do with the identity of Islam per se."[27]

All in all, the intensity of the discrimination reported by Muslims, accumulated across all the indices is "around 50 percent higher in comparison to people who state they are not religious," a pattern more pronounced in education, work, and public services: only "Muslims still encounter more discrimination in housing than in health."[28] Therefore, the religious affiliation of a minority indeed comprises the potential vector of a collective condition insofar as it transcends ascriptive markers (gender, age, and origin) and class membership. The theme of Islamophobia, unlike issues surrounding the practice of a faith, symbolizes this collective exposure to social discrimination and thus contributes to the construction of the Muslim condition.

Many critiques have been leveled at the TeO survey, which have been synthetized by sociologist Olivier Masclet,[29] particularly the risk of essentializing social groups and neglecting individuals' class position. One of these critiques, which is more directly relevant here, relates to the difficult relationship between the various grounds for discrimination, especially race and religion. This relationship is discussed in most historical, sociological, and psychosocial analyses of Islamophobia, whether in descriptions of how they complement one another, their interactions, their "family" relationship, or in efforts to establish a kind of homological relationship based on the concept of racializing the religious field. Researchers Yael Brinbaum, Mirna Safi, and Patrick Simon are correct to use the term "interferences" to refer to statistical uncertainties between "origin" and religion. This caution stems from the difficulty in statistically controlling for each of these markers. By statistically neutralizing "origin," they point out that "among immigrant groups, Muslims are no longer significantly discriminated against," while for the descendants of immigrants, there is still an effect on their experience of discrimination that is specific to the religious variable. Despite this, they underline that the religious criterion "is very difficult to separate from the effect of origin precisely because the groups facing the most discrimination are by a large majority, Muslim."[30]

We have to remember that the grounds for discrimination are recorded in TeO are based on the victim's own statement.[31] By requiring the respondents to separate out the grounds themselves, the survey uses the theory and induces the idea that the various suggested grounds refer to easily distinguishable events. However, as Valérie Amiraux astutely notes, "the act of religious discrimination brings into play [a] plethora of parameters" and does not always allow what derives from class, gender, race, or religion to be distinguished from one another.[32] Variables that can be separated statistically cannot necessarily be distinguished sociologically. "Origin," just like religion, may summarize, be a shorthand for, or conceal other variables, and it is not clear that they are independent from one another. Moreover, "what the world of statistics refers to as 'race' is not an exact match to what is perceived by the actors who contribute to the decision-making and selection processes."[33] This reasoning could be extended to the variable of "religion," particularly by positing that "origin" and religion "interfere" as much from the perspective of the perpetrators as of the victims of discrimination or racism. On this specific point, the initial findings from the EU-Midis Survey are invaluable.[34]

The EU-Midis program constituted a break with tradition in the European bodies' monitoring practices through the establishment of massive victimization surveys.[35] Since 2001 several reports had identified the shortcomings of quantitative evaluations of racism and discrimination in Europe and set out plans for specific surveys, or even the incorporation of modules of questionnaires dedicated to the racist and discriminatory issues within existing surveys.[36] The 2008 EU-Midis Survey had a sample of 23,500 people across the twenty-seven EU member states.[37] It enabled minorities' experiences of discrimination to be studied by focusing on two particular groups within each country. In France, the study concentrated on "North Africans" and "Sub-Saharans" who had been living within the country's borders for at least a year prior to the survey and self-identified with these groups.

In the EU-Midis survey, discrimination is examined across a multitude of spaces: place of work, housing market, contact with workers in the health, social, and educational services, the hospitality sector (cafés, restaurants, and bars), shops selling textiles, and access to banking services (opening an account and getting a loan). One report from the survey, on the experiences of "Muslims," was published, and here we highlight its salient points. One in three Muslims in Europe states they have experienced an average of eight incidents of discrimination over the previous twelve months (34 percent of the men, and 26 percent of the women). As in the TeO survey, it emerges that the likelihood of reporting incidents decreases with age. Moreover, new arrivals and noncitizens report higher levels of discrimination on the basis of their origin. On the other hand, the report highlights that wearing traditional or religious clothing (such as the hijab) do not have a significant impact on experiences of discrimination, although it is impossible to identify the rate of such incidents for each country. Indeed, on the thorny issue of grounds for discrimination, only 10 percent of respondents state "religion or beliefs" alone as their cause, which is three times less often than "ethnic or immigrant origin." However, when the option of combining these two grounds is available, it receives 43 percent of responses. Whether this score expresses confusion or not in how to determine grounds for discrimination, it encourages caution in the measurement and analysis of Islamophobia that relies on asking questions of the victims.

Muslimness as a Labor Market Penalty

Some researchers have tried to transcend this uncertainty by using the "situational test" method. Live field experiments aim to establish whether there is a religious penalty in a multi-individual comparison. This experimental method is supposed to mimic a discriminatory situation by isolating one marker, which is then tested. This is an operation that assesses the social reception given to individuals (customers at discos, applicants for jobs, or for accommodation), distinguished solely by the specific marker being tested in real conditions. It aims to neutralize one or more factors likely to contribute to making a socially discriminatory decision. In France, Claire Adida, David Laitin, and Marie-Anne Valfort compared the attempts to find work by French Muslims and Christians from Senegal based on sending applications with two virtually identical (fictional) résumés in which only the religious marker differed.[38] They revealed a considerable level of discrimination against the Muslim applicant, who got 2.5 times fewer interview offers than the Christian applicant. In other words, for every hundred positive responses received by "Marie Diouf," "Khadija Diouf" only got thirty-eight.

In a larger-scale survey on religious discrimination, Valfort observes that "the probability of practicing Catholics being contacted by the employer to offer an interview is 30 percent higher than their Jewish counterparts; and 100 percent higher, i.e., twice as high, in relation to practicing Muslims."[39] This result is twice as high as discrimination between Whites and Blacks in the USA, as demonstrated by a study with comparable methodology carried out in the secretary and sales job markets.[40]

However, field experiments have theoretical and methodological limits. Such experiments are difficult to establish, requiring a considerable logistical effort and a high level of rigor at every step of the protocol (drafting of applications, collection of recruiters' data, etc.). The survey must be quickly completed to avoid excessively large time gaps, and the sample size is limited by the number of jobs on offer. Moreover, field experiments reveal actions more than they do processes, and their major disadvantages are their sporadic nature and the difficulty of generalizing the results. Adida et al. sought to fill this gap in another study aimed at understanding the basis for this discriminatory treatment. The study used a series of experimental games, in which the researchers focused on separating what is due to "discrimination by taste"—that is, an "altruism deficit"—from what is due to a more rational ("statistical") form of discrimination, that is, a problem of trust between French natives and Senegalese Muslims. Their findings purport to reveal that "the weakest type of cooperation by the French in relation to Senegalese Muslims in the simultaneous interplay of trust is due to discrimination by taste, and thus has no rational basis."[41] "Irrational" behavior seems linked to what the authors call "the Hortefeux effect," in reference to the comment made on 5 September 2009 by former minister of the interior Brice Hortefeux: "When there's one of them it's ok [...] It's when there are a lot that there are problems!" According to Adida et al., "In fact it is enough to go from a session containing one Senegalese Muslim player to a session containing two Senegalese Muslim players for French people's unconditional altruism toward Senegalese Muslim recipients to erode."[42] Here we reach the principal theoretical limit that profoundly undermines this experimental approach: it essentializes the "Indigenous French" and "Senegalese Muslim" groups, etc., and fuels the scientifically unfounded and politically dangerous idea of a "threshold of tolerance."[43]

PART II

A History of the Concept of Islamophobia

CHAPTER 4

From Anti-Orientalism to the Runnymede Trust

According to some Parisian media intellectuals, the term "Islamophobia" deserves no place in the French language. One of the main arguments used to justify its removal from French vocabulary is the oft-made statement that the term was allegedly coined by "Iranian fundamentalists" in the 1970s, both to undermine those women refusing to wear headscarves and prevent any form of criticism of the Islamic religion. This argument is put forward for example by journalists Caroline Fourest and Fiammetta Venner, in 2003: "The word 'Islamophobia' has a history that should be understood better before it is used lightly. It was used in 1979, by the Iranian mullahs who wanted to label women who refused to wear headscarves as 'bad Muslims' by accusing them of being 'Islamophobic.' [...] Actually, far from referring to any form of racism, the word Islamophobia has been clearly designed to invalidate the claims of people who resist fundamentalists, beginning with feminists and liberal Muslims."[1] With this myth having spread, "philosopher" Pascal Bruckner used it himself a few years later: "Coined by Iranian fundamentalists in the late 1970s to counter the claims of American feminists, the aim of the term 'Islamophobia,' modeled on 'xenophobia,' is to place Islam beyond criticism unless you want to risk being accused of racism."[2]

These media intellectuals actually have no grounds for this assertion. There is no real equivalent of "Islamophobia" in Farsi (Persian) or Arabic, and this type of neologism is very rare in both languages. *Islam harâssi* seems to be the Farsi term to mean "hostility towards Islam," while *eslam setizi* means "antagonism toward Islam." However, there is no adjective like "Islamophobic." *Eslam setiz* seems a feasible source for this claim, but is rarely used.[3] Two terms are used in Arabic, but they rarely go together to make up an equivalent term to "Islamophobia." There is firstly the "traditional" *adâ'al-islâm* (hostility toward Islam), and then the slightly more learned term, *ruhâb al-islâm* (phobia of Islam), but the latter appears only to have emerged in the 1990s.[4] However, this difficulty in finding Farsi and Arabic origins for the term "Islamophobia" stems from the fact that far from being an "oriental" invention, it is actually a French invention!

An Orientalist Critique of Orientalism

As Fernando Bravo Lopez, who carried out the first study of this subject, emphasizes, we owe the invention of the neologism "Islamophobia" and its initial uses to a group of "administrator-ethnologists" who were specialists in the study of West African (especially Senegalese) Islam: Alain Quellien, Maurice Delafosse, and Paul Marty.[5] At the beginning of the twentieth century, knowledge of Islam was a necessity for administrators in the colonial civil service who sought to maintain imperial domination over colonized Muslim populations. The production of knowledge for both administrative and academic ends is thus intrinsically bound up in the project of colonial domination. This desire for knowledge was realized in the proliferation of often dense and erudite ethnological research into "Black Islam" in sub-Saharan Africa. In France, the connection between ethnology and colonial policy can be illustrated by two elements. First, the publication of the prestigious journal, the *Revue du monde musulman* (Journal of the Muslim World) by the Moroccan Academic Society, and secondly, the movement of its administrator-ethnologists back and forth between the colonial bureaucratic space and the academic space, especially in their journeys as pupils and teachers, through the higher education institutions such as the École coloniale and the École spéciale des langues orientales (School for Middle and Far Eastern Languages) in Paris.[6] For these civil servants, what was primarily at stake was to establish the "right" colonial policy by winning the trust of the colonized, and some degree of legitimacy in their eyes. From this viewpoint, Islamophobia could be split into two versions: government Islamophobia, and academic Islamophobia.

In a 1910 article about the state of Islam in French West Africa, Delafosse criticizes the element of the colonial administration that openly asserts its hostility to the Islamic religion. "Whatever those for whom Islamophobia is a tenet of administration of the indigenous population may say," he argues,

in West Africa, France has no more to fear from the Muslims than it does from the non-Muslims. [...] Islamophobia therefore has no good reason to be present in West Africa, where Islamophilia, meaning a preference afforded to Muslims, would in turn create a feeling of distrust among the non-Muslim populations, which are in the majority. The interests of European power, as is the case for the interests of the indigenous populations, mean that we must assume the obligation to seek to maintain the status quo and remain rigorously neutral in respect of all religions.[7]

Islamophobia is thus defined as an erroneous form of governance, that is, differential treatment based on religious criteria. Delafosse instead asserts that the value of governance should be unconnected to any moral considerations and rather determined by a pragmatic policy of domination. Islamophobia is therefore the opposite of "Islamophilia," the preference given to Muslims, which is not necessarily the most appropriate mode of governance in West Africa either, because it would end up provoking the enmity of the majority of the non-Muslim colonized group. Government Islamophobia is moreover linked to what Marty calls "ambient Islamophobia,"[8] which is not exclusively restricted to the circles of the colonial civil service.

However, for these administrator-ethnologists, "ambient Islamophobia" is based on academic Islamophobia. In a review of the book *L'âme d'un peuple africain: Les Bambara*, by Abbé Henry (1910), Delafosse criticizes the "ferocious Islamophobia" of its description of Bambara customs.[9] However, it was Quellien who developed the most systematic critique of academic Islamophobia. In his law thesis on "Muslim Policy in French West Africa," defended and published in 1910, he defines Islamophobia as "anti-Islamic prejudice": "Islamophobia has always been, and still is, *a widespread prejudice against Islam* held by people from Western and Christian civilizations. For some, the Muslim is the natural and implacable enemy of the Christian and the European. Islamism is thus the antithesis of civilization, while barbarity, bad faith and cruelty are the best that can be expected from Muslims."[10]

However, Quellien argues that "this hostility to Islam goes a little too far, as the Muslim is not the natural enemy of the European but could become it, consequent to local circumstances and especially when they mount armed resistance to colonization."[11] To show that the Muslim is not the enemy of the European, Quellien uses testimonies from "explorers" Adolf Overweg and Heinrich Barth, members of an 1849 British scientific expedition in Africa, and Louis-Gustave Binger, a French colonial officer and administrator in Côte d'Ivoire, who were "very well received in the Muslim towns and by the Muslim tribes," and in Binger's case, "was never anxious about their religion."[12] Quellien thinks Islam has "an incontestable moral value" and that it "raised the moral sensibility of the people it ripped from the grasp of fetishism and its degrading practices." He thus refutes the opinion of the German explorer and geologist Oskar Lenz, who feels that "Islam is the enemy of all progress, and it exists purely by the force of its own inertia, which leaves it unassailable"[13] and that therefore "Islam means immobility and barbarity, whereas Christianity represents civilization and progress."[14]

Quellien then undertakes to contradict the main "criticisms" of Islam (the "holy war," slavery, polygamy, fatalism, and fanaticism) by using anti-essentialist and historical arguments. He goes as far as to assert that Islam "does not seem [. . .] opposed to the idea of the conquest of Muslim countries by European powers"[15] insofar as, according to some Islamic religious legal scholars, "when a Muslim people have resisted a Christian invasion, as hard and as long as their means of resistance have allowed, they may give up the struggle and accept the conquerors' domination if the latter guarantee Muslims both freedom of worship and respect for their wives and daughters."[16]

It is from the similar standpoint of critiquing Orientalism as a set of biased Western forms of knowledge that both Étienne Dinet (1861–1929) and Sliman Ben Ibrahim (1870–1953) write. Dinet was a painter from a middle-class Catholic family who moved between France and Algeria, while Ben Ibrahim was a highly educated practicing Algerian Muslim. They met when Ben Ibrahim "saved" Dinet from a brawl with Algerian Jews.[17] Dinet converted to Islam in 1913 and became an "activist artist." Parallel to his activity as a painter (within the genre of Algerian Orientalist painting),[18] he campaigned during the First World War for the repatriation and burial of Algerian Muslim infantrymen and for the building of the Grande Mosquée de Paris (initiated in 1926). He is part of the same intellectual family as the administrator-ethnologists, without ever having belonged to the colonial administration. He enthusiastically supported "the Franco-Muslim union" and equality between colonizers and colonized (in the context of empire), in order to avoid anticolonialist separatism and the victory of communism in colonized lands. It was only in the wake of the failure of Algerian governor-general Maurice Viollette's proposals aimed at giving national recognition and political rights to a minority of Algerian Muslims that Dinet despaired of and abandoned politics, thereafter going on the pilgrimage to Mecca.

For Dinet and Ben Ibrahim, "Islamophobia" refers firstly to "modern-day Orientalists" who had introduced "innovations" into the biography of the Prophet Muhammad.[19] They state that "the study of the innovations [. . .] introduced into the Prophet's story enables us to observe that sometimes they were inspired by an Islamophobia that is difficult to reconcile with science, and unworthy of our historical era." They criticize the "stark ignorance of Arab customs" evidenced in these studies and instead attempt to convey a history of the Prophet based on the writings of classic Muslim authors (Ibn Hicham, Ibn Saâd, etc.) and that of a modern historian, Ali Borhan'ed Dine El Halabi. Dinet and Ben Ibrahim formulate a critique of Orientalism from within: for them, Islamophobia is a prejudice incompatible with scientific methods.

Moreover, Dinet uses the term "Islamophobia" as a synonym of "Arabophobia" to identify and criticize particular political actors and Algerian settlers. He writes twice to his sister in January 1929: "If the [Viollette] Bill is rejected, it will be a triumph for the Arabophobes and for militarism that the whole world can see, at the very moment of the Centenary [of the conquest of Algeria in 1830], and will be an everlasting wedge driven between the French and the Muslims despite the protestations of love that will have been dictated to the local tribal chiefs when they are showered from turban to toe with Légions d'honneur. The politicians steeped in Arabophobia, seeking to mobilize the Settlers [...] against their true interests."[20] In March of the same year, he continued in the same vein: "I wonder what Viollette thinks of Tardieu's speech [opposing the bill] to the Centenary Commission for Reforms for Indigenous People? Here, the Islamophobes are over the moon because the Bill is well and truly buried [...] There is no doubt of the boost that this has just given to Bolshevism!"[21]

At the end of their pilgrimage, Dinet and Ben Ibrahim published a travel account, in the conclusion of which they expand on the three aspects of the trip that had made the strongest impression on them: "the vitality of the Muslim faith, the formidable power of the Muslim faith, and the persistence of a loosely disguised European hostility toward Islam."[22] The latter element is the basis for the definition of Islamophobia they provide, elaborating it further along three dimensions.

First, they place the definition in the long-term historical context going back to the Crusades. They argue that "unfortunately, Europe has political traditions dating back to the Crusades that have not been abandoned and, if one is tempted to forget them, Islamophobes such as [William E.] Gladstone [former British prime minister], [Lord] Cromer [British consul in Egypt], [Arthur J.] Balfour [former British prime minister and foreign secretary], the Archbishop of Canterbury, and the missionaries of all religions, etc., immediately step forward to remind us of them."[23]

Next, Islamophobia is posited as an ideology of conquest that should logically diminish at the same pace as armed resistance to colonial conquest is broken: "As it is no longer able to contribute anything, Islamophobia should therefore diminish and disappear. If it did persist, it would prove once and for all to the whole of Asia and Africa that Europe seeks to hitch them to an increasingly tyrannical yoke. [...] If, on the contrary, Europe engaged in friendly relations with Islam, world peace would be ensured."[24] The alliance between Europe and

Islam, defined in this essentialist way, would thus be an "unbreakable barrier" to both the "yellow peril" and the threat of communism.

Lastly, Dinet and Ben Ibrahim set out a typology of Islamophobia, distinguishing "pseudoscientific Islamophobia" from "religious Islamophobia."[25] To illustrate these two types, they only give a single example: the book *Islam*, by Samuel W. Zwemer, professor of the history of religion at Princeton University, whose translation of the verses of the Quran leads the reader to believe that Islam is a polytheistic religion . . . and which includes a genuine appeal for war against Islam.[26] According to Dinet and Ben Ibrahim, "when a scholar studies a subject, he is passionate about it and discerns all the beauty imaginable in it,"[27] but "there is only one exception to this rule, and again Islam is the victim of it." Indeed, they argue that there is a group of Orientalists who only study the Arabic language and Islam "in order to taint and denigrate it."[28] These scholars, "who have forgotten the principles of impartial science," have "left the missionaries overjoyed, and they have redoubled their proselytizing zeal."[29] They thus continue their critique of Orientalists begun in *L'Orient vu par l'Occident*,[30] in which their targets are works by Belgian Jesuit Arab "expert" Henri Lammens, and *Mohammed et la fin du monde* by Paul Casanova, a professor at the Collège de France.

Although the term "islamophobie" was invented by the French, there was a long passage of time before the appearance of an English translation. When Dinet and Ibrahim's *La vie de Mohammed* was published in English in 1918, the "islamophobie" was translated as the expression "feelings inimical to Islam";[31] it did not migrate from French to English at that point. It appeared for the first time in English in 1924, in a review of *L'Orient vu par l'Occident*, but the author merely quotes Dinet and Ben Ibrahim, rather than using the term independently.[32] It reappeared in English only in 1976, in a piece of writing by an Egyptian Dominican Islamic scholar, Georges C. Anawati, who gives the term a completely different meaning from that accorded it by Dinet and Ben Ibrahim. According to him, the task of the non-Muslim Orientalist is even more difficult because the latter would be "compelled, under penalty of being accused of Islamophobia, to admire the Koran in its totality, and to guard against implying the smallest criticism of the text's literary value."[33] Anawati suggests this "hostage to Islamophobia" scenario is an obstacle to the advancement of Orientalist knowledge.

A Postcolonial Critique of Orientalism

After the Second World War, the uses of the term "Islamophobia" became more disparate. It was used in 1951 by Charles-Vincent Aubrun, a specialist in the scholarship of Spain, in his review of a book on fifteenth-century epic poems from Navarre that were hostile to Muslim Spain.[34] He refers to "anti-French and Islamophobic sentiments" expressed in a poem that is part of the Western Christian tradition of the *Chanson de Roland* (the oldest surviving piece of French literature, from the eleventh century). The term seems to be used often in the academic discourse about Medieval Spain to describe poetry hostile the "Moors."[35] In 1985 ethnographer Anne-Marie Duperray writes of "the latent or explicit Islamophobia of the (colonial) administrators" in her book on the Yarse people of Burkina Faso.[36] In 1978 Tunisian historian and Islamic specialist Hichem Djaït refers to Islamophobia and Arabophobia to describe "the Islamophobic orientalism" in his book *L'Europe et l'Islam*.[37] However, his study of Orientalism is scarcely at the same level of depth as Edward W. Said's 1985 comparative work on Islamophobia and anti-Semitism (see chapter 11).[38]

According to the Oxford English Dictionary, the first occurrence of Islamophobia is in 1991 in the U.S. journal *Insight*. Although this article is insubstantial, by following the thread of its sources and citations, the readers end up at an interview with the Russian Islamic specialist, Stanislav Prozorov, member of the Saint Petersburg Institute of Oriental Studies. The interview was held after a lecture in Leningrad called "Islam: Traditions and Innovations," which was published in the youth section of the *Leningrad Smena* newspaper (December 1989) and reprinted in *Komsomolets Uzbekistana* (17 January 1990). In it, Prozorov defines Islamophobia as an ideology that legitimized the Soviet conquest of Central Asia (General Budennyi's campaign), Stalin's repression of Muslims, and the destruction of mosques and religious books. If Islam represented an "immediate danger" in Central Asia after the fall of the Berlin Wall, this was not due to the Muslims but rather to Soviet policy. For Prozorov, the Afghan War would never have been waged if the Soviet leadership had had sufficient knowledge of the reality of the Muslims in that country: "Not only did we not know the basic facts about Muslim groups, but in general, all the information about the history, traditions and culture of Islam had been twisted for dozens of years by our ideological dogma. [...] Islamophobia was nowhere more pervasive than among the country's political leadership."[39]

Time to Mobilize: From London to the United Nations

So far, the uses of the concept of Islamophobia remained siloed in the intellectual sphere, particularly within the critique of Orientalism. From the 1980s, a political use of the category of Islamophobia emerged, this time not in relation to hostility to, and prejudice about, colonized Islam or Muslims, but instead in reference to Muslim immigrants in Europe. According to British sociologist

Chris Allen, a specifically anti-Muslim form of racism became a major concern for British Muslim communities in the early 1980s, particularly for political activists based in the London borough of Brent.[40] The emergence of this "new" racism was explained by the conjunction of two phenomena: the construction of a specific "Muslim identity" ("British Muslim") in the context of the various immigrant communities, and the shift in forms of racism from "biological" to "cultural."

The first postwar generation of migrants in Great Britain, from the Caribbean, Pakistan, India, and other Commonwealth countries, had initially defined itself by nation and religious membership. Muslim communities therefore fell into the category of Black and Asian.

But British-born Muslims would identify themselves differently from their parents' generation. For them, the role and preeminence of their religion, Islam, became increasingly significant,[41] which created the conditions for the emergence of a "Muslim consciousness."[42] The period therefore witnessed a transformation in the frames that people used to collectively identify themselves, with the category "Muslim" first competing with, and then replacing, "Asian."

Moreover, the political discourse on immigration also went through a significant change, from focusing on color in the 1950s–1960s to an emphasis on race and Blackness in the 1970s–1980s.[43] Robert Miles and Annie Phizacklea maintain that the anti-racist movement was a response to the racism underpinning the laws on immigration control.[44] According to Tariq Modood, it was the implementation of the 1976 Race Relations Act that led to a consensus around the umbrella term "Black"; suddenly, its hegemonic character excluded Asians. New forms of self-identification emerged to shatter the dominance of political Blackness, to the point where, by 1989, Muslim identity had become the principal one.

Indeed, perhaps the 1976 Race Relations Act caused tensions insofar as while it ensured protection of the law to racial groups, religion was not included as a legitimate communal marker. Thus, the legislation afforded no legal protection to multiethnic groups such as Muslims. Although some Muslims, particularly Pakistanis and Bangladeshis, were protected in relation to their national origin or ethnic group membership—as are Blacks, Asians, Sikhs, Jews, etc.—in this legal framework, religious group membership was a secondary matter. Despite the various campaigns by British Muslim organizations aimed at extending the law's field of application, the enduring loophole in the legislation was exploited by right-wing and far-right political groups, whose new discourse was sometimes labeled "new racism."[45] British conservative discourse thus underwent a fundamental change. It no longer focused on the "traditional" markers of race but used new ones, based on cultural and religious difference, that were not so well protected under the law. Unlike "classic" racism, this neoracist discourse was much less explicit, with its evocation of threats to the "British way of life."

The British anti-racist movement thus failed to recognize not only the shift in self-identification within Muslim communities but also the growing antipathy and hostility toward the latter. In this context, only a handful of Muslim activists acknowledged and fought against the embedding of a distinct anti-Muslim racism (see chapter 13). This struggle was spearheaded by organizations like An-Nisa and activists such as Fuad Nahdi, director of *MuslimWise* and *Q News* magazines. Other groups discussed the phenomenon, like the UK Action Committee on Islamic Affairs (UKACIA) and the Muslim Council of Britain (MCB). After the Rushdie Affair in 1989, during which various Muslim groups across the world protested against Salman Rushdie's novel *The Satanic Verses* and the anti-Muslim discourse propagated during the debates around it, more and more articles were published on anti-Muslim prejudice (in *MuslimWise*, the *Muslim Update*, and *Q News*), although the term Islamophobia was not used. Recognition of this phenomenon and identification with the Muslim faith also owe much to the publication and reception of Kalim Siddiqui's book *The Muslim Manifesto: A Strategy for Survival*.[46]

It was in this context, of affirming a Muslim identity and transforming the racist discourse, that the term Islamophobia began to be deployed in Great Britain. The first acknowledgement of Islamophobia by non-Muslims appeared in a report from the multiculturalist think tank, the Runnymede Trust, *A Very Light Sleeper: The Persistence and Dangers of Anti-Semitism*, published in 1994.[47] The report, which focused only on anti-Semitism and Islamophobia and did not look at any other forms of racism, was the catalyst for the Runnymede Trust's creation of the Commission on British Muslims and Islamophobia in 1996.

In a ten-year period, Islamophobia had gone from a shared social experience of Muslims in North London to a global, historical, and racial phenomenon, reinterpreted and redefined by both Muslims and non-Muslims as well as academics, state actors, and activists. From this perspective, the publication in 1997 of the second Runnymede Trust report, *Islamophobia: A Challenge for Us All*, not only influenced the meanings accorded to Islamophobia but granted it public and political recognition.[48] It was the first contemporary work to put forward a relatively detailed and up-to-date definition of Islamophobia. Despite its numerous criticisms, this definition has been highly influential in the anglophone world and has been cited by many researchers and in other public reports, at both national and international levels.

When the Runnymede Trust report came out, Muslim organizations were becoming increasingly active. These were the early days of the MCB and the establishment of the Forum against Islamophobia and Racism (FAIR) in 2001, which set their sights specifically on tackling Islamophobia. Despite the success of these organizations, their strategies were to be severely challenged by the events of 11 September. A few days after the attacks, FAIR and the Islamic Human Rights Commission (IHRC) joined with other NGOs at the World Conference against Racism in Durban and managed to obtain formal UN recognition for Islamophobia. The term had now been legitimized on the international stage and become a political "fact," even if the UN had not provided a precise definition. Moreover, the Copenhagen Declaration on Islamophobia should be stressed. This was produced at the end of a conference organized in 2006 by the UK-based television station, Islam Channel, and defined Islamophobia as the "demonization of human beings for no other reason than their Muslim faith."

After 11 September, a number of studies were carried out under the aegis of European Union (EU) institutions, particularly the European Monitoring Centre on Racism and Xenophobia (EUMC), which, by mobilizing fifteen member states, organized the broadest ever project of "vigilance" around Islamophobia. Several reports were published (in 2003, 2005, and 2007), but although the EUMC contributed to the institutional legitimization of the concept of Islamophobia, it did not produce a clear definition.

CHAPTER 5

Academic Research

The first form of institutional recognition granted to Islamophobia was in the Runnymede Trust report in 1994, which did not provide a definition. More specifically, it ignored other forms of racism and established links between Islamophobia and anti-Semitism without further developing them. Still, the report led to the establishment of the Commission on British Muslims and Islamophobia (CBMI), an organization whose 1997 report was based on information gathered from NGOs from several towns and boroughs (Bradford [in the north], Tower Hamlets and Waltham Forest [London and surrounding area]), plus data collected by a number of local authorities (Bradford, Kirklees, Manchester, Rochdale, and Sheffield in the North, Birmingham in the Midlands, and the London Boroughs of Camden, Haringey, and Newham). The CBMI had eighteen members and a chair, Gordon Conway. One of the members, Zaki Badawi, explained to Chris Allen that they preferred to give the chair's role to a non-Muslim to afford the commission greater credibility.

Shortcomings of the 1997 Runnymede Report

Before the publication of the 1997 report, thirty-five hundred copies of an interim report, *Islamophobia: Its Features and Dangers*, were sent out to well-known figures and organizations for feedback. However, only 140 responses were received. The 1997 version agreed on a two-part definition of Islamophobia: "1. The abridged formulation of it which refers to a fear or hatred of Islam — and consequently, the fear of, and aversion to all or a group of Muslims"; "2. A phobia of Islam [. . .] a recurring characteristic of closed views."[1]

In *Islamophobia* (2010), Chris Allen formulates several critiques of the Runnymede report, which seem absolutely valid.[2] First, although the report acknowledges the legacy of the past, it sees Islamophobia as a totally new, ahistorical phenomenon. This approach differs from that adopted in the 2004 report on anti-Semitism, which saw the past as a determining influence. However, this perspective is missing in the case of Islamophobia. This contemporary phenomenon is allegedly sui generis, with the issue of historical legacy not taken seriously into account.

Moreover, the 1997 report sets out a list of "closed views" that are argued to be characteristics of Islamophobia:

1. Islam is seen as a single monolithic bloc, static and unresponsive to new realities.
2. Islam is seen as separate and other—(a) not having any aims or values in common with other cultures; (b) not affected by them; and (c) not influencing them.
3. Islam is seen as inferior to the West—barbaric, irrational, primitive, sexist.
4. Islam is seen as violent, aggressive, threatening, supportive of terrorism, engaged in "a clash of civilizations."
5. Islam is seen as a political ideology, used for political or military advantage.
6. Hostility toward Islam is used to justify discriminatory practices toward Muslims and exclusion of Muslims from mainstream society.
7. Criticisms made by Islam of "the West" are rejected out of hand.
8. Anti-Muslim hostility accepted as natural and "normal."

This list is particularly problematic due to its normative dimension. Little is known about the ways in which it was constructed, but Chris Allen's interview with Robin Richardson (head of Inservice Training and Educational Development) provides some partial answers, as he was the member of the commission who "translated" the consultations, meetings, visits, and discussions into the text of the report. He had initially suggested seven features that characterize Islamophobic discourse, features that are to all intents and purposes identical to the views adopted in the final report. A subgroup of the commission was tasked with turning this list into a table. As Richardson explains, "I agreed [with this method] but did not realize straightaway that this way of doing things would open it up to the critique that the only alternative put forward to Islamophobia was Islamophilia."[3]

In other words, the discourses analyzed in the report were either Islamophobic or Islamophile, and the analysis of Islamophobia becomes an unsophisticated, normative exercise. For example, discourse hostile to Islam, as a religious dogma, could be labeled Islamophobic, even if this type of discourse could indeed have nothing at all to do with racism against Muslims as a group. Nor did the definition offered by the Runnymede Trust enable the thorny issue of the distinction between criticizing Islam and the stigmatization of Muslims to be satisfactorily resolved.

Moreover, the commission's subgroup mainly based its findings on the work of social psychologist Milton Rokeach, particularly his concept of "closed" and "open" minds. Rokeach's typology, developed in the USA between 1951 and 1954, seeks to understand psychological reasoning, based on beliefs and values. Rokeach's goal was to find "a single set of concepts, and a single language for analyzing personalities, ideologies and cognitive behaviors [...] and to produce a theory of intolerance and prejudice which is also argued to be ahistorical."[4] From this perspective, the work established a "dogmatic scale" that is highly problematic from a sociological viewpoint. His work is also strongly influenced by the context of the 1960s insofar it distinguishes between the minds of Blacks and whites, as well as between the minds of right-wing people and left-wing people (communists). Rokeach's methodology is thus very much open to question, and the CBMI's use of his analytical framework reveals its conceptualization of Islamophobia as a psychological, that is individual, and ahistorical phenomenon.

Moreover, the open/closed binary ends up paradoxically reinforcing the closed views, as these are utterly distinct from the historical context in which they are produced. In a way, the Runnymede Trust report achieves the same outcome as the Orientalists (see chapter 11): it implicitly excludes even Muslim individuals and groups that do not fit into the mainstream Islam bracket. Those who do not share the Runnymede Trust report's vision of Islam are neglected and ruled out of campaigns against Islamophobia. According to the report's logic, just stating that "some Muslims are intolerant about other religions" could itself be considered an Islamophobic attitude. There again, disagreement and debate cannot be placed on the same footing (i.e., considered to be completely legitimate common sense) as prejudice and discrimination, which are illegitimate and invalid. The report does not satisfactorily address this problem. As sociologist Michael Banton emphasizes, the Runnymede Commission's approach is "ill-informed" in that it "attributes all problems to a single form of harm, which it misinterprets."[5]

As Allen emphasizes, the concept of Islamophobia introduced in the Runnymede Trust report is reduced to a simplistic, superficial, individualized, and ahistorical phenomenon, defined more by the features of the victim than by the motivations and objectives of those who put it into practice. The report does not define a clear concept with analytical and empirical credibility. Despite these shortcomings, it still exerts a substantial influence over the public discourse and on the work of some scholars.[6]

A Contested Concept

However, none of these political and institutional discourses have provided an incontrovertible definition of Islamophobia; hence the proliferation of critiques put forward by recognized researchers after the Runnymede Trust reports were published.[7] Some of them were skeptical and even challenge the academic relevance of the concept of Islamophobia. For Professor Fred Halliday, the use of the term "Islam" in the 1997 Runnymede Trust report turns it into something completely abstract.[8] The use of the term "Islamophobia" reproduces two misrepresentations: it leads to the idea that there is a single "Islam" and prevents theological debates internal to Muslim communities: conservatives can accuse reformers of Islamophobia and "the first Islamophobes would then be found among the Makkan aristocracy who opposed to the Prophet."[9]

The way in which the report interprets the "closed views" could end up with either of two conclusions: either it is Islam as a religion that is being attacked, or it is the identity shared by all Muslims interpreted in the abstract, irrespective of the diversity and heterogeneity of Muslim communities. According to Halliday, the hostility weighed more heavily on Islam as a religion in the past, whereas in the current context this hostility has been displaced toward Muslims as a group, or as individuals. Non-Muslims' proximity to Muslims in a given country is said to provide a focus for contemporary hostility.[10] Consequently, for Halliday—supported on this point by anthropologist Esra Özyürek[11]—the neologism "Islamophobia" is not justified: we should instead use the term "anti-Muslimism."

From the perspectives of Jocelyne Cesari and Marcel Maussen,[12] Islamophobia is an imprecise term too often applied to diverse phenomena, from xenophobia to the justification for war in the Middle East, via the war against terrorism. It brings together various forms of discourse and action by suggesting that they stem from a single ideology and respond to a "fear," or a "phobia" of Islam. For Maussen, various types of discourse (academic, political, private/public, etc.) should be distinguished from one another and not considered equivalent or comparable parts of the same ideology. Cesari asserts that "Islamophobia" is therefore a "misleading" term because it assumes the preeminence of religious discrimination when other forms of discrimination, particularly racism and classism, may be relevant.[13] Robert Miles and Malcolm Brown, British sociologists of racism, maintain that "Islamophobia" should be used only if a specific and identifiable hatred of Islam can be evidenced.[14] It is not necessary to have a different category, such as "anti-Muslimism," and the phenomenon may be absolutely incorporated into theories of racism and xenophobia. According to anthropologist Pnina Werbner, Islamophobia is merely a form of "differentialist racism," or at a pinch, "anti-Muslim racism;" alternatively, sociologist Rachad Antonius's original expression, "respectable racism" (later picked up and popularized by sociologist Saïd Bouamama), could be deployed.[15] In this latter formula, it is not so much the sign to which anti-Muslim racism is applied that matters but rather the legitimacy from which it benefits in Western public space.

As we stressed in the introduction, the arguments leveled against the use of Islamophobia as a concept can be easily contradicted. Social sciences can redefine the term by going beyond its "phobic" dimension. Islamophobia cannot be reduced to anti-Arab racism; the censorship of the anticlerical critique of religions has less to do with the concept itself than the uses to which it can be put. Moreover, Allen is correct to be skeptical about the term "anti-Muslimism" since the 2002 EUMC report shows that both Islam as a religion and Muslims as a group are its targets. If the term "anti-Muslimism" is adopted, then "anti-Islamism" would also then have to be used, but given the polysemy of the term "Islamism," this would add to the confusion. Allen therefore prefers "Islamophobia" despite its flaws, especially since unlike its competitors, the term has acquired a "reasonable level of appropriation" in public discourse.[16]

It is for the same reason that anthropologist Matti Bunzl utilizes "Islamophobia," despite its imperfections: "Antisemitism and Islamophobia are simply the European terms of debate, and although there is no consensus over their meaning (particularly the former), I consider that ultimately, my objective (as a researcher) is to provide clarification."[17] The comparison with anti-Semitism is useful from this perspective: it is a term invented and claimed by nineteenth-century anti-Semites, who fostered the confusion between the "Jewish race" and Judaism. Despite its overtly racist origins, anti-Semitism is widely used in social sciences, from where a variety of academic definitions have been put forward, for the very goal of distinguishing it from a common-sense racist meaning (see chapter 12).

"Islamophobia" has thus become a freestanding category of public policy legitimized by international organizations (United Nations, European Union, etc.), by the propagation, over more than twenty years, of social science PhD dissertations, articles, and books published by the most prestigious anglophone publishers (Oxford and Cambridge University Presses, Routledge, Palgrave, etc.), and by the establishment in late 2012 of the academic *Islamophobia Studies Journal* (by the University of California–Berkeley).[18] Social and publishing "profitability" certainly plays an important role in the appropriation of the term by researchers who must "deal with it" since no alternative category has so far successfully replaced it. For example, despite her criticisms of the term, Jocelyne Cesari uses it in the titles of some of her publications and justifies it by stipulating that it is a "departure point."[19]

Plural Approaches to Islamophobia

Despite the criticisms leveled against it, the term Islamophobia has thus become embedded in the vocabulary of the anglophone social sciences. What is at stake is less the choice of terms than its definition from an academic, rather than a normative, perspective. While critiquing the Runnymede Trust's definition, numerous intellectuals and researchers, primarily from the English-speaking world, have produced definitions of Islamophobia delineating a battery of theoretical approaches, strands of which may overlap and cut across each other.

The first such approach sees Islamophobia as a racist ideology. This perspective draws on Miles and Brown's definition of racism,[20] and has three components: a political program or ideology very much codependent with nationalist ideology and providing a framework for knowledge and interpretation of power relations; a set of prejudices, opinions, and attitudes held by individuals, groups, communities, or societies, or by a combination of these; and lastly, a raft of exclusionary practices resulting from these prejudices and forms of discrimination in employment, housing, and other socioeconomic spheres, as well as the use of violence as a tool of exclusion.

The ideological dimension must therefore be distinguished from its translation into popular culture by the construction of prejudices, and from the practices of exclusion, given that the relationships between these three levels are not set in stone. The exclusionary practices can thus be thought of as the outcome of Islamophobia once they can be proven to have been motivated by the victim's "Islamic-ness" (see chapter 11), or that all Muslims are implicated, independently of variations in class, gender, ethnicity, race, etc.

Moreover, Miles and Brown identify two forms of exclusionary practice: those that are explicitly justified by racist discourse and those that are not, with the latter having other types of justification. It is therefore not the practice itself that is racist, but the motivation or underlying cause. So, hostility toward wearing the headscarf, as a symbolic form, becomes Islamophobic due to the meanings given to it. From this perspective, Islamophobia is not an action, a practice, or a form of discrimination, but rather the meaning determining an action, practice, or discrimination. It is basically an ideological phenomenon, as Allen's definition illustrates:

> Islamophobia is an ideology, similar in theory, function and purpose to racism and other similar phenomena, that sustains and perpetuates negatively evaluated meaning about Muslims and Islam in the contemporary setting in similar ways to that which it has historically, although not necessarily as a continuum, subsequently pertaining, influencing and impacting upon social action, interaction, response and so on, shaping and determining understanding, perceptions and attitudes in the social consensus—the shared languages and conceptual maps—that inform and construct thinking about Muslims and Islam as Other.[21]

In the same vein, Stephen Sheehi defines Islamophobia as a "new ideological formation whose expression has fully evolved since the collapse of the Soviet Union [. . .] [*and which disseminates*] anti-Muslim and anti-Arab stereotypes and beliefs circulated in order to naturalize and justify U.S. global, economic and political hegemony."[22]

Islamophobia fits into the pattern of all the transitory anti-Muslim historical phenomena, whose intensity varies from one period to another. Allen argues that this is endemic to European and Western culture and that it can be recognized and observed in different cyclical periods of latent and acute Islamophobia, which can reach the threshold of an "epidemic" after particular incidents (such as the attacks on New York on 11 September 2001 and the 7 July 2005 attacks on London). For British Pakistani intellectual Ziauddin Sardar, the contemporary manifestations of Islamophobia embody the reemergence of an enduring anti-Muslim phenomenon.[23] Dilwar Hussain argues that it would be better to refer to "Islamophobias" in the plural, in that the features of Islamophobia are contingent upon the historical context, in which it is expressed, bound to, but never completely dependent upon, the past.[24] This perspective is shared by sociologist Vincent Geisser, who sets out a typology of Islamophobias ("occupational," "municipal," "institutional," "latent," etc.). He maintains that the "new" Islamophobia "is indeed a profoundly modern anti-Muslim racism embodied in a postrevolutionary racialist ideology,"[25] but his approach is less compelling when it tries to explain the relationship between the concept of Islamophobia and those of "religiophobia" and "islamistophobia."[26]

This trend of interpreting Islamophobia as an essentially ideological phenomenon has led to most researchers prioritizing the analysis of representations of Muslims in public discourse (press, television, and cinema), especially after the 1979 Iranian revolution, and 11 September 2001 (see chapter 7). Most research

on Islamophobia thus addresses public discourses on Muslims in the context
of international conflicts, while few studies focus on social practices or deploy
original empirical and quantitatively significant material.[27] The overwhelming
majority of academic book chapters and peer-reviewed journals deal with media
discourse, for example, the bellicose rhetoric of George W. Bush or the discourse
of neoconservative intellectuals, etc. This ideological preference is probably due
to the fact that anglophone researchers who write about contemporary Islamophobia are mostly located within disciplines such as Islamic studies, religious
history, communication, literature, etc.

However, we argue that the ideological, warlike perspective is insufficient for
grasping the social structures of Islamophobia, in that it is not only an ideology of
conquest and reaction to terrorist attacks. Islamophobic discourses can be identified beyond and well before the military conflicts engaged in by Western countries. For instance, in France, the racialization of immigrant workers occurred
prior to the first Iraq War (1990) and the extension of the Algerian civil war to
mainland France in 1995 (see chapter 6); in Great Britain, it functioned in the
1980s even though the British government was not participating in armed conflict with Muslim countries. From a sociological perspective, while the ideological
dimension is clearly important, Islamophobia cannot be reduced to these causes.

The second approach to Islamophobia involves analyzing the processes of
racialization of Muslims and the embedding of race with religion. As sociologist Colette Guillaumin underlines, the "signifier" must be distinguished from
the "signified," that is, the process of racialization can be split into several elements (the division between identity and otherness; naturalization/essential-
ization; hierarchization and exclusion) and could be based on a wide variety of
signs (such as race, skin color, class, sex, religion, etc.).[28] From this viewpoint, researchers "should not restrict the use of the concept of racialization to situations
in which a group is distinguished from another by reference to skin color,"[29]
while the concept of racialization enables "research and political argument to
escape from the unproductive debates seeking to determine whether such and
such an individual or discourse, claim or doctrine is or is not 'racist.'"[30]

Nasar Meer and Tariq Modood assert that "anti-Muslim sentiment [. . .]
simultaneously draws upon signs of race, culture, and belonging in a way
that compels us to consider how religion has a new sociological relevance because of the ways it is tied up with issues of community identity, stereotyping,
socio-economic location, political conflict and so forth."[31] If it is accepted that
racism is not necessarily based on somatic or biological features, then the conclusion should be that "cultural racism is not merely a proxy for racism but a
form of racism itself."[32]

In other words, one should analyze the long—contingent, unnatural, and arbitrary—historical process of racialization that assigns a religious identity ("of Muslim origin," or "of Muslim appearance") to individuals and that is making Muslims—a socially, politically, nationally, geographically, spiritually, ethnically heterogenous religious group—into a homogenous and unchanging one. We suggest calling this process a religious racialization,[33] understood as the construction of identity ("us") and otherness ("them") based on religious affiliation. What is at stake theoretically is therefore the process of racialization of a set of individuals that justifies exclusionary practices.

While most work on the racialization of Muslims has analyzed public discourses, a new trend emerged in the 2010s: a focus on empirical studies and ethnography. Racialization is not only enacted in public discourses but is also the result of everyday social practices and interactions between Muslims and non-Muslims that could lead to forms of stigmatization and discrimination. For example, Steve Garner and Saher Selod edited a special issue of *Critical Sociology* in 2015, with case studies on the experiences of middle-class U.S. Muslims, young working-class British-Pakistani men, the peculiar situation of white British converts to Islam, the policing practices targeting Muslims in Ireland, and the construction of Muslim identities in the media, in particular through online comments about a reality TV show.[34]

The third approach to Islamophobia assumes a global historical and geographical perspective. In this "decolonial" framework, developed by sociologists Ramón Grosfoguel and Éric Mielants, Islamophobia is a phenomenon "constitutive of the international division of labor" that should be analyzed from a "world-historical perspective." It is a "form of cultural racism" corresponding to "the subalternization and inferiorization of Islam" produced by the "modern/colonial European/Euro-American Christian-centric capitalist/patriarchal world system" from 1492,[35] the year marking the Reconquista, the deportation of Jews and Muslims from Spain, and the conquest and colonization of the Americas. Contemporary Islamophobia here sinks its roots into the "hispanophobia" generated against the Muslims of Al Andalus.[36]

Other researchers interpret global Islamophobia through the prism of the control of bodies and the disciplining of Muslim subjectivity. Sayyid and Vakil argue that Islamophobia should be distinguished from racism for three reasons. First, anti-Muslim discrimination cannot be reduced to racism since Muslims do not comprise a single ethnic group: the concept of Islamophobia enables the multiethnic dimension of such discrimination to be accounted for. Second, Islamophobia transcends the borders of the nation-state and goes beyond racism based on nationalist ideology. Lastly, Islamophobia demonstrates the West's anxiety about its continuing cultural, economic, and military domination. They conclude that Islamophobia "emerges in contexts where being Muslim has a significance which is political. What Islamophobia seeks to discipline is the possibility of Muslim autonomy, that is, an affirmation of Muslim political identity as a legitimate historical subject."[37] Deploying concepts developed by Michel Foucault, David Tyrer analyzes Islamophobia as a form of "racialized governmentality," that is, the governance of the Muslim body, which is translated into reality particularly in the distinction made between "extremist" and "moderate" Muslims.[38] In these ways, the authors seek to shed light on the "inflections of Islamophobia, its variations and accents [which] are products of specific histories and trajectories."[39]

Another global perspective developed by some researchers is to use Stanley Cohen's theory of "moral panic." A moral panic arises when "a condition, episode, person or group of persons emerges to become defined as a threat to societal values and interests."[40] The construction of "folk devils" by "moral entrepreneurs" often entails xenophobia and racism that racialize both the folk devils and the "threatened moral community." For Cohen, the characteristics of a moral panic are volatility (temporary panic), hostility toward the threat, the projection of social malaise onto the folk devils, disproportionate state responses to them, the pinpointing of the threat in national space, and the importance of mass media. The aim of George Morgan and Scott Poynting is "to demonstrate the globalization of contemporary Islamophobia" and refresh Cohen's theory; they suggest that the Islamophobic "moral panic" is characterized by permanence, relocation, and the compression of time and space brought about by new media.[41]

One final approach consists of a focus on gender and sexuality in the production of Islamophobia ("gendered islamophobia"). For example, Jasbir K. Puar develops the concept of "homonationalism" to describe the "rise in homonormative Islamophobia in the North" and the contribution to the stigmatization of Muslims by particular homosexual political movements and actors, such as Pim Fortuyn in Holland and OutRage! in Great Britain.[42] Others refer to "sexual nationalism" or the instrumentalization of feminist and homosexual causes for nationalist and Islamophobic ends.[43] Partly reproducing the categories of colonial Orientalism (see chapter 11), the Islamophobic discourse thus carries differential representations of the "Muslim man" (violent, sexist, anti-Semitic, homophobic, etc.) and the "Muslim woman" (submissive, needing emancipation, etc.), whose reception by Muslim women has for example been studied in Great Britain and Lebanon.[44]

All in all, it is hard to put forward a single definition of Islamophobia that transcends all the theoretical approaches mentioned here. However, for us,

Islamophobia is a complex social process of racialization based on the sign of actual or perceived belonging to the Muslim religion, whose forms of operation vary according to the national contexts and historical periods. In contemporary France, this "total social fact" stems from an insider/outsider relationship, with the legitimacy of the presence of postcolonial immigrants on national territory at stake. It is a global and gendered phenomenon because it is influenced both by the international circulation of ideas and people and by gender relations. We theorize that Islamophobia is the consequence of the construction of a "Muslim problem," whose "solution" would be to discipline the bodies and even the minds of actual or perceived Muslims.

Islamophobia and French Academia

Confronted with the growing phenomenon of contemporary Islamophobia, the French social sciences have paid scant attention to it as an object of research.[45] This difficulty is not specific to the issue of Islamophobia, since it is also found in the relation to the topic of race in general.[46] The publication of sociologist Vincent Geisser's *La nouvelle islamophobie* in 2003 did not spawn new research projects until 2011, when the first university seminar series on Islamophobia was held at the *École des hautes études en sciences sociales* (EHESS).[47] Since then, the French academic field has been torn between two opposing trends. On the one hand, there has been a timid recognition of the emerging research on Islamophobia, for example through the publication of the first special issue devoted to the subject in the journal *Sociologie*.[48] A few academic conferences have been organized on Islamophobia by French researchers but also, revealingly, by British or American academics working (or not) in France.[49]

On the other hand, there is an academic underinvestment in studying this form of racism, since no French social science PhD dissertation contains the term Islamophobia in its title,[50] and very few of them deal with Islamophobia as a research subject.[51] Worse still, in a national context where academic freedom is threatened, some university conferences dealing with Islamophobia have faced attempted censorship, from both inside and outside the university, and one of them, at the University of Lyon 2, was even cancelled in 2017 as a result of pressure from far-right movements.[52]

Thus, as one of us has shown, there is a striking contrast between French academic production and that of English-speaking countries, where the academic field has largely engaged in a discussion of Islamophobia as both a concept and a social phenomenon.[53] The French academic controversy related to Islamophobia raises the general question of the autonomy of social sciences in relation to the political-media field and the capacity of researchers to be reflexive and to distance themselves from common-sense Islamophobic discourse.

The study of publications produced by French academics about Islamophobia shows that the controversy does not occur in the mainstream social science journals but on their periphery, or even externally to academia. For instance, no articles in the *Revue française de sociologie* mention the term, except in three book reviews.[54] Compare this to the number of articles in *Current Sociology* (thirteen), *Sociology* (fifteen), the *British Journal of Sociology* (seventeen), and the *American Sociological Review* (five). Major French social science journals such as *Annales HSS, Politix, Genèses, Sociétés contemporaines*, and *Actes de la recherche en sciences sociales* have published fewer than ten articles each containing the term Islamophobia. Most of the articles on Islamophobia in French are published in more specialized academic journals, but above all in the national press (*Le Monde, Le Figaro, Mediapart*, etc.).

One can also observe the logic of avoiding the (rare) French accounts on Islamophobia, which not only results in a lukewarm academic debate but also in the concept of Islamophobia being discredited, with arguments similar to those of political-media discourses being marshaled. Most of the time, in articles or books explicitly devoted to the subject of Islamophobia, the existing literature is avoided. For example, the sociologist Gérard Mauger, senior researcher at the CNRS and a specialist in working-class studies, contributed three of them to the "Reactionary Rhetoric" section of the journal *Savoir/Agir*.[55] According to him, "to get an idea of these controversies, one can consult the very complete Wikipedia entry."[56] Despite the history of the word and the variations of its meaning being well documented (chapter 4), he claims that "this long history of the concept runs the risk of anachronism: there is no guarantee that [the meaning of the idea] in the contemporary media space during jihadist attacks is identical to that of a concept previously 'confined to the intellectual sphere and to criticism of orientalism.'"[57] This peremptory assertion is made as if the work of contextualization had not already been done. In a similar vein, the anthropologist Jeanne Favret-Saada, senior researcher at the *Ecole pratique des hautes études* (EPHE), republished and expanded her 2007 book on the famous Muhammad cartoons controversy,[58] but without citing any of the scholarly accounts of the affair, whether Danish or foreign, that had been published in the intervening period.[59] These two examples show that French academia is strongly influenced by mainstream neoconservative discourse on Islamophobia, making the academic debate quite difficult.

The Construction of the "Muslim Problem"

PART III

The Construction of the
"Muslim Problem"

CHAPTER 6

The Postcolonial
Immigration "Problem"

Since the early 1980s, the French public realm has witnessed the construction of a "Muslim problem." An objection could be raised here: Islam could be seen as problematic because of the increasing number of violent acts legitimized by an Islamic religious discourse (the attacks in Paris, 1995–2020; New York and Washington in 2001; Madrid in 2004; London in 2005, etc.) and by a change in how Islam is practiced in France (an increase in the number of places of worship, and the emergence of Salafism).[1] Although these tangible facts are undeniable—and linked in part to changes in global political violence and in part to changes in Muslim religious practices across Europe—there are just as many non-Muslim violent acts and religious practices that are not classed as public issues, such as the campaigns of traditional Catholics against abortion and same-sex marriage and the growth of the African Pentecostalist movement in working-class areas in France.[2] Moreover, "separatist" movements are overrepresented in the category of acts that Europol labels "terrorist."[3]

Drawing on the theoretical framework put forward in the sociology of public problems,[4] our departure point is the principle that while not every social fact is naturally a public problem, it can become one if the three conditions for the possibility of collective belief in the existence of a "problem" are satisfied, through a complex social process.[5] This belief is primarily the outcome of a substantial production of knowledge about Islam and Muslims (see chapter 7), which selects and interprets the facts deemed problematic in the light of what we are calling here the "anti-Muslim archive," a changing set of negative representations of Islam and Muslims that has been constructed from the Middle Ages to the present time (see chapter 11). It then develops via the mobilization of a number of individual and collective (private and state) actors, who, without concerted efforts, contribute to fuelling the idea that Islam—in itself—is a problem (see chapter 8). The exploitation of the anti-Muslim archive functions in various national and political contexts, but in every case, it offers a religious framework for interpreting the social realities that inform struggles at national (for example, between immigrant workers and their French bosses) and at international levels (e.g., between jihadist groups and the U.S. government). This belief ultimately depends on meeting a particular norm, that is, a rule that is the basis for a fact being considered "problematic" (see chapter 9). In the case of France, this is the norm of national homogeneity, supposedly challenged by the emergence of Muslim religiosity among postcolonial immigrants and their descendants. Conforming to this norm is to be accomplished through establishing a new form of secular discipline.

Taking the gaps in the literature on Islamophobia into consideration—particularly the lack of focus on the conditions of production of media discourses—we would like to suggest some ways to help us think through and analyze the process of "universalizing" the "Muslim problem." In many European countries, the local specifics of the construction of the "Muslim problem" mean that, like the "Jewish question" at the turn of the twentieth century, it suddenly becomes "the only issue capable of generating near unanimity in public opinion."[6] The question for us, then, is how to understand the way in which a veritable national consensus can be built around the ideas that "Islam is a problem" and that "Islam is incompatible with the secular French Republic."

To grasp why and how the "Muslim presence" has become such an obsession in French public space, the three criteria that make a collective belief in the existence of such a problem possible—knowledge of the problem; the norm from whose perspective a social fact is considered to be problematic; and a mobilization that convinces the entire society that there is such a problem—should all be examined, as we know that they are bound up in one another and that they are basically the subject matter of the sociology of elites. Indeed, it is above all administrative, political, media, and academic elites who are the key actors in the construction of the "Muslim problem." We use the term "elites" in the plural to designate that this is not a homogenous social group. On the contrary, there are many fragmented and competing factions, each developing in different social spaces. The question is therefore to understand why and how, despite the divisions and tensions between these various elements of the ruling classes, the "Muslim problem" has become the subject of such a consensus among elites.

Strikes in the Car Industry and the Discrediting of
Immigrant Workers

The construction of this consensus has been achieved by yoking the "immigration problem" to the "Muslim problem."[7] Several studies by historians and sociologists have shed light on the mechanisms by which the "immigration problem" in particular has been constructed.[8] The current phase of problematizing immigration was not initiated by the Front national's breakthrough into the political arena in the early 1980s but stemmed from within the administrative area responsible for immigration, especially the DPM (Direction de la population et des migrations, Population and Migration Secretariat, established in 1966) in which, after Algerian independence, senior civil servants from the Ministry of Labor and a significant number of civil servants who had returned from Algeria were brought together in one state agency. The creation of the DPM saw the invention of a new institutional culture in which "controlling migratory flows" became the key issue. Having first been used experimentally on Algerians (sending back "fake tourists," limiting family reunion, creating personal case files, etc.), the French state's restrictive policy was then extended to cover all categories of foreigner, most of whom were nationals of former colonies.

Thus, contrary to popular belief, the official "suspension" of immigration in 1974 was not the Chirac government's response to the 1973 oil crisis. It was above all the result of a mobilization of administrative actors convinced that immigration was a problem to be managed. After the promulgation of the Marcellin-Fontanet Circular in 1972, which made the conditions for allocating residence cards more stringent, these civil service actors succeeded in normalizing their point of view by convincing both the economically liberal employers, usually very reluctant to restrict migratory flows, and the Chirac administration to support their strategy. Suspending immigration was justified not primarily by unemployment and the economic situation but by a set of other factors: demographic imbalances with developing world countries (French society was said to be threatened by "anarchic immigration"); the risk of a "new May '68, supported by a critical mass of foreign workers"; the "spectacular effect" of such a policy on official immigration (an end to illegal immigration and "fake tourists"); and the consequent savings in the national budget (particularly in cuts for foreign workers' housing).[9] The objective of being able to control migration thus became a taken-for-granted notion for the civil service, as well as political and media "elites" from the early 1970s. It is therefore hard to argue that this was a consequence of the "Lepen-ification of attitudes," a suggestion implying that the

latest politicization of the public immigration debate, begun in the early 1980s
with the rise of Jean-Marie Le Pen, kick-started the spread of such ideas into the
public debate.

Although the construction of the "immigration problem" is relatively well
known, the development of the "Muslim problem" is not very well understood.
Much of the scholarship takes 1989 as the departure point for controversy surrounding Islam, the year in which both the first headscarf affair in Creil and the
Satanic Verses incident occurred.[10] There is thus a surreptitious slippage from
the "immigrant problem" to the "Muslim problem," because the schoolgirls in
that first episode wore headscarves and the Ayatollah Khomeini put out a fatwa
against Salman Rushdie. Some explain this shift in emphasis by changes in forms
of self-identification among postcolonial immigrants. According to this view, a
"Muslim identity" took the place of an "immigrant identity." The generation of
the March for Equality and against Racism (Marche pour l'égalité et contre le
racisme) (1983) is thus labeled "secular," while the following generation of activists is argued to have yielded to the siren song of "Islamism."[11] If there is a Muslim problem, it is ultimately because Muslims segregated themselves or opted for
identity politics, worrying states of affairs to which the "elites" merely reacted
legitimately. Both this timeline and this line of argument seem historically unfounded. Well before 1989, the initial stage of the politicization of the Muslim
problem, in the aftermath of the Algerian War, emerged in the context of strikes
against large-scale redundancies in the car-manufacturing industry.[12] Strike action at the Citroën Aulnay and Talbot-Poissy plants (in April and May 1982,
respectively) was initially undertaken from within the traditional format of the
workers' movement: that is, the claims were basically about conditions, pay, and
individual and union rights, etc. However, the layoffs were eventually confirmed,
and immigrant workers occupied the factories and carried out a tougher course
of action, supported most of the way by the unions. This is the context in which
the Muslim question burst into the public debate. According to the mainstream
discourse, religious conflict had supposedly replaced the class struggle, bearing
in mind the decline of the reference to class as an identity in the public domain,
which goes back at least to the post–May 1968 period (when the dominant neo-
liberal discourse held sway during Valéry Giscard d'Estaing's presidency).

Since the early 1970s, unions had responded positively to religious requests
from Muslim workers in the name of freedom of worship.[13] The first mosque at
the Renault-Billancourt factory was opened in October 1976, hence the presence in the list of claims of one for a place of worship, in 1982. This request,
together with pictures of workers praying at the factory and the use of Arabic
and religious references by union leaders to mobilize workers,[14] were tangibles

used by opponents of the strikes as tools for criticizing and stigmatizing them. Thus, as Vincent Gay and others demonstrate, the debate's consequent focus on Islam is the result of actions carried out by three sets of actors: employers, media, and politicians.[15] Firstly, it was the leadership of the PSA Group (the owner the car manufacturers in question) that interpreted the strikes as a manipulation of Muslim workers by the trade union Confédération générale du travail (CGT, General Labor Confederation)—an idea echoed by some experts.[16] According to an internal PSA memo from May–June 1982, "the original thing about the strikes [at Citroën-Aulnay and Talbot-Poissy] is that without a shred of doubt, one of the CGT's main aims was to control the Muslim (mainly Moroccan) element of the workers."[17] The memo goes on to claim that there is thus a "not insignificant risk of seeing fundamentalist movements, whether ad hoc or based in the Near East, striving to take advantage of this agitation [. . .] [given that] certain Moroccan leaders, especially at Talbot, are known for their links to fundamentalist movements in their home countries."[18] With the Red Scare converging with the "green" one, according to the PSA leadership, an emerging "Muslim problem" would justify not only the intervention of the police but also the deportations of immigrant workers from France.[19]

The media then addressed the strikes through the lens of international current affairs, particularly the 1979 Iranian revolution.[20] Certain newspapers printed numerous photographs of skilled Maghrebi and African workers praying at the mosque and published caricatured cartoons in which cars were manufactured covered in Islamic veils, etc. This kind of religious othering is all the more effective as the twisting of social reality is legitimized by the political class, both in the speeches of right-wing politicians and in those given by the government ministers of the Left in the 1980s.[21]

In January 1983 Minister of the Interior Gaston Defferre complained in an interview on radio station Europe 1 about "holy strikes, fundamentalists, Muslims, and Shi'ites."[22] In February, Prime Minister Pierre Mauroy criticized the immigrant workers "whipped up by religious and political groups that define themselves according to criteria that have little to do with French social realities."[23] In a similar vein Minister of Employment Jean Auroux claimed, "There is clearly a religious and fundamentalist stake in the disputes we have witnessed, which gives them a twist that is not just to do with trade unions. That said, we live in a secular state and we have every intention of staying that way [. . .] I stand opposed to the institutionalization of any religion whatsoever at a workplace. I am against religions in businesses just as I am against politics in business."[24] These public statements are certainly based on a memo written by a Ministry of Employment advisor—according to which "fundamentalist Islamic theories" were filtering into "some French companies that had Muslim workers"[25]—and news from the government communications department, whose role in the politicization of the Muslim question is not very well documented in the period prior to 9/11.[26]

When the employers sought to stigmatize striking workers by depicting them as fundamentalists, the media broadcast pictures of groups at prayer to attract a large audience and the Socialist government first distanced itself from the strikers before changing economic policy by adopting austerity.[27] Media and political explanations of the immigrant workers' intransigence in clinging to their jobs ignored social factors, such as the ongoing class struggle, and posited religious factors (i.e., Muslim fundamentalism) instead. This was a completely different way of looking at the social world, in which religious affiliation allegedly determines both individual and collective behavior.

The construction of the "Muslim problem" can therefore be explained less by Muslims' actual actions and discourse, which above all focused on wages, than by the ideological convergence between employers and the political and media elites. Yet the "Muslim problem" only involved immigrant workers—whose presence is considered temporary—and not their children, who were to burst onto the public stage in the Marche pour l'égalité et contre le racisme.[28] While the Muslim problem was virtually absent from the discourse of the marchers and the media coverage of their anti-racist campaigning, it was to become a major theme in the debates held by the 1987 Marceau Long Commission on Nationality.

The Immigrant Children "Problem"

On 22 July 1987 French prime minister Jacques Chirac established the Commission on Nationality after the withdrawal of a bill to reform the nationality laws. The bill's proposal to challenge the legal right to nationality acquired through birth on French soil by introducing the criterion of "demonstrating a desire to be French" for French-born children of foreigners had, at the time, provoked an outcry.[29] Although the process of setting up a "blue-ribbon committee" is not specific to immigration, this was actually the first time in French history that a commission aiming to produce a national, public consensus about "the immigration problem" and "national identity" had been established.[30] Well before wearing hijab had become the subject of various political and media "affairs" (1989, 1994, 2003–2004, 2009–2010 and 2012–2013) and terrorist attacks had been committed in France (1995–1996, 2012) and other Western countries (11 September 2001, 11 March 2004 in Madrid, 7 July 2005 in London, etc.), several dozen well-known figures from academia, politics, the civil service, unions, the voluntary sector, and the media were recruited to reflect on what the place of postcolonial immigrants should be in French society, thus illustrating the embeddedness of the construction of the "immigration problem" within the construction of the "Muslim problem."

The "Long Commission" was to be the site of a struggle around the definition of Islam, whose outcome enabled the formation of what Edward Said terms a "community of interpretation."[31] There were two antagonistic positions, which map roughly onto an opposition between "orthodox neo-Orientalist" knowledge and "antithetic" (or heterodox) knowledge of Islam. The former was represented by Bruno Étienne (1937–2009), a famous scholar of Islam and professor at the l'Institut d'études politiques (Institute of Political Studies) at the University of Aix-en-Provence. "Muslims cannot be integrated," he explained to the Long Commission. "I am completely consistent on this. My answer is that it is very hard for Islam to tame the private sphere, which in our society is distinct from the public sphere. I don't think we should kid ourselves [...] This is a genuine issue. It should therefore be addressed. However, my theory on this is that the free space that France represents in the separation of church and state may facilitate the emergence of a form of Islam—and this should not come as a shock—that I would call cozy and quiet, homely even, and which indeed exists in the private sphere."[32]

The hegemonic perception of Islam imputes to it a set of negative intentions and characteristics. These include Islam's "difficulty" in distinguishing the public from the private spheres and its plan to impose itself on the public sphere. In other words, the essence of "Islam" is said to consist of regulating every aspect of life, for all members of society, and consequently, challenging the secular French state's monopoly of government, for example through "Islam's 'desire'" to impose a personal status that runs contrary to the dispositions of French civil law. "Islam" thus poses "a problem" by claiming to govern society. However, this perspective assumes that "Islam" is just another word for "French Muslims." The various components of the quasi-natural definition of "Islam" are thus attributed to all populations that are supposedly Muslim. A consequence of this metonymy is that Muslims "cannot be integrated" if they are "really" Muslims and must "naturally" refuse to be subject to the authority of the state and of French civil law.

This vision of Islam is in stark contrast to the one outlined by a minority of those giving evidence to the commission and by some of its members. A counter vision was expressed by Islamic studies scholar Mohammed Arkoun (1928–2010), director of the Institute for Islamic Studies at the University of Paris III-Sorbonne Nouvelle. He stated, "I'd like to draw your attention to the problem of secularity [laïcité]. It is said—and it's a kind of dogmatic principle, even for scholars of Islam—that Islam totally collapses the spiritual into the temporal, that it makes no distinction, whereas, in the French tradition, of course, this distinction is very sharp, and, from a legal perspective, has been for a very long time. And this point is considered as one of the compelling arguments that make, or would make, Muslims in France, unable to assimilate, as they say. There isn't enough time to show you that this is a myth."[33]

This "myth" has been constructed using Orientalist knowledge, which dehistoricizes and essentializes Islam and Muslims,[34] making a plethora of past and present experiences,[35] of a secular state and "Republican Islam" unthinkable.[36]

The dominant groups within the academic field, hostile to the idea of a secular Islamic experience, have had a considerable political impact on the public debate. The Long Commission interpreted the debate through the dominant neo-Orientalist frame and de facto marginalized the anti-Orientalist discourse. According to the commission, "historians stress the resistance exerted by Islam to Christian civilization over the centuries" and that "the conflicts possibly provoked through living side by side with, and being part of, the same national unit as groups whose history and traditions are not the same, cannot be denied."[37]

Islam can thus "pose a specific problem because of individual rights: such as polygamy, and gender inequality" and "it seems inconceivable that some of the population should be following a different form of law, in the name of cultural relativism."[38] In as far as "Islam is more than just a religion," it "may contradict the customs, internal legal order, and even the values of a non-Muslim society," and "the effort made by the most devout Muslims in France (i.e., those most attached to Islamic law) to comply with some of our society's rules should not be underestimated."[39]

The "specific problem" posed by Islam, however, is put into perspective by what sociologists have observed about the reality of Muslims' religious practices. According to Bruno Étienne, "only 5 percent of Muslims practice all the religion's required rituals." In other words, there are no authentic Muslims in France.[40]

Those supposed Muslims are not really Muslims, since according to the commissioners, "it should be noted that most children of Muslim immigrants (or French Muslims), who are not very religious, have only acquired knowledge of Islam from pictures that they are shown in French schools. [...] Studies also show that most young girls from Muslim immigrant backgrounds end up imposing significant changes to family traditions."[41] Children of postcolonial immigrants are thus of "Muslim origins." Although they "can be integrated" as "immigrants," they might pose problems as "Muslims." As they are not devout, they can eventually be "integrated." This "community of interpretation" of Islam that emerged from the Commission on Nationality constitutes an important step in the construction of the "Muslim problem." In 1987 the French ruling classes considered that if Islam "posed a problem" in general, this was not really translated into social reality. Ultimately, the report exuded an "optimistic" vision for the future of postcolonial immigrant children: unlike their parents, who are attached to religious traditions, they are not very religious and are caught up in an ongoing process of "integration," especially through secular state education. The overall process of secularization can only result in the extinction of Muslim religious practice.

This belief in the inevitable assimilation-integration of immigrants' children, deeply rooted in "elite" republican categories of thought going back to the end of the nineteenth century, was to be comprehensively turned on its head by young French girls with postcolonial immigrant backgrounds who wore head-scarves.[42] Just before the 1989 headscarf affair, Henri Tincq, religious affairs editor of the daily *Le Monde*, neatly expressed this "elite" perspective: "We first thought that Islam would be a fleeting phenomenon based on the supposedly transitory presence of immigrant workers from the Maghreb on French soil, and then, that the assimilation of this population, reluctantly or not, would foster the rise of a secularized 'sociological' Islam. This two-part forecast turned out to be inaccurate. [. . .] Far from becoming westernized, Islam has become one of the principal sources of identity, in a context of uprootedness, and even exclusion."[43]

The challenge to the belief in the disappearance of Muslim religious practices among postcolonial immigrant children reverses this (assimilationist) perspective: the children's integration is no longer conceptualized within a logic of expansion, wherein the state is responsible and must make them integrate, but in a logic of exclusion, according to which they are responsible for their own integration and the most "integratable" must be selected. The challenge to the legitimacy of their presence in France therefore depends on their capacity to satisfy the injunction to integrate.[44] Some social actors mobilized, especially during the September 1989 headscarf affair, to communicate the interpretation of wearing a headscarf to a state school as a national threat, and of Islam in general as a worldwide problem.

The (interior, national) headscarf affair was therefore connected to the (exterior, international) *Satanic Verses* affair, which thus enabled the emergence of an "imaginary Islam," to use Thomas Deltombe's term.[45] Yet the idea of taking steps to counter the "Muslim problem" by, for instance, banning the wearing of headscarves in state schools, was not a subject of consensus in the 1990s. Prohibitionists like Élisabeth Badinter, Élisabeth de Fontenay, Régis Debray, Alain

Finkielkraut, and Catherine Kintzler, co-authors of the "Profs, ne capitulons pas!" (Teachers, don't give in!) appeal, were in the minority, unable to convince the government, the Conseil d'État (French Supreme Court for State affairs, to be distinguished from the Cour de cassation, Supreme Court for Private Affairs), or even all the dominant media outlets.[46]

Just over a decade later, the "elites" stance on "solutions" to the Muslim "problem" had shifted dramatically. Excluding young women in headscarves from state schools, deemed by the Conseil d'État in 1989 to be a form of religious discrimination against the principle of secularity guaranteed under the Constitution, had become "legitimate" and seemed justifiable, according to the same principle of secularity, by 2004.[47] While racist attacks against North Africans had been on the decline since the difficult 1980s,[48] the Ministry of the Interior and anti-racist organizations identified a rising trend, with attacks especially targeting people wearing visible religious signs of Islam (see chapter 2). Stigmatizing discourse and appeals to the hatred of North Africans as a national or racial group, decreasingly legitimized in public discourse, had been usurped by "respectable" or "virtuous" racism targeting North Africans as an Islamic religious group, which was justified, or at least downplayed, by the highest levels of the state.[49]

CHAPTER 7

(Lack of) Knowledge about Islam

The strikes of 1982–1984 and the 1989 headscarf affair demonstrate the degree to which robust knowledge of the social roots of the ideological convergence around the "Muslim problem" encourages us to examine the logics underpinning the ways in which the economic, political, media, administrative, university, and not-for-profit-sector fields function. Doing so is an indispensable prerequisite for understanding not only the production of knowledge about Islam but also the project seeking to impose the idea that there actually is a "Muslim problem." The conditions of knowledge and campaigning are fulfilled at the intersection of several social fields, which follow their own rules and are crisscrossed with tensions specific to each of them.

Media Mechanisms for Stigmatizing Muslims

The press and the television undeniably play decisive roles in constructing "the Muslim problem" insofar as these are vast arenas for the production and dissemination of often inaccurate knowledge about Islam and Muslims: most residents of Western countries rely exclusively on the audiovisual and text-based media as the source for their ideas about Islam and Muslims. It is therefore not a coincidence that media discourses have hitherto comprised the main field of Islamophobia studies.[1] However, despite the profusion of books and articles on media coverage of Islam and Muslims, seldom does this work move beyond an internal analysis of finished products, in other words, of the often stereotypical, essentialist, and threatening representations and images of Islam and Muslims (see chapter 11).[2] Yet the internal analysis of these discourses is often open to the twofold critique of insufficiently engaging with the way media structures work and encouraging the trend toward "mediacentrism," that is, considering the media to be a monolithic bloc and thus underestimating the influence it has over the categories of readers', listeners', and viewers' perceptions of reality.[3]

In other words, although an internal analysis of media discourse is necessary, it does not suffice on its own. It needs topping up by a sociological analysis both of the conditions of production of information and of the routine practices of journalists, that is, by a "sociology of media logics that exclude Muslims."[4] The following question is thus raised: Why do journalists so frequently publish articles laying out the "Islamic threat"?[5] In the absence of a sociological study,[6] the hypothesis could be that, as is the case for other social facts extensively covered by the media—such as "the banlieues," "foreign delinquents," and "insecurity"[7]—its obsession with "Islam" is the product of multiple economic and structural constraints specific to the field of media, which facilitate the direct or indirect stigmatization of Muslims.

As much for the regional as for the national press, the exclusion of Muslims might be explained firstly by the marginalization and even exclusion of Muslims from the cozy social world of media owners and journalists, whose newspapers and audiovisual media are part of the specific social relationships of regional and national "elites." Since most Muslims are working class, completely outside media circles, and Muslim journalists seeking to present a less essentialist and stereotyped vision of Islam are generally distanced from the dominant media[8] to the advantage of those who demonstrate "political goodwill,"[9] Muslims are more often media "subjects" than media agents.

Moreover, the exclusion of Muslims may be enabled by press and audiovisual media marketing strategies for promotion and broadcasting: "If there is racism, it turns out to have been 'engraved' into the typologies of marketing, as sociologically fantastic as those may be, produced by so-called experts' surveys, but having functioned for several decades."[10] Indeed, these marketing surveys view the working classes and immigrants, some of whom are Muslims, as "indifferent" to the local and national press. They are therefore not a marketing target group, due to their supposed "indifference" and low spending power. The economic survival of the print and audiovisual media depends on advertising. What is essentially at stake is to maintain readers, listeners, and viewers, whose characteristics vary depending on the type of media, and win over a new, solvent audience, preferably located in the middle and upper classes. Outside the media specifically targeted on North African, Black African, and Muslims audiences, where adverts for typically Muslim products (halal, pilgrimages, etc.) appear, Muslims generally seem to be ignored by media marketing specialists and advertising agencies because they do not (yet) make up a commercially viable target group.[11]

If the media produce increasing numbers of articles, headlines, and cover stories focusing on the Islamic threat, this could also be due to the trend in the press toward publishing more and more small news items (called *fait-divers* in French), which began at the end of the nineteenth century[12] and continued, through the twentieth, into television broadcasting.[13] Islam is actually a stigmatizing subject of discourse in the "Other news" and "Society" headings, which is a feature in the mass media's economic survival. The subjects likely to fill those parts of the newspaper must be of interest to the usual audience and a potential new audience: the Islamic threat is thus one of the "old chestnuts," that is, social topics (like "insecurity," the "freemasons," etc.) that are relatively popular editorially, as measured by sales figures and "market share" of audiovisual audiences. We have witnessed an editorial and visual overproduction aimed at illustrating the idea of the Islamic threat:[14] "The Specter of Islam," "Shameless Islam" (*Le Point*, February 2012 and October 2012), "The Disturbing Truth about Islam," "The West Confronts Islam," "Fear of Islam" (*L'Express*, June 2008, October 2008, and September 2012), etc. Fully knowing that publishing cartoons of the Prophet Muhammad was very likely to provoke a public controversy, some newspapers became specialists in this field. For example, while the average sales per issue of the weekly *Charlie Hebdo* stood at 45,000, the issues published on 8 February 2006 (a reprint of the cartoons from the far-right Danish newspaper *Jyllands-Posten*) and 9 September 2012 (cartoons of Muhammad following the release of the film *The Innocence of Muslims*) sold 560,000 and 150,000 copies respectively.[15]

Moreover, the logic of competition between media outlets to get "scoops" leads to a constant need for news items, whose stock is basically provided by the government, the police force, and the justice system. Journalists depend on official sources, to such an extent that "a form of co-production of news with official sources" has been established.[16] This dependent relationship hampers journalists' capacity to maintain distance between themselves and their sources, and at the same time facilitates the circulation and uncritical reproduction of police categories in the media. Media coverage of Islam thus owes much to police frameworks, according to which Muslim religious practices (wearing headscarves, niqab, beards, djellaba, observing Ramadan, going to mosque, using a satellite dish, etc.) may be clues to Muslims' "ethnic divisiveness" and their political "radicalization." This phenomenon, in which the media reproduce categories used by the police to make sense of their work is then conveyed following the logic of "circular circulation of news" analyzed by Bourdieu:[17] insofar as journalists read each other's work and publish the news that others have already published, these categories are surreptitiously spread, to the point that they fudge the distinction between "Islam" and "Islamism." A religious practice thus becomes, according to media common sense, a threatening political practice.

Another politico-media mechanism—the use of opinion polls—facilitates discrimination against Muslims.[18] Pollsters are new hegemonic actors in a political situation where everyone can say and even believe what "public opinion" thinks and wants. Despite the critiques formulated by sociologists, polling institutions have succeeded in imposing their definition of public opinion because it is presented as both more "democratic" and more "scientific." These polls are firstly a technique of statistical sampling that enables a small group to represent the whole population. Around one thousand people "representative of the French population are polled" from which we can deduce what "the French people" supposedly "think." However, the apparently expert measurement of public opinion by polling industry organizations blinds us to the fact that this concept belongs less to the register of science than to political metaphysics. As Pierre Bourdieu emphasizes, public opinion as measured by polling organizations in the form of a percentage is an artefact, that is, a result produced by an instrument and with a distance from social reality.[19] This measuring technique is based, inter alia, on the assumption that there is an agreement about the questions that deserve to be asked, via the selection and setting out of the questions (vocabulary, order of presentation, choice of answers suggested, etc.) and the imposition of problematics by those commissioning the survey.

The polls regarding Islam published in the French press reveal more about top-down Islamophobia (of the polls' commissioners) than bottom-up Islamophobia (the hundreds of respondents supposed to represent "the French").[20] For example, one of the questions in the IFOP poll carried out for *Le Figaro* (25 October 2012) is worded thus: "Would you say that the presence of a Muslim community in France is: more of a threat for our country's identity; more of an enrichment of our country's culture; none of the above." This assumes that there is a "Muslim community," a national "identity" and a "threat"—whose contours are not defined at all. Although it was the actual wording of the question in the poll that used the idea of a Muslim threat, the commissioning newspaper concluded that 43 percent of those polled considered Islam as a "threat," "linked to Islam's steadily increasing 'visibility' in the public and media arenas."[21] We can thus observe a media construction of Islamophobia, which satisfies both the ideological orientations of the poll's commissioners and the advantages of sensationalism in terms of sales.

Some media outlets are owned by overtly Islamophobic figures, like the 24/7 news channel Cnews (Canal+ group, Vivendi holding), taken over by Vivendi's main shareholder, Vincent Bolloré, who hired the polemicist Eric Zemmour, convicted numerous times by the courts for incitement to racial hatred against Muslims without this harming his career in the slightest. Other examples include the daily *Le Figaro* (for which Zemmour writes a regular column)—which is part of the group owned by aircraft manufacturer Serge Dassault—and the weekly *Valeurs actuelles*, belonging to the Iskandar Safa holding group (the owner of dockyards where warships are built), via the Valmonde Groups and Privinvest Médias, in association with two high-profile media personalities, Étienne Mougeotte and Charles Villeneuve, who had successful careers with the most popular French television channel, TF1. Movement between the Far Right and the mainstream media can also be witnessed, as demonstrated by *Valeurs actuelles* recruiting journalist Louis de Raguenel into the private radio station *Europe 1* in 2020.[22]

Media logics of stigmatizing Muslims thus reveal the powerful heteronomy in which the media field is located, that is, the rules of the journalistic method (in-depth inquiry, triangulation of sources, intellectual and financial independence, etc.) have been marginalized in favor of logics that are both economic (viewing figures) and political (submission to the will of the owners). This is the way to properly grasp the meteoric rise of particular columnists and "media intellectuals," who have attained dominant positions due to their propensity to think and act in compliance with media expectations. It would not be possible to understand the enduring success of certain journalists, despite their openly racist comments, without knowing that they are skilled improvisers who can provide a "ready to go" response to the soundbite-style "analyses" imposed by media logic.[23]

Intellectuals, Pseudo-Intellectuals, and So-Called Experts

Given the stereotypical visions of Islam produced by the dominant media, one might wonder about the lack of visibility of academic researchers and teachers. Academia is indeed the preeminent site of the a priori detached, dispassionate production of knowledge about Islam and Muslims.[24] Yet even in that world, Islam is still a "hot topic" (according to the term used by Jean Leca in 1988).[25] Academics feel the pressure of the public space and, de facto, it is difficult for them to systematically adopt the detached position that should be assumed by any knowledge producer. Several ideal-typical academic profiles can thus be demarcated, based on the degree of independence of their scholarly strategy in relation to social and political demands ("intellectuals," "pseudo-intellectuals," and "so-called experts"), with the caveat that the same person may move between categories depending on specific pieces of writing or time periods.

As Max Weber and Norbert Elias emphasize, there is no such thing as completely "objective" social science insofar as it is always in some way "engaged" with the social world.[26] In other words, as feminist studies have elucidated, knowledge is always socially "situated." However, the degree of research independence (its "scientific nature") relies on compliance with the rules of scientific method and the effort at detachment made by the researcher. From this perspective, intellectuals are those who seek to comply with these rules; pseudo-intellectuals (a reference to philosopher Pascal's *demi-habiles*) are those who distance themselves from these rules, despite a certain level of erudition; and so-called experts are those who adopt the framings of issues that are imposed via social, and particularly government, demand.

Yet it is so-called experts and pseudo-intellectuals who monopolize public discourses on Islam and Muslims. As political scientist Vincent Geisser has demonstrated, almost none of the French specialists in the study of Islam are interested in studying Muslims resident in France, in contrast to the sociologists and anthropologists who have actually spent time carrying out research on Muslim religious life.[27] But, since the pioneering work of such sociologists as Nilüfer Göle, Françoise Gaspard, Farhad Khosrokhavar, and Jocelyne Cesari, inter alia, in the 1980s, a new generation of researchers has focused on Muslim religious practices as "normal" social facts.[28] The observation of the "hegemony of political science discourse" in research on Islam in France can be explained by the fact that "political scientists seem [...] the best placed to respond to political and institutional demands in terms of knowledge about Muslims resident on French soil."[29] In fact, since the 1980s, "complex entanglements between the political science and political fields" have been established.[30] This is how political scientists such as Rémy Leveau, Gilles Kepel (professors at Sciences Po-Paris), and Bruno Étienne (Sciences Po-Aix) have become so-called experts on "Islamist" movements and Muslim communities in Europe. These political scientists are not a monolithic group, their trajectories are not identical, and they do not all have the same relationships with the authorities. However, it should be noted that Kepel's many books and articles have been the subject of stringent criticism from political scientists specializing in Islam and the Muslim world because he is one of the "skilled craftsmen in the process of developing and bolstering of a particular type of religious gaze on the world" who stand astride the academic, political, and media fields.[31] Thus, according to academic Gilbert Achcar, Kepel's book *Le Prophète et Pharaon* (The Prophet and the Pharaoh)[32] "gave us a glimpse of the model which would characterize his prolific later output: a mass of useful information—which would later be facilitated by his privileged access to government sources—with limited theoretical conceptualization, becoming increasingly superficial with each book published. He became a media darling [...] as well as an advisor to Western and other governments in their struggle against radical Islamic fundamentalism."[33] The "neo-Orientalists"[34] have indeed played the role of so-called experts on Islam both for political authorities and the media, which generally reproduce the neo-Orientalist categories of perception of Islam and Muslims: "We might therefore talk of collusion between docile and shoddy academic research and relatively opaque political interests."[35]

The neo-Orientalists therefore reproduce the idiosyncrasies of Orientalist knowledge and help convey the most caricatural stereotypes and prejudices about Islam and Muslims forged over centuries (see chapter 11). As Valérie Amiraux points out, "the idea of an 'orientalist premise' linking together cultural and religious specifics like the key to reading and interpretation of political, social, economic and changes in an area that is sometimes the Middle East, and sometimes the Muslim world, is ongoing, year in year out, in the exclusive context of the colonial experience."[36] In the United States, the most obvious example is the historian of Turkey Bernard Lewis (Princeton), the inventor, in 1957, of the concept of "the clash of civilizations" (a self-fulfilling prophecy revisited and popularized by Samuel Huntington in 1993) and very close to the U.S. neoconservative movement supportive of the wars in Afghanistan and Iraq.[37] Despite his considerable erudition, his deliberately provocative books and articles, vigorously challenged by his academic colleagues, illustrate the essentialization of Islam typical of colonial Orientalism, insofar as he considers Islam immutable and believes that "any political, historical and academic approach to Muslims must begin and end with the fact that Muslims are Muslims."[38]

Since the attacks of January and November 2015 in Paris, neo-Orientalist academics have been highly sought after in the fight against "radicalization."[39] In *Les territoires conquis de islamisme* (Lands conquered by Islamism, 2020),[40] political scientists Bernard Rougier, Hugues Micheron, and Gilles Kepel develop the concepts of an Islamist "ecosystem" and "separatism," in which Islamist ideas spread through "contagion" and "atmosphere" across several sites: mosques, prisons, halal shops, sports clubs, etc. The idea of separatism was picked up by the major media outlets, including *Le Monde*, and by President Emmanuel Macron, whose antiradicalization policy assumes that there are overlaps between Muslim not-for-profits and terrorist organizations. However, this analysis has been vigorously criticized by researchers specializing in jihadist movements, particularly political scientist Laurent Bonnefoy, according to whom *Les territoires conquis de l'islamisme* is an "academic legitimization of a xenophobic discourse."[41]

The profile of the "neo-Orientalists" with academic qualifications must nevertheless be differentiated from that of "security experts," whose source of legitimacy is external to academia.[42] These so-called experts have managed to become fixtures in the European media and challenge the authority of academic specialists on Islam and Muslims on their own territory. By accusing the latter of "benevolence" toward Muslims and of "looking for sociological excuses" for the acts of violence perpetrated by Muslim terrorists, these so-called experts project on the contrary a "genuine" neutrality, by "telling the truth" about Islam and Muslims. This group basically comprises journalists, essayists, former political (often far-right) activists, or members of government information units who have reinvented themselves as so-called experts on Islam and terrorism (the two being for them closely linked). This process has been institutionalized through multiple and repeated invitations to appear on the media, publish books (for example Xavier Raufer's *Atlas mondial de Islam activiste* [Global atlas of Islamic activism]), and write for journals (for instance *Les Cahiers de l'Orient*), and the establishment of think tanks focused on this topic, such as the Centre d'études et de réflexion sur le Proche-Orient (Centre for Study and Reflection on the Middle East) directed by Antoine Sfeir, the Observatoire des pays arabes (Observatory on Arab Nations) led by Antoine Basbous, the Observatoire international du terrorisme (International Terrorism Observatory) run by Roland Jacquard, etc.

Some so-called experts on Islam, who completely sidestep the requirements of academic research and even those of journalistic ethics, are the inventors and the propagators of the myth of "Islamization" of Europe (Oriana Fallaci, Alexandre Del Valle, Gisèle Littman—alias Bat Ye'or, Christopher Caldwell, etc.)[43] A sociological study of this movement remains to be written. However, the "chimera" is one of the features of anti-Semitism (see chapter 12) and seems to have become a major feature of contemporary Islamophobia: we are witnessing the construction of a "political fiction," a fear of Islam based on the supposed advent of "Eurabia," that is, a Europe dominated by Muslims with the complicity of "multiculturalist elites."[44] An odd thing is that this political fiction is sometimes conveyed by academics with recognized scientific legitimacy. For example, this is the case of demographer Michèle Tribalat, who wrote the preface of the book by *Wall Street Journal* journalist Christopher Caldwell, whose title is evocative: *Une révolution sous nos yeux: Comment Islam va transformer la France et l'Europe* (A revolution under our noses: How Islam is going to change France and

Europe).[45] Myth building may be the last phase of the construction of the "Muslim problem" because it is completely cut off from social reality and becomes all the more open to challenge, producing a self-fulfilling prophecy that "begins with a false definition of the situation, provoking new behavior that ends up making the original false idea into a reflection of reality."[46] This fantasy of Islam perfectly illustrates sociologist William Isaac Thomas's theorem, according to which when people think particular situations are real, they become real in their consequences.

Popularizing Islamophobia

The description of the various forms of knowledge of Islam would be incomplete if we did not refer to those that can be categorized as popularization: school textbooks, graphic novels and comic books, children's magazines, books and films, etc.[47] From this point of view, a specific literary genre has been hugely successful on a global scale and, in terms of what comprises the main forms of disseminating scenarios that generate the "Muslim problem," deserves particular attention. This literary genre is composed of an intellectual twist, the anti-Muslim essay written by media intellectuals, and in a romantic or biographical alternative, stories by "women oppressed by Muslim men," often written by a woman whose name evokes Muslim culture (Karima, Leila, Souad, etc.) and whose cover shows a woman wearing a headscarf, a veil, or a burqa.[48] Here is a nonexhaustive list of books like this published in France: *Not without my Daughter* (Betty Mahmoody, 1987, sold 3.4 million copies globally by 1992); *Sold* (1993); *Burnt Alive* (2004); *My Forbidden Face* (2004); *Infidel* (Ayaan Hirsi Ali, 2005); *Married by Force* (2005); *Down with Veils!* (Chahdortt Djavann, 2006); *In the Name of Honor* (2006); *Dead among the Living* (2006); *Disfigured: When a Crime of Passion Becomes an Affair of State* (2006); *The Price of Silence* (2007); *Fatwa: Living with a Death Threat* (2008); *Sultana's Daughters* (2008); *Prisoner of Tehran* (2009); *Convert* (2009); *I Am Nujood, Age 10 and Divorced* (2009); *Burqa: Aicha's Revolt* (2009); *Unsubmissive and Unveiled* (2009); *Beneath My Veil* (2010); *Unveiled* (2010); *Dying to Live Again* (2010); *The Veil of Fear* (2010), etc.

This point is not made in order to challenge the authenticity of these narratives or to debate the authors' intentions; rather, we seek here to question the media positioning of such books, when others written by women with "Muslim" names are not so successful.[49] There is scope to carry out a sociohistorical study on the trajectories of the authors, preface writers, the selection process at the often conservative publishing houses specializing in this literary genre,[50] the forms of the authors' circulation through political and media space, the conditions under which literary and "woman of the year" prizes are allocated, and the controversies provoked by particular books, etc.

Moreover, while the analysis of the construction of the "Muslim problem" boils down to a sociology of French and European elites, the existing work has totally ignored the question of the reception of the media discourse by readers, listeners, and viewers. Analyzing hostility toward Muslims based on opinion polls can be challenged due to the epistemological issues that arise, not only in the design of the questionnaires but also in relation to how the data is dealt with (see chapter 2). The cultural studies approach enables us to offer more nuanced analyses, for example in support of the three forms of reception in the "encoding/decoding" model (i.e., "hegemonic," "negotiated," and "oppositional") explained by Stuart Hall as varying by individuals' social properties.[51] Several case studies could be focused on the forms of appropriation by certain categories of readers of newspapers, magazines, and the "women oppressed by Muslim men" literary genre, or by listeners and viewers of particular television or radio programs.[52]

The Islamophobic Political Cause

The knowledge about Islam produced by various actors generally entails calls for political action to "solve" the "Muslim problem." Viewed from this angle, the conditions of production of knowledge about Islam may be determined by the "solution" put forward, which may vary significantly depending on its architect's diagnosis of social reality. The myths propagated by security experts and some media intellectuals often go hand in hand with calls for tightening migration policy, mass deportations, the withdrawal of citizenship rights and even, in some cases, physical violence targeting Muslims. Other media intellectuals and neo-Orientalists stand out from the crowd by advocating a strategy of "restriction," that is, aiming to reduce the "Islamic threat" and block the "rise in ethnically divisive activity," particularly via laws prohibiting the visibility of religious practices in public space.

These appeals still need the support of political actors and not-for-profit organizations to be transformed into action. The construction of the "Muslim problem" thus owes much to the support it receives within political circles and the "mobilization space," around what we suggest calling the "Islamophobic cause." This refers to the set of campaigns, whether partisan or not, aiming explicitly or implicitly to apply a regime of "exception"—that is, a legal regime that derogates from common law—to all or some French and foreign Muslims, as a social group.[1] This regime of exception is the direct and practical consequence of the construction of the "Muslim problem" and is imposed in the name of grand republican principles, particularly "néo-laïcité." This concept should be distinguished from "laïcité," since while the latter guarantees the freedom of religious expression, the former intends to restrict it and should be analyzed as a disciplinary tool used to assimilate supposed Muslims. In what follows, we analyze the political uses of the Muslim issue, which must be looked at in the light of the rules governing how the political field and the mobilization space operate.

The Politicization of the Muslim Problem

The political field can be defined by three principal features: a competitive space around a particular stake, that is, politics (the struggle to occupy government positions) and the political (symbolic struggles over what principles are used for conceiving of, and dividing up, the world); a relatively autonomous and structured space, organized into a hierarchy of dominant and dominated positions, according to (ownership and access to) political capital; and lastly, a space into which access is restricted, that is, dependent on the accumulation of political capital that is both representative (measured by the number of voters) and reputational or popular (which can be accumulated outside the political field and converted into political capital). The political field is thus structured but partly autonomous: the accumulation of political capital depends on the institutionalized participation of the electorate and the logic of reputation/popularity (hence the growing importance of the media).

Political capital is formed from elements external to the political field, but paradoxically, a logic of steady closure can be observed: the formulation of political issues is monopolized by the political class. Certain economic and social issues (the housing crisis, the conditions of working-class areas, nuclear risk, energy policy matters, etc.) are barely translatable politically. The problem is that the "smooth" functioning of the political field depends above all on the "smooth" functioning of the mechanism of representation. Belief in the principle of representation is based on the simple idea that the political field is homologous with society in general. In other words, the structuring of, and divisions within, the political field must match the structuring and dividing lines of society (a left/right split deriving from that between working and dominant classes).

However, since the early 1980s, this relationship has withered away. Although the parties of the Right still—objectively—represent the interests of the dominant classes, left-wing parties no longer position themselves as speaking for the working classes (socialist think tank Terra Nova even promotes reconfiguring their appeal to the middle classes).[2] This disconnect can be partly explained by the social composition of the political and administrative elites (a high degree of social homogeneity and the phenomenon of reproduction) and the close links between political, economic, and public-service elites, established via commonly experienced education trajectories (especially Sciences Po, but also l'École nationale d'administration, HEC, Polytechnique, etc.) and the "revolving door" practices of ENA graduates (known as "énarques").[3] These patterns have facilitated the ideological transformation of the Left in power (since the high watermark of the austerity policies of 1983, not breaking with the capitalist economy, etc.) and overturned the logics of distinction between political parties. Insofar as the differences between the economic programs of the main political parties have eroded, the competition between them has generally shifted onto other political issues, particularly to matters labeled "social," beginning with immigration and Islam.

Indeed, these campaign themes have the advantage of maximizing electoral potential, that is, targeting all French citizens, especially the voters most likely to go to the polling station, to the exclusion of foreigners (for legal reasons) and (for symbolic reasons) French Muslims, who are considered minorities and/or poor and therefore likely to be nonvoters.[4] The issues also refer to a "compensatory overproduction"[5] around foreigners and Muslims—tied to the disarray of governments, which are deliberately powerless vis-à-vis financial, economic, and social crises—made possible by keeping migration policy and nationality tucked into the bosom of national sovereignty (unlike economic policy, which is highly constrained by European treaties). Once all the major political parties consider that there is both an "immigrant problem" and a "Muslim problem," the distinctions between them are only about which "solutions" to provide, as Socialist leader Laurent Fabius claimed in 1984, when he stated that "the Le Pen phenomenon derives from 'genuine questions' to which the extreme Right provide the wrong answers."[6]

This comment illustrates the impact of the rise of the Front national (FN), renamed Rassemblement national (RN) in 2018, within the political field: "If the threshold of sensitivity to the intolerable is lowered, this movement has taken hold first among the actors of the political game and due to the emergence of the FN and the reorganization of political competitions around it."[7] Indeed, the focus on immigration and Islam has been facilitated by the dominant electoral analysis—developed particularly by the Cevipof (the politics research center based at Sciences Po, formerly known as Centre d'études de la vie politique française [Center for the Study of French Political Life])—of the Far Right's success. The analysis posits that since the "FN vote" is allegedly the translation of "working-class xenophobia" into votes, the electoral successes of other parties are said to depend on their capacity to attract "FN voters." However, this analysis, highly contested by sociologists who specialize in elections has become dominant in the public space, thanks to the efforts of campaign managers and political communications advisors.[8]

The "electoral profitability" of Islamophobic political discourse needs further analysis. Some researchers suggest there is a link between the success of Islamophobic discourse and the improvement in the Far Right's electoral fortunes in Europe, above all in the wake of the attacks of 11 September 2001, 7/7 in London, and case of the cartoons of the Prophet (in 2005). Yet this idea is much floated but barely and seldom empirically demonstrated.[9] In the British case, there are suggested correlations between the significant numbers of Pakistanis and Bangladeshis in some constituencies and the rise in xenophobia and votes for the British National Party (BNP).[10] Following this logic, it is the "visible presence" of Muslims that fosters xenophobia and ultimately results in voting for a racist party. This spurious reasoning has little basis in the sociology of electoral behavior, a highly complex phenomenon.[11] We conclude therefore that the relationship between the reception of Islamophobic discourse and electoral behavior is still relatively unexamined and deserves to be the subject of an in-depth analysis, particularly through work with a local focus.[12]

As we have noted, it is not a coincidence that political actors campaigning around the "Muslim problem" are not confined to a single party, on the right or the far right. Although the intellectuals in the French extreme Right (FN, GRECE, Club de l'horloge, etc.) have been theorizing Arab and Muslim otherness since the 1960s, these negative representations of Islam have tended to be shared across the entire political field since the early 1980s via the three transformations in racist ideology—the shifts from race to culture; racial inequality to cultural difference; and heterophobia to heterophilia[13]—and the idea that Islam is a "religion incompatible with our cultural traditions."[14]

The social evidence of the "Muslim problem" is so widely shared that Islamophobia has become a major stake not only in the struggle between competing parties but also of intraparty competition. As sociologist Frédéric Lebaron shows, "Islamophobia is now at the core of competition between the various factions of the UMP [main right-wing party renamed Les Républicains in 2015], and of course between the UMP and the FN. It has become the very terrain where the organizational and ideological future of the French Right is playing out in its most direct form. It is certainly also one of the keys to understanding the intensity of the divisions on the right, even though the clan-style fractures made visible by the economic crisis do not precisely map onto the strategic oppositions."[15] The logic of inter- and intraparty competition thus fosters forms of symbolic outbidding, to the extent of becoming a conduit for real Islamophobic myths, such as the "Roissy mosques" (invented by Philippe de Villiers before the 2007 presidential election),[16] the "forced sale of halal meat to non-Muslims" (invented by Marine Le Pen during the 2012 presidential campaign),[17] and the "stolen pain au chocolat" (picked up again in 2012 by Jean-François Copé, then fighting François Fillon for the leadership of the UMP).

One of the signs (and determinants) of Islamophobia's centrality to the development of political capital is the use of the Muslim issue by certain outsiders, whether activists or politicians, attempting to occupy the best positions in the political field or within their party. "Pioneering" political parties in the struggle against "Islamization" are Pia Kjærsgaard's Danish People's Party and Geert Wilders Freedom Party (Netherlands), which managed to politically impose themselves by developing a violently Islamophobic discourse.[18] The FN under Marine Le Pen, which positions itself as an outsider in the French political field, followed the "Nordic path" with its strategy of "un-demonization." "To understand Marine's FN," explains Laurent Chambon,

> you have to know that Pia Kjærsgaard founded the Danish People's Party (Dansk Folkeparti) out of the ruins of an anguished xenophobic, nationalist party that had suffered a great deal from internal divisions. After changing the name and the party structure, Kjærsgaard spent ten years building a well-oiled and compliant electoral machine. She then succeeded in becoming a government coalition partner that could not be ignored, by either right-wing or liberal parties, for ten years. To pull this off, she developed several themes that resonate with those of Marine's FN: no official contact with the racist, homophobic and anti-Semitic extreme Right; a party that obeyed its leader without dissent; a discourse based on Islam as an ideology threatening for European civilization; the ad nauseam parading of classic nationalist, nativist themes; defense of the Welfare State and social benefits against profiteers from outside; the people against the system stolen by the multi-culturalist Left; and a reinforced concrete Zionism.[19]

However, the practice of accruing political capital through exploiting the Muslim issue is not specific to the extreme Right. It crosses the left-right political divide.[20] Indeed, several case studies could be carried out on both the left and the right of the French political landscape: Ernest Chenière—the headteacher of the school in Creil who excluded Samira Saidani and Leila and Fatima Achaboun for wearing headscarves to school in 1989, became an RPR deputy for the Oise (north of Paris) in 1993, and put forward three bills on banning hijab in state schools; the up-and-coming generation of right-wing politicians (Thierry Mariani, Éric Raoult, Hervé Novelli, Guillaume Peltier, etc.), many of whom started out in far-right groups, managed to change the balance of power within the Right in their favor, to the detriment of the "Gaullists" in the 2002–2012 period; Françoise Laborde, a senator for the Parti radical de gauche (Radical Left

Party) drafted a bill on banning employees in nursery care from wearing hijab; André Gérin, Communist mayor of Vénissieux (just outside Lyon) from 1985 to 2009, and a deputy for the Rhône since 1993, drafted a bill, during the campaign for the Communist Party leadership, banning the wearing of the niqab in public; leaders of left-wing parties Lutte ouvrière (Georges Vartanianz) and the Ligue communiste révolutionnaire (Pierre-François Grond) played roles in the exclusion of Alma and Lila Lévy in Aubervilliers in 2003 etc.[21] All these French examples illustrate the symbolic retributions that some activists and politicians can extract by producing Islamophobic discourses, even if they are not necessarily based on the same logic: those on the left usually base their engagement on anticlericalism, the fight against Islamism, and antisexism (claiming to oppose a religion that oppresses women) whereas on the right it is more to do with class contempt or racism pure and simple. Yet despite the different logics of engagement, néo-laïcité seems to have created a consensus that transcends the traditional political divisions (as we will see in chapter 9).

In contrast, the centrality of Islamophobia in the political field means that assumed or fictitious membership of the Muslim religion might sometimes be a way to discredit someone politically. This phenomenon can compound a class-based obstacle, which is well known in political science; however, this is not systematic and differs depending on the relevant party and local or national political arena.[22] During the 2012 French presidential campaign, the candidate Nicolas Sarkozy sought to discredit his opponent, François Hollande, by declaring that the intellectual Tariq Ramadan and seven hundred imams had called for people to vote for Hollande, the Parti socialiste candidate.[23] In 2017 Emmanuel Macron was accused of "Islamo-leftism" because he refused at that time to endorse the néo-laïque political agenda (he changed his mind in 2019 when he decided to use far-right rhetoric for his own purposes).

The social evidence of the "Muslim problem" also results in effects on the ways minorities are included within partisan structures. Several studies have analyzed the discourse on "diversity" in politics and the practices of the main political parties, particularly in the process of setting up local and national leadership committees and the selection of electoral lists.[24] But few have underlined the fact that minorities with access to stable positions of political power have a highly specific sociological profile. They are mainly upwardly mobile women with middle-class backgrounds, university graduates, display no signs of Muslim affiliation, and support the Act of 15 March 2004 that prohibits Muslim headscarves in public schools. The antithesis of the "good" "diversity" candidate, whose silhouette is visible behind this image, instead has a working-class background, few or no educational qualifications, is visibly affiliated to Islam, and opposes the Act of 15 March 2004. We could therefore suggest the theory that the criteria for selection of minority candidates is linked to the Muslim issue, as illustrated by the controversy surrounding the candidature of Ilham Moussaïd in the 2010 regional elections in Provence-Alpes-Côte d'Azur, which generated deep internal divisions within the Nouveau parti anticapitaliste (NPA).

The Islamophobic Mobilization Space

Islamophobia's pivotal position in the political field links with the recent developments in Islamophobic "mobilization space,"[25] which refers to the whole set of collective, conflictual phenomena committed to the fight for Islamophobia. A "loose Islamophobic network" exists in France (and Europe), whose borders are fluid and whose activist legitimacy has been built on the social evidence of the "Muslim problem."[26] The network's extensive heterogeneity and the gaps in academic research on it make an in-depth analysis difficult. Indeed, it must be studied with the help of the traditional tools of the sociology of social movements, which focus on the determining factors of commitment, activist careers, the activist division of labor, the forms of disengagement, and the logics of alliance and opposition, etc.

The loose network's first component is incorporated into the "galaxy" that we can qualify as "European neoconservative,"[27] which is united against the "Islamization of Europe" (and the USA), and propagates the myth of "Eurabia." This comprises a very diverse set of movements varying according to the situation pertaining in their country of origin,[28] from the neo-Nazi extreme Right to some elements of the European Left, via some Zionist groups, which could form alliances or split from one another. Some are linked to political parties and some are not. They have either built on existing structures or have constructed new ones, particularly through the use of websites, social networks, and online fora and blogs. Not only do they carry out violent activities (physical attacks on Muslims, especially on women wearing hijab, attacks on mosques and halal restaurants, the desecration of Muslim cemeteries, deadly bomb attacks, etc.) but also symbolic actions (conferences, occupations, demonstrations, concerts, holding public "sausage and wine appetizers" in public parks, "pork soup" for the homeless, etc.).

On 18 December 2010, the first International Tribunal against the Islamization of Europe (held in Paris)[29] revealed to the general public an alliance that seemed improbable only a few years earlier[30] between small groups and parties from the extreme right well known to political scientists and antifascist activists (Bloc identitaire [dissolved in 2021 for hate speech and military actions against migrants], English Defence League [EDL], Union démocratique du centre [UDC] etc.), leftist activists (Pierre Cassen's Riposte laïque),[31] a "traditional" feminist group (Anne Zelensky-Tristan's Ligue du droit des femmes),[32] women's campaigns against fundamentalism (Christine Tasin's Résistance républicaine and Michèle Vianès's Regards de femmes),[33] neofascist literary circles (Renaud Camus's Parti de l'innocence, fervent supporters of Richard Millet),[34] etc. This alliance illustrates an ideological convergence based on Islamophobia and a re-definition of secularity (where *laïcité* becomes néo-laïcité). As for the political field, "the rejection of Islamization has only become a winning formula for the Bloc identitaire [and other participants in the Assises] to break out of the mar-gins and into the mainstream."[35] Here again, the "Nordic path" has been taken to obtain media recognition and political legitimacy in mobilization spaces, and even in the political field.

However, it is essential to separate out another component of the loose Is-lamophobic network from those movements we have just listed, that is those groups whose objectives have to do with secular feminism and those for whom it is about the struggle against fundamentalism and defending néo-laïcité. It is important to identify them because the loose network is itself a competitive space: the former groups (Riposte laïque, etc.) accuse the latter (Prochoix, etc.) of Islamophilia, while the latter accuse the former of xenophobia, revealing the robust ideological oppositions that are part of the struggle for definition of how the "regime of exception" should function.[36] Whereas some want to ban all Muslim religious signs from public space and forbid any mosque construction, while favoring the mass deportation of Muslims, others distinguish between the types of sign (hijab or niqab) and public places (the ban on hijab in state schools but not in the street) and are relatively keen on freedom of conscience and state-guaranteed freedom of worship. While some feel that the "Muslim problem" actually stems from the core beliefs of Islam (with the Quran often be-ing compared to "Mein Kampf") others distinguish between "fundamentalist" and "moderate" Muslims.

Movements that are so far apart ideologically and politically cannot be amal-gamated. The fact remains, however, that their common denominator is the conviction that there is such a thing as the "Muslim problem," and with it, the desire to establish a regime of exception for all or a section of the Muslim popu-lation. In France, these are basically movements seeking a ban on wearing hi-jab to state schools, in the street, and even in private companies in the name of néo-laïcité, according to the term used by right-wing politician François Baroin (see chapter 9). They include the not-for-profit Ni putes ni soumises, the activist journal *Prochoix* (Caroline Fourest, Fiammetta Venner, Claudie Lesselier, etc.), the Comité laïcité république set up in 1990 by Pierre Bergé and directed by Patrick Kessel (Laïcité Info and "Prix de la laïcité"), and the Ligue internationale contre le racisme et l'antisémitisme (Licra), which created the "Certificat diversité et laïcité" for public and private-sector organizations, etc. So the issue is to understand how the construction of the "Muslim problem" has opened up a mobilization space enabling the political and media ascendance of certain figures such as Fourest (a columnist for *Le Monde*, state radio station France Culture, and then *Marianne*, and on the teaching staff at Sciences Po, etc.) and the emergence of new types of political collective actions unthinkable a few years previously (public "sausage and wine appetizers" and "pork soup" events for the homeless, etc.).

Overall, the construction of the "Muslim problem" has been the contingent product of a particular historical conjuncture in which an ideological convergence among various factions of the dominant classes can be observed, which became very clear around the (second) headscarf affair of 2003–2004. As Françoise Lorcerie, a senior researcher at CNRS (French National Research Center) demonstrates, the evolution of the bill banning the wearing of headscarves in state schools into the Act of 15 March 2004 was the result of a social and political configuration that had fostered alliances between different components of the French "elites."[37] But what does this ideological convergence mean from the perspective of the production of the dominant ideology and the composition of the French "elites"? As Pierre Bourdieu and Luc Boltanski emphasize, the dominant ideology helps express and produce the logical and moral integration of the dominant class.[38] In other words, it enables internal divisions to be transcended and alliances to be forged between the various fractions of the dominant classes. The theory could thus be floated that the construction of the "Muslim problem" is one of the main channels of unification of French, and even European "elites" at the very moment when the capitalist/anti-capitalist (or market economy/socialist economy) split has been challenged by the strategic change of tack toward austerity policies by the governing Left.

CHAPTER 9

Legal Discrimination by a Capillary-Like Process

Since the late 1980s, multiple individuals and groups have developed knowledge about and built campaigns aimed solving the "Muslim problem." Yet many institutions outside the media, political parties, and nongovernmental organizations have also played definitive roles, particularly the Marceau Long Commission on Nationality (1987), the Haut Conseil à l'intégration (HCI, the High Council for Integration, 1989–2012),[1] and the Stasi Commission (2003). The case of the HCI is especially interesting due to its activities focused on the "Muslim problem" over a long period, as well as its political and media influence.

The High Council for Integration and Néo-Laïcité

The HCI was composed of members drawn from the various elements of the French dominant classes (left-wing and right-wing politicians, academics, activists, senior civil servants, journalists, etc.). It published reports, position papers, and recommendations and is used as much by the political authorities as by the press. Insofar as it brings together actors belonging to different fields of activity (politics, civil service, justice system, media, intellectuals, economics, NGOs, etc.), the HCI seems to be a "neutral space,"[2] that is, a space enabling dominant ideology to be produced via homogenizing the categories of thought through which the strands of "elites" interpret the social world. From this perspective, the bourdieusian concept of a "neutral space" appears very apt for considering alliances between elements of the dominant classes. These are spaces of meeting and exchange in which participants do not abandon the values of their original group, and which are located at the intersection of the intellectual field and that of power. These spaces are "neutral" because the attendance is on an individual basis (with no group mandate) and loyalty toward the original groups is unchallenged.

From this perspective, the HCI is an essential channel for the dominant "community of interpretation," following Edward Said's expression, of Islam and secularity (laïcité). In fact, secularity has been the subject of an intense symbolic struggle in which multiple actors are seeking to impose their own definition, which generally depends on their diagnosis of the "Muslim problem." The tensions caused by this symbolic struggle have had ramifications within the HCI, which experienced an ideological swing in the 2000–2003 period, after the imposition of a new, néo-laïc definition of secularity. This definition was articulated in the 2003 parliamentary report by François Baroin, *Pour une nouvelle laïcité*,[3] as well as by the Stasi Commission, nine of whose members are, were, or would later become members of the HCI (Jacqueline Costa-Lascoux, Nelly Olin, Gaye Petek, Hanifa Chérifi, Marceau Long, Rémy Schwartz, Alain Touraine, Patrick Weil, Gilles Kepel). The flagship measure stemming from the Stasi Commission report—the banning of "conspicuous" religious signs in state schools, enshrined in the Act of 15 March 2004—should therefore be understood as the extension of a new framing of the "Muslim problem" by the HCI.

In 2001 the majority of the HCI, consonant with Conseil d'État jurisprudence, concluded that wearing hijab in state schools was not in itself contrary to secularity. For some, the ban even boiled down to challenging the freedom of conscience and worship, recognized by the Constitution and international conventions. From 2002 secularity was redefined via the rearticulation of the opposition between private and public spheres, hitherto less inflexibly distinguished from one another in the legal definition of secularity.[4] Whereas, according to the HCI's previous interpretation, the 1905 Act had guaranteed the freedom of religious expression for pupils within the confines of state schools, néo-laïcité seeks, on the contrary, to restrict it. It therefore means reconfiguring the division between the public and the private by rejecting the expression of "conspicuous" religious signs in public space and the intrusion into private intimacy in order to assess compliance with republican values (with the criterion of assimilation being made a prerequisite for obtaining French nationality, for example).[5] Néo-laïcité is thus a disciplinary tool used to assimilate supposed Muslims.

The HCI's change of ideological tack is not only the consequence of virtually all its membership having been replaced in 2002 (only the néo-laïcité supporter Gaye Petek survived the reshuffle) but also the result of framing the Muslim question in a new way, marked (as we saw in chapter 3) by the hegemony of media discourses and the marginalization of any expertise on Islam and Muslims that directly counters the dominant discourse. As soon as edifying witness statements "prove" the veracity of the Muslim threat, it becomes necessary to redefine the secular norm to contain the "Muslim problem": the Act of 15 March 2004 is therefore justified by the desire to make the integration of pupils via state schools possible. The power of witness statements should not be underestimated as a mode of knowledge in the social world, as—combined with the way the commission functioned[6] and the mobilization of political actors—it appears to have brought about the change of attitude of several academics in the Stasi Commission.[7]

For example, sociologist Alain Touraine, a member of the commission who had signed a petition against the proposed act in 2003, justifies his U-turn by referring to the impact of the witness statements: "Since the Intifada [in 2000], France has become an ethnically divided country. It is not accurate to say that I changed my mind, it is France that has changed, and profoundly so: in the schools, you're Jewish or Arab, people no longer identify themselves by class or even the branded clothing their parents have had to pay for, but by religion." He summarizes his own journey thus: "Three years ago I used to deny that ghettoes existed in France. The dean of a community college gave evidence to the Commission in which he admitted that 98 percent of his pupils were of foreign origin, while another told us that Jews and Arabs were fighting in the courtyard."[8] In his opinion, these selected witness statements seem to be more accurate than many years of sociological accounts of Islam, schools, and working-class neighborhoods.

The redefinition of the secular norm owes much to the ongoing mobilization of an informal group of HCI members within the Mission laïcité, which initiated the "Charte de la laïcité dans les services publics" (Charter for Secularity in the Public Services, 2007) and the position paper "De la neutralité religieuse en entreprise" (On religious neutrality in businesses, 2011).[9] The social trajectory of the person leading the Mission laïcité group, Alain Seksig—a Ministry of Education inspector, editorial board member of the journal *Hommes & Migrations*, and activist close to the Licra, etc.—reveals the social reach (accumulated social capital) and capacity enjoyed by this set of actors to move between the civil service, academic, political, cultural, and not-for-profit fields. Their multiple positioning—their capacity to hold positions simultaneously within several social fields—plays a determining role in the making the "Muslim problem" into a society-wide issue, insofar as it enables the "circulation of discourses, ways of working, topics, and issues," contributes to producing shared framings of the "entire dominant classes," and feeds into the "integration work undertaken by the dominant class in producing a feeling of familiarity and solidarity amongst its membership."[10] It is therefore not by chance that the advocates of néo-laïcité

have, in a capillary-like process, gradually and organically succeeded in imposing the idea of a "politico-spiritual power grab in relation to French youth of
Muslim heritage in a disadvantaged economic and social position in areas abandoned by the state."[11]

The HCI is in some ways the government's "secular avant-garde." To adopt
the phrase used in one of its reports, it "has opened up avenues of questioning
and made proposals—often followed up too late by political leaders," especially on the theme of secularity.[12] This is how, borrowing Seksig's phrase, the
"field of secularity" is formed.[13] It is enabled by the institutionalization of the
public issue and the multiple positioning of the actors. The construction of a
new secular norm has indeed helped construct a new social space with restricted autonomy, located at the intersection of a number of fields (civil service,[14] media,[15] not-for-profit sector, academia, etc.), which corresponds to a
new area of specialization, expertise in secularity, itself codified by a new "secular
code"[16] conveyed in the fields of teaching and research (e.g., academic training
at the master's level)[17], in specialist journals and NGO magazines,[18] and even
in private practice.[19] It uses its own vocabulary: "laïcité" ("secularity"); "ostensible" ("conspicuous"); "communautarisme" ("ethnic divisiveness"); "territoires
perdus de la République" ("no-go areas," literally, "territories lost to the French
Republic"); "désintégration" (the opposite of "integration"); "omnisacralisa-
tion" (the general sacralization of things/ideas, etc.), etc., invented by flagship
experts and "orthodox" translators of concepts into popular culture (including
members of the HCI). These concepts are challenged by heterodox intellectuals
and NGOs.[20]

The field of secularity has thus emerged at a time when state institutions are
turning néo-laïcité into a domain of state policy whose "targets" are not only
(supposed) French and immigrant Muslims but also civil service employees. The
disciplinary logic of néo-laïcité is extended outward. In fact, the HCI "wanted
to carry out its consciousness-raising work by alerting public authorities to the
risks of fracturing national cohesion and by setting out some potential strategies."[21] Whereas prior to 2002 the HCI was opposed to teachers who held too
restrictive an idea of what secularity should be, it was now ready to execute a
"vast plan for training staff in the various branches of the civil service, beginning with management."[22] The HCI "advocates the adoption of a genuine pedagogy of secularity, aimed as much at civil service staff as at the service-users,
so that all citizens understand the shared objective of not claiming or imposing their religious convictions in public spaces."[23] Néo-laïcité is assumed to be
something about which public servants have insufficient knowledge, which is
why the HCI, in partnership with several ministries, the Centre national de la

fonction publique territoriale (National Center for the Civil Service), and the not-for-profit Ligue de l'enseignement organized the seminar "La laïcité dans la fonction publique" (Secularity in the civil service); according to Seksig, the seminar "was aimed primarily at civil service management."[24] Thus, the political desire to establish homogeneity in the implementation of néo-laïcité can be seen across the civil service.

In fact, the speeches delivered in the course of this seminar illustrate the interiorization of the new secular norm by some of the Ministry of Education's senior managers. While the religious question had previously been far from a major concern for teachers and senior ministry officials,[25] it appears to have become one between 2003 and 2012, as the Obin Report demonstrates[26] and by the speeches given by important senior civil servants.[27] For example, the director-general of schools stated that "by preserving state schools of all levels, whose role is to provide all children with education, whether they are believers or not, protected from the pressures that may result in conspicuous manifestations of religious belonging, the law guarantees everyone freedom of conscience."[28] It is not surprising that the chair of the HCI, Patrick Gaubert, proudly noted the "convergence of opinions between the Ministry of Education and the HCI"[29] or that Seksig could thus celebrate the victory of néo-laïcité: "After fifteen years of confrontations and applications of the principle of secularity reconfigured to fit local circumstances, tensions within and around education establishments, in the end, Élisabeth Badinter, Élisabeth de Fontenay, Régis Debray, Alain Finkielkraut, and Catherine Kintzler who had written [...] a resounding appeal published in the Le Nouvel Observateur, 'Teachers, let's not capitulate!' [2–8 November 1989] had been proven right."[30]

The definition of secularity proposed by the "prohibitionists" of 1989 appears to have won over a section of the Ministry of Education civil service elites. Despite this "victory," made tangible by the passage of the Act of 15 March 2004 and the fall in the number of "conspicuous" religious signs identified in educational establishments,[31] suspicion of Muslim pupils is still particularly acute. This is why Head of the Inspectorate Claude Bisson-Vaivre repeated witness statements according to which compliance with the new secular norms is relatively superficial: young women wearing headscarves allegedly simply change into "secular mode" before entering their schools. Such witness statements, emphasizes Bisson-Vaivre, "show that there is still work to be done. Indeed, although the law has produced positive outcomes in terms of fewer visible signs of religious affiliation, especially headscarves, the principle of secularity is still not definitively guaranteed."[32] It is based on this "observation" that the advocates of néo-laïcité seek to impose a new form of secular discipline on pupils and extend the scope of the secular struggle.

"No Secularity without Discipline": The Extension of the Scope of the Secular Struggle

The "genuine pedagogy of secularity" for schoolchildren is above all destined for teachers, in particular history teachers. According to the HCI, those who have "inherited the legacy of the "hussards de la République" [the first secular teachers during the Third Republic] must "convey to pupils the feeling of belonging to a single people, united by basic principles, even when their ethnic origins, political, and religious convictions are different."[33] From this perspective, the educational institution's objective is "to form a homogenous social body around the principles of freedom of opinion and expression in compliance with the secularity of the public services."[34] To achieve this, it is necessary for "pupils as free individuals, to learn how to demonstrate a sufficiently open mind to accept that the specificity of their own cultural habitus is challenged by the diversity of opinions prevalent in a democratic society."[35] The special use of terms like "social body" and "cultural habitus" signals an important dimension of the demand to integrate, which is not new in the history of French power relations.[36] Indeed, echoing the revolutionary policy of linguistic unification, it is a "conflict over symbolic power with the formation and reformation of mental structures at stake."[37] Once the essentialist way that the (supposed) Muslims are supposed to have different "cultural habitus" and specific "mental structures" (based on religious dogma) is taken into account, one is meant to think that they have not interiorized the "national habitus" despite their socialization in France. It is therefore their religious identity that is the cause of their "failure to integrate." If Muslims have a habitus that does not sit squarely with that of everyone else, it is easier to understand the surprising question posed by the head of the Inspectorate of Life and Earth sciences: "Is it possible that the same brain contains both a scientific vision and one revealed by a higher power? It is up to each of us to decide that. Secularity here is engaging with the distinction between the private sphere, where each person resolves this potential conflict that coexists in them, and the public sphere. It revolves around this framing of the question about a clear distinction of disconnected intellectual fields. In other words, there can be no secularity without discipline."[38]

This speech reveals a desire to discipline bodies and minds: the bodies and minds of Muslims are racialized and allegedly undisciplined, as they refuse to adapt to "republican" mental structures and must thus be subjected to a special form of discipline. As the dean of the "School Life" group states, citing a doctor consulted by the HCI for the report *Les défis de l'intégration à l'école* (Challenges to integration in the school system, 2010): "'To enter secularity you must know your own body,' but there are many teenagers who don't know theirs."[39]

This disciplinary logic lies on a line of continuity between the 1987 Commission on Nationality that, as we saw, considered that the integration of children of Muslim immigrants was possible because of their low levels of religious observance, and the Advisory Board's trust in the integrative capacity of state schools. Yet the HCI is now convinced that these Muslim pupils reject schooling for religious reasons—glossing over the large-scale exclusion that removal from schooling and leaving the school system with no qualifications equates to—and that they are practicing in increasing numbers. However, as the HCI report on the challenges to integration in the school system explains, "it was because children of immigrants were born on French soil and educated at the schools of the Republic that they were granted automatic French nationality at the age of eighteen—but this right may be problematic once the state school no longer plays this integrating role."[40] We can thus grasp how the logic that had resulted in the challenge to the right to citizenship through birthplace (1993–1998), legitimized by the Commission on Nationality, may absolutely be reused in the future.[41]

Moreover, this disciplinary logic is compounded by the rationale of extending the scope of the struggle for secularity, which is an outcome of the process of rationalizing the "Muslim problem" and turning it into a universal issue: néo-laïcité has become a legitimate and universal state norm, which must therefore be applied universally. Insofar as it is an integral element of "state thinking,"[42] it is now possible to subject more and more social situations to the requirements of the new secular norm. In fact, the Stasi Commission hearings allowed HCI members to "discover" other social spaces beyond state schools, in which the "Muslim problem" was being raised and where a "demand for secularity" seemed to be making itself felt: the "closed" public services (hospitals, prisons and the army), the public services that greet people (ticket offices, public facilities and ceremonies), and private companies.[43] The process of constructing the "Muslim problem" in these other social spaces followed the same rules as it did in state schools: production of knowledge (personal testimonies, media, and academia), mobilizations of internal and external actors, and the transformation of the secular norm.

The statements gathered by the HCI were not only about Muslim pupils but new categories of citizens to be disciplined: "Muslim teachers" accused of "breaking the fast [of Ramadan] with their pupils in a high school North of Paris,"[44] "certain adults in the group of monitors and school mediators" accused of "making claims based on religious affiliation,"[45] women wearing headscarves and volunteering to accompany school trips, etc. What is at stake is the imposition of néo-laïcité not only on public service employees but also in intermediary organizations providing public services (with the exception of private Catholic, Jewish, and Muslim schools), on people who occasionally work with the public services (court juries and parents accompanying school trips), candidates for political office and elected representatives, and lastly, on public service users.[46] It is from this angle that the creation of the "secular code" must be understood,[47] that is, as envisaged by the HCI as a "working tool" for the implementation of secular pedagogy.[48]

Yet disciplinary néo-laïcité extends beyond the civil service and into a hitherto untouched space: private companies. In the HCI's opinion, "in the absence of clear legislation on this subject, or of consensus on these issues, CEOs and heads of HR are usually left to be judge and jury where there are requirements that, if they are not satisfactorily fulfilled, may give rise to complaints about discrimination."[49] The shedding of light on a "Muslim problem" in private companies is justified in the same way as it was for state schools: "In private companies also, people have the right to work in a religiously neutral setting, where individuals can avoid any pressure exerted by religious or ethnic communities."[50] CEOs, like teachers and head teachers, thus stand alone on the frontline against "ethnic divisiveness," knowledge of which is based again on the accumulation of witness statements and pseudoscientific expertise.

This knowledge is basically drawn from the report on major corporations by the First and 42nd consultancy group, which sets out a table of "problematic cases" (see fig. 3).[51] The HCI feels that the issue of Islam in companies would be difficult to address (out of fear of accusations of racism), and that certain requirements could be dealt with flexibly (Ramadan, dietary practices) while others could contravene the smooth functioning of the company (hijab, kippa, demands for prayer rooms, sexism between employees, etc.). It concludes that there has been an increase in religious infringements in companies: "It is as if breaches of legality are justified in the name of religion."[52] Just like the mediation process with pupils wearing headscarves in school—before the passing of the 2004 law, they were asked to stop wearing them but few agreed to—the sporadic treatment of "the problem" in this case by the Association nationale des directeurs de ressources humaines (National Association of Heads of HR) and the association Dynamique diversité (created by Dounia Bouzar) is deemed insufficient. This is the reason why the HCI is in favor of a legislative amendment

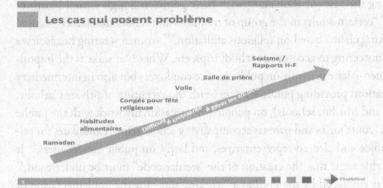

FIGURE 3.
Problematic cases. (Terms in table, from left to right: Ramadan; Dietary practices;
Days off for religious festivals; Hijab; Prayer rooms; sexism/M-F relationships)
Source: Cabinet-conseil First and Forty-Second, "Business and Religion: Full Review of Problems
and Actors," 2010 (cited in the HCI recommendation, *Expression religieuse et laïcité dans l'entreprise*,
(Religious expression and secularity in the company setting, 1 September 2011, p. 23).

to make néo-laïcité apply to private-sector companies, too. Yet if religious neutrality can only be required in a private law employment contract, there is in the
HCI's opinion at least one exception: private companies carrying out work for
or within the public service. It is not a coincidence then that one of the final
arenas of struggle faced by néo-laïcité is that of private organizations working in
the social or care sectors and nurseries.

Islamophobia and the Legal Regime of Exception

On 7 December 2011, the French Senate debated a bill introduced a few weeks
previously by Françoise Laborde, a Radical Party senator from the Haute-
Garonne (southwest France) since September 2008, whose goal was to "extend
the obligation of religious neutrality to private organizations responsible for
nurseries and to ensure compliance with the principle of secularity." The law was
passed in the Senate on 17 January 2012 and debated in the National Assembly.
In the report by the Senate's Laws Commission, drafted by Alain Richard, Socialist Party senator from Val-d'Oise (northwestern suburbs of Paris), the bill
may be interpreted as "a further step" after the passage of the Act of 15 March
2004 and makes explicit reference to the "Baby Loup case," named for a nursery run by a not-for-profit organization (Baby Loup) in Chanteloup-les-Vignes
(northwest of Paris) where Fatima Afif, deputy head and employee of Baby

Loup since 1997, had been fired "on 19 December 2008 for insubordination, threats, and gross misconduct."

Ms. Afif allegedly infringed the organization's in-house regulations because she wore a headscarf to work. She then appealed to the HALDE (High Authority for the Struggle against Discrimination and for Equality), which decided, in compliance with its own case law (decisions of 14 December 2009 and 21 March 2011), that this constituted discrimination based on religious criteria (decision of 1 March 2010) before officially changing its ruling in October 2010, following the arrival of Jeannette Bougrab—a member of the Conseil d'État and the right-wing UMP—as the new head of the HALDE (decision of 28 March 2011). In the meantime, Ms. Afif appealed to the Conseil de prud'hommes (employment tribunal) in Mantes-la-Jolie, which in December 2010 endorsed her sacking for "gross misconduct" and "repeated serious insubordination." This court also deemed the nursery's in-house rules, which banned the wearing of religious signs in the name of the principle of "neutrality," to be "lawful,"[53] a verdict confirmed by the Versailles court of appeal on 27 October 2011. In its ruling, the appellate court stipulated that, "bearing in mind the age of the children [using the nursery] had not been exposed to conspicuous manifestations of religious affiliation," the "restrictions [on employees' expressing their religious convictions] thus set out [in the in-house regulations] now seemed justified—by the nature of the work to be accomplished—and proportionate." This ruling was well received by the HCI, which, in its recommendation of 2 September 2011, justified Ms. Afif's dismissal and exhorted the government to pass a relevant law.

Without rehashing the details of the controversy, we would like to highlight one of the main legal elements at stake in the sacking of Ms. Afif, namely the "public service mission" dimension attributed to the role of nursery manager. Since the nineteenth century, employees of the French civil service have had to demonstrate "religious neutrality" for the very reason that it is a public service, but this religious neutrality requirement was not previously applicable to the private sector. From this viewpoint, the initial deliberation in the Afif case at the HALDE found that the in-house regulations at the not-for-profit organization Baby Loup were unlawful: "It emerged that these two principles [secularity and neutrality] do not apply to employees of a not-for-profit organization that is not carrying out work within a public service remit. Besides, the in-house rules, such as they were applied by Baby Loup, boiled down to a general but total ban on freedom of religion within it. The in-house rule as applied seemed unlawful. [...] In the absence of objective elements of the case outside of any type of discrimination, the severance of the plaintiff's contract was carried out on the basis of her religion and therefore discriminatory." It is no surprise that the HALDE's second deliberation recommended that the government "examine the option of extending the obligations of neutrality that are applicable to public-sector organizations to private-sector organizations that are responsible for social work, caring and nurseries in the framework of general interest or public service mission." In fact, the Laborde Bill simply rearticulated this recommendation by seeing to extend the "public service mission" to activities in the private sector.

Although it has no relation to an occupation (whether paid or unpaid), the same legal principle has been utilized by advocates of preventing parents who wear hijab from accompanying pupils on school trips. The school rules at the Paul Lafargue Elementary School in Montreuil (eastern suburbs of Paris) state that "parents who volunteer to accompany school trips must comply with the neutrality of secular schools, both in their dress and their comments." This provision has been challenged at the administrative tribunal of Montreuil by Sylvie Osman, a parent of pupils at the school and a member of the Mamans toutes égales (MTE, All Mums Are Equal) collective, but the court ruled in favor of the head teacher and the director of the Créteil regional education administration. The tribunal's decision on 22 November 2011 stipulates that "the parents of pupils who volunteer to accompany school trips are part of [. . .] the educational branch of the public service." From this perspective, the school rules are merely an "application of the constitutional principle of neutrality of the public service to the school trips on which pupils' parents accompany them."

The Baby Loup case ended with the court ruling against Ms. Afif.[54] A Cour de cassation ruling (19 March 2013) states that the principle of secularity does not apply to employees in the private sector who do not run a public service. However, for a private-sector organization to be considered a "public service," the civil service itself must initiate the creation and delegation of the relevant service, as well as imposing its own objectives, constraints, and state-legitimized control, which was not the case for the Baby Loup nursery. Yet on the same day, the Cour de cassation published a second ruling, about an employee of the Caisse primaire d'assurance-maladie (equivalent to the Medicare administration in the United States) in Seine-Saint-Denis who wore a headscarf at work. This second ruling legitimized the woman's dismissal and "extends on this occasion the field of secularity to all employees participating in a public service remit, whether public or private-sector employees, whether they are hired by a public or private-sector organization, whether they hold positions of authority or low-ranking positions, and whether or not they have contact with the public."[55]

Yet the Baby Loup case had a twist to it. In 2013 the Cour de cassation had stated that the principle of secularity did not apply to employees in the private sector who do not run a public service. But on 25 June 2014, the Cour de cassation's plenary assembly finally agreed with the appellate court's, which stated that the dismissal had been "justified by the employee's refusal to give in to the employer's lawful requests to desist from wearing the headscarf, and by the repeated gross insubordination described in the dismissal notice, which made a continuation of the employment contract impossible." In other words, one section of the Cour de cassation was in revolt against the other section. Ms. Afif had not wanted to involve the European Court of Human Rights, but in June 2015 she presented a statement to the UN's Human Rights Committee arguing that the French state had violated the International Covenant on Civil and Political Rights(ICCPR). On 10 August 2018, the committee found in favor of Ms. Afif, stipulating that the nursery had violated articles 18 and 26 of the ICCPR, which guarantee freedom to show religious affiliation, and had established an "intersectional form of discrimination based on gender and religion." However, the committee's ruling is not binding on French courts.

The main legal basis for the exclusion of women wearing the headscarf in schools or workplaces is thus the extension of the public service remit. However, the extension proposed in the Laborde bill would go further, as it introduces a mandatory neutrality clause into the legislative measures on professional and workplace qualifications (article L. 2324–1 of the public health code) and the licensing of people to work with young children (article L. 227–1 and article L. 423–23 of the Social Action and Families code in relation to childminders and nurseries). In other words, were parliament to pass this bill, women wearing headscarves would be banned from working not only in the various collective organizations (nurseries, drop-in centers, children's playgrounds) but also from home (family-run nurseries, childminders). The law would therefore exclude several thousand women, especially immigrants, for whom the childcare/nursery sector is the only means of providing for their households or of topping up low income.[56] In November 2008, there were over 283,000 nursery assistants registered with the Pajemploi center (an agency within URSSAF [Unions de recouvrement des cotisations de sécurité sociale], the national body that manages social security contributions), looking after more than 800,000 children. It is not known how many of these are women who wear headscarves, but that group may well no longer be able to obtain documentation allowing them to work as nursery assistants. The Laborde Bill was not passed, but the willingness to pass such legislation still exists among both right- and left-wing members of Parliament.

The idea of an exclusion justified by the integration of a private workplace into the "civil service" is not a new one. This legal argument was crucial in the nineteenth century to legitimize the exclusion of foreigners (especially Jews from Eastern Europe), women, and naturalized citizens from occupations that were not part of the civil service, and for which elections were held. Public law specialist Serge Slama demonstrates how the "privilege of the national" was enforced in French law and analyzes the process by which exclusion, confined to political positions after the 1789 Revolution, was extended first to public and ministerial officials (bailiffs, court employees, etc.), then to third parties in the legal system (arbitrators, experts, etc.), and finally to specific occupations requiring professional qualifications (lawyers, doctors, etc.). The lawyers' association was the first to campaign for the exclusion of foreigners from its ranks, and "lawyers entirely constructed the exclusion of foreigners by successfully imposing the idea that their work is a public service which, like all public services, should be reserved for French nationals."[57] In the late nineteenth century, the requirement for the status of French national in order to practice law was not stipulated by the representatives of the people but by the lawyers' Councils of Order, endorsed by the courts and supported in academic doctrine. It was by a decree issued on 20 June 1920 that the exclusion of foreigners from the bar association was formalized.

The comparison elucidates our understanding of how the construction of new social evidence and the power of this legal argument work. An area of employment comes under the "public service mission" once actors mobilize to produce this outcome and succeed in making their point of view the mainstream one—but, in the case of the parents of pupils on school trips and the women wearing the headscarf and employed in childcare, this exclusion has nothing to do with foreigners. Indeed, if the law were to be passed, it would usher in a system of de jure discrimination in the world of employment within the French national community, legally comparable to those that, at various periods in French history, impacted on French women, naturalized citizens, and French Jews, who were banned from accessing certain occupations. In the cases of the exclusion of the young schoolgirls (Act of 15 March 2004), pupils' parents on school trips, female childcare workers, etc., a gradual and organic spread of legal discrimination—by a kind of capillary motion—is occurring: the logic of exclusion is steadily transmitted into several social spaces and the next step is based on the legal arguments that had served as the basis for the previous step, which is an essential criterion for legal legitimization.

As legal scholar Emmanuel Dockès underlines, obvious legal discrimination against Muslims can be observed. The Conseil d'État does not apply néo-laïcité to habit-wearing nuns who are paid for their work in prisons (rulings of 27 July 2001 and 29 May 2002). According to the Constitutional Court, the principle of secularity does not apply to the regime dealing with worship in the Alsace-Moselle region, which, however, is funded by the state and which excludes Islam (ruling of 21 February 2013). Therefore, "secularity seems to be a principle of neutrality that can be amended and flexible ... except when it is directly or indirectly related to Islam and particularly hijab. [...] When the neutrality [of the judge] can no longer be respected, when the law tries, increasingly clearly, to combat particular religions, perhaps we would do better to speak of discrimination, or even xenophobia."[58]

CHAPTER 10

The Depoliticization of Violence and the Politics of Compensation

After the January 2015 terror attacks, a new phase in the legal regime of exception emerged.[1] Instead of dealing with the social and political roots of violence at home and abroad, most politicians consider, as Prime Minister Manuel Valls put it, that "to explain is to excuse" (*expliquer, c'est excuser*). Thus, social scientists, especially those who analyze Muslim communities, Islamic organizations, and Islamophobia, have been criticized as "naïve" or "incapable" of "preventing" such violence and even complicit with takfiri groups—that is, those who use excommunication (*takfir*) as a justification for political violence—since the former are supposed to share the latter's denunciation of Islamophobia. In other words, the "gatekeepers" of rationality, detachment, and reflection, which social scientists are meant to represent, have been overtly blamed, allowing political elites to turn to the politics of emotion, fear, and order, depoliticizing the political violence and leading to what we call here the *politics of compensation*. While failing to address the real issues, the government must *appear* to address the problem of violence and find quick, visible solutions: it compensates for its political weakness by an increased focus on law and order. Thus, the "politics of compensation" is based on political communication rather than policy informed by social science.

Using material collected from print and television media, observations, and statistics, this chapter aims to show that the "double-bind" relationship between the takfiri political violence and the French government has led to an escalation in the level of violence toward the point of no return: indiscriminate mass physical violence and the persecution of Muslims. We would like to show how this vicious double bind has provoked a complete depoliticization of political violence and ushered in the politics of compensation. This has converted a political problem—state violence in the Middle East and discrimination against Muslims—into a racial/religious problem—"is Islam compatible with French society?" The depoliticization of political violence is the Trojan horse of the ra-cialization of Muslims, which might be identified in various phenomena: the idea of Muslims' "hidden solidarity" with the killers, the lack of recognition of Muslim organizations' statements against the attacks, the invisibility of Muslim heroes and victims, the kind of "collective punishment" implemented against Muslims, and the néo-laïc (secularist) framework that impedes any effort at es-tablishing a clear analysis of takfiri political violence.

"Hidden Solidarity" and the Impossibility of Being a Muslim Hero or Victim

In 1903 W. E. B. Du Bois wrote, "How does it feel to be a problem?"[2] That is the nagging question that so-called "Muslims," both French citizens and foreigners living in France, have asked themselves for the past three decades. Recent attacks have served as morbid realizations of prophecies by both literary (Michel Houel-lebecq) and journalistic (Eric Zemmour, Alain Finkielkraut) Islamophobes who conceive of the "Muslim community" as "a people within a people," whose prob-lematic presence can only be remedied by "remigration" (Renaud Camus), a eu-phemism for "deportation." Many other intellectuals, who may not link Islam to terrorism, have nonetheless argued for a "reformation of Islam," to be initiated by theologians and Muslim leaders. This solution is proposed by intellectuals such as Abdennour Bidar, Laurent Bouvet, and Gilles Kepel, according to whom the "disease of Islam" explains political violence.

Both approaches fail to consider the most basic sociological evidence: the "Muslim community" does not exist. Muslim organizations do not represent so-called Muslims. So-called Muslims constitute a diverse population in terms of social class, nationality, and political and ideological leanings, all of which are erased entirely by the call for *désolidarisation* (disassociation). This neologism assumes that solidarity already exists between the killers and all other supposed Muslims. In other words, so-called Muslims are presumed guilty by their simple association with Islam, and thus being Muslims automatically makes them part of the problem.

This guilt prevails even in the context of all Muslim organizations, including the Salafi ones, univocally condemning the attacks. After the ISIS-related assassi-nation of two police officers perpetrated by Larossi Aballa in Magnanville (forty miles west of Paris) in 2016, a demonstration against takfiri political violence was organized by local Muslim leaders, bringing thousands of people together in front of the Mantes-la-Jolie police headquarters. Considering that many politicians have accused Muslims of not being vocal enough against the attacks, one could have expected full media coverage. However, only one journalist covered the event and revealed that the organizers had not been invited to come into the police station, as if public statements against takfiri violence were not sincere enough and were in fact an instance of duplicity.[3] The idea of "hidden solidarity" remains unquestioned, even when Muslims are in the line of fire as victims or heroes—such as Ahmed Mrabet, a police officer killed in cold blood in front of the *Charlie Hebdo* office, and Lassana Bathily, a former illegal immigrant who saved several lives in the hostage situation in the kosher supermarket in 2015. In the Nice attack in 2016, more than a third of the eighty-four victims were Muslims.[4] The notion of "hidden solidarity" and the types of discourse associated with it—Islam as a threat or "disease"—draw their power from updated racialized relationships.

Let us now turn to the reasons behind the general blindness which followed the 2015 attacks. The emotional response incited by the killings—on both the national and international levels—tends to discredit social science researchers and journalists, whose job it is to deconstruct the mechanisms behind this violence. They are discredited for being "excessively idealistic" or "politically correct," or because of their perceived "inability to see what is directly in front of them." The historical context is like that of the post-9/11 period, when armchair journalists and pundits gave geography lessons to political scientists, sociologists, and journalists who had for years conducted research on violent groups. For instance, former director of *Charlie Hebdo* Philippe Val published an essay after the January 2015 attacks to denounce what he calls "sociologism," which is alleged to "completely remove responsibility [for their acts] from individuals [such as takfiri fighters]."[5] Because they seek to locate the social causes of the violence, social scientists are accused of legitimizing the latter and attenuating takfiri fighters' responsibility. What is at stake here is the possibility of producing a rational discourse based on empirical research, at the very moment when Islamophobes are taking advantage of a window of opportunity to proclaim the return of the concept of "the clash of civilizations."

In the case of *Charlie Hebdo*, with the blame solidly heaped on so-called Muslims, scorn was generally heaped on those journalists and commentators criticizing the editorial choices of the victimized magazine. For example, the journalist Caroline Fourest and the politician Jeanette Bougrab called out associations such as les Indivisibles, cofounded by the journalist Rokhaya Diallo, for having armed the killers with ideology: "By saying that *Charlie Hebdo* is Islamophobe, [Les Indivisibles] are of course guilty."[6] According to them, anti-Islamophobia activists might even be "responsible" for the killings and ought to explain themselves, as if their articles and speeches against racism had somehow inspired the killers. This accusation attributes a degree of media influence to these activists that they do not actually have, since reaching a wider public is in fact much more difficult than often assumed. Furthermore, to make such an accusation is to misunderstand the real ideological influences of the killers, which are rooted in the religious takfiri writings and the loose networks that are al-Qaeda and ISIS. With emotion prevailing over reason, there is a risk of censuring all types of university, journalistic, and protest speech denouncing the very real social phenomenon of Islamophobia. The risk is that collective responsibility becomes collective punishment, which takes three forms: Islamophobic hate speeches and crimes, the biased implementation of the law against the "apology for terrorism," and the way the government policy under the state of emergency has targeted the so-called Muslim community.

Collective Punishment

The proliferation of anti-Semitic acts committed during periods of violence in Palestine clearly shows that so-called Jews are punished collectively and held responsible for Israeli war crimes.[7] Similarly, as well as the extremely problematic perceived "defense of terrorism" discussed above, so-called Muslims have been subjected to a form of collective punishment, which has manifested itself in an increase in Islamophobia. Data from the Ministry of the Interior show that almost as many Islamophobic acts were committed in the month of January 2015 (128) as in the whole year of 2014 (133). Police sources recorded thirty-three acts committed against mosques and ninety-five threats; some of these acts involving grenades or firearms.[8] This racist violence was nourished by the "fascosphere" within social media that relayed appeals for murder.[9] However, considering the extreme tension that blanketed the country, one cannot help being struck by the difference between Islamophobic and anti-Semitic acts. Although anti-Semitic acts have become less frequent over the last decade, they are more violent and have often involved murder (the Toulouse killings by Mohamed Merah in 2012, for instance). Conversely, Islamophobic acts occur much more frequently, and while they can be very violent (the Ajaccio Mosque was burnt down in November 2015, a Muslim was shot and injured at the Bayonne Mosque in October 2019), only rarely do they lead to homicides.

The only such case recorded after the *Charlie Hebdo* events is that of Mohamed El Makouli, a forty-seven-year-old Moroccan killed at his home in Le Beaucet (Vaucluse, in the south of France) on 14 January 2015 by his neighbor, who stabbed him seventeen times while screaming, "I am your god, I am your Islam" (the offender was not prosecuted, since he was considered "not responsible" because of mental illness).[10] Islamophobia-related physical attacks are thus more common, relatively less violent, more anonymous, and generally directed at women wearing hijab.[11] This is where the point of no return becomes clear: by exacerbating existing social tensions, ISIS aims to provoke far-right calls for murder. As the director of the French domestic intelligence service Patrice Calvar stated before the National Assembly in July 2016, "We will, at one time or another, have to provide resources to deal with other extremist groups because the confrontation is inevitable. This confrontation, I think will take place. Even one or two attacks and it will happen. It therefore behooves us to anticipate and block all those groups who would, at one time or another, trigger communal clashes."[12] Since 2015 several underground violent Islamophobic groups have been identified and neutralized by the French intelligence service, such as Action des forces opérationnelles (Operational Forces Action) or Réseau libre (Free Network), founded in 2018 and 2019 respectively by former police officers and military, who intended to bomb the Nanterre Mosque (west of Paris), attack Muslim women wearing a headscarf, and poison halal food in supermarkets, etc.[13]

This discrepancy between anti-Semitic and Islamophobic violence is reinforced by the differing levels of legitimacy assigned to different types of racist speech. Whereas anti-Semitic speech is largely denounced by the entire French elite, as the latest "Le Pen affair" demonstrated,[14] Islamophobic speech appears to be much more acceptable, and certain public figures such as the philosopher Elisabeth Badinter readily embrace the label "Islamophobic."[15] The link between the level of physical and symbolic violence is not easy to determine but examining it might allow us to problematize analyses of "racism" in general. The mainstream media's reluctance to go down that slippery slope could be witnessed in the aftermath of the *Charlie Hebdo* attack and may have prevented even more physical violence. For example, on 7 January 2015, the commercial radio station RTL broadcast a daily show hosted by Marc-Olivier Fogiel,[16] in which extreme right-wing editorialist from *Le Figaro* Yvan Rioufol called upon the so-called Muslim journalist Rokhaya Diallo to disassociate herself from the killers. Diallo began to cry and was comforted by the other participants in the show, including Fogiel and Laurence Parisot, the former head of the French employers' union MEDEF. This kind of situation, which we find elsewhere in the media universe, can bring about a call to stop symbolic Islamophobic violence for fear of provoking a civil war. It was as if the link made between terrorism and Islam, which is usually the bread and butter of the mainstream print and television media, had been suspended for the short time around the killings in order to avoid France sinking further into an ever-widening hole of violence.

The second form of collective punishment relates to the law against "defending terrorism" and its increasingly stringent implementation. Until the antiterrorism law of 14 November 2014, this offense fell within the guidelines of the 1881 law about the freedom of the press: proceedings were usually very long and handled by a special judicial committee because freedom of expression could only be limited in very special cases. Today, however, "defense of terrorism" is included in the penal code (article 421–2–5), can be invoked by any judge in a criminal court, and can compel an immediate court appearance. The violent reaction in response to the attacks in January and November 2015 led the Syndicat de la magistrature,[17] Amnesty International, and prominent attorneys such as Maître Eolas to sound the alarm and denounce "swift justice" that contradicted the original goal of the law. Instead of challenging the defense of political violence related to Islam, the judicial system charged people absolutely unrelated to political violence.[18]

Indeed, what little information is available in the media is enough to show that the implementation of the antiterrorism-defense law after the January 2015 killings has mostly impacted those who had nothing to do with violence relating to Islam. Out of a total of forty-six cases reported by the press (there have actually been about 117),[19] only the three following cases related to people who subscribed directly to the ideology of ISIS or al-Qaeda. On 13 January in Elbeuf (Normandy), Franz Petermann, a temporary worker and Muslim convert, told police officers during an altercation: "I'm not gonna move, asshole. [. . .] it's not enough for you that we killed three cops? There are a lot of us and we have AK47s." Petermann was placed under arrest for "criminal association with intent to commit acts of terrorism" in Syria. Though the charge of "defense of terrorism" was dropped, he received a three-month suspended prison sentence and five years' probation for insulting an officer and a death threat. On 19 January in Lille, a fifty-eight-year-old bookseller allegedly sold ISIS flags and then declared at the police station, "I am not Charlie, I am Coulibaly, I am a terrorist."[20] He was given a suspended prison sentence of one year for "defending terrorism." On 22 January in Valence (southeast France), a divorced forty-five-year-old man allegedly forced his children to look at "extremely violent" images that "defended terrorism," with the supposed goal of indoctrinating them (unknown verdict). It should be noted that these sentences are lenient for a crime that can lead up to five years in prison and a €75,000 fine or, in the case of defense of terrorism online, up to seven years in prison and a fine of €100,000. The real targets of the law were, in the end, given suspended sentences.

On the other hand, severity seems to be the norm for all other cases. For example, an eighteen-year-old man, who made an "offensive gesture" toward a police station and screamed "100 percent Kouachi!"[21] several times (9 January, Nice), was sentenced to a one-month mandatory prison sentence; a thirty-four-year-old man charged with driving under the influence of alcohol, refusing multiple times to take a breathalyzer test, involuntary assault, and defending terrorist acts by screaming, "There should be more Kouachis. I hope you will be next. [. . .] You are a blessing for terrorists" (Valenciennes, 10 January), got a four-year mandatory prison sentence, lost his driver's license for two years, and was stripped of his civil and family rights for three years. Between these two extremes, most of those convicted were given prison sentences (rarely suspended) of a few months.

Victims of this disproportionate reaction were numerous: an eight-year-old third-grader named Ahmed was referred to the police by his school in Nice for having allegedly declared, "I am with the terrorists";[22] another student, nine years old, was referred to the police and accused of breaking the one minute's silence in Villers-Cotterêts (northeast of Paris), following another ill-intentioned student's tattling;[23] a left-wing activist and high-school philosophy teacher in Poitiers, Jean-François Chazerans, was accused by students' parents of defending the Nice attacks. He was suspended from teaching for several months and finally moved to another high school.[24] Lastly, a metal worker represented by the SUD union was fired for having allegedly made some "shocking" remarks defending the attacks while working at the Bombardier factory in Crespin.[25] The first child did not even know what the word "terrorism" meant but nevertheless suffered stigmatization at the hands of faculty who, if those remarks really had taken place, should have turned the situation into a teachable moment. The second and the third are the victims of what amounts to hearsay by a student and by the parents of a student, respectively. The fourth is the result of union pressure within the context of a serious conflict with management. The accusation of "defending terrorism" has become an easy weapon to wield when one wishes to spread rumors about an enemy, whether in the playground, the political sphere, or the workplace. Similar accusations were made by waiters at an Angoulême restaurant (southeast France) against four men later released by a judge and then jailed for two months after the Court of Appeal contradicted the first judge's decision. Accused of "celebrating January 7 in a bar," they were, in fact, celebrating a successful bet on a horse race.[26]

The gap between the spirit of the law and its real-life application is even more surprising when we consider the conditions that led these people to "defend terrorism." At least twenty cases were related to a direct challenge, either to a police authority (BAC, CRS, police, gendarmerie) or to public transport staff. In other words, the new crime of "defense of terrorism" is treated as a crime of contempt and rebellion, a classic judicial tool used by police to maintain social order. The only difference is the use of words such as "AK–47" or "Allahu Akbar" (God is great)—as if "Allahu Akbar" were synonymous with the defense of terrorism—and the explicit reference to the Kouachi brothers, or to Coulibaly. As political scientists Laurent Bonelli and Fabien Carrié point out, these alleged criminals match the profile of "agonistic radicals."[27] Far from being ISIS ideologues, these individuals made crude but not ideologically motivated reference to the killings in order to taunt, insult, and provoke those who represent the authorities and social control. The height of absurdity was reached when judges issued extremely severe sentences to seven people under the influence of alcohol. One intoxicated thirty-one-year-old man got a ten-month mandatory prison term for saying, while in a police station on 11 January, "Dirty Africans, Allah Akbar, fuck France, the Arabs are here" and "that's not good, AK 47 better, I'll smoke you with an AK 47." The lawyers tried to argue that the state of drunkenness was responsible for these "stupid" comments, but the judges were unmoved. They were equally unmoved in the case of two people with serious mental health issues. One of them, a thirty-eight-year-old Moroccan man from Paris, who insulted police officers on 15 January, was given a three-month mandatory prison sentence despite psychiatric evidence proving his mental health condition. Ultimately, the law of 14 November 2014, as applied since the January 2015 killings, has been used to compensate for the inability of the government to deal with the problem of takfiri political violence. Government authorities have convicted around fifty people, mostly of North African origin or of Muslim faith. Those cases that have been made public, especially the case of young Ahmed, show that so-called "Muslim" men and women are suspects from an early age.

The third form of collective punishment deals with the state of emergency. The politics of compensation also lies at the core of the state of emergency implemented after 13 November 2015, and the same process of collective punishment has occurred. As was the case in January of that year, the condemnation of the November killings was massive, and the desire to show solidarity with the victims was unanimous. But, in the so-called Muslim community, these feelings were mitigated by the fear of retaliation from far-right groups and of the brutal government response during the state of emergency. According to the Ministry of Interior,[28] 3,021 searches were conducted and 318 home arrests were made between 15 November 2015 and 7 January 2016. While 464 offenses were discovered (from carrying illegal weapons to drug dealing), only twenty-five were related to terrorism. In the end, the antiterrorism prosecutor initiated only four proceedings. Again, aberrations have dominated the news: those relating to a Muslim humanitarian organization (Baraka City), a practicing Catholic, environmental activists, protesters against the state of emergency, and others who were arrested or put under house arrest despite having no links with any armed group.

The Strength of the Néo-Laïc Framework

One cannot understand the logic of collective punishment and the politics of compensation in France without what we call here "the néo-laïc framework," based on the idea of néo-laïcité developed in the previous chapter. As we observed in the introduction and chapter 9, laïcité as defined by the 1905 law corresponds more or less to the separation of church and state, and the guarantee of the freedom of religion and worship, even in public spaces. Néo-laïcité however, distinguishes itself by expanding the realm governed by laïcité, which now includes the *use* of public services (no longer only public-service workers) and religious practice, not only in public areas but also in private companies. The defining characteristic of néo-laïcité is that since 1989 it has striven to erase Islam from public view, all in the name of a perceived threat to "national identity": that is, the persistent belief in and practice of Islam by the children of postcolonial immigrants. From an assimilationist point of view,[29] which is precisely the type of perspective that has inspired néo-laïcité, this persistence is considered an anomaly within the "republican model" and constitutes the source of the "Muslim problem." It is therefore not an accident that the first institution summoned to "respond" to the killings was the national school system, and that the first tenet deployed was that of laïcité. From that point of view, the solution to the problem of political violence might lie in teaching about laïcité in public schools; hence the extensive teacher training program, the institution of 9 December as "National Laïcité Day" and the "counter-radicalization" policy in public schools. Moreover, other parts of the public sector, from the "left hand" of the state— that is, the welfare state, according to Pierre Bourdieu—have been involved in the "counter-radicalization" policy. For instance, the Ministry of Interior, the "right hand of the state," asked the Juvenile Protection Administration,[30] which is supposed to help youngsters with family difficulties to integrate into society, to prevent any "new Kouachi brothers" and detect any "radicalization indicators" (invented by the so-called Islam expert Dounia Bouzar), such as wearing a beard, starting to pray, etc.[31] Some local authorities and Caisses d'allocations familiales even closed community centers, where many social activities are organized for working-class families and young people, because of a suspicion that some rooms may be used as prayer spaces.[32] In other words, *the right hand of state has been "colonizing" the left hand.* The néo-laïc framework has been the Trojan horse of the racialization of Muslims in the public sector.

This néo-laïc framework has also manifested itself in the legislative branch of the government. On 18 February 2015, the UMP National Assembly representative Eric Ciotti introduced a bill seeking to extend the principle of laïcité to include public institutions of higher education. On 2 March Secretary of State for Women's Rights Pascale Boistard went further, declaring that the veil might not belong in a university setting. On 12 March a bill adopted by the Senate in January 2012 in response to the "Baby Loup" affair, and subsequently relegated discretely to the fringes of the legislative agenda, resurfaced; it was again submitted for adoption by the National Assembly in May 2015. The bill sought to ban the wearing of religious symbols in private day-care facilities that receive any government funding, which is to say most such centers in France. It is thus apparent that representatives on both the right and the left have conflated the killers with women who wear hijab in universities and nurseries; this conflation holds those women responsible for acts that they did not commit but are suspected of secretly supporting. Thus, one of the likely effects of the killings has been a process of entrenched legal discrimination that aims to construct a special legal statute that subverts the right to education and the right to work.

PART IV

Compiling an "Anti-Muslim Archive"

CHAPTER 11

Construction and Circulations of European Representations of Islam and Muslims

For several centuries, Islam and Muslims have represented the figurative embodiment of the enemy par excellence in Western theological and political thought.[1] From Muslim invasions of European countries in the Middle Ages (Spain, the Balkans, etc.) to the European (then U.S.) imperialism of the nineteenth and twentieth centuries, religious and political conflicts have generated a set of European discourses aimed at challenging a new, heretic religion, justifying social segregation and legitimizing military conquests. This set of discourses about Islam and Muslims is a discursive legacy upon which each generation of state, NGO, and academic actors draws, depending on their social position and the historical and political contexts. A look back at this "anti-Muslim archive"—in other words, the construction of what can and cannot be said on the subject of Islam and Muslims—is indispensable for an understanding of contemporary discourses.

However, it is imperative to avoid the twin pitfalls of anachronism and an ahistorical vision of discursive Islamophobia. There is no such thing as a global, multisecular Islamophobia intrinsic to European identity: a visceral and endemic hostility whose "nature" has allegedly remained identical from the Middle Ages up to the twenty-first century and which varies only in intensity from one historical period to another. Instead, there are actually contingent discourses, produced by a highly diverse group of actors (theologians, philosophers, scholars, diplomats, governments, scientists, journalists, etc.) in specific sociohistorical contexts (responses to Muslim conquests, Crusades, the decline of the Ottoman Empire, European and U.S. imperialism, immigration to the West from Muslim nations, etc.). While basing our account on the existing literature, we will look at the construction and circulation of European representations of Islam and Muslims by focusing on the discursive continuities and discontinuities. This rapid scan of the horizon will enable us to think about comparing the "anti-Jewish Archive" and the "anti-Muslim archive," that is, comparing anti-Semitism and Islamophobia.[2]

Discourse in the Early Christian Middle Ages

From the seventh century onward, Christian Europe's political and religious authorities developed a number of strategies to address the expansion of Muslim civilization into the world:[3] theological rejection, Crusades, sending missionaries, martyrdom, etc. The first representations of Islam and Muslims in Europe were the product of anti-Muslim works—the term "Islamophobic" did not exist. These texts were produced by Christians (in the seventh to eighth centuries), living either in Christian and Muslim Europe (Spain or the Balkans), or in Eastern, Muslim countries, whose objective was to combat both Muslim religious dogma and the political enemy.

Over time, polemical arguments were refined and the Muslim enemy was designated using several, often interchangeable, categories: Arabs, Saracens, Moors, Ishmaelites (Ismailis), Hagarites, Turks, etc.

The terms "Arab" and "Saracen" are mentioned in the Bible and the writings of the Fathers of the Church, so it is clear that "the construction of a controversial image of the Saracens began before the expansion of Islam."[4] But it was indeed the expansion of Muslim civilization and the conquest of Christian lands that provoked an anti-Muslim discourse, with three objectives: to prevent conversions to Islam in the conquered territories; to legitimize military action against the invader; and to justify the legal segregation and social repression of the Muslim subjects of Christian princes.

Christianity thus produced a "body of beliefs,"[5] an "arsenal of controversial images" or "intellectual weapons"[6] that are part both of a defensive ideology (against invasion and the status of *dhimmi* Muslims) and an aggressive ideology of conquest that builds a feeling of superiority among Westerners in relation to Muslims and Arabs. This superiority was at that time defined basically in religious terms, and the arguments marshalled against Islam and Muslims were above all theological. From a Christian perspective, the military victories of Muslim armies did not result from their great warlike or strategic qualities but from a plague or divine punishment visited upon Christians who had strayed from the path of Christian orthodoxy. There were numerous theological disagreements between Islam and Christianity, based specifically on the nature of the Revelation, the concept of the Holy Trinity, the status of the Prophet

Mohammed, etc. Islam was depicted as a heresy to be fought against, both intellectually and militarily, because it was viewed as a form of paganism, or even a polytheist religion, invented from scratch by a false prophet. In a highly successful literary genre, biographies of the Prophet Mohammed,[7] he is described as an impostor whose revelations expressed not the word of God but that of the Antichrist or the Devil in person.

There were many caricatures of the Prophet that mocked his religious message: some engravings show the Devil in the form of a small bird who dictates his word to Mohammed . . . Muslims were thus argued to be obeying a charlatan who had simply constructed a religious doctrine from the Old and New Testament, on the advice of a "sparrow" that had instructed him.

Generally speaking, Christian discourse established the relational structures that were to become crucial in the common perception of Islam and Muslims. On one side, Islam became a synonym of irrationality, passion, emotion, and barbarity, while on the other, Christianity represented reason, civilization, and spiritual uplift. These types of relational structures were expressed through the discourses about Saracens as a group labeled a "treacherous race" by Riccold de Monte Croce (1243–1320) (the term "race" did not have biological connotations at that time), one that was violent, aggressive, uncivilized, and whose sexual customs were intolerable (the "fornication" of Muslims is contrasted with the celibacy of Christian priests). John of Damascus (676–749), one of the Fathers of the Early Church, "began the long tradition of attacks on Mohammed based on the idea that he used God—by simulating the Revelation—in order to justify his own sexual pleasures."[8]

The arguments deployed by Christian authors against Muslims were not very different from the ways used to invalidate the Jewish people and religion: both Muslims and Jews, as irrational infidels, were "accommodated in the same premises."[9] The "Muslim connection"[10] that bound Jews and Muslims together was accompanied by legal and political connections (see below). From the seventh century, Christian religious and political authorities passed laws constraining the legal status of Jews and Muslims and aiming to limit the "contamination" of Catholics by infidels, by avoiding sexual contacts, social bonds, and religious contamination via syncretic rites, etc.

According to historian John Tolan, the Medieval period, particularly after the Crusades, is definitive in the construction of negative representations of Islam and Muslims in the West: "The Europeans were never again to mount a stronger intellectual effort against Islam comparable to that waged by their ancestors to explain, refute, and convert."[11] After the crystallization of eighth-century European representations of Islam, the latter would undergo only "minor variations" until the Enlightenment, and even up to the twentieth century: "Between 1300 and the Enlightenment, little new was written about Islam."[12]

Philosophy of the Enlightenment and Orientalism

The period from the Reformation to the Enlightenment indeed witnessed a greater heterogeneity in the European discourse on Islam and Muslims.[13] The traditional prejudices were still very widespread in Europe: for instance, stereotypes of the Prophet Mohammed as an impostor were still in circulation, especially in popular literature. Yet the consensus underlying the European discourse was shattered by in-fighting in Europe (Protestants and philosophers against the Catholic Church), a transformation of international power relations, and greater knowledge. From the fourteenth to the eighteenth centuries, the Muslim world was represented by the Ottoman Empire, to such an extent that "Turk" became the synonym of "Muslim." In their struggle against Catholic orthodoxy, some Reformation Protestants thought they had found useful arguments within Islam. Martin Luther, for example, used the Turkish idea of "morality" to oppose Catholic "immorality," while fearing a coalition between "Papists" and the Turks. Conversely, the Counter-Reformation sought to invalidate Protestantism by comparing it to heretical Islam.

However, following an extension of Muslim-held territory as far as the gates of Vienna in 1683, the eighteenth century saw the decline of the Ottoman Empire. As Europe gradually caught up with, and then overtook, the technological level of the Muslim world, "the growing consciousness of its weakness in relation to the European powers made the Ottoman Empire more an object of curiosity than of fear."[14] In other words, the reversal in power relations between the Ottoman Empire and Europe meant that Islam was no longer just subject to negative prejudices but also became an object of relatively far-removed knowledge. The discourses were no longer strictly theological and Christian but had become more secular and ambiguous. For example, this ambiguity can be identified in Count de Boulainvilliers's biography of the Prophet (*La vie de Mahomed*, 1730), which presented simultaneously an impostor, the inventor of a false religion, and a conqueror just as admirable as the Emperor Alexander and Caesar. This ambiguity can also be identified in Voltaire, who used the traditional Medieval arguments to justify his enduring antipathy toward the "fanatical" Prophet (*Fanaticisme ou Mahomet le Prophète*, 1736) but diverged from Medieval discourses by engaging in an analysis of Muslim faith from a secular perspective (*Essai sur les moeurs*, 1756) and by contrasting the intolerance of the Christians with the goodness of Muslims: Islam was thus a weapon for the heterodox and the deists to use against the Catholics.

However, "the 'philosophical' sympathy for Muslims (including the Turks) that could be found in the work of some thinkers from the first half of the [eighteenth] century seemed to have evaporated" by the end of it.[15] This change in attitude can be explained by the inclusion of the Ottoman Empire in the system of international alliances and the desire for conquest expressed by influential diplomat-writers such as Count Volney in France (*Voyage en Égypte et en Syrie*, 1787) and William Eton in Great Britain.

The latter made effective use of the concept of "oriental despotism" conceived by Montesquieu (*De l'esprit des lois*, 1748), who sought to describe an "oriental" situation, according to the author, in which submission to a single person was total; fear rather than law was the dominant force; and in which the reign of the arbitrary turned subjects into slaves doomed to total obedience. However, Volney and other philosophers saw Islam itself as the primary cause of the obedience of its people and the barbarity of the despot. Muslim power must therefore be driven out of Europe in order for the freedom of subject people to be restored. Thus, "instead of making them less Other in the eyes of enlightened authors," the integration of the Ottomans into the European diplomatic game "actually pushed them further away into a more radical otherness, as representatives of a uniquely fanatical and despotic state that did not belong in Europe."[16]

This radicalization of Muslim otherness in the eighteenth century went hand in glove with the birth of a new discipline, Orientalism, the fruit of an intellectual endeavor unprecedented in European history, aimed at comprehending the Orient in general, and Muslim civilization in particular.[17] Orientalism is the study of the arts, languages, sciences, history, religions, cultures, and people of the Orient by theologians, academics, and scientists from both the natural and social sciences.[18] These Orientalist authors interpreted the Orient as a group of societies to explore and colonize for economic (raw materials, workforce, etc.) and political reasons (power struggles between France, Great Britain, Germany, etc.). These colonial explorations produced a three-way split in the world: civilized Western Europe, the world with no history or culture of the "savages" and, between the two, the Orient: composed of great civilizations in decline. As Edward Said emphasizes, the production of Orientalist knowledge is bound up in, but not reducible to, European imperialist power. While producing a set of new knowledge about Oriental societies, Orientalism enables not only an academic legitimization of colonial conquest but also active participation in the conquest: desire for knowledge and for power were often embedded in one another. From this perspective, the numerous scientific explorations, the best known of which is the military expedition to Egypt (1798–1801),[19] contributed to the construction of academic disciplines in Europe (anthropology, sociology, ethnology, philology, etc.) and of a specific body of knowledge about Muslim societies, which is essentially rooted in two basic assumptions or claims.

The Orientalists first claim that the history of Oriental societies cannot be analyzed in the same way as the history of European ones: they tend to downplay the technological, economic, and social factors because, according to them, it is primarily the spiritual and the religious aspects that predominate in Oriental cultures, unlike in the secularizing West. This view contributed to legitimizing the idea that individual and collective behavior of Muslims is above all determined by their religious affiliation, and not by political, economic, and social determinants. This religious determinism also leads to a concentration on religious texts, especially the Quran, that are supposedly crucial to understanding the Muslim world: the textual analysis of surahs of the Quran are argued to be easily sufficient to enable the comprehension of Muslim history. The Orientalist interpretation of the Quran thus leads to the formulation of "criticisms" addressed specifically to Muslims: jihad (holy war), slavery, polygamy, fatalism, and fanaticism are, for Orientalists, inherent to Islam and constitute immutable features of Muslim communities.

This ahistorical vision of the history of the Muslim world links up with a second claim: the existence of separate races within the human race, each one with inherent biological and psychological features. By including the theory of "race war" and the pseudoscientific work in racial anthropology in their own arsenal,[20] the Orientalists studied the dynamics of the history of the Muslim world as simultaneously a struggle between religious movements and a race struggle, specifically between the Semitic and Indo-European races (see below). By connecting religion to race, they therefore helped racialize religious belonging, which became an intrinsic feature of Muslim populations in such accounts.

It is thus no coincidence that colonial domination was founded on a racial definition of nationality and citizenship.[21] For example, after the conquest of Algeria (1830), the defeated indigenous Muslims were, in legal terms, both nationals (imperial subjects) and noncitizens (they had no right to vote or stand for election) and were subject to their own parallel penal code, with specific offenses and tougher sentences, called the *code de l'indigénat*: this legal discrimination is explained both by the colonizers' desire to retain the monopoly of political power and by the belief in the racial inferiority of Muslim Algerians and their civilization. The 1865 senatus-consult (command by the Senate) afforded them the option of demanding naturalization, on condition that they give up personal status as a Muslim. Yet even this renunciation was not enough to acquire citizenship, in as far as Muslims could not escape their "Islam-ness" by conversion to Christianity: as a Court of Alger ruling underlined (5 November 1903), "it is obvious that the term 'Muslim' does not have a purely religious meaning, but that it refers on the contrary to the group of individuals of Muslim origin that, not having been granted citizens' rights, have of course retained their personal Muslim status, without there having been an opportunity to identify whether they belong to the religion of Islam."[22] The colonial situation had thus produced a distinction between Islam as a religion and Islam as a race ("Muslim origin"). To paraphrase Hannah Arendt (see below), it could be argued that the transformation of Islam-religion into Islam-race is a very dangerous intellectual step, because even if Muslims were able to escape Islam by conversion, none of them could escape from their racialized Islam-ness.

Ultimately, the colonial period witnessed a pseudoscientific radicalization of Muslim otherness, a difference made not only religious or theological but also racial and psychological. This racializing vision of the Orientalists can also be observed in public space (colonial exhibitions,[23] the press, popular songs,[24] Orientalist literature, etc.), constructing the mythical figures of the "Muslim man," described as barbaric, duplicitous, and a sexual predator,[25] and the sensual and oppressed "Arab woman."[26] As many studies have shown,[27] European perceptions of social relations in the Muslim world are replete with distorted and ambivalent images of unbridled and deviant sexuality on the part of both men and women (descriptions of the harem and polygamy, etc.), as well as an allegedly "specific" masculine domination, that is, one that is more oppressive for the completely "submissive" women in the Muslim patriarchal order.

However, although these representations of Islam and Muslims were very popular in Europe during colonial times, what happened to them in the postcolonial period? This era, which began in the wake of the Second World War, saw a greater diversification of the discourses about Islam and Muslims, helped by the emergence of the mass media, the proliferation of wars in the Middle East, the growing role of countries without histories as colonial powers (especially the United States) in the Muslim world in the production of discourses, and the split in academia between the neo-Orientalist and scientific approaches to Islam and Muslim societies.

"Neo-Orientalism" in the Age of Mass Media

In academia, Western ways of understanding Islam and Muslims, either living in Muslim countries or the West, were completely turned on their head by the rise of Arab nationalist movements, the decolonization process, and the challenge to Western hegemony by colonized people. The history and sociology of Islam and Muslims started to become an academic specialization that challenged the assumptions and claims of colonial Orientalism and was split into specific subfields: Islamic studies or Islamology, philological and literary analysis, the history of the various religious groups, the sociology of religion, political science, and specializations on the "cultural zones" (Maghreb, Mashrek, Iran, etc.). Academically speaking, knowledge of Islam and Muslims had never been so advanced, due to the intellectual independence of research and collaboration between Western researchers and those from Muslim nations, some of whom taught at the most prestigious Western universities.[28] Yet some researchers began to step away from academic requirements in order to take up stances as experts with state organizations, as the case of neo-Orientalism referred to in chapter 7 illustrates.

Media discourse about Islam and Muslims prioritizes caricatural and stereotyped neo-Orientalist representations, but there are significant variations within them, depending on historical contexts and national specifics. A distinction must be made between the European nations, who have a long experience of direct contact with the Muslim world, and the United States where, according to Said, "it is only when a political crisis occurs that a public debate on Islam begins"[29] (the capture and enslavement of U.S. sailors by "barbaric" Mediterranean corsairs in the 1780–1850 period,[30] the Iranian revolution of 1979, the Iraq Wars of 1990 and 2003, 11 September 2001, the invasion of Afghanistan in 2001, etc.). Although Said's comment about the construction of a Black Islam "problem" should be put into perspective,[31] this distinction is important for understanding that in France, for example, the essentialist discourse about Islam and Muslims dates back to a period well before the initial "crises" around Islam in France, that is, the 1989 "Islamic headscarf" affair and the terrorist attacks attributed to the Algerian Groupe islamique armé algérien (GIA, 1995–1996). The differences in the discourse at national levels also explain some variations between the *New York Times'* and *Le Monde's* coverage of the 1979 Iranian revolution.[32] While the American newspaper ignored the many experts on Islam and Iran in the U.S. academy and published cobbled together and anecdotal articles by journalist Flora Lewis, the French daily seemed at that time more open to the academic approach and invited Maxime Rodinson, an eminent French Orientalist and Marxist to provide a detached analysis of events, based on sophisticated knowledge of the political and social Iranian actors of the period.

However, media coverage of Islam by the French press and television has deteriorated over the intervening years. Despite the diversity of national contexts, we have witnessed an international convergence, or the formation of a dominant media consensus transcending national borders, which, however, has never been a monolithic bloc. Indeed, "it does not, however, dictate or determine the news involuntarily: it is neither the result of deterministic laws, nor of conspiracy, nor of dictatorship."[33] It was the social construction of a dominant ideology that became "obvious" in the course of the long labor entailing selection and interpretation of social reality.[34]

Having analyzed hundreds of television programs between 1971 and 2004 (television news on the TF1 and France 2 channels, plus debates and freestanding reports), Thomas Deltombe shows how media coverage of Islam has contributed to the construction of an "imaginary Islam" through the "Islamization of the (media) gaze."[35] In the 1970s Islam was perceived through the frame of the 1973 oil crisis and the Iranian revolution, in which the threatening figures of the rich, potbellied mustachioed Muslim from the Gulf states and the Muslim woman dressed in a chador appear. The Muslim question was linked to the immigration debate during the strikes against the layoffs of the early 1980s, when the paternalist vision of a domesticated Islam were expressed, succeeded by that of a threatening Islam (as we noted in chapter 6). In the 1990s, two crucial events— the Iraq War (1990–1991) and the Algerian civil war (1991–1998)—provided the opportunity for the theme of the "clash of civilizations" to be popularized, for the term "Islamism" to be imposed, and for an artificial and ideological opposition between "fundamentalists" and "moderates" to be constructed.

During the 1990s and even more in the wake of 11 September 2001, the essentialization of Islam became radicalized via the construction of a continuum between Islam, Islamism, and terrorism. The media thus repeatedly made false equivalences and fallacious semantic slippages while promoting a worldview overdetermined by the religious element and concomitantly neglecting socioeconomic factors, unable to conceive of the diversity within Islam. These phenomena have been more widely spread by the logic of how the media works, which we outlined in chapter 7. This entails a fixation on viewing and readership figures; the primacy of the "scoop" and "breaking news"; the hegemony of television to the detriment of the daily print press and editorials; and exacerbated competition between the various television channels. The increasingly unequal division of journalistic labor (with an inflated value attached to the industry's "stars" and the simultaneous increase in precarity of the lower-level employees, plus the increasing rarity of correspondent and senior reporter's jobs) are also structural constraints whose effects include distorting frames and filters in news production. The dominant media representations associating Islam with violence are so prevalent in public space that the Oklahoma City bombing (1995), the explosion at the AZF factory in Toulouse (2001), the urban uprisings in France (2005), and the Utoya massacre in Norway (2011) were "automatically" attributed to Muslims/Islamists by most of relevant media.

There is also a "resemblance"[36] between colonial Orientalism and postcolonial neo-Orientalism in terms of religious affiliation being deemed preeminent in both cases for understanding the action of Muslims, whose violence, barbarity, and duplicity are intrinsic and immutable features. Neither is it a coincidence that Islamophobic films that have provoked international controversy—*Submission*, by Dutchman Theo van Gogh and the Dutch-Somalian Ayaan Hirsi Ali (2004); *Fitna* by Dutchman Geert Wilders (2008); and *Innocence of Muslims* by U.S. Coptic Christian Nakoula Basseley Nakoula (2012)—lean heavily on the surahs of the Quran to "explain" the actions of political movements such as al-Qaida.

However, notable variations within the colonial Orientalist discourse can be identified, especially on the theme of sexuality. Although there are "several continuities between the old orientalist certainties and the evocations [...] that link North African men and sex" just after decolonization,[37] this theme disappears in French songs of the 1980s,[38] and contemporary discourse is critical of both repressed sexuality (wearing the hijab; the niqab, the burqa, and authoritarian control of women's bodies, etc.) and Arab and Muslim sexual violence.[39] A comparative analysis of media discourses in France and Great Britain reveals a "paradigm shift from an old exotic and sensual stereotype of Islam to a more recent stereotype of Muslim fanaticism."[40] As Éric Fassin points out, "eroticism has changed sides."[41] There is thus no identical reproduction of Orientalist representations and discourses, but rather a reactivation of them depending on the political and national contexts.

Despite these ruptures between the Orientalist and neo-Orientalist discourses, both connect the Arab to the Muslim, even though these two categories refer to associated but distinct social and historical realities.[42] The Arab world cannot be reduced to the Muslim world because there are Arabs who are not Muslim (Christians, Jews, atheists, agnostics, etc.), just as the Muslim world cannot be reduced to the Arab world, since the vast majority of Muslims in the world are not Arabs (but Indonesians, Iranians, Indians, Pakistanis, Europeans, etc.). However, despite the fact that "Arab" and "Muslim" are categories split by nationality, social class, religion, and written and spoken language, neo-Orientalist discourse homogenizes and essentializes the "Arabo-Muslim" world as if it is a unique reality. This monolithic vision leads to the production of a kind of imaginary atavistic solidarity between individuals whose only common characteristic is that they are (or are assumed to be) Muslim: the French atheist whose parents were Algerian immigrants is thus assumed to be responsible for, and to feel solidarity with, the murderous actions of a French jihadi against French soldiers and Jewish children (Mohamed Merah) and with a Saudi Wahabi millionaire who carried out terrorist attacks (Oussama Ben Laden); the practicing British Muslim with Pakistani heritage is assumed to feel solidarity with the London bombers of 7 July 2005; the French Muslim association leaders (Conseil français du culte Muslim) should be accountable for and do everything to free the French journalists taken hostage by Iraqi Muslims and those resisting the Western occupation. There is a never-ending supply of examples of bizarre scenarios in which "Muslims" living at the four corners of the planet are all grouped together due to the fallacious connection made between Islam, Islamism, and violence and terrorism.

In these circumstances, only the sharpest mind could distinguish Islamophobia from anti-Arab racism or anti-Indian/Pakistani racism, as is demonstrated by the difficulty of producing reliable statistics on racist or Islamophobic acts (chapter 2). This difficulty can be partly explained by the othering process in itself: the construction of the border between "Them" and "Us," between the Other and the Self, can be developed from a wide variety of signifieds (sex, race, class, religion, ethnicity, etc.), which change according to national and historical contexts.

In the contemporary Western world, the figurative embodiment of the absolute Other is that of the Muslim man and the Muslim woman, just as the Jew was the figure of Otherness par excellence in the recent past.

CHAPTER 12

Anti-Semitism and Islamophobia

The comparison between the extremely complex phenomena of anti-Semitism and Islamophobia has been the subject of several debates in the anglophone world: anthropologists, philosophers, historians, and sociologists—especially British and U.S. specialists—as well as specialists in European societies, have begun the process of reflection. In as far as these debates have developed in their own siloes, we will follow in the footsteps of Gil Anidjar and Fernando Bravo Lopez, author of the first PhD thesis comparing anti-Semitism and Islamophobia,[1] and make connections between medieval history, modern history, political philosophy, anthropology, and sociology.[2]

This comparison immediately runs into a problem of definition, which arises for both Islamophobia (see chapter 5) and anti-Semitism. Indeed, although the latter term is widely used in the social sciences, it is criticized in ways that resonate with critiques leveled at the term Islamophobia. Attempts to compare the two thus derive from the ways in which various authors define these concepts, but overall, two main theoretical approaches can be identified: one from history and the philosophy of ideas, the other drawn from sociology and historical anthropology.

While the former approach focuses on the symbolic forms assumed by anti-Semitism and Islamophobia (representations, stereotypes, prejudices), the latter is particularly interested in the position of Jewish and Muslim minorities in European societies. The two approaches are of course not mutually exclusive, but it is rare to find an account that genuinely links both the symbolic and social dimensions of anti-Semitism and Islamophobia. Moreover, things get more complicated when some researchers compare the two across different historical periods such as the Middle Ages, the Enlightenment, the modern era (industrial capitalism and imperialism), and the contemporary period. The heterogeneity of the historical contexts and protagonists of anti-Semitism and Islamophobia between these different periods makes the comparative task extremely perilous. Nevertheless, we seek to present some lines of inquiry that seem relevant to a better understanding of both phenomena: "Since Jews and Muslims define themselves—and are defined by others—through reference to race and religion, it is reasonable to consider whether they have shared any similarities in their representation as constitutional religious minorities in the State."[3]

Similar Symbolic Forms

Without claiming to address all the stakes and protagonists in the struggle over the definition of anti-Semitism,[4] the most widely accepted definition—according to historian Leon Poliakov—is of "an effective sui generis attitude of gentiles toward Jews, an endemic hatred pregnant with explosive outbursts, reducing the children of Israel to pariah status, and exposing them, as traditional scapegoats, to numberless and endless massacres."[5] This dominant vision presents anti-Semitism as an "animosity toward Jews that is radically different, due to its intensity and enduring nature, from all other historical conflicts and hatreds."[6] It is thus argued to be a thousand-year hostility from Antiquity to the present day, with the same "nature" regardless of the various "forms" and varying levels of intensity it assumes in different historical periods: there is seemingly a symbolic continuity between pagan anti-Judaism (in Antiquity), Christian anti-Judaism, Enlightenment anti-Judaism, and the racial anti-Semitism of the nineteenth century: "In place of divine interpretation came the racial interpretation, the preserve of the elite in the eighteenth century, and property of the masses in the nineteenth, which provided the ideological justification for the gas chambers in the twentieth."[7]

From this perspective, the critique of the Jewish religion as a religious dogma is considered a form of anti-Semitism. For Poliakov, the violent attacks on Judaism perpetrated by Enlightenment thinkers, especially Spinoza and Voltaire ("the prestigious propagandist of 'anti-Semitism' in this form"), spread the idea that "the Jewish people were grossly ignorant and fundamentally perverse," and these writings also "contained embryonic proto-racism." Thus, Poliakov argues that "the thread leading from Spinoza, to Herder, Fichte and Hegel" bears "immense responsibilities" for the philosophical justification of twentieth-century anti-Semitism.

The problems that this vision of anti-Semitism raises are clear: it corresponds to Zionist historiography in that it only analyzes "ideas," without taking the

sociohistorical contexts of the production of these ideas sufficiently into account.[8] It is hard to defend the position that ahistorical and "visceral" forms of
anti-Semitism and Islamophobia are intrinsic characteristics of European societies. This approach takes account of neither the social construction of otherness
nor the specific features of modern anti-Semitism. Some locate the latter in the
nineteenth and twentieth centuries, where it was translated into action through
an unprecedented policy of persecutions and exterminations, unparalleled in
Christian anti-Judaism. Yet recent historical research has challenged this neat
distinction between premodern Christian anti-Judaism and the anti-Semitism
of the nineteenth and twentieth centuries: "The renewal of research into medieval and modern history [. . .] helped challenge the evidence of this differentiation."[9] As Jean-Frédéric Schaub emphasizes, a racial dimension to the stigmatization and exclusion of Jews (and Muslims) can be identified from the end of the
fifteenth century, especially after the Spanish Reconquista of 1492.[10] One of the
main elements of distinction between Christian anti-Judaism and modern anti-
Semitism lay in its justificatory logic: the movement from a religious discourse
to a pseudoscientific discourse of racial anthropology, based on a philosophy of
history, and then to a "chimeric" discourse generated by a conspiracy theory.

For historian Gavin Langmuir, a distinction must be made between, on the
one hand, xenophobic discourse, which consisted of using an empirical fact to
generalize it to the entire subaltern group that becomes a threat, and on the
other, a chimeric discourse (or "chimeria" to use Langmuir's phrase) not based
on any tangible reality.[11] The xenophobic discourse would for instance entail arguing that "Jews are, relative to the whole population, disproportionately found
in the banking sector, so they threaten Christian identity and the economy." A
connection is made between the "Jew" and an abstraction or social peril (in-
debtedness, national disunity, international conflict, etc.). Individual variations
among Jews are denied because the xenophobic discourse is not supposed to empirically describe Jews. The abstraction does not refer primarily to Jews but to a
broader phenomenon of some kind: belief in the existence of a threat, one which
is hard to understand and of which the Jews are "just" a symbol, its embodiment. This is why even the physical destruction of the group that symbolizes
the threat is "not enough" to erase the belief in the threat but can only reduce
awareness of it. The xenophobic discourses and actions may also function to re-
press the awareness of the difficulty in changing the social conditions at the root
of the belief in this threat, particularly the difficulty in transforming a complex
economic system. According to Bravo Lopez, the construction of a threat is the
main feature shared by anti-Semitism and Islamophobia: they are discursively
constructed in the same way insofar as they are "two essentialist discourses on

Judaism—and the Jews—and Islam—and Muslims—built on a threatening image."[12] Reza Zia-Ebrahimi argues that the common point of anti-Semitism and Islamophobia is the process of "conspiratorial racialization" that attempts to racialize Jews and Muslims as the ultimate "Other" determined to destroy "Us."[13]

However, xenophobia can be distinguished from "chimeria," which refers to fantasies, that is, purely products of the imagination completely unconnected to reality. The Jews have for example been accused of carrying out "ritual murder" when a child or young adult disappeared without a trace from a village. These ritual murders have never been witnessed, but the accusations change the image of the members of the target group into that of inhuman monsters. The chimeric discourse is more potent than the xenophobic one because it incites immediate action against the group and cannot be refuted using empirical facts. For this reason, Langmuir reserves the term anti-Semitism for situations in which there is socially significant chimeric hostility toward the Jews.[14] Consequently, anti-Semitism is defined as a chimeric discourse or an irrational prejudice against Jews, whose emergence can be situated in the twelfth and thirteenth century Northern Europe and which can be explained by a major change in Medieval Christian attitudes.

Although Langmuir's timeline in regard to the specifics of modern anti-Semitism is highly debatable, his definition of "chimeric discourse" is particularly relevant to grasp the specifics of discourses hostile to Jews, Blacks in the USA (e.g., the myth of the "Black rapist"),[15] and women (e.g., the myth of "witches").[16] "Chimeria" as proposed by Langmuir appears to have become a major feature of contemporary French Islamophobia. On 21 September 2001, the AZF factory in Toulouse exploded and a Muslim victim was wrongly accused of causing the explosion because he was wearing "five pairs of underpants and long johns on top of one another," a ritual supposedly enacted by jihadists before their terror attacks. In 2006 the far-right politician Philippe de Villiers published a book, *Les mosquées de Roissy* (The Mosques of Roissy [Roissy is a small town north of Paris, where Charles de Gaulle airport is located]), where he describes the so-called process of Islamization of Paris airport staff based on fake news. In 2012 the right-wing politician Jean-François Copé invented the story of Muslims pupils who supposedly harassed non-Muslim pupils during the month of Ramadan, stealing pains au chocolat from them.[17] As Ivan Jablonka and Raphaël Liogier point out, we are witnessing the construction of a "fictional politics," of a fear of Islam based on the "myth of Islamization" and the supposed advent of "Eurabia."[18]

Nevertheless, modern anti-Semitic discourse is more complex than even the chimeric elements of Christian anti-Judaism because it draws on theories of "race war," racial anthropology, and conspiracies.[19] These frames for the perception of reality have led to the transformation of the forms of othering Jews via the construction of the racial concept of "Jewishness." As Arendt emphasizes, "the transformation of the 'crime' of Judaism into the fashionable 'vice' of Jewishness, was dangerous in the extreme" because "Jews had been able to escape from Judaism into conversion [...] from Jewishness there was no escape."[20] And although crime can be punished (by assimilation or emigration), "vice can only be exterminated."[21]

In his study of comic cartoons depicting "the Arab" after the Arab-Israeli Wars of 1967 and 1973, Edward Said argues that "these Arabs are clearly 'Semites': as their distinctly crooked noses and 'bad moustache' smiles testify (to people who are mainly not Semites) that 'Semites' are the cause of 'our' troubles, which, in this case, are about the petrol shortage. Popular anti-Semitic animosity has smoothly transitioned from the Jew to the Arab, since the visual image is almost the same."[22] The historian Enzo Traverso outlines this transferal from anti-Semitic to Islamophobic representations. Anti-Semitism is thus defined as a "repertoire of stereotypes, images, places, representations, stigmatizations, and reflexes bearing a perception and interpretation of reality that condenses and codifies into a stable, ongoing discourse."[23] As this discursive practice is "likely to entail a transfer of object, anti-Semitism has therefore transmigrated toward Islamophobia."[24]

Anti-Semitism and Islamophobia thus converge in several analytical frameworks. To take the example of Great Britain, Nasar Meer and Tehseen Noorani attempt to show that modern discourses on the "nonassimilation" of Jews (at the turn of the twentieth century) are not far from the contemporary discourses on the "nonassimilation" of Muslims.[25] In each case, the putative lack of capacity to assimilate is explained by an essentialist discourse: "racial difference" for the Jews and religious/cultural difference for Muslims. The othering of Jews and Muslims revolves particularly around the representation of specific physical features (hooked noses, protruding ears, bushy beards, etc.) and specific religious practices (not eating pork, circumcision, religious clothing, etc.). However, other groups are also subjected to the injunction to assimilate and forms of othering in the history of representations: for example, Blacks, Gitanes and Roms, immigrants (even European ones), communists, etc.[26] It could be argued that the specificity of anti-Semitic and Islamophobic discourse is above all the constant relationship between race (or culture) and religion: religious belonging is supposed to be the ultimate determining factor in both individual and collective behavior.

Politically speaking, analogies can be made between the loyalty of Jews and

Muslims in the context of a major political or military crisis. Challenges to their loyalty to the state manifest themselves in the construction of the "Judeo-Bolshevik" or "Judeo-Anarchist" threat and that of "Islamic/Islamist terrorism": "The specter of Islamist terrorism has replaced that of Judeo-Bolshevism."[27] Violence committed by some Muslims becomes inherent to the Islamic religion, which is argued to be intrinsically fanatical and bellicose, just as the anarchist attacks at the end of the nineteenth century were interpreted as an illustration of an international Jewish conspiracy. The construction of a threat from within (nonassimilation) is connected to that of a threat from without (Judeo-Bolshevism/Islamism). While Jews are perceived by anti-Semites as global conspirators wielding a hidden power, Muslims are "problematic" because of their visibility, aggression, and desire to establish hidden Muslim power (the myth of Eurabia). In France in 2003, some media intellectuals such as Pierre-André Taguieff forged the notion of *islamo-gauchisme* (Islamo-leftism), which means the so-called political alliance between radical leftists and Islamists. This conspiracy theory has become the main symbolic tool to stigmatize Muslim and non-Muslim activists, politicians, and scholars who denounce Islamophobia.[28] The notion was mainly used by far-right movements but gained intellectual and political legitimacy in 2020 and 2021 when important members of the French government—Minister of Education Jean-Michel Blanquer and Minister of Higher Education and Research Frédérique Vidal—called for an "official inquiry" to investigate the "islamo-gauchisme" in French academia and its supposed complicity with jihadist terrorism.

In summary, anti-Semitic and Islamophobic discourses share a number of elements: essentialization, dehumanization, the fallacious interpretation of religious imperatives, conspiracy theories, the fantasy of Islamization/Judaization and Judeo-Bolshevism/Islamo-leftism, the notion of "parallel communities," or a "state within a state," threats from within and without, religious belonging as an identification afforded total explanatory power for individual behavior, etc.[29] This being the case, the comparison does have its limits: there are significant symbolic differences. Whereas Jews were described by their desire to self-segregate and surreptitiously acquire political and financial power, Muslims are characterized by their refusal to conform to liberal and secular values.

While Jews were accused of seeking to establish a "new Jerusalem" in Europe, Muslims are accused of living in separate communities and "no go areas." Although Jews did not have antidiscrimination legislation available to them, the ethnic groups making up Muslim communities have effective legal protection. Moreover, certain imaginary embodiments of the "Jew" constructed through anti-Semitic and philosemitic discourses bear the mark of the specifics of Jewish history.[30] This is true of the "Jew" of anti-Judaism (arrogant moneylenders, blasphemers, desecrators of sacred objects, throat-cutters of small Christian children, etc.), the rich capitalist Jew of modern anti-Semitism, and the enlightened Jewish universalist and pacifist intellectual of philo-Semitism.[31]

The Semitic Hypothesis

The comparison between the symbolic repertoires of modern anti-Semitism and of contemporary Islamophobia neglects an important reality, raised by Said when he compares the two phenomena within Orientalist knowledge, in his 1985 article, "Orientalism Reconsidered." Here, Said goes back over the reception of his seminal 1978 book, *Orientalism*, and responds to some critiques that did not grasp the "connection—explicitly made by two authors [that he] cites in Orientalism, [Ernest] Renan and [Marcel] Proust—between Islamophobia and anti-Semitism."[32] According to Said, anti-Semitism and Islamophobia share the same ideological root: "Hostility toward Islam in the modern Christian West has always gone hand in hand with, has stemmed from the same source, and has been nourished at the same stream as anti-Semitism."[33] A critical analysis of Orientalism therefore comes back to studying anti-Semitism as well: "A critique of the orthodoxies, dogmas, and disciplinary procedures of Orientalism contribute to an enlargement of our understanding of the cultural mechanisms of anti-Semitism."[34]

This line of inquiry is explored using different disciplinary approaches, and with sometimes diverging findings, in the work of James Pasto, Jonathan M. Hess, and Gil Anidjar.[35] These researchers seek to theorize the construction of the "Jewish problem" and the "Muslim problem" in European political thought by examining the relationship between modern anti-Semitism and colonial Orientalism. In his history of the enemy constructed by "Christian Europe," Anidjar posits that "the enemy [...] is structured by the Arab and the Jew, that is to say, by the relationship of Europe to *both* Arab *and* Jew," relationships which are "distinct but indissociable."[36] Whereas the figures of the Jew and the Arab are nowadays considered to be two polarized and conflicting identities, particularly due to the perpetuation of the Israeli-Palestinian conflict, Anidjar suggests turning our contemporary gaze on its head by revealing the connections and associations between them over the history of European "theological-political" thought.

This connection has existed since the Middle Ages. As noted above, Arabs were at that time defined through several categories (Saracens, Mohammedans, Muslims, Hagarites, Ishmaelites, pagans), but "Jews and Arabs [...] were linked together several times, placed in the same categories and even attacked at the same time."[37] In order to understand the novelty of Islam, the Christian West required help: the long-standing discourses barely provided any keys to comprehension and, "intellectually, the closest parallel to the position of Islam was that of the Jews."[38] Christian discourses thus used to refer to Muslims as "new Jews" and "consistently characterize Islamic beliefs and practices as Jewish, or at least as Jewishly influenced."[39] It is no coincidence that several medievalist historians have connected Christian anti-Judaism to Christian hostility toward Muslims,[40] which historians Alan and Helen Cutler call "anti-Muslimism."[41] The Jews were indeed accused numerous times of collusion with, and treason in support of, Muslims when the latter conquered several European countries.[42] At the seventh Council of Toledo (in 694), Egica, the Visigoth King of Spain, accused the Jews of Spain who had converted to Christianity of having been in contact with Jews in Africa to fight the Christians. They were the targets of the same accusations after the conquests of Bordeaux (848) and Barcelona (in 852).

The persecution of the Jews attained an unprecedented intensity from the beginning of the eleventh century: it witnessed a radical change in its geographical scope, due to the convergence of perspectives between the civil and religious authorities, and above all, because of the new accusation leveled against the Jews: treason "in support of the Muslims."[43] In the wake of the destruction of the Church of the Holy Sepulcher and other holy places in Jerusalem by Sultan Hakim (1009), the Jews of Orléans were the victims of such an accusation: they had allegedly warned the sultan about threats that Christians had made against him and encouraged him to carry out the destruction of the tomb of Christ. When news of this destruction reached the West, "it became obvious that the Jews had been the instigators of this crime. It was then decided by all the Christians that the Jews would be expelled from their countries and cities."[44]

The outburst of anti-Jewish persecution from the early eleventh century thus led to a brutal split between Jews and Christians. Perceived as a growing threat that had to be totally expelled from Christian lands, the Jews were systematically removed from Christian armies: "The first warlike Western endeavor necessarily carried out without the support of the Jews was the Spanish War of the eleventh century, not unreasonably labeled the Crusade of Spain."[45] From then on, a military brotherhood-in-arms between Jews and Christians was no longer possible, which meant "a major change in the situation of the Jews and was in no way an outcome of Judeo-Christian relations."[46]

It is because Jews and Muslims were considered enemies in alliance against Christianity that during the famous Fourth Lateran Council (1215) Pope Innocent III decided on the establishment of the distinctive clothing to be worn by both Jews and Muslims (the origin of the yellow badge worn by Jews). The pope's reasoning was based on the idea that the second coming of the Messiah would take place in 1284: to prepare for this eschatological event, the Muslims of the Middle East would have to be converted to Christianity, by sending missionaries and the Fifth Crusade, and the conquered Muslims would have to be socially degraded by the compulsory wearing of a distinctive article of clothing. The Jews were the allies of the Muslims, and they too had to be distinguished from Christians.[47]

As historian Carlo Ginzburg shows, collusion between Jews and Muslims was used as a theme in fourteenth-century Christian anti-Judaism, and both groups were even linked to leprosy in the myth of poisoning the waters in the wells and fountains. According to certain chronicles of the 1320s, the Muslim King of Granada, "incapable of victory over the Christians by force, had come up with a trick to defeat them. He approached the Jews, offering them an enormous quantity of money to devise and carry out a criminal plan to destroy Christianity. The Jews had agreed, but stated that they could not act overtly because they were a suspect community: it would be better to entrust lepers with the implementation of the plan since they were frequently in contact with Christians and could easily poison the water."[48] This myth spurred the edict issued by King Philippe V of France (Philip the Tall), who in 1321, enabled the mass killing and imprisonment of lepers, as well as the massacre, incarceration, extortion, and expulsion of the Jews from France.

The connection between the Jew and the Muslim is, in a completely different way, also a feature during the period when Orientalism flourished, in the nineteenth century. Without being able to review the controversy surrounding the complex relationship between anti-Semitism and Orientalism here,[49] we agree with Anidjar's emphasis that European "theologico-political" thought strove to link Jews and Muslims around the concept of "Semites." From this perspective, the "Semitic hypothesis [. . .] refers to the invention of the Semites, that is to the historically unique discursive moment when everything that could be said about the Jews could also be said about the Arabs, and vice versa."[50]

Actually, the concepts of "Semite" and "semitic" had been invented in the late eighteenth century by historian August Ludwig von Schlozer, who used them to define both a language family and the people who spoke these languages.[51] This invention bound Jews to Muslims, and Orientalist knowledge, particularly the writings of Ernest Renan, helped racialize the category "Semite" and anchor it in immutable characteristics. As Edward Said underlines, Renan's philology is a "secular science." Following the discovery of the chronological precedence of Sanskrit over Hebrew, the divine origin of language, bestowed by God in the Garden of Eden, was challenged. Philologists then located the origin of language in the Orient and contributed to the renaissance of Orientalism and the classification of languages: Indo-European and Semitic. Renan's work on Semitic languages comprises "virtually an encyclopedia of race prejudice directed against Semites (i.e., Moslems and Jews)."[52] The Semitic (race and language) thus emerges as a degraded form, in both the moral and biological senses of the term, a stable form of decadence characterized by its irregularities (in contrast to the regularity of the Indo-European): Renan is—according to his own terms—"the first to acknowledge that the Semitic race, compared to the European race, really constitutes an inferior combination of human nature."[53]

However, the Semitic hypothesis does not work systematically, either in the discourses about Jews and Muslims or in the practices of the state.[54] For example, following the conquest of Algeria by the French Empire, the senatus-consult of 1865 gave indigenous Jews and Muslims the chance of individual naturalization, on condition that they gave up their personal Jewish or Muslim religious status. Yet, the 1870 Crémieux decree afforded collective naturalization to Algerian Jews, who would automatically become French citizens.[55] According to French republican racial thought, the Jews were generally considered part of the white race, whereas Muslims belonged to the exotic races.[56]

This nineteenth- and twentieth-century discursive decoupling of Jews from Muslims is indeed challenged in modern anti-Semitism, which seeks to somewhat "Orientalize" the Jews and exclude them from the white race. Philosopher Giorgio Agamben reminds us that this connection reemerged in an especially tragic place: the Nazi concentration camps.[57] In the language specific to the Nazi machinery, several words to describe the world of the concentration camp were invented ("Häftlinge" for prisoners, "Kapos" or "Kamaraden-Polizei" for police informer, etc.). The word "Muselmann" (plural "Muselmänner") referred to "the weak, the inept, those doomed to selection."[58] This meant "men in decay [...]: they have no distinguished acquaintances in camp, they do not gain any extra rations, they do not work in profitable Kommandos and they know no secret method of organizing [...] they suffer and drag themselves along in an opaque intimate solitude, and in solitude they die or disappear, without leaving a trace in anyone's memory."[59] The use of the term "Muslim" to refer to "weak" Jews condemned to be exterminated links back to typical Orientalist representations of the weak, fatalistic Muslim, submitting to the authority of "Oriental despotism" without any individual will. In the concentration camp, the "weak" Jew became the "Muslim," that is, "the nonman who obstinately presents himself as a man, and the human that is impossible to distinguish from the nonhuman."[60]

After the Second World War, European discourses about Jews and Muslims were completely disrupted: the concept of race, fundamental to the justification of anti-Semitism, was discredited, from the 1950s and 1960s, both within the social sciences and public space. As sociologists of racism have demonstrated, overt biological racism could no longer be voiced, but cultural racism could more easily be articulated: the othering of Jews and Muslims (like that of other minorities) was based on the idea of cultural or religious difference. This is why researchers agree that modern anti-Semitism from the nineteenth and twentieth centuries has virtually disappeared from European public space, and according to some (Albert Memmi, Pierre-André Taguieff, etc.), it would be more accurate to talk of "Judeophobia" to refer to the discourses and actions hostile to Jews (rather than to a religion).

The association between Jews and Muslims almost disappeared. The idea of a "Judeo-Arab" plot can be found in the discourse of the French colonial information services in Algeria, from the 1930s to the War of Independence (1954–1962), because of the participation of Algerian Jews in the anticolonialist movements, including the FLN (Front de libération nationale).[61] Yet it returned with a bang in the 2010s, both in Europe and the USA, where the billionaire Georges Soros and his Open Society Foundation, for example, have been accused by the Far Right of bias toward the rights of Muslim migrants and being the accomplices of European Islamists.[62]

Reactions of Majority Population to the Integration of a Minority

The second comparative approach focuses specifically on the economic and political position of Jewish and Muslim minorities in European societies. It stresses the distinction between Christian anti-Judaism and modern anti-Semitism, revealed in the pioneering work of Abraham Léon, James Parks, Jules Isaac, and Hannah Arendt.[63] This distinction is based on two elements, which are as much overall factors explaining modern anti-Semitism in Europe. First, the birth of anti-Semitism can be explained by the transformations of the position occupied by the Jews in European economic systems, which were overturned by the development of industrial capitalism in the twentieth century. Under the feudal system, the Jews held a position in which they were both privileged and discriminated against. While most Jews were poor and part of the working class, some of them were bankers to monarchical states, moneylenders to the aristocracy and peasantry, and merchants in international trade. These groups were indispensable to the smooth running of the precapitalist economy and state enterprises. The capital they had accumulated was enough to fuel state activities and they monopolized a form of knowledge that was unique to the trade and finance sector, in which other social groups, especially the aristocracy, refused to invest, for various historical reasons, such as religious bans and the allegedly low yield from investment in state enterprises, etc. The Jews therefore enjoyed a quasi monopoly of the trade and credit sectors in that economic system. Every court and every landed aristocrat had their own "court Jew," who would enter into a relationship of dependency with the state on their behalf. Despite prejudices about them, Jews were tolerated because they occupied a specific niche in the structures of the feudal economy and fulfilled a particular relationship with the state and its authorities.

However, the Jews suffered social discrimination due to specific laws and segregationist allocations of space (the establishment of ghettos), which shows how ambiguous and precarious the position of the Jews in the feudal system actually was. Aristocratic and monarchic authorities had a stake in protecting the Jews, but these authorities were also the major debtors. It was always possible for kings and aristocrats to deploy their power of coercion to shut down claims for repayment and free themselves from debts. Using this frame, we can see an explanation for the persecutions targeted on the Jews in the feudal system, illustrated in the statutory shakedowns (e.g., collective fines for fictitious acts such as poisoning the wells or the "ritual murder" of Christians), massacres, expulsions, and confiscation of goods.[64]

This precarious position was eliminated altogether by the birth of industrial capitalism and the construction (followed by the decline) of European nation-states. The emergence of a new social class, the bourgeoisie, plus industrial development, ended the Jewish monopoly over international trade: "Because the Jews represented a primitive form of capitalism (trade and money-lending), the development of modern capitalism dealt a death blow to their social situation."[65] From this point, Jews' economic activities filtered into the banking sector, but only via loans to the state and consumer credit. They did not invest in the productive, industrial sector. Since the Jews belonged to the old feudal order, "they were unable or unwilling to develop along industrial capitalist lines."[66] The Jews thus no longer fulfilled functions of production in the new capitalist system and now even constituted "an obstacle for a normal capitalistic development."[67] Their position deteriorated even further because new actors put an end to the Jewish monopoly over state transactions (non-Jewish businessmen turning to imperialist expansion, private shareholders involved in state lending) and consumer credit (Christian banks).

Thus, the development of industrial capitalism ended up generating genuine social differentiation within Jewish communities, which had to either integrate into the structures of the capitalist economy and new sectors of economic activity (working class, craftsmen, food sales, the professions, cultural institutions such as the press, music, the theatre, etc.) or emigrate to more clement surroundings, that is, from Eastern to Western Europe and the USA. Assimilate or emigrate were the two alternatives offered to European Jews, in particular those in the East, where industrial capitalism developed later. In other words, "while in Western Europe it enabled them to assimilate, capitalism uprooted Jews from their secular economic positions in Eastern Europe."[68] Moreover, "although Judaism had not completely disappeared from the West, this was due to the massive influx of Eastern European Jews."[69]

It was precisely the moment when the Jews of Europe made their massive and collective (no longer individual) entrance into the process of assimilation into European societies that witnessed the development of modern anti-Semitism. For Arendt, "Antisemitism reached its climax when Jews had similarly lost their public functions and their influence, and were left with nothing but their wealth."[70] This loss of influence was reflected in a transformation in attitudes toward the Jews among the various components of European societies, which can be explained by the transformations in power relations between social groups. The declining aristocracy of the end of the nineteenth century was the first social group to construct political anti-Semitism: by attacking the Jews, the aristocracy attacked the egalitarian nation-state that tended to emancipate them. The aristocrats succeeded in forming an alliance with the conservative forces of the Catholic (especially the Jesuits) and Protestant Churches to fight political liberalism. Meanwhile, the liberal and radical opponents of reactionary regimes developed a real "left-wing anti-Semitism"(the distinction between the Jew who could be assimilated individually, and the Jews who could not be, collectively),[71] which reduced banking capitalism to the "figure" of the Jew. The petite bourgeoisie, badly impacted by a series of financial scandals and corruption cases, in which Jewish individuals played intermediary roles, developed an anti-Semitic discourse by fallaciously identifying Jewish bankers as representing the capitalist system. This convergence of hostilities against European states, whether monarchies or reforming democracies, turned the Jew into a "parasite" and a representative of the power of the state, even though "when emancipation was for the first time an accomplished fact for the Jewish masses, the power of the privileged Jews had disappeared."[72]

Therefore, at the end of the nineteenth century, modern anti-Semitism had steadily spread through all the strata of European societies, with the notable exception of the organized working classes, to such a degree that anti-Semitism "emerged suddenly as the one issue upon which an almost unified opinion could be achieved."[73] Across Europe, certain corporations and professions mobilized against the integration of the Jews within them, particularly the universities and the army. The Dreyfus affair in France can partly be explained as the reaction of the officer class (Catholics and Jesuits) to the accession of assimilated Jews into positions of command (Dreyfus was the first Jew to reach the senior rank of Staff officer [*officier d'état-major*]): "When the Jews began seeking equality in the army, they came face to face with the determined opposition of the Jesuits, who were not prepared to tolerate officers immune to the influence of the confessional."[74] This anti-Semitic hostility, deeply engrained in European societies, was the fulcrum of anti-Semitic and pan-European political parties' efforts to take state power.[75]

From this perspective, modern anti-Semitism is intrinsically bound up with the birth of industrial capitalism and the disruption of political power relations between social classes. After the Second World War, European Jews who had survived the genocide either resumed work in their home countries or emigrated to another Western country or Israel. In any case the social differentiation process begun in the nineteenth century continued, enshrining their position in European societies. The legitimacy of their presence as Jews in the various sectors of the economy and society is no longer publicly challenged by the main reactionary and xenophobic movements in Europe (apart from in certain places, particularly Eastern Europe, and in tiny neo-Nazi groups). However, although public anti-Semitic discourses have gradually disappeared, anti-Semitism has been transformed into an "ideology in reserve" for internal use in far-right parties and at the local level (a distinction must therefore be made between public and hidden discourses).[76]

The consolidation of social positions and the normalization of the Jewish presence sits in stark contrast to the challenge to the legitimacy of the Muslim presence on European soil. From this standpoint, anthropologist Matti Bunzl compares modern anti-Semitism with contemporary Islamophobia in relation to the construction of *nation-states in the nineteenth century and the European Union in the twentieth*. In his view, anti-Semitism played a defining role in the invention of national identities, and Islamophobia has an equivalent function in the context of the construction of European identity: "Whereas anti-Semites questioned Jews' fitness for inclusion in the national community, Islamophobes are not particularly worried whether Muslims can be good Germans, Italians, or Danes. Rather, they question whether Muslims can be good Europeans. Islamophobia, in other words, functions less in the interest of national purification than as a means of fortifying Europe."[77] This argument is also suggested by his-

torian Shlomo Sand, who wonders whether "the role played by political Judeophobia in nation-building in Europe be compared with that of Islamophobia in
the renewed continent-building effort?"[78]

Although the hypothesis of the connection between the construction of the
EU and the rise in Islamophobia is worth discussing, Bunzl's and Sand's reasoning should be nuanced because it tends to underestimate the importance of the
colonial experience in the discourses about formerly colonized Muslims; furthermore, it assumes an identification of anti-Semitism with nationalism. Yet, as
Arendt argues, the original feature of anti-Semitic parties was to have "at once
started a supranational organization of all antisemitic groups in Europe, in open
contrast to, and in defiance of, current nationalistic slogans."[79] Indeed, political
anti-Semitism had a supranational preoccupation that referred to Jews' alleged
desire to build an "inter-European government 'above all nations'" after the
phase of taking power at the national level.[80] In this way, political anti-Semitism
assumed a supranational form because it conceived of its enemy, the Jews, as a
supranational group, even if the unification of European anti-Semites was never
really achieved (outside of the German domination of the continent during the
Second World War).

Indeed, the advocates of contemporary Islamophobia find themselves in a
logic analogous to this (see chapter 8). The myth of Eurabia imagines Muslim
populations as a threat not only on the national but also the European (and even
Western) level. Historian Wolfgang Benz is therefore correct to highlight that
"the concept of the Other as an enemy was an antimodern reaction to the emancipation of the Jews [...] [and] it is possible to see in the current generalized
demonization of Islam in Germany [and in Europe] a reaction to the process of
Muslim integration, during which this population has become visible."[81] From
this point of view, anti-Semitism and Islamophobia share an analogous logic of
rejection of equality, which is based on the split between national and foreigner.
Here lies the great distinction between the anticlerical critique of religion and
anti-Semitic and Islamophobic discourse: whereas in the former the stake is the
fight against religious institutions and dogma, in the latter it is the legitimacy of
the presence of Jews and Muslims on national soil.

PART V

Islamophobia: Denial versus Recognition

CHAPTER 13

The Denial of Islamophobia

Although the "Muslim problem" has become an obvious part of the social landscape for the French and European "elites," can the same be said about the "Islamophobic problem"? The acknowledgement of Islamophobia as a public issue has encountered structural hurdles that can be explained primarily by the state of power relationships between critics of Islamophobia and their opponents. Despite the international legitimization of the term and the knowledge production around it based on press coverage, academic work, essays, and statistical reports, campaigns against Islamophobia have come up against obstacles that are difficult to surmount. Basing our account on existing research and our own observations, we attempt here to shed some light on the confrontation between deniers of—and activists for—the recognition of Islamophobia as a public issue. Over and above the reasons already referred to in the introduction, the social logic of denial is based on the rallying of actors located in the political, media, or intellectual fields, as well as in the anti-racist movement, which is highly divided over the matter. These forces oppose those—particular anti-racist organizations, global justice activists, Muslims, feminists, and members of ethnic minorities, journalists, politicians, and others—who seek to impose the struggle against Islamophobia as a legitimate cause. We will therefore analyze the dialectical movement of discrediting and legitimizing the struggle against Islamophobia, which is occurring in the historical context of a powerful secularizing culture; suspicion targeted at Muslim political and campaigning commitments; and the national fallout from international events (11 September 2001, the entrenchment of the Israel-Palestine conflict, "the War on Terror," etc.).

The Structural Denial of Islamophobia: The Question
of "Religious" Discrimination

The slow, difficult process of acknowledging and understanding forms of rejection and discrimination based on religious affiliation can probably be ascribed
to profound cultural, political, and legal resistance cutting across most social
groups, including the academic world, still suffering from "intellectual myopia"
on this subject.[1] Historical experiences of incomprehension of, contempt for,
and hostility toward religion have existed in all European societies, including
the UK, which have experienced the secularization process (the withdrawal of
ecclesiastical authority from political and social life, a drop-off in the practice
of religion, and the crisis in recruiting priests and nuns) and the de-escalation of
conflict between state, society, and organized religion throughout the twentieth
century. Although the law of 9 December 1905 on the separation of church and
state in France did not end the struggle between the "two kingdoms"—Catholic
and anticlerical—it did help assuage the tense relationship between organized
religion and the secular republic (*la République laïque*) in France.[2] The constantly evolving stakes underlying the separation of powers and the secularization of society rested on a fragile balance characterized by frequent changes in
regulations and adjustments. Until the 1980s those public freedoms bound to religious affairs (freedom of conscience and freedom of worship) were not up for
debate and seemed not to require the legislature's involvement. Taking religion
into account as a variable was almost dismissed as irrelevant during the drafting
of the law against racism of 1 July 1972, where the legislators "feared discrediting
the initiative by using such an obsolete frame."[3]

Religion as a social problem became a live issue again in the early 1980s, particularly when Catholics campaigned against the Savary Bill (1982–1984). The
so-called Free School movement indeed managed to wreck the bill aiming to
integrate private (mainly Catholic) schools into a "broader public service" and
helped bring down Pierre Mauroy's socialist administration on 17 July 1984.
The initial politicization of the Muslim issue after the Algerian War occurred
during this same period (1981–1984), during the widespread strikes in the car-
manufacturing industry, which several observers analyzed using the frame of
conflict between the secular state and Muslim religious "fundamentalism" (see
chapter 6). The Muslim issue was thus not the only one to raise questions about
the relationships between society, the state, and religion—as the Catholic activism aimed at thwarting the bill on same-sex marriage in 2012–2013 demonstrates. It did however focus attention, especially through a series of public
controversies about the visibility of places of worship, on both the wearing of

religious signs and ritual practices in public places (Ramadan, consumption of halal meat, circumcision, etc.).

The possibility of Muslims getting Islamophobic prejudice acknowledged and measured depends largely on their capacity to impose their own definitions and meanings of their religious observance.[4] However, it is very difficult for Muslim minorities to define what their "religion" is within a "European space of belief, structured above all by historical divergences and specific uses of terms such as worship, confession, belief, and religion."[5] The public manifestations of belonging and the forms of religious commitment that underlie them give rise to numerous struggles over interpretation. There is a profound dissonance between spiritual and moral intentions, sometimes coupled with the affirmation of identity, articulated by Muslims themselves, and the dominant interpretative frames that equate Muslim religious practices with failure to integrate and the rise of Islamism. However, the dominant community of interpretation that has steadily established itself in France means that "religious signs—particularly to do with dress—come into conflict with dominant normative frameworks that render them partly incomprehensible."[6]

Unsurprisingly, the public visibility of the Muslim religion clashes with the rationalist and materialist bases of secular European spaces and is still relatively "unintelligible for the policies and public imaginaries built on the conviction that the modern rationality of public space is the opposite of the intimate and private space of the religious experience."[7] The foundation of the denial of Islamophobia is the illegitimacy that cloaks Muslim religious practice. This seal of illegitimacy crystallizes several logics that function alone or cumulatively: anticlericalism (the danger of religion); the struggle against Islamism (dangerous religion); antisexism (religion oppressing women); classism (religion of the poor); and pure racism (religion of the foreigner).

The second rationale for denial of Islamophobia is fueled by the legitimization of practices that may be considered, sociologically, as discriminatory, not only in media and politics but also in the legislative and legal arenas. Once it is justified by the law and in jurisprudence for example, can it be interpreted as discriminatory to exclude girls wearing hijab from state schools and women wearing niqab in the street? Legally speaking, discrimination is defined as differential treatment based on illegitimate criteria. However, can it still be considered discrimination if the variable on which it depends (in this case the fact of wearing a "conspicuous" religious sign) is deemed legitimate (as a basis for discrimination) by parliament and the courts? A kind of "ratcheting up effect" is operating, in that a discriminatory law that legitimizes discrimination is no longer challenged, and in turn, legitimizes another discriminatory law. To this is added the fact that unlike the traditional anti-racist consensus stemming from the necessity of combatting discrimination based on gender, race, nationality, or disability handicap, there is no such consensus on Islamophobia that requires manifestations of hostility toward Muslims to be taken into consideration.

The third and final basis for denial, which makes it hard to consider whether there is a religious penalty, is the nature of the relevant markers of rejection. Indeed, markers that correspond to *ascribed status*, that is, assigned at birth or imposed from outside, must be distinguished from those that correspond to *acquired status*, that is, natural, or stemming from a personal initiative. An Arab or Black man or woman cannot be penalized for who they are (ascribed), but their cultural or religious choices (acquired) can more easily be opposed because they are perceived as being reversible. Prohibition laws do not target Muslims—as a religious group—but the religious practices of some Muslims can be targeted. This tension between ascribed and acquired status can be seen very clearly in the forms of resistance to, and the acknowledgement of, Islamophobia as a specific form of rejection equivalent to racism, sexism, and ableism. Therefore, compared to the more equitable deployment of action against discrimination in other European countries, particularly in the UK with the Equality Act,[8] forms of discrimination based on religious pretexts are in France "characterized, by a secular indifference, or even a rationalist justification," explains the director of the Institut du droit local alsacien-mosellan (Alsace-Moselle Regional Legal Institute), Jean-Marie Woehrling.[9]

The use of antidiscrimination law in relation to religion has particularly struggled to make practical headway in terms of furnishing official legal proof, which often involves statistical data. Indeed, "'religious' discrimination raises two sets of issues: problems in pinpointing the reason for differential treatment; and the difficulty of constructing a relevant comparative framework." Some legal practitioners state that "so-called religious discrimination is usually based on something other than religion" and consequently proves difficult to demonstrate.[10] This viewpoint can be challenged in the light of sociological studies of discrimination that highlight the distinction between, or rather the articulation of, the racial and the religious, but there is a serious legal argument denying the pertinence of Islamophobia as a specific reality.

Discrediting the Struggle against Islamophobia: The Suspicion of Fundamentalism

In as far as Muslim religious observance is explicitly or implicitly perceived as illegitimate in France, it is hardly surprising that the suspicion of fundamentalism lies at the core of the argument of those opposed to recognizing Islamophobia. This logic of suspicion aims to counter and delegitimize the struggle against Islamophobia by establishing a kind of "buffer zone" around organizations and figures linked to Islam based on a rule of "pariah status." This norm is based on the idea that beyond the domestic and "domesticated" (docile, "enlightened," or "moderate"), cultural. and traditional expressions, Islam is a problem *in itself*, as a manifestation of "fundamentalism." Consequently, it should not be normalized by any form of recognition or dialogue whatsoever. It is logical from that point on that the use of the term "Islamophobia" be rejected, along with the very notion of a mobilization against this phenomenon, because doing so means "playing the enemy's game," which everyone should be resisting. Recognizing Islamophobia is thus seen as the equivalent of recognizing the legitimacy of Islam as it is practiced, and so betraying the only struggle worth engaging in, that of the "fight against fundamentalism." This desire to banish ideas by making the public sphere a sanctuary regularly manifests itself in the reactivation of the principle of "pariah status" that reproduces the public illegitimacy of Islam.[11]

The main targets of this principle are neither the immigrant generations, whose public investment is often split between constructing buildings and management of worship at the local level, nor adherents of the most hard-line and radical streams of Islam, who stand out due to the degree to which they have internalized this rule and their political illegitimacy (and by a desire to make a total break with the society around them).[12] The rule of "pariah status" mostly impacts on the movements and figures who reject the isolation imposed on them by the climate of defiance surrounding Islam, and who foster an active presence in the public sphere. These committed Muslims are mostly French-born college graduates enjoying a degree of academic and political capital. They generally display a comfortable and open-minded version of Islam. Some of them are responsive to the ideas of Tariq Ramadan. Moreover, the fate of this Swiss intellectual and those movements that support his line of thought are symbolic of the pervasiveness of the suspicion and the application of this norm of "pariah status," that is, cancelled lectures and a refusal to sign petitions or to take part in international seminars to which he is invited, etc.[13] This was the rule applied when Patrick Cohen (France Inter) criticized Frédéric Taddeï (France Télévision) due to the latter's repeated invitation for Tariq Ramadan and other "sickos" to appear on his television show.[14]

The treatment meted out to the Collectif contre l'islamophobie en France (CCIF) is equally revealing of this climate. Despite its decade of existence and the organization's international recognition, the Ministry of the Interior chooses to ignore it, preferring to work with the CFCM's Observatoire de l'islamophobie, run by Abdallah Zekri, and the data provided by the ministry itself. "Pariah status" owes much to the symbolic work of discrediting carried out by media intellectuals, such as Caroline Fourest and Fiammetta Venner, who deem the activists of "the Indigènes de la République and the Collectif contre l'islamophobie more indulgent of Islamism than secular and anti-racist groups."[15] *Le Figaro* stated in a piece by a recognized but anonymous expert that "the CCIF embodies an aggressive version of Islam driven by identity-politics."[16] In his essay entitled "Quatre-vingt-treize," neo-Orientalist political scientist Gilles Kepel equates "anti-Islamic gateways such as Riposte laïque," the "Observatoire de l'islamisation," the "Bloc identitaire," and "fdesouche," with the "Indigènes de la République," a website he calls "francophobe" and "anti-white," the Islamist site "Forzane Alizza," and the "Comité [sic] contre l'Islamophobie en France (CCIF)." The latter is allegedly characterized by a "mental twinning process" in which it reduces the "execrated Other to its caricatural features," stigmatizing and dehumanizing the Other through this essentialization.[17] These accusations contribute to the establishment of a "principle of precaution": all those who would be tempted to criticize themselves, or even to engage the CCIF in dialogue, in turn risk "contamination" by the shadow of suspicion that certain "experts" and "journalists" cast over this collective. The smear campaign against the CCIF reached its peak following the murder of teacher Samuel Paty on 16 October 2020 by Abdullakh Anzorov, a Chechen influenced by the Islamic State. Minister of the Interior Gérald Darmanin accused the CCIF of complicity with the terrorist and of provoking racial hatred for having denounced the Islamophobia of state agents, even though there was no evidence to support this. But he issued a decree dissolving the association on 2 December 2020, which was validated by the Council of State on 24 September 2021, causing consternation among human rights organizations. Beyond the CCIF, the suspicion of fundamentalism and Islamism thus becomes a formidable weapon with ramifications for the anti-racist movement.

The Anti-Racist Movement Split over Islamophobia

France is among the most reluctant of European countries with a large Muslim minority to take responsibility for the struggle against Islamophobia, and this reluctance surprisingly includes NGOs and bodies that fight against racism and defend human rights. The role of the anti-racist movement in hampering the development of the struggle against Islamophobia is a decisive one, in that their institutional and political positions enable them to set out the parameters of the anti-racist struggle. Acknowledging the existence of an Islamophobic penalty runs into difficulties in a space of anti-racism built around ethnoracial and anti-Semitic cases, which mainly neglects antireligious discrimination altogether.

The French anti-racist movement, officially recognized and funded by the state, is split over the question of Islamophobia, both in terms of the idea and the actual phenomenon it refers to. Such divisions did not appear when the "Muslim problem" emerged but can be traced back to the pivotal role played by the "Jewish question" in the history of the development of the anti-racist NGOs.[18] The priority accorded to anti-Semitism, always very clear in Licra and SOS-Racisme, is now diminished at the LDH and the MRAP, whose action has altered in response to changes in society, international current affairs, and shifts in racism in France. Since the Second World War, the balance within the anti-racist movement has been intrinsically bound up in the conflicts taking place in the Middle East, which underscores the way the various stakes of hierarchizing the various struggles are embedded in one another, in relationships with minority groups, and in international issues.[19] The Israeli-Palestinian conflict is the origin of numerous tensions, fueled by the growing identification of French people whose ancestry originates from the Maghreb with the Palestinian cause, and by the bolstering of pro-Israel commitments of SOS-Racisme and the Licra, in line with the main Jewish institutions in France. Indeed, the 2000s were a period of significant realignment for the French anti-racist movement, with the emergence of new stakes and demarcations. On one side, Pierre-André Taguieff's theory of the "new Judeophobia" critiques a convergence of interests between the anti-Zionist extreme Left, anti-imperialists, anti-capitalists, and "Arab-Muslim" circles.[20] On the other, the "new Islamophobia" expresses the rejection—en masse—of Islam and Muslims and demonstrates the growing influence of the "clash of civilizations" thesis, which has fostered a political convergence between the republican, anticlerical and secular, and the extreme right nationalist worlds around the "Muslim problem."[21] For the anti-racist movement, this configuration is relatively unheard of insofar as the same social group, the "Arab-Muslims," is deemed both driver and victim of racism. A real dilemma stems from choosing which framework to adopt: there is a risk of reinforcing racism by indiscriminately accusing the Muslim minority or by concealing the growing forms of hostility such as Islamophobia.

Consequently, new splits have developed, with the LDH and the MRAP on one side and SOS-Racisme and Licra on the other, while also generating internal divisions within some of these organizations. The stark increase in anti-Semitic actions, correlated with the second intifada (2002–2004), was thus the opportunity for a growing challenge to be made to "Arab-Muslim" circles, even more so because at the various other controversies emerged at the same time over the headscarf and the presence of Muslims in France. These two concomitant developments fueled the emergence of a new interpretative framework linking the idea of a crisis both of minorities (in terms of morals, socioeconomic conditions, and identity, etc.) and of the condition of their homelands.[22]

Over the course of the 2000s, the splits within the anti-racist movement manifested themselves on numerous occasions. For example, in April 2002, the MRAP refused to take part in demonstrations against anti-Semitism, due to Ariel Sharon's explicit support for them. The same year, SOS-Racisme and the UEJF jointly published a survey of anti-Semitic incidents in France, in the same vein as the Licra, prioritizing the struggle against anti-Semitism.[23] In May 2004, amid the desecration of a Jewish cemetery, SOS-Racisme organized a demonstration against anti-Semitism supported by the Licra and the UEJF. The LDH and the MRAP, as well as left-wing parties like the Greens, the Communists, and the LCR, stressed that this march should be an opportunity to denounce all forms of racism. When the organizers refused, those organizations turned round and marched out. In November 2004 the MRAP and the LDH organized another rally against racism, anti-Semitism, and discrimination. SOS-Racisme and the Licra refused to join in with the march due to the participation of the Union des organizations islamiques de France (UOIF). Dominique Sopo, director of SOS-Racisme, stated that his organization could not march with individuals who were opposed to sexual equality and who had not made their positions clear on secularity, homophobia, and anti-Semitism.[24]

Therefore, the historic split over the Israel-Palestine question was now embedded in another split, about which stance to adopt regarding "Muslims" deemed to have "pariah status."[25] The shift from defending people discriminated against due to the color of their skin or their origins to the defense of people discriminated against because of religious affiliation has proven far from easy. On the contrary, the public appearance of an "Islamophobic problem" accentuated a two-way split. On one side were those who considered the practice of Islam and its public manifestations to be illegitimate: signs of "fundamentalism," rampant "self-segregation," and "fundamentalist" maneuvers.[26] On the other were those who felt the rejection of Muslims due to their religious affiliation transgressed the principle of nondiscrimination and eroded freedom of conscience and worship. Accusing the latter group of naivety and complicity with "Islamists," postcolonial blindness, and self-guilt, the former group, like SOS-Racisme or the Licra, declared they were fighting the emergence of a harmful "ethnically divisive" approach to anti-racism,"[27] based on victimhood, against which they advocated a form of anti-racism aiming to be "republican" and "universalist," that is, in line with the national ethos and tradition. According to Belgian intellectual Henri

Goldman, this is a tension inherent "in the anti-racist approach," which is usually transformed into an "explosive contradiction" when it entails choosing between, rather than combining, "the affirmation of the universality of humanity and acknowledgement of its diversity."[28]

During the Stasi Commission in 2003, the MRAP led an active campaign against the ban on religious signs being worn at school. One of the MRAP legal team, Laurent Levy, was personally involved as his two daughters, converts to Islam, had been excluded from their lycée because they wore headscarves. The four anti-racist organizations—the MRAP, the LDH, SOS-Racisme and the Licra—were initially, and for different reasons, opposed to the idea of such a law.[29] Yet in the run-up to the vote, in 2004, SOS-Racisme ended up siding with the prohibitionists,[30] which caused quite a stir within the organization and led to the defection of one of its founders—the lawyer Francis Terquem—to the MRAP, who declared that the ban was a thinly veiled instance of latent and very perceptible racism."[31]

As Timothy Peace underlines, many of those opposed to the law banning the headscarf feel it is based on racism concealed by euphemisms and justified by reference to secularism, gender equality, and the struggle against fundamentalism. However, until 2003, the distinction between anti-Arab and anti-Muslim racism did not exist. Then the game changed, with the public dissemination of the idea of Islamophobia. The CCIF was founded, Vincent Geisser's *La nouvelle islamophobie* was published, and the MRAP invested in the idea, with Director Mouloud Aounit organizing a colloquium on the topic at the National Assembly.[32] Moreover, the Ministry of the Interior and the CNCDH established instruments for measuring the rejection of Islam and Muslims (in terms of attacks and opinions) and Prime Minister Jean-Pierre Raffarin, in a speech delivered at the Paris Mosque on 17 October 2003, "said he was 'concerned [...] about a certain Islamophobia that was growing incidentally in France." A week later, on the TV news channel LCI, Claude Imbert, editor of *Le Point* and a member of the Haut Conseil à l'intégration (High Council for Integration, HCI), responded to him indirectly in an editorial by declaring himself to be "Islamophobic."[33]

These multiple initiatives against Islamophobia immediately provoked resistance and pushback well beyond anti-racist circles. In autumn 2003 a media counteroffensive entailed philosopher Pascal Bruckner, followed by journalist Caroline Fourest deprecating the word "Islamophobia,"[34] on the pretext that it was an "invention by the Iranian mullahs" aimed at prohibiting all criticism of Islam and establishing the offence of blasphemy. This erroneous idea was still being propagated despite a decade of attempts to reframe the concept historically and served the arguments marshalled by the Licra and SOS-Racisme,[35] which committed themselves to the prohibition of its use. The "semantic" dimension of this opposition is a sign of political positioning since, as we have seen, the denial of Islamophobia (as a social fact) is often achieved via a denial of the term's validity.[36]

Tensions within the MRAP

The MRAP's commitment to the struggle against Islamophobia has not occurred without breaking some eggs. To reduce the serious tensions within the movement, in May 2004 its national executive decided on a moratorium on the use of the word "Islamophobia" until the congress held in December of that year.

The debates on the use of the term and the organization's commitment to counter this form of racism dominated the congress. As *Le Monde* journalist Sylvia Zappi reports, "the split was perceptible from the first workshops of the congress on the Friday evening. Heated debates took place between supporters of fierce secularism and the universality of racism, and those who think that the movement must be on the side 'of the victims of exclusion,' the expression of a certain growing Islamophobia in French society."[37] The "civil war" was waged by a group of dissidents, whose line of argument was very close to that of the Licra and SOS-Racisme, against the MRAP and its director, picking up the idea of the "pariah status" of Muslim organizations, both independent and orthodox, perpetuating the demonization of Tariq Ramadan and those who adhere to his thinking in the name of the fight against fundamentalism, and equating recognition of Islamophobia with "ethnic divisiveness."[38]

The motions passed by the 2004 national congress reveal the divisions around ideology and the terms of the debate on a national scale. On one side, one approach (motions one, two, and seven) views Islamophobia simply as a fear and the expression of a critical distance from the Muslim religion. The term Islamophobia leads to a conflation of the rejection of believers and the criticism of religions, by underscoring the necessity of "condemning religious texts and ideologies, when they express hatred and oppression of others, because of their religion, origin, culture, or gender."[39] Islamophobia "confuses a phobia of the religion with phobia of Muslims" and thus becomes an "opportunity for fundamentalist religious groups that do not participate in the fight for universal values but adhere to an ethnically divisive conception of society." Moreover, the understanding of Islamophobia as merely a critical stance regarding, or defiance toward the Muslim religion, is systematically accompanied by the condemnation of the fundamentalist peril. This standpoint is based on a dichotomous and conflictual vision of French society and its Muslim population (as motion two from the Marseille branch puts it), with "progressives from all backgrounds" on one side and "fundamentalists from all religions" on the other. Suddenly, unlike "the defense of universal human rights," the recognition of Islamophobia—equated with defense of Islam—equates to "ethnic divisiveness" and contributes to an unacceptable and antisecularist legitimization of the religious field.

On the other side (motions three, four, and five), a vision of Islamophobia as a "new form of racism," distinct from anti-Maghrebi racism, is put forward. It functions by "demonizing Muslims," has "practical repercussions," and requires the MRAP to engage in a specific campaign. The proponents of this view deem equating Arab-ness and Muslim-ness unsatisfactory for the purposes of labeling an emergent form of racism "whose target is religion"; Islamophobia is therefore a necessary concept (motion two, Menton branch). According to this logic, the critique of religions, which must be defended, is a pretext, a mask, and a way to euphemize a latent racism. Islamophobia as an idea is a response to a new need for conceptualization (motion four, Paris Nineteenth and Twentieth Arrondissement branches). On this point, these motions reiterated that concepts and their actual uses are not the same thing and that, if there is indeed a risk of Islamophobia being instrumentalized by radical movements as a way to silence any criticism of Islamic dogma, the accusation of anti-Semitism targeting critics of the State of Israel's policies is part of the same deflection exercise.[40]

In the end, the congress voted in favor of recognizing Islamophobia as a concept and axis of struggle by 131 votes to 83 (with forty-six abstentions). It was also decided that this action must be carried out "within the framework of the statutory definition of incitement to racial hatred." This restriction would later give rise to divergences in interpretation, which would restart the internal struggle over the MRAP stance on Islamophobia. After the congress, the controversy kicked off again, fueled by the same small set of people opposed to the organization's director, Mouloud Aounit (2004–2008). Criticisms were then focused on his presence at events in which organizations explicitly flagged up as Muslim took part. Critiques pinpointed Aounit's appearances with Tariq Ramadan in public debates, with girls wearing headscarves at demonstrations, and with the religiously affiliated institutions within the Une école pour tou-te-s (One School for All) collective.

Following the national executive meeting on 15 January 2005, these opponents of the majority line published an "internal press release targeted at the entire MRAP membership," which stated that "many activists, leaders, and senior leadership of the MRAP are keen to state that some of the Secretary General's statements as they are perceived in the media do not reflect the membership's dominant feelings." Blaming Aounit for having come up with the idea of campaigning for the introduction of "differentiated" meals, in relation to a case of school of children refusing to eat meat and being excluded, the signatories interpreted this as a claim for religious (rather than secular) order. Other similar internal tensions were common during Aounit's various periods in charge, particularly when Jean Ferrat and Albert Memmi symbolically left the organization.

Similar, albeit less acute tensions were felt in the LDH. In its 2003 report, the CNCDH claimed that the LDH refused to use the term Islamophobia, which it considered a mask for concealing fundamental social problems. The LDH however, did participate in several activities against the exclusion of women wearing hijab, contributed to the dissemination of analyses and events concerning Islamophobia, and enabled the Islam and Laïcité Commission to remain as a viable entity after the Ligue de l'enseignement had abandoned it. Moreover, the "Redeker Affair"—from the surname of a philosophy teacher, Robert Redeker, who wrote an Islamophobic column in *Le Figaro* in September 2006—was the moment when two important LDH members (Antoine Spire and Cédric Porin) made striking exits,[41] blaming the Ligue for not having supported freedom of speech because it had criticized Redeker's text, engaged in dialogue with Muslim actors, and held a position deemed too pro-Palestinian.

Countermobilizations in Jewish Not-for-Profits

Some of the groups representing Jewish communities in France have also had issues with recognizing Islamophobia or have fought vehemently against its recognition. Of course, there is no such thing as a single "Jewish voice": many Jewish intellectuals and movements recognize the existence of, and deplore, Islamophobia.[42] There are many contributions to the debates from various communities, and they cannot be separated from the stakes endogenous and exogenous to Jewish communities and institutions. Analyzing the attitudes of Jewish institutions during the 2003–2004 headscarf affair, Vincent Geisser emphasizes that the public interventions made are part of a "competitive struggle to publicize Jewish opinion."[43] In fact, the "prohibitionist overkill" of the UEJF and the umbrella group, the CRIF (Conseil représentatif des institutions juives de France, Representative Council of Jewish Institutions in France), cannot be reduced to their rallying behind the "Islamic threat" thesis.[44] It also makes sense to understand it within the context of competition aimed at hindering the growing public visibility of religious groups, especially the Consistoire central israélite de France, which opposed the law banning headscarves.[45]

In terms of the struggle against Islamophobia, the CRIF's commitment has been expressed particularly through its former director Richard Prasquier, in "Reflections on Islamophobia," a text published in November 2012, which compares anti-Jewish and anti-Muslim racisms and prioritizes the former: "I have never heard of any demonstration in which Muslims are doomed to hell. I have never heard of bullying carried out against Muslims at school. I have never heard of books comparing Muslims to the children of animals. I have never heard of a network of hateful trolls carrying out attacks on places linked to Islam."[46]

Thus, while completely ignoring the data collected by the Ministry of the Interior and the CCIF (see chapter 2), the CRIF director agrees that "discrimination against Muslims is a grim reality of our society," whereas "discrimination against Jews has gradually disappeared." After stating that the criticism of religions is legitimate, that Islamism is not a desirable horizon, and that it is one of the causes of Islamophobia, he concludes by reaffirming the fundamental difference between the rejection of Muslims and anti-Semitism: "The ease of comparison is tempting but misleading, because Islamophobia is not a duplicate of anti-Semitism." In this text, which is not a brutal denial but a form of dilution, Islamophobia is reduced to a secondary form of rejection (vis-à-vis anti-Semitism), limited to obstacles on the employment and housing markets. He makes no reference to the violence of discourse, threats, or attacks aimed at Muslim institutions.

Another press release dated 16 April 2013 states that Richard Prasquier sought to meet the state legal ombudsman,[47] Dominique Baudis, to ensure that the latter "consider the boycott [of Israeli products] was discriminatory," but mainly, in relation to the word "Islamophobia," in order to remind him that "the criticism of religions, which is an individual right, must not be confused with the hatred of certain persons and violent acts perpetrated against them due to their membership of such or such human group."[48] In other words, the CRIF was critical of the instrumentalization of a category of racism—Islamophobia—for political ends, whereas that organization regularly does exactly that, by labeling a number of people critical of Israeli state policies anti-Semitic, thus equating anti-Zionism with anti-Semitism.[49] During the annual gala dinner in 2003, Roger Cukierman, then-director of the CRIF, who had just been reelected, strongly criticized a "brown-green-red alliance" between the Muslims and "an extreme left anti-globalization, anti-capitalist, anti-American, anti-Zionist movement."

Moreover, the CRIF was involved in a campaign against a bill introduced into the Belgian senate in February 2013 on the struggle against Islamophobia. By showing solidarity with the Centre communautaire laïc juif (CCLJ, Secular Jewish Community Center), the campaign sought to support its position in France but also to fight the recognition of Islamophobia at the European level. The bill aimed to have Islamophobia recognized as a form of racism and to widen the anti-racist "penal net," based on an acknowledgement of the rise in the rejection of Muslims in Belgium. In its particularly bellicose press release, the CCLJ refused to recognize Islamophobia, felt to be a strategy of "Organization of Islamic Cooperation (OIC) member states" whose goal they claimed was to "prevent any criticism of Islam and make sure the most basic rights are not applied in their states in the name of the respect given to all religions." The statement, once again, was based on the idea that "the concept of Islamophobia was invented by the Iranian theocracy and the fundamentalist Muslims of India and Great Britain to justify the death threats (fatwa) called on Salman Rushdie, the British author of Indian origin."[50]

Thus, the idea that the concept of Islamophobia restricts the freedom of speech and minimizes anti-Semitism is frequently deployed by political institutions within the Jewish community. Yet the contempt for Islamophobia is undiminished. Since the early 2000s, changes in the relationship between French Jewish institutions and the Muslim question have been perceptible. Borne by anxieties and anguish felt across the various Jewish groups, these changes have translated into the emergence of defiant discourses and stances vis-à-vis Muslims. This anxiety-inducing climate is linked to the ongoing worsening of the political situation in the Middle East, the succession of rebellions and military interventions in Palestine, and their ramifications for anti-Semitic actions in France, whether spikes in attacks or extremely serious acts such as the killing of Ilan Halimi and the murders committed by Mohamed Merah. These anxieties, which have generated or exacerbated fears, defiance, and racism within Jewish communities against the relevant minorities (a strand of racism that has not been studied),[51] have led community representatives to adopt a virulent language, reactivating, entrenching, and essentializing the categories of "Jew," "Arab," and "Muslim." Vincent Geisser observes that "the most striking element is this general pattern of 'Islamizing' [...] the perceptions of people whose origins are in migration from North Africa." This process has ended up constructing an "Arab-Muslim" enemy—and his "Islamo-Lefty" accomplice—who embodies a new form of anti-Semitism, "acting like a kind of mediator of Arab-Muslim community cohesion."[52]

This essentialization and defiance were expressed in a high-profile way the day after Jean-Marie Le Pen got through to the second round of the presidential election in 2002, when the director of the CRIF told the Israeli newspaper *Ha'aretz* (23 April 2002) that "Le Pen's success is a message to Muslims to keep quiet because he has always been against Muslim immigration." This frame posits that the "new" Muslim Judeophobia is the key issue and is thus manifested in a (Jewish) rapprochement with neo-Conservative authors, the Far Right, and supporters of an Islamophobic, pro-Israeli line.[53] The dominant Jewish institutions thus embraced a logic of confrontation in the name of intercommunity competition, as a reaction against the "new Judeophobia" and due to the Israel-Palestine conflict, which may conclude in Muslims being discredited and Islamophobia being denied.

If the CRIF's stance is officially restricted to expressing reservations about the degree to which the category "Islamophobia" shuts down free speech, we might speculate that other, maybe fundamental stakes have become attached to this position. One avenue to explore is more specifically the involvement of many Jewish institutions in the defense of Israeli policy against the pro-Palestinian movements in France. However, the campaigns against Islamophobia partly overlap with the Palestine Solidarity movement, which leads various left-wing movements into shared struggles alongside activists identifying with (among other things) Islam and working-class neighborhoods.

The ways in which the campaigning around Palestine and Islamophobia have bled into one another has not escaped academic Pierre-André Taguieff. For him it is in "this victim-oriented space of the politically correct Far Left, focused on the unconditional defense of certain categories of victim (Palestinians, immigrants from outside Europe, 'undocumented migrants,' Muslims, etc.) that the controversial use of the word 'Islamophobia' makes sense. Unlike the word 'arabophobia,' it enables a safety belt to be drawn tightly around everything to do with Islam."[54] He critiques the possible instrumentalization of the concept of Islamophobia by the confusion between "what comes under the legitimate critical analysis of a religious culture, and what is a desire to stigmatize, discriminate against, and exclude." But that is not all, because the introduction of the idea of Islamophobia, for him, also has a more strategic goal in that it is part of a "new anti-Jewish language" aiming to "demonize 'Zionism' and Israel." "The modern-day anti-Jew," states Taguieff, "no longer admits to racism, but on the contrary condemns it just as he condemns 'Islamophobia' and, by stigmatizing the 'Zionists' as 'racists,' he legitimizes his 'anti-racist' and 'pro-Palestinian' credentials. The anti-Jews have recovered their path to a clear conscience."[55]

For Taguieff, then, the "condemnation of Islamophobia" is actually "a vehicle for culture war" with violent implications. As evidence, he cites "the brutal murder of film-maker, columnist, and declared enemy of Islamism, Theo Van Gogh, for the sin of Islamophobia, in Amsterdam on 2 November 2004. This shows that the incendiary remarks of Islamist preachers and 'anti-racist' activists calling for 'Islamophobics' to be hunted down can be followed up with violent actions."[56] While in Taguieff's opinion the idea of Islamophobia is used first and foremost to demonize Israel and Zionism, according to another academic, Schmuel Trigano, it is more a device for relieving Muslims of responsibility for their anti-Semitic impulses."[57]

Therefore, for those fighting and attempting to undermine the legitimacy of the alliances between Muslim minorities and the pro-Palestine Left, the defenders of the struggle against Islamophobia are considered strategic enemies whose political coverage and reach must be as limited as possible. Recognizing the legitimacy of Islamophobia as a stake and as a concept is to risk giving credit to actors hostile to Israel and suspected of embodying the "new Judeophobia." These ideas, firmly anchored in the clash of civilizations paradigm, are brought into contact with one another via the anxiety generated over seeing the decline of national memory and guilt over Nazism's Jewish victims.[58] Although the academic legitimacy of these analysts is seriously dented by their absence of political restraint and lack of subtlety, their analyses still exert a genuine influence in certain Jewish and pro-Israel contexts, as well as within the Licra and certain politically powerful circles.[59]

It remains to be understood why the CRIF, SOS-Racisme, the Licra, and the CNCDH, which actively deny Islamophobia, use the concept "anti-Muslim racism." There is no evidence that this distinction enables any instrumentalization aimed at preventing freedom of speech to be avoided. What prevents potential promoters of the offence of blasphemy from instrumentalizing the expression "anti-Muslim racism" in the same way as they could employ the idea of Islamophobia? The difference between these two ideas is not located at this level. They differ by their semantic and political breadth: the word "Islamophobia" allows a broader understanding of the rejection of Islam, unlike the term "anti-Muslim racism," which immediately sets up an interdependent relationship between the racial and the religious, the preeminence of the former over the latter, and suddenly, restricts the phenomenon to one of xenophobia. We might also consider the theory that the refusal to acknowledge the idea of Islamophobia also aims to cut off critiques targeting the ideological work of discrediting and marginalizing Islam, which functions via false equations and essentialization. It is one way to spare the elites by decoupling Islamophobic discourses from anti-Muslim actions.

This position does not necessarily work by denying "anti-Muslim racism," but rather does so by reducing it to just individual or small group cases of violence and isolated differences, with no connection to the discourses to which the perpetrators of such violence refer in order to justify it.[60] This is therefore a strategy of "withdrawing responsibility," which usually disconnects Islamophobic ideologies and discourses from racist acts against Muslims and which enables the political "laundering" of those, particularly on the left, who are active participants in the construction of the "Muslim problem." The case of the Licra and SOS-Racisme is relevant here, as they have expended more energy fighting the use of the term Islamophobia than in fighting what they call "anti-Muslim racism."[61]

Ambiguities and Paradoxes of the CNCDH

The Commission nationale consultative des droits de l'homme (CNCDH) is a state agency tasked with ensuring the interface between the government and civil society and putting forward proposals on racism and xenophobia. The countermobilizations against the recognition of Islamophobia referred to above must be borne in mind in order to understand the ambiguities of the CNCDH on the subject of Islamophobia. In 2003 the commission sought to develop a position on the rejection of Islam and Muslims, and what to call it. Several leading figures and organizations gave oral statements on the position of Islam in France (Alain Boyer and Bruno Étienne); secularity (Union nationale des syndicats autonomes, UNSA); and Islamophobia (Dalil Boubakeur, Mohammed Arkoun, the Licra, and the MRAP). On the latter point, two positions were expressed. On one hand, the MRAP underlined the urgency of fighting Islamophobia, considered as a "new expression of a hatred that extends anti-Arab racism."[62] Favorable to the establishment of an observatory on Islamophobia, the MRAP indicated the relative independence of racial and religious markers, while stressing the extension of "anti-Arab racism."

On the opposing side, the Licra rejected the use of the term Islamophobia, considering it "useless" and "dangerous," picking up the line of argument invented by Pascal Bruckner and Caroline Fourest. Yet beyond the word itself, the Licra challenged the very existence of Islamophobia: "It is not certain, and it is even unlikely, that there is a rejection of Islam." They argue that there is "rather a rejection of fundamentalist practices."[63] This position was relatively new considering that a few weeks prior to giving evidence to the CNCDH, the Licra had again suggested the "establishment of an observatory on anti-Semitism and Islamophobia" to the CFCM and the Conseil des démocrates musulmans (on 19 October) had labeled "inappropriate" the comments made by Claude Imbert, who had claimed the label "Islamophobic" for himself and stated on that occasion that "the defense of secularity should not be achieved via Islamophobia" (26 October). The Licras's sudden change of tack was not clarified, but it could be linked to the internal struggles and to the national political context of the 2003–2004 headscarf affair.

The CNCDH also addressed the fundamentalist threat argument, basing its stance on the contribution given to its hearing by rector of the Paris Mosque Dalil Boubakeur. When questioned on the existence of a repudiation of Muslims, he felt that there "was indeed some Islamophobia in the air," before adding that "it's more like 'Islamist-ophobia.'"[64] The CNCDH and the Licra only referred to the second part of the sentence, removing it completely from the context of the struggles for influence among the principal Muslim federations, related to the stakes of which organization would get to represent Muslims; crucially here, Boubakeur's use of "anti-Islamist" rhetoric aimed to invalidate his competitors' claims and perpetuate his own privileged position vis-à-vis the state. This position enables us to understand why it is the rector of the Paris Mosque—rather than other religious actors who are more engaged in campaigning against Islamophobia—who gets invited by the CNCDH and the government to give evidence.

In the end, "the Commission distanced itself from the use of the term Islamophobia" in its study because the term is controversial."[65] The Commission thus came around to the same stance as the Licra, feeling that a "precise and fixed definition" of Islamophobia had not been arrived at, as it allegedly ends up "often being conflated with anti-Maghrebi racism."[66] According to the CNCDH, "it seems that some fundamentalist circles are trying to have anti-Maghrebi racism revalidated under the banner of 'Islamophobia' in order to more effectively benefit from people's frustrations, manipulate the withdrawal of the Maghrebi-origin population into its own religious identity community, and make religion the absolute criterion for differentiation and division."[67]

However, the CNCDH's position is more ambiguous than the Licra's because the rejection of the word "Islamophobia" does not imply a denial of hostility against Islam. While making hostile opinions and attitudes toward Islam visible, as referred to in chapter 3, the commission has constantly minimized their scale and diluted their intensity. From 2001 onward, the shockwave of the 11 September attacks led it to acknowledge that "the targets of these acts of violence are not exclusively North Africans or 'beurs' of immigrant origin, as in the past, but now, more broadly, Arab-Muslims in general."[68] Yet hostility toward Muslims, which had previously been incorporated into "acts hostile to North Africans," is referred to in the expression "anti-Islamist acts," a term that relativizes Islamophobia by equating Islam with Islamism and by reducing post 9–11 Islamophobia to Al-Qaida's very high level of unpopularity. Moreover, the expression "Arab-Muslim," whose use has been on the increase since Islam became more publicly visible, is part of the recurring conflation of origin and religion, and of Islam and the Arab world.

TABLE I
Experiences of Racism

	Yes (%)
Has witnessed racist comments	54
Has witnessed anti-Semitic comments	31
Has witnessed anti-Muslim comments	48
Has witnessed anti-Arab comments	55
Has witnessed racist behavior	48
Has witnessed anti-Semitic behavior	20
Has witnessed anti-Muslim behavior	32
Has witnessed anti-Arab behavior	38

By 2003 the term that the CNCDH used to refer to Islam in their opinion polls had been called into question. A "split sampling" test was carried out, whereby the sample was split into three, with each group given a different term. The first group had to express an opinion on the word "Islam," and the other two, on "Islamic religion" and "Muslim religion," respectively. The first term— the most frequently utilized in public discourse and journalism—is the one that provoked the most negative opinions (40 percent) and the lowest "sympathy index" score (the ratio between positive and negative opinions). Each of the other two words generated 31 percent negative opinions. Ultimately, the CNCDH chose to use "Muslim religion" for future polls; the phrase ranked the highest both on its positive opinion score (30 percent compared to 24 percent for the other two) and the "sympathy index."[69] In other words, the CNCDH would from then on use the category that most minimized the hostility against Muslims as its standard term for measuring hostility against Muslims.

Moreover, unlike the tone of the analyses of racism and anti-Semitism, the tone of those focused on the extent of Islamophobia are often subject to a form of dilution. The 2001 CNCDH report states, without offering proof, for example, that "France has not experienced [...] waves of attacks on Muslim places of worship, organizations or individuals."[70] In 2003 the CNCDH withdrew a section of its questionnaire that focused on the first-hand experiences of those being polled, who had been asked if they had witnessed "racist," "anti-Semitic," "anti-Arab," or "anti-Muslim" comments or behavior. Whether it was perceived as a direct (having witnessed) or indirect question (having been a perpetrator), this question constituted a break with convention, because it was explicit and powerful, as well as having the capacity to exceed the simple analysis of representations and opinions (table 1).

In as far as this type of question calls on the lived experience of those polled and has a very low proportion of "no responses," the question should have deserved a different outcome, all the more so because its scores were significant and stood out from the general caution exhibited by analysts, who felt at the time that polling offers "highly contrasting answers [which] allowed nuance to be introduced into the extent of 'French Islamophobia.'"[71] The scores recorded seem to prove the opposite, revealing a context in which racist behavior and comments are common and aimed mostly at "Muslims" and "Arabs." Almost half those polled had heard "anti-Muslim" comments, whereas one third had witnessed behavior of the same kind. This is a society in which Islamophobia is overtly expressed in the social relationships set out in this table.[72]

This excess of unevenly applied caution can also be found in the ways the rise in Islamophobic acts and ongoing hardening of opinions are interpreted. Until 2010 only the MRAP and a few rare Muslim representatives appearing in the media emphasized the deleterious role played by Islamophobia in politics and the media.[73] Neither the CNCDH nor the Ministry of the Interior made the explicit link between the heated nature of public controversy and the levels of rejection quantified in their polls. Thus far, the statistical increase was basically explained by matters relating to recording procedure. It is only in 2010 that the ministry resolved to make the link between the tenor of public debates and the increase in the attacks aimed at the Muslim community. The ministry's note thus points out that "social debates on the building of minarets, wearing the full veil, and national identity" are liable to fuel "anti-Muslim feeling within a certain fringe group of the population."[74]

However, this minimalist and cautious connection was immediately relativized by the CNCDH. It stated that its data "demonstrates an upward trend in violence specifically aimed at people belonging to the Muslim religion," but it "is not however sufficiently significant for real change to be deduced from it, all the more so because the convention agreed between the CFCM and the Ministry of the Interior could have improved the recording of these acts."[75] When those words were written, the CNCDH cannot have been unaware that the—barely open—observatory in question did not actually record anything and limited itself essentially to communicating statistics provided by the ministry. In fact, for the commission, these "feelings of contempt could in time entail a genuine significant rise of such patterns and legitimize anti-Muslim behavior." The media and political construction of the "Muslim problem" is thus thought to represent a risk, a potential, but not something that already exists. This level of caution in interpretation differs starkly for instance, from the interpretation and analysis of the patterns of anti-Semitic acts.[76]

TABLE 2
The categories of racism mentioned in the National Assembly by number of occurrences across all fields (including questions to the government, in brackets)

	1997–2002	2002–2007	2007–2012
Racism	417 (165)	868 (361)	867 (381)
Anti-Semitism	72 (15)	320 (160)	245 (132)
Islamophobia	8 (0)	19 (7)	47 (19)
"Anti-white" racism	0	6 (3)	10 (5)
Anti-Black racism	0	0	1 (1)

Failure of the Concept of Islamophobia to Gain Purchase in the World of Politics

The institutional space of anti-racism is not the only one to resist recognizing Islamophobia. The position of denial specified in 2003–2004, and based on the arguments put forward by Caroline Fourest, Pascal Bruckner, Pierre-André Taguieff, the Licra, SOS-Racisme, and the CNCDH, was widely disseminated through the media and was also shared in the political field. Even if the term Islamophobia had been used a few times by national political figures (Jean-Pierre Raffarin as prime minister and Nicolas Sarkozy as minister of the interior at the Paris Mosque, then again when he was president during his speech in Algiers),[77] the term was scarcely heard in parliament between 1997 and 2012. Most of its mentions came in debates prior to the vote on the law banning the wearing of hijab in state schools (2003–2004) and wearing the niqab in public space (2010) (see table 2).

Even though the numbers are small, the use of the word "Islamophobia" rose in the latter period covered by this table. Between 2007 and 2012, it appeared six times as frequently as it did between 1997 and 2002. But if the figure is restricted only to written or oral questions to government (the figures in brackets), that is, where mentions come only from within parliament (and not including the publication of public hearings or exchanges with EU partners and institutions), the gap is all the more stark. In twenty years, the term "Islamophobia" was used twenty-six times in questions to the government, that is, eleven times fewer than the word "anti-Semitism" and thirty-four times fewer than the word "racism": a gap whose size grows further still if it is borne in mind that several deputies were using it specifically to sap the term of its value, empty it of its descriptive and analytical functions, or to defend themselves from accusations of it.

Only a minority of the parliamentarians recorded used it to refer to an emerging form of "racism." There is little distinction between the use by the political left, right, or center, except for the parties and factions for which "the struggle against Islamization" is the key to their doctrine. The two deputies most committed to the recognition of Islamophobia are Ecologist Noël Mamère, who argued that the laws against the headscarf are discriminatory, and the UMP deputy Éric Raoult, who was on the contrary a supporter of and contributor to the two laws in question, but whose stance is primarily based on his local alliance with the Union des associations musulmans de Seine-Saint-Denis (UAM 93). No clear line separates Socialist and Communist Party deputies' relationship with the concept of Islamophobia. Speaking on 4 February 2004 about the difficulties for Muslims organizing their worship, Paris deputy Jean-Christophe Cambadélis (Parti socialiste) felt that a lack of state action on this matter risked "weakening the Republic and leaving space for detractors to insert an Islamophobia that they claim exists." On 11 May 2010, Jean Glavany, a Parti socialiste deputy from the Hautes-Pyrénées (southwest France), responded to criticisms that the banning of the niqab in public space was discriminatory by stating that "this trial for Islamophobia doesn't make sense."

In contrast, Socialist Party deputy from Val-d'Oise François Pupponi targets the xenophobic downward spiral of the right-wing government by accusing it of "refusing to see the human tragedies occurring and being more interested in satisfying an electorate sensitive to the alarm bells around immigration, the sirens signaling Islamophobia and now, the condemnation of unemployed people accused of sponging off the state." In the PCF, the gulf is just as visible. On one side is Jean-Pierre Brard (Seine-Saint-Denis), who on 18 October 2010 called for a "boycott of the BRED" (a national co-operative bank), which he alleged had "violated the principle of secularity" for having organized a forum on Islamic finance, under the sponsorship of Minister of Economy and Finance Christine Lagarde. On the other hand, Jean-Claude Lefort (Val-de-Marne) stated on 4 February 2004 that the headscarf bill was underpinned by "the execrable ideology of the 'clash of civilizations,' an unhealthy Islamophobia, and the stench of an unaddressed colonialist past."

However, in over twenty years, and despite the quantity of debates held on Islam and Muslims, the deputies have overall barely addressed Islamophobia as a social phenomenon, and even less as a framework for understanding the reality for Muslims in France. Although the frequency of occurrences of the categories in the public debate makes sense, Islam is first and foremost considered a public issue and not as a marker at the origin of an illegitimate form of hostility. The political trajectory of this idea requires further research.

It is highly likely that in common with the stakes of secularity and controversy around the headscarf, the recognition of Islamophobia as a phenomenon

TABLE 3

The categories of the "Muslim problem" referred to in the National Assembly by number of occurrences across all fields (including questions to the government)

	1997–2002	2002–2007	2007–2012
Islam	113	255	328
Islamism	127	266	296
Fundamentalism	134	243	242
Islamophobia	8	19	47

distinct from anti-Arab racism and as a relevant category will continue to divide opinion. On the UMP's website, the only reference is to a joint press release signed by the director of the CFCM and government spokesperson Jean-François Copé after the "Pains au chocolat" affair. However, statements by former prime minister Alain Juppé highlighted the prevalence of an "Islamophobia [. . .] contrary to republican principles," that is "one of the fundamental points of division" separating the various factions and candidates for the leadership of the UMP.[78]

On the Parti socialiste website, two mentions of the word "Islamophobia" can be found: the first in a text written by activists on Euro-Mediterranean relations, in which Islamophobia is seen as a form of racism to fight against[79]; the second is published in the *L'Hebdo des socialistes* (Weekly socialist party newsletter) concerning a decade of attacks against laïcité. The text criticizes Nicolas Sarkozy's parallel, drawn when he was president, between anti-Semitism and racism, "which remains for all humanists the most violent and most unbearable evils," and the 'phobia' of a religion." "He talks about 'Arabophobia' which is a form of racism, which is understandable. But what is 'Islamophobia' doing here?" asks the PS weekly.[80]

Within the Front de gauche (FDG, Left Coalition) this opposition can be identified around the definition of Islamophobia, considered alternatively as a critique of religions and as a form of racism. On 16 September 2012, Pascale Le Néouannic and Alexis Corbière, leaders of the Parti de gauche (PG) and close to presidential candidate Jean-Luc Mélenchon, condemned the interruption, on the previous evening, of a debate about the Front national at the Fête de l'humanité (Annual festival of the Communist Party newspaper *L'Humanité*) to which Caroline Fourest had been invited. Labeling the instigators of the trouble as "tiny violent groups" seeking to "reestablish a kind of a totally unacceptable offence of blasphemy," the authors—defining Islamophobia as merely a critique of the Muslim religion—emphasized that the criticism of religion is free and that "the term 'Islamophobic' does not figure in their vocabulary."[81]

This last assertion was not unanimously accepted within the Far Left, as proven by the *Mediapart* article "Appeal to FDG Activists and Sympathizers," uploaded on 20 April 2012. It states that "Islamophobia is one of a set of discriminations" to "fight using theory, political means, and on the ground."[82] This position is shared by certain "anarchists, libertarian communists, anarcho-syndicalists, independents, artists, whether organized or not organized" who share their "utter condemnation of Islamophobia in all its forms."[83] As for the Fédération pour une alternative sociale et écologique (FASE, Federation for a Social and Ecological Alternative), a member of FDG, it stated that "along with xenophobia and anti-Semitism, Islamophobia is an evil on the rise in France. These troubling downward spirals are enabled by media campaigns devoted to a media construct of 'Islam' aimed at creating fear, and ignoring the desire for peace among the vast majority of Muslims; and also by the adoption of positions originating from across the whole political spectrum."[84] The FASE called for solidarity with "people who are victims of Islamophobia [as with] victims of every other form of discrimination, which make up one of the tools for division constantly used and abused by the dominant order." Lastly, after the death of Mouloud Aounit, in August 2012, Pierre Laurent, national secretary of the PCF, acknowledged that the former MRAP secretary general "was one of the first to courageously condemn the rising Islamophobia, exacerbated by the Far Right and part of the mainstream Right, defying certain criticisms to do so."[85]

Judging by the political field's cautiousness in accepting the word "Islamophobia," the divisions that the term generates, its tenuous purchase in parliamentary discourse, and low level of legitimacy in decision-making circles, it appears that the various forms of mobilization against the recognition of Islamophobia have proven quite effective. Yet the political field is barely homogeneous. It cannot be reduced to the activity of the large organizations, political parties, and the government and is not limited to actions with a national dimension. In terms of the struggle against Islamophobia, there is so far very little scholarship about local and intermediate-level campaigning, or extraparliamentary politics.

Upsurge in Islamophobic Acts and Intense Media Scrutiny

2013 was a major turning point in the history of campaigns against Islamophobia.[86] During the 2000s third-sector religious and political movements comprising the "anti-Islamophobia front" labored to have the existence of Islamophobia and the legitimacy of their anti-racist cause recognized. From 2013 the French denial of Islamophobia, based on a combination of historical, political, and institutional factors (chapters 12 and 13), seemed weaker than previously among political and media "élites." Although the unanimity on Islamophobia had not yet dissipated, several indicators signaled that it had partially broken; these included, inter alia, the media coverage of Islamophobic attacks that contributed toward the embedding of the term Islamophobia in popular discourse and academic advances in the official recognition of both the concept of Islamophobia and the nongovernment actors working against Islamophobia, in the CNCDH's 2013 annual report.[87] It is probably true to say that the increasingly widespread use of the term helped secure the acknowledgement of the social phenomenon that it describes and contributed to the legitimization of the struggle against Islamophobia. However, it is not because a term is deployed that it is necessarily legitimate, insofar as for a long time the term Islamophobia was used precisely to discredit it. Although the statistical data we collected should not be over-interpreted,[88] it does enable two main periods in the use of the term to be approximately distinguished from one another, namely the "discrediting" period (2001–2010) and the "routine use" period (2010–2015).

In the early 2000s, the use of the term was very infrequent. Although the 2003–2004 headscarf affair saw a rise in the number of articles utilizing the term (fig. 4), the first decade of the 2000s prior to 2003 witnessed a lack of NGO actors to mobilize around this concept; furthermore, after 2003, the prohibition of the term proclaimed in a series of controversial articles by Caroline Fourest, Fiammetta Venner, and Pascal Bruckner proved highly effective.[89] In our discussions with several journalists, we were actually astonished by the censorship effect of these articles, as if speaking about Islamophobia boiled down to taking sides with "Islamists" or Muslim fundamentalism. However, in the context of ideological conflation between three distinct phenomena (Islam, "Islamism," and "jihadism"), journalists who defied the ban, particularly Xavier Ternisien (Le Monde) and Alain Gresh (Le Monde diplomatique) were rare.

From 2010 we can see a significant increase in usage in the French press. While the number of articles mentioning Islamophobia stood at around 30 in 2002, it rose to 342 by 2010 and took off in 2013 and 2015, reaching 1,468 and 2,924 respectively. It is hard to explain this upsurge, but the print press had never used the term as much prior to 2010, bearing in mind that the overall figure conceals varying uses by specific newspapers (fig. 2), which can be measured by their use of Agence France Presse (AFP) dispatches. These actually comprise the journalists' raw material and help impose particular topics that often get recycled by editorial teams. The latter's dependence on dispatches leads to what Pierre Bourdieu calls the "circular circulation of news." However, the number of AFP dispatches using the term "Islamophobia" increases noticeably from 2010 and

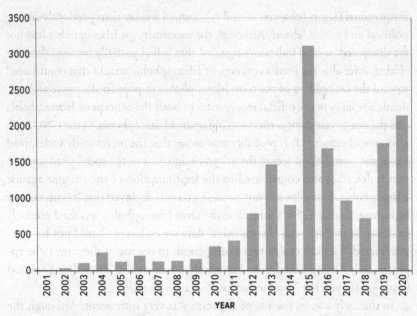

FIGURE 4.
Occurrences of the word "Islamophobia" in the French press between
1 January 2001 and 31 December 2020 (by number of articles).

takes off in the 2012–2015 period. A sociohistory of the journalists specializing
in Islam and Muslims has yet to be written, but we might float the theory that
this increase is the manifestation of a generational shift, as new journalists took
over the religion and discrimination desks at newspapers between 2003 and
2014.[90] As we have been able to observe, the journalists who were not around for
the 2003–2004 headscarf affair, and those most open to the social sciences, were
far less reluctant to address the question of Islamophobic discrimination. Nonetheless, this increasing use of the term "Islamophobia" came to a dramatic halt
after 2015. It seems that the violence of January and November 2015 terror attacks had an impact on the legitimacy of the term in the press. Since the victims
of *Charlie Hebdo* massacre had been accused of Islamophobia, many journalists
became more reluctant to use the word, as if to do so would equate to a kind of
complicity with the terrorists.

However, how AFP dispatches were dealt with differs from one editorial team
to the next. Thus, in the major national daily press (fig. 5), the increase recorded
at the AFP had the greatest impact on *Le Parisien* and above all on *Le Monde*,
which published 296 articles containing the term between 2001 and 2009, compared to 528 between 2010 and 2013, and used it with increasing frequency in its

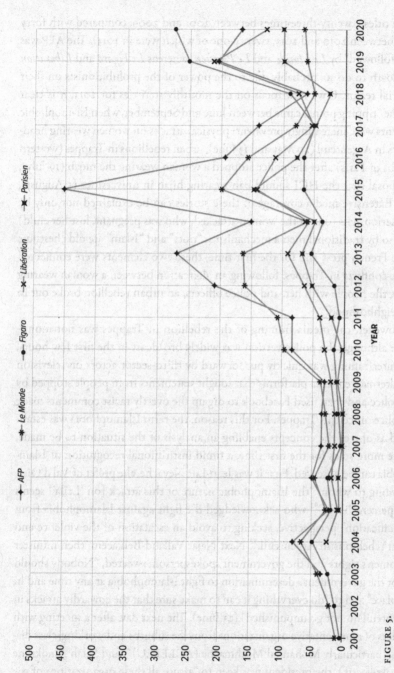

FIGURE 5.
Occurrences of the word "Islamophobia" in the major national daily press between
1 January 2001 and 31 December 2020 (by number of articles).

article titles (twenty-three times between 2001 and 2009, compared with forty times between 2010 and 2013, twenty-one of which were in 2013). The AFP was thus "followed" by *Le Monde* and *Le Parisien*, whereas *Le Figaro* and *Libération* were loath to do so, probably due to the power of the prohibitionists on their editorial teams. If we now focus on the monthly statistics for 2013, it is clear that the "tipping point" came between June and September, when Islamophobic incidents were increasingly prevalent; physical attacks on women wearing head-scarves in Argenteuil (20 May and 13 June), urban rebellions in Trappes (western suburbs of Paris) after the police stopped a woman wearing the niqab (19 July), a proposal that the HCI should ban wearing hijab in universities (5 August), etc.[91] Extensive media coverage of these stories can be explained not only by their seriousness (one of the women attacked, who was pregnant, lost her child) but also by traditional media mechanisms: "riots" and "Islam" are old chestnuts of the French press and for the first time, these two elements were connected by the conflicts in Trappes: following an altercation between a woman wearing niqab, the people with her, and police officers, an urban rebellion broke out in the neighborhood.

However, the media framing of the rebellion in Trappes was not mono-lithic: although the police version was widely broadcast in the first few hours, a counterframing was quickly put forward by third-sector actors on television and alternative media platforms that sought statements from people stopped by the police and then used Facebook to dig up the overtly racist comments made by police officers in Trappes. For this reason, the term Islamophobia was estab-lished as one of the concepts enabling an analysis of the situation to be made, all the more so as for the first time, a timid institutional recognition of Islam-ophobia can be observed. First it was Jean-Luc Névache, the préfet of Val d'Oise, according to whom "the Islamophobic nature of this attack [on 'Leïla'] seems 99.9 percent likely,"[92] who acknowledged the fight against Islamophobia from a "pacification" perspective, seeking to avoid an escalation of the violence and urban rebellions in Argenteuil.[93] Next Najat Vallaud-Belkacem, then-minister of women's rights and the government spokesperson, tweeted, "Nobody should doubt the government's determination to fight Islamophobia at any time and in any place" and to "do everything it can to make sure that the cowardly attacks in Argenteuil do not go unpunished" (23 June). The next day, after a meeting with "leaders of representative organizations from the suburbs and working-class dis-tricts," particularly Mohamed Mechmache (ACLEFEU)[94] and Salah Amokrane (Tactikollectif), the president was keen to "assure all these organizations of the government's determination to fight all racist acts, especially those against Mus-lims, which constitute unacceptable threats to the unity of the Republic."[95] Summer 2013 thus witnessed the conjunction of several media and political factors that favored lifting the censorship around the term Islamophobia.

The New Publishing Season 2013: A Symbolic Turning Point

Media and political coverage of summer 2013 saw a proliferation in the breaches of the previous Islamophobic unanimity, and they opened further when the new publishing season started in September, as four books on Islamophobia, in different registers, were published: *Nos mal-aimés* by Claude Askolovitch, *Ce populisme qui vient* by Raphaël Liogier (a year after his *Mythe de l'islamization*), the *Dictionnaire de l'islamophobie* by Kamel Meziti, and the original version of this book.[96]

Askolovitch's book made a very significant contribution to challenging the doxa underpinning the ban and the denial of Islamophobia, in that unanimity about Islamophobia was broken "from the inside." Indeed, this author is a member of the group of very influential journalists, having moved between several Paris outlets since the beginning of his career: Europe 1, *L'Événement du jeudi*, *Marianne*, *Le Nouvel Observateur* (2001–2008), *Le Journal du dimanche* (2008–2011), *Le Point* (2011–2012), I-télé (2010–2011, 2013–2016), Arte (2013–), France Inter (2016–), etc. He was also well known for having accused Muslim intellectual Tariq Ramadan of anti-Semitism, in an article on "ethnically divisive intellectuals," published the day before the Saint-Denis European Social Forum in 2003. It was therefore difficult for Islamophobic journalists to accuse Askolovitch of "complicity" with "Islamism" given that he had criticized the person most viewed as embodying "Islamism" in France. But it is also because he was a member of the "inner circle" that it was possible to engage in dialogue with him. While he could have been completely ostracized and undermined as "a useful idiot for Islamism," several media outlets hostile to Askolovitch's book in fact did in-depth interviews with him, often in the format of face-to-face encounters between him and an opponent. However, his stances showed that he was quite close to third-sector activists, both Muslim and non-Muslim, who had been fighting Islamophobia for over a decade:

> Old-fashioned racism reeked of slobbishness and arrogance: it was the white man beating the inferior, the indigenous, and the "swarthy" with a truncheon. Islamophobia is not arrogant but fearful, an ideology for people who have lost before they begin [...]. Racism was just vomit, so easy to condemn, whereas Islamophobia stakes a claim on our values, its justification is rooted in the horror

of Islamism, it douses itself in modernity and disguises itself as republican, and
we will sing love songs [...] and their sound will be mistaken for the ball sack of
the former Republic.[97]

To understand the publication of this work, which was risky even for an established journalist, we need to analyze Askolovitch's social trajectory and the
politico-media configuration in which these stances make sense. The same is
true of the cofounder of *Mediapart*, Edwy Plenel, who published *Pour les mu-*
sulmans (La Découverte), a rare anti-racist bestseller (with over fifty thousand
copies sold) in 2014. Whatever the case may be, these journalists can be considered "rebels of the élite," according to the meaning offered by anthropologist and
political scientist James Scott:

> The members of élites who do not comply with the official scenario [...] in this
> way represent a much greater danger than their small numbers might suggest.
> Public dissent, although seemingly trivial, actually shatters the naturalization of
> power made possible by the imposition of a united front [...] This is why the de-
> fection of part of the élite has a much greater impact on power relations than the
> same message being conveyed by members of subordinate groups.[98]

Indeed, the dissent over Islamophobia within the dominant media helps de-
naturalize the Islamophobic *doxa*: socially, it is no longer so easy to discriminate against and stigmatize presumed Muslims, since the Islamophobic "united
front" is broken, making a heterodox discourse on the subject possible. So it was
no coincidence that certain journalists, who had been walking on eggshells in
relation to Islamophobia, felt authorized to contradict the logic of denial. This is
what we observed during the promotion of the original version of this book, carried out by the communications office of our publishing house, La Découverte.
Again, it is not within our remit to study the media and political reception of
our book, but we could at least state, without being accused of bias, that, overall,
our work was well received by a French press that is reluctant to recognize the
existence of Islamophobia. Announced in an article in *Le Monde* about the "season of ideas,"[99] the book received a certain amount of media coverage;[100] it also
led to numerous invitations from local community organizations as well as institutions.[101] This media and publishing industry coverage reveals a transformation
of the dominant ideology:[102] far-reaching denial had been replaced by a limited
recognition of Islamophobia, to which the book made a contribution, insofar as
all the academic work on Islamophobia over several years was part of the process
of legitimizing the concept, making Islamophobia visible.

However, when the evidence of denial gradually dissipated, those with a stake in upholding the *doxa* of Islamophobia reacted via appeals for symbolic order. In its edition of 21–22 September 2013, *Libération* put a set of articles about Islamophobia on its front page for the first time. Its contents illustrated the editorial team's internal tensions. Certain passages acknowledged the existence of Islamophobia, while others denied it. Editorial writer Fabrice Rousselot advocated banning the word because of its "instrumentalization" by "extremists" while acknowledging the existence of "anti-Muslim discrimination," but ended his column ambiguously, reproducing the neo-Orientalist binary opposition between "Islam" and "Secular Republic": "Islam—like all religions—must accommodate itself to the laws of the Republic in our secular country. Not the other way round." The following weekend, in its 28 September edition, *Le Monde* also offered an editorial plus an interview with us by journalist Stéphanie Le Bars. The title of the editorial, "Islamophobia: From Fantasy to Reality," marked a major ideological swing:

> The term has long been controversial, all the more so because it seemed to be a tool for discounting any criticism of Muslim fundamentalism. However, it began to be recognized by political leaders and intellectuals. The reality of hostile acts perpetrated against Muslim places of worship and citizens is now acknowledged at the highest levels of State. This recognition is welcome. Naming and identifying a problem can only help resolve it.

Thus, for *Le Monde*, the fantasy of a concept allegedly invented by the Iranian mullahs was swept away by the statistically measured and academically studied tangible realities.

Although the *Libération* special issue did not provoke a reaction, *Le Monde*'s editorial triggered two "wake up" calls. The first came from Fourest in her weekly column on *France Culture* (1 October, and published in *Huffington Post*), where she directly attacked our book. She reiterated her attacks in *Islamophobie: La contre-enquête*, published in October 2014, and her book, *Éloge du blasphème*.[103] While the main argument for banning the word Islamophobia was its alleged invention by the Iranian mullahs in 1979 to prevent any criticism of the Muslim religion, she had shifted position: "We did not say that the fundamentalists were the only ones to use this term. It was just to explain that the attack aimed at feminists criticizing the headscarf, by labeling them racist, already had a precedent in our recent political history [. . .] The fact that a man in the nineteenth century used the term with a different meaning changes nothing."[104] This symbolic pirouette cannot hide the journalist's annoyance as she discovers the real origin of the word, Islamophobia, revealed by Fernando Bravo Lopez, Alain Gresh, and Thomas Deltombe, and in fact, in 2013, the editors of the ProChoix website changed the text dated 2003, deleting the phrase "for the first time."[105] Alongside the falsification of an old text came the technique of discrediting. Fourest alleged we were "activist-researchers" and that our book was "guided in principle" by the CCIF, "an ethnically divisive association" influenced by Tariq Ramadan and funded by billionaire George Soros and Qatar.[106]

The second "wake-up call" was the publication of a feature with the revealing title "'Islamophobia': Is It an Illusion?," in *Le Monde*'s "Ideas" section (1 November). While the editorial of 28 September had concluded that Islamophobia was real, a few days later, political cartoonist Plantu drew a typical caricature of Islamophobic logic, equating Islam with fundamentalist religious groups (1 October). This contradiction showed the tensions within *Le Monde*: Plantu and the coeditor of the "Ideas" section, Nicolas Weill, probably did not share the analysis of the "Religious Affairs" editor (Stéphanie Le Bars). In any case, two columns (Thomas Deltombe's and Saida Ounissi's) stressed the reality of Islamophobia, and three others contradicted them (Gilles Kepel's, Pierre-André Taguieff's, and Pascal Bruckner's). Nobody working in the Muslim third sector was asked to give their opinion, although they are in the forefront of the issue, and it is highly noteworthy that Deltombe's column was partially censored. His simple reference to the editorial of 28 September and condemnation of Plantu's Islamophobic caricature were deleted without the author being warned.[107]

Without analyzing the entire section, two important elements can be highlighted. First, political scientist Gilles Kepel stuck with the logic of denial when he criticized "the incantations against the 'Islamophobia' that French elites are guilty of spawning, a postmodern avatar of anti-Semitism of which Muslims are allegedly the quintessential victims." The use of the concept Islamophobia he argues, would simply "construct positions of power, in the intellectual field for the former [us and other scholars], and the religious arena for the latter [Muslim NGOs], in order to mobilize political support on the basis of identity at the next election."[108] One can only be amazed by the scant regard that Kepel, a senior professor at Sciences-Po, has for the hundreds of pieces of academic research on Islamophobia, including those carried out by his colleagues at Sciences-Po, and by the reduction of our book to a desire to hold positions of power. These comments were another illustration of his specific position in the academic field, as we write elsewhere in this book (chapter 7).

Next, we should also note the change of tack by philosopher Pierre-André Taguieff, hitherto a supporter of the ban on the concept of Islamophobia. Before 2013 he effectively considered Islamophobia to be a "sham" and a "very flexible category whose advantage is that it can be applied, not without confusion, to both the criticism of Islam and blasphemy, just as it can to forms of xenophobia targeted on immigrant populations of Muslim culture." For him, it enables "an alignment with the positions of Islamists, whether they are fundamentalists or jihadists, by thoroughly distorting the struggle against racism from the bottom to the top, and by abandoning the defense of human rights to cynical manipulators."[109] On 2 October 2013, he shifted his stance:

> Acknowledging the dubious or strictly tactical uses of the word "Islamophobia" in no way implies its outright rejection. It is a question of defining it clearly, which the professional "anti-Islamophobics" never do, causing a permanent malaise in the public debate. The term Islamophobia should be strictly reserved for the designation, at the level of opinions, appeals to hatred, discrimination and violence aimed at the Muslim religion, and at Muslims as such. Or, to put it more conceptually, the essentialization and demonization of Islam and Muslims.[110]

So, far from rejecting Islamophobia, he put forward a definition in his *Le Monde* column: "This term should be used to refer to appeals for hatred, discrimination and violence aimed at Muslims and/or their religion. Islamophobia cannot be reduced to a phenomenon of opinions. In practice it also takes the form of discrimination and physical attacks. It can be understood as a form of heterophobia aimed at a transnational community of believers."[111] Although Taguieff's definition seems limited to us, it is not far from what we have suggested: it is necessary to distinguish between the concept and the reality it refers to on the one hand, and on the other, the political uses of the concept.

CHAPTER 14

The Struggle for the Recognition of Islamophobia

The reluctance of the main anti-racist organizations to acknowledge Muslim actors and invest themselves in the struggle against Islamophobia pushed other social actors to commit themselves to this fight. The divisions within mainstream anti-racism turned out to be determining within what could be called the minority, anti-Islamophobia mobilization space. This space was particularly boosted by the small groups campaigning against the ban on headscarves, which developed between 2002 and 2004, functioning "like a net [and] bringing together the secular, Muslims and feminists, a heterogeneous network but bolstered by a high degree of interconnectivity."[1] This was a fragmented world, made up of a multitude of tiny activist grouplets that were sporadically capable of plugging into greater support (political parties and trade unions) and of campaigning figures from the media, the arts, or academia. However, these groups had their own political agendas and developed various, sometimes contradictory, strategies.

Cautious Religious Actors: A Generational Divide?

Due to their privileged relationship with practicing Muslim populations, it could be expected that the actors in leadership positions within the Muslim faith would be at the forefront of campaigning against Islamophobia. This is the scenario that emerges very clearly from the way the equivalent bodies function in the USA and the UK, where faith-based organizations (Council on American-Islamic Relations, Muslim Council of Britain, etc.) are actively engaged in the fight against Islamophobia. Yet, in France, the main Muslim organizations invest little effort or support as such into this field, despite the involvement of some of them in the defense of the young women wearing hijab caught up in the headscarf affair.

The "headscarf cause" and that of the struggle against Islamophobia partly overlap.[2] Even though the majority of the recorded victims of Islamophobia are women who wear headscarves, other manifestations of the Muslim faith are also objects of discriminatory treatment. The struggle against Islamophobia is a broader cause, liable to trigger a wider-based rallying of forces and to spread within spaces usually reluctant to engage with the situation of Muslims. However, the space of the struggle against Islamophobia has, like the "headscarf cause," witnessed a "fragmentation into stages," into "discontinuities and vacillations of collective action [. . .] that reveal obstacles that the 'Muslim community' have been encountering for nearly two decades in terms of having a voice in both public discourse and collective action."[3]

Unlike "relatively consensual subjects, such as the construction of places of worship or even religious worship practices,"[4] the struggle against Islamophobia unites little of the country's mosque leadership. Of course, the main Muslim federations, including the Paris Mosque, one of whose members co-ordinates the Observatory on Islamophobia in France, regularly express their "concern" about the rise of anti-Muslim acts and discourses.[5]

Yet beyond a few sporadic responses when public figures "get out of hand," or when places of worship or tombs are desecrated, this concern does not translate into any significant action. The increasing number of indignant press releases issued by the Conseil français du culte musulman(CFCM), the Paris Mosque, the Union des organizations islamiques de France (UOIF), and the Fédération nationale des musulmans de France (FNMF) sits in stark contrast to their lack of formal commitment: their investment in the "headscarf cause" would predict a constant provision of manpower, funds, and materials, but this is not the case.[6]

To understand this caution and withdrawal we need to make a short historical detour. Since the first headscarf affair in 1989, the UOIF and the FNMF have actively invested in defending girls wearing headscarves and consequently getting excluded from school, both in the name of freedom of worship and in order to compete with the monopoly on the representation of French Islam hitherto held by the Paris Mosque (and the Algerian state). The progressive and faltering steps forward this initiative took to achieve public and state acknowledgement was at the time supported by the Conseil d'État's liberal case law on the application of the principle of secularity in education institutions (November 1989, see chapter 6). At that time, this investment assumed the "allure of consecration," with the establishment of the CFCM in 2003 enabling organizations competing with the Paris Mosque, including those frequently labeled "Islamist" or "ethnically divisive" (particularly the UOIF), to get official recognition.[7] This co-optation by the government, however, was accompanied by a step backward in terms of the law, with the vote on the act banning hijab.

As Claire de Galembert demonstrates, the institutional consecration of those organizations and the vote on the act went hand in hand because "the reopening of the [headscarf] affair [in 2003] resulted specifically from the booing that engulfed Nicolas Sarkozy [then minister of the interior and religion], when he stated during the speech he made to the UOIF annual congress that no special exemption from the law would be made to women wearing hijab when it came to carrying identity papers. [...] For those criticizing the minister of the interior for having let the Islamist wolf into the Republican sheep pen and enabling ethnic divisions, this episode became irrefutable proof of the debatable political loyalty of what would become the main partner of the state and other authorities."[8]

For many Muslims, the Act of 15 March 2004 seemed to be a victory for Islamophobia because it legitimized exclusionary measures affecting everyday life and the future of hundreds of teenagers and, more widely, opened the door to anti-headscarf excesses, as evidenced by the witness statements collected by the CCIF. Moreover, participation in CFCM forced its members to prove both their loyalty and a form of pragmatism that completely wiped out their tendencies to challenge and critical capacity, all the more so as the CFCM was wracked by in-fighting and squabbles between the sponsoring consulates, all of which absorbed a lot of energy. The consequent institutional enshrining of the organizations involved thus assumed the form of a "dissociation from initiatives aimed at representing Muslims and supporting the cause of women wearing headscarves. The latter, impacted by the consequent reconfiguration of the type of actors committed to defending them, cut ties with Islam in order to join the anti-racist cause instead."[9]

This dissociation process was fueled by a generational gulf between young French descendants of immigrants, excluded from the process of representation from the outset, and their parents, in leadership positions at most places of worship,[10] already built or under construction, whose agenda for the Muslim community focused first and foremost on the management of rituals and spiritual education.

Moreover, as reflected in the findings of the TeO survey (see chapter 3), immigrants are overall less sensitive to the question of discrimination than their children. Therefore, it is a generational, cultural, and political divide separating Muslim immigrants—whether from the generation of workers or that of the religious leaders who came to France to study for degrees—and their descendants (born and raised in France) that structures campaigning against Islamophobia.

Although confronted with brutal forms of rejection and many administrative and political obstacles, the former group turned out to be more reluctant to commit themselves to the fight against Islamophobia, a battle borne above all, under a variety of names, by groups and movements involving more members of the next generation seeking—sometimes unsuccessfully—to universalize their struggle.

The most dynamic Muslim campaigns against Islamophobia are thus the work of converts and the children of immigrants, who are bringing new causes to the fore and deploying new forms of collective action.[11] What distinguishes these new actors in the French Islamic landscape is their desire to establish new forms of civic engagement and social and political participation, through education, publishing, nonreligious third-sector activism, popular education, etc. The not-for-profits and collectives created in this period (e.g., the Union des jeunes musulmans since 1987, the Jeunes musulmans de France, the Collectif des musulmans de France), have thus committed themselves actively—in the name of equality and the rejection of discrimination—against the exclusion of headscarf-wearing teenagers.

This strategy differs from that of previous generations, since it sometimes draws on activist capital already accrued through union campaigning and work in urban working-class areas (especially by the pioneers of such work from the Greater Lyon area) and has no compunction in inciting "young Muslims to assert themselves, through their commitment to voluntary work, as fully autonomous actors [and] to use their votes. [These not-for-profits] thus promote new forms of social activism that have, in the name of Islam, begun to rival social educators and social workers on their own territory, as well as the leadership of not-for-profits set up in the 1980s."[12] One fringe of this new wave of Muslim leadership draws particularly enthusiastically on the ideas of Tariq Ramadan who, since the 1990s, has encouraged participation in social movements. This dynamic of openness and participation in wider social struggles has helped spread the struggle against Islamophobia, which has coalesced around various, often connected spaces of campaigning, characterized by an intense level of circulation among actors.

The Development of the Fight against Islamophobia beyond the Muslim Community

Although the term Islamophobia was not used then, the premises of a minority struggle can be detected in the 1990s, through the profile of the actors and their ripple-like spread through politics aimed at combatting anti-Muslim discrimination. In a context where tension between France and Algerian Islamist movements was acute (the killing of five French citizens in Algeria in summer 1994), an initial campaign brought together several Muslim not-for-profit organizations and the network of the Mouvement de l'immigration et des banlieues (MIB) to protest the decision by Minister of the Interior Charles Pasqua to place several dozen activists and leading figures from the Muslim community under "house arrest" in Folembray (in the Aisne department, northeast of Paris), notably Larbi Kechat (the rector of the Da'wa mosque in the nineteenth arrondissement of Paris), all accused of membership of the Algerian Front islamique du salut (FIS, Islamic Salvation Front). The following year, a Committee for Free Speech for Muslims in France was set up following the ban on Tariq Ramadan entering the country.

Subsequently, the fight against anti-Muslim discrimination developed in spaces of exchange and training, bringing together activists from various backgrounds, Muslim or not, some of whom are still active, like the Laïcité et Islam Commission (renamed Islam et laïcité) and the Une école pour tou-te-s collective. The former was established in 1997 under the aegis of Michel Morineau and Pierre Tournemire of the Ligue de l'enseignement (Teaching League),[13] before being taken over from 2001 by the LDH and *Le Monde diplomatique* (which withdrew in 2006 when the commission became a not-for-profit organization under the Act of 1901). The commission's objective was to gradually and objectively analyze Muslim life in France, in order to reflect upon and evaluate its political and social inclusion, particularly in relation to the discrimination experienced by its worshippers and their institutions. At this time, the Ligue de l'enseignement did not focus on Islamophobia as such, as the concept was barely on the radar in the public sphere,[14] but was more interested in the relationship between French society, its institutions, and Muslims. The Ligue therefore adopted a statement on "secularity and the Act of 1905" during its board meeting of 14 November 1995, in which it demanded equality of treatment of religion, aware that "basically motivated by ideological considerations, obstacles have been placed—by elected representatives—to the freedom of worship of the Muslim faith."[15] Moreover, it reiterated its support for the liberal direction of the Conseil d'État's ruling of November 1989.

The Ligue's strategy of openness and exchange with Muslim actors, as well as its liberal take on secularity, drew much criticism, especially from the other institutional pillar of secularity in France: the Grand Orient de France.[16] The strategy pursued by the Laïcité et Islam Commission consisted of developing dialogue with the various components of Muslim life, which broke with the dominant political attitude that sought to select rather docile and compliant interlocutors.[17]

Despite the numerous exchanges, lectures, and publications, the knowledge acquired and the relationships woven between its members, the commission was caught up in the controversy surrounding Tariq Ramadan and the movements inspired by his work. In a similar way to what was playing out in the antiglobalization movement, the strategy of isolation adopted by Muslim not-for-profits gradually impacted on the commission. Picking up the baton from Jean-Louis Debré, who had briefly banned Tariq Ramadan from entering France in 1995, Jean-Pierre Chevènement (minister of the interior from 1997 to 2000), fired a second salvo, showing his concern about the Swiss intellectual within the Laïcité et Islam Commission. "This inquiry," states Michel Morineau, "would have consequences. Indeed, a few months later, in early 2001, the Ligue's board decided that the commission had exhausted its subject matter and the organization should move on to another dimension of the problem."[18] Shortly afterward, Morineau was forced to resign, but "in September 2001, the majority of the membership had a hard time accepting this decision, and the commission, now called 'Islam et laïcité,' decided to continue its work with the Ligue des Droits de l'Homme, with the very obvious support—funding included—of *Le Monde diplomatique* and the Fonds d'action sociale pour l'intégration et la lutte contre les discriminations [FASILD, Fund for Social Action for Integration and the Fight against Discrimination]."[19]

Despite the LDH having taken over responsibility for the commission, some tensions remained within the Ligue de l'enseignement. Michel Morineau particularly emphasizes the unhelpful role played by high-profile best-selling publications, "among others, the poorly documented and error-strewn book" published by Caroline Fourest on Tariq Ramadan in 2004.[20] One of the central arguments and criticisms leveled at Islam et laïcité was, according to her, "the presence of Tariq Ramadan, his work and frameworks running counter to the surrounding ideology, and his highly critical analysis of publications by intellectuals deemed 'Islamophobic'": these media-profile books "definitely created a fantasy representation of a 'mysterious and Machiavellian place,' a genuine 'crucible' in which ethnically divisive theories liable to overturn the 'one and indivisible' Republic tomorrow were being crafted!"[21]

In spite of losing some of its overall reach, the Islam et laïcité Commission remains active, producing ideas and organizing public demonstrations. Across all the areas it focuses on, it plays a considerable role in the dissemination and publication of texts and news about events relating to Islamophobia, the question of the hijab and, more broadly, discrimination in general. The commission's experience reveals two stakes underlying all the campaigning against Islamophobia. First, their anchoring outside the Muslim community, which represents the fruit of the mobilized Muslim organizations' desire to share and universalize their struggle, and second, the existence of a countercampaign striving to drive a wedge between these alliances in the name of the fight against "fundamentalism" (of which Ramadan and the groups close to him are viewed as the most blatant embodiment). This pattern can be identified in all the activist arenas in which an independent and protesting Muslim component committed to working in civil society has taken up a position.

From the ESF to Mamans Toutes Égales

Within the Islam et laïcité Commission, the struggle against Islamophobia remained for years a secondary concern, restricted to the narrow space of intellectual exchange. However, it acquired a more political status in both France and Europe after the 11 September attacks and the reignition of the controversy around wearing headscarves. It was from within the antiglobalization movement that this process took shape. According to Timothy Peace, author of a detailed study of relations between Muslims and the antiglobalization activists, the synergies triggered at the European Social Forum (ESF) enabled the establishment and strengthening of links, alliances, and joint action between human rights organizations, not-for-profits from working-class areas or the Muslim religious movement, and members of the radical left and feminist movements. By allowing action decoupled from geographical space that exceeded the boundaries of the local and the national, these meetings contributed to the circulation of expertise and repertoires of collective action, the strengthening of the intersections, and the injection of momentum for a new dynamic of anti-Islamophobia campaigning.

Indeed, since the beginning of 2000, and particularly at the first ESF in Florence in 2002, the participation of European groups and movements that identified as Muslim in various forms contributed on one hand to the spread of the theme of Islamophobia through activist worlds that had been less engaged, and on the other, enabled alliances to be developed, some of which are ongoing.[22] The initial connections are greatly indebted to the action carried out by the Mouvement de l'immigration et des banlieues, whose track record and legitimacy in the struggle against inequalities, racism, and police violence opened the way to collaborations with "many groups and not-for-profits which would later be the founding members of the 'No Vox' network. The MIB [. . .] played a pivotal role in bringing together the different campaigns under one umbrella and acting as a bridge between the various groups."[23] Other convergences were facilitated by the antiglobalization movement's interest in the Palestine question, particularly through the participation of activists from various strands within the same civil society missions.[24]

These convergences did not all run smoothly. The majority of the "anti-globalization actors did not support such campaigns, and the efforts of the people who did want to incorporate Muslim groups into their campaigns mainly failed. The groups themselves were restricted by lack of financial resources, hence their absence [from the FSE] in Athens in 2006."[25] It was not so much the presence of actors with religious affiliation that was fundamentally the problem— as the presence and engagement of the Secours catholique and many others shows—but rather the fact that activist commitment could be tied to Islam and that those not-for-profit organizations embodying this approach and involved in the ESF (Collectif des musulmans de France and the Présence musulmane network) were associated with Tariq Ramadan, the target of a discreditation campaign that heated up in 2004 (in particular in the wake of the publication of Caroline Fourest's book).

The FSE then witnessed the same scenario as the Islam et laïcité Commission had, with the same grievances in play, often driven by the same actors (Caroline Fourest, Pierre-André Taguieff, SOS-Racisme, etc.). These affairs have marked both the antiglobalization movement and Muslim actors. As Timothy Peace emphasizes, "the most noteworthy thing about this Muslim campaign was its impact on the anti-globalization groups themselves, and the way it challenged their own representation as an open, tolerant movement."[26]

Despite their strong representation in international fora, the Muslim collectives in question also reinvested resources in national space, inter alia in the form of the revamped Forum social des quartiers populaires (FSQP), whose first meeting was held in Saint-Denis on 22–24 June 2007. This "inward-facing" strategy, countering the resistance of the antiglobalization movement to the Muslim presence, highlighted the fact that Islamophobia is as much a local as a national concern and that it is embedded in multiple social problems such as class, urban segregation, racism, and the cause of Palestine. But above all, a number of committed actors in these movements and the ESF were to turn their alliances into practical realities around the specific struggles more directly linked to the fight against Islamophobia.

This was indeed the case in early 2004, for the collective Une école pour tous-tes—contre les lois d'exclusion (CEPT, One School for All—Against Exclusionary Laws). The way this collective was set up was new in terms of its scope and eclectic composition, since it included groups close to Tariq Ramadan (Présence musulmane and the Collectif des musulmans de France, CMF), anti-racist and human rights organizations (the MRAP and LDH), left-wing political parties (the Greens and the LCR), LGBT not-for-profits (Act Up), old-school feminists (Christine Delphy), and groups active in the struggles over immigration and the banlieues (MIB, Saïd Bouamama), etc. All of these actors were, according to their own political agendas, opposed to the exclusion of teenagers wearing headscarves from state schools. So for the first time since the beginning of the headscarf affair, "a bridge between the Islamic groups campaigning for the headscarf and some of their potential allies that had broken away from that protest" presented itself.[27]

The demonstrations and events held by the CEPT in February 2004 conveyed the desire to both universalize and "detach the headscarf cause from its faith-based origin," based on a traditional repertoire of activism.[28] Out of step with the forms of campaign engaged in by faith-based organizations, having broken with the strategy of confrontation pursued by the Parti des musulmans de France and embracing French society's cultural and religious plurality (especially in the way it designed processions and the content of its slogans), the collective enabled the struggle against the exclusion of the girls wearing headscarves to be removed from religious terrain and be embedded instead in anti-racism and feminism. The open nature of the collective also fostered the development of a support network, albeit a sporadic one, emerging from trade union, academic, political, and artistic circles, which facilitated the dissemination of the collective's claims by means of a multitude of forms of support (books, documentaries, petitions, public meetings, etc.). This scenario was reproduced later by some of the same actors from that collective, beneath the banner of Mamans toutes égales (MTE, All Mums are Equal), which campaigned against the ban on mothers wearing headscarves accompanying their children on school trips.[29]

An Anti-Islamophobic Stream of Feminism

While women were on the frontline of Islamophobic acts and legal bans, the feminist movement was highly divided. An active fringe made active contributions to the struggle against Islamophobia but, as in the case of the Muslim presence in the antiglobalization movement, the issue of wearing hijab revealed internal contradictions as well as the unspoken rules of the feminist movement.[30] As Nicolas Dot-Pouillard stresses, these controversies "led many activists—male and female—to reflect on the colonial past, the religious question, and the nature of the republican state school, food for thought that had been abandoned a long time ago."[31] Moreover, these controversies also "heralded the start of a political reconfiguration within the French feminist movement," which split into three distinct groups: one refocusing on the issue of republican secularity; a second seeking to preserve the historical heritage of feminism; and lastly, a third, which adopted a stance against the school exclusions and asked questions that cut across the 'colonial continuum' of ideas developed during colonial times and racist and Islamophobic discrimination."[32]

The historical and majority stream, represented by the Collectif national pour le droit des femmes (CNDF, National collective for women's rights), certainly did not support the Act of 15 March 2004 but refused to participate in the campaigning against the prohibitionist laws, or against Islamophobia in general. As Dot-Pouillard explains, this strand of feminists actually retained the conventional framework for interpretation, considering the hijab as a "fundamentalist and backward" sign and as a claim for recognition of a religious and reactionary identity fueled by "'essentialized' Islamism, seen as homogenous and perceived as a threat to women's rights, in a way that seems totally controlled and organized."[33] The CNDF was thus explicitly opposed to the "interpretations provided by certain researchers, activists, and journalists, like Alain Gresh, Editor of *Le Monde diplomatique*, for whom the headscarf held several political and social meanings and was not ipso facto a conspicuous sign of fundamentalism and claims for a regressive kind of identity."[34] This reading, which usually reduces wearing a headscarf to an act of antisecular, antifeminist defiance, as well as behind the scenes male fundamentalist maneuvering,[35] was the subject of profound and still lively divisions within the CNDF.[36]

Public and feminist debates witnessed a struggle over the meaning of the hijab. According to one line of thought, wearing headscarves is the symbol of regression, both in terms of religion and identity, produced by the worsening of social conditions in working-class areas: from this perspective the hijab expresses an (ethnically divisive) inward-facing turn in identity that should disappear when economic conditions improve.

A second approach, developed by the dominant media and a minority of the historical feminists, focused "its strategy and program on the interlinked questions of secularity and the Republic," through a "defensive movement, in which the Republic and universalism were highlighted and became the foundation of all women's strategies for emancipation."[37] This group concluded that wearing hijab demonstrated a coordinated and organized desire to chip away at the egalitarian gains of the Revolution and women's struggles, revealing an underground offensive of Islamist movements against the secular Republic. Here it linked in with the dominant discourse on the "fundamentalist plot." "This new republican feminism is basically embodied in the Ni putes ni soumises (Neither Whores nor Submissives) group and the magazine *Prochoix*," asserts Dot-Pouillard, while being "supported by a composite raft of not-for-profits, unions, and political groups"[38] that include SOS-Racisme, the Union des familles laïques, Lutte ouvrière, activist forces within the Parti socialiste and, subsequently, the UMP.[39] Some of the feminists in this strand have tilted steadily toward what historian Michelle Zancarini-Fournel calls an "Islamophobic feminism" fueled by a few activists such as Michèle Vianès and Anne Zelenski (see chapter 8).[40]

In contrast, the feminist campaigning against Islamophobia objected to the other two strands above in the name of "féminisme métisse" (hybrid feminism), which seeks first "to elucidate the complex relationships between colonial past, racism, and Islamophobia, and the essentialization of Islam." And it was within the CEPT and the CFPE that feminist reflection on, and commitment against, Islamophobia took shape, in opposition to the "neither law nor hijab" position held by the CNDF, the republican feminism of Ni putes ni soumises, *Prochoix*, Élisabeth Badinter, and the radically Islamophobic feminism whose voice had already been heard in the "Tribunal against Islamization" (see chapter 8). This anti-Islamophobic strand was the source of significant intellectual, academic, and activist contributions to the debate and led to the organization of public events and establishment of mixed feminist collectives. These latter included "'historic feminists' (Monique Crinon, Christine Delphy, etc.), the social movement's architects (Catherine Samary, head of Attac), and leaders of Muslim not-for-profit organizations, both with and without headscarves (including Siham Andalouci, member and spokesperson of the CMF)."[41]

This third path, and the campaigning that it opened up, are based on an interpretation of hijab that clashes fundamentally with the other readings.[42] Without concentrating on the political and religious meanings, this stance argues that "the act banning headscarves is essentially sexist (as it punishes only women), racist (in that it particularly focuses on one religion, Islam), and lastly, essentialist (since it describes the hijab as a universal sign of oppression, notwithstanding its various meanings)."[43] This approach constituted a direct attack on Islamophobia—defined as the othering and racialization of the religious—in which the colonial theme is crucial, thus facilitating the convergence of struggles of a number of activists and within several movements sensitive to this way of framing the issue. Indeed, the Act of 15 March 2004 "is argued to fit with a specific heritage of representations drawn from colonialism. This link between the colonial continuum and the law on wearing headscarves lies at the heart of the thinking of another group of women and girls (of immigrant background), also born out of the Une école pour tous-tes collective: 'Les Blédardes.'"[44] Houria Bouteldja and Djamila Bechoua were the highest profile leaders of this group, which "traces itself back to a critical feminism, open to the plurality of strategies for emancipation and challenging the French style of universalism, which is bound up in the colonial subconscious."[45]

This postcolonial critique of majority feminism follows in the footsteps of U.S. Black feminism in that the Islamic headscarf affair opened the way to a radical critique of some of the foundations and unspoken rules of majority feminism.[46] This critique is focused on challenging the "universalist" character of the category "woman," in the name of the diversity of experiences, priorities, and feasible trajectories as well as modes of emancipation. This critique helped put the first cracks in the dominant encoding of the feminist question. While in United States the critiques produced by minority feminism concentrated on the experiences of Black women, in France it was the recent emergence of Muslim feminism, and moreover, feminism engaged in by women wearing hijab, that provoked an outcry and the opening up of debate.[47]

The two forms of feminism—"Black" and "Islamic"—do have links. Chandra Mohanty, a prominent figure in postcolonial feminism, has put forward an analysis based on analogies between American slave-owning culture and French colonialist culture. As was the case for Black women in a different era, Mohanty critiques the habit of dominant feminism that imposes a single, monolithic, and negative meaning of the hijab, regardless of the opinion and subjectivities of the women wearing it.[48] The rejection of Islamophobia is thus articulated with critical, pluralist, and postcolonial feminism, which posits the diversity of emancipatory strategies and suggests another agenda for feminist struggles in which the fight against racism and sexism based on a "critique of all patriarchal and macho models is prioritized, without [. . .] abandoning responsibility for a culture and a religion."[49]

Although the majority of campaigns were focused, logically, on defending women wearing headscarves being excluded from an increasing number of public spaces, the struggle against Islamophobia was to steadily broaden and diversify its base. As Claire de Galembert notes, in relation to the cause of the headscarf, "a corollary of the reconfiguration of actors in the campaign was their investment in a new field of debate, the struggles against discrimination and Islamophobia, brought about by the new opportunity structure that [now] constituted the implementation of a policy of fighting discrimination."[50] This opportunity structure, more broadly, was also constituted by the growing investments of international organizations (the European Commission and the UN) and by several international NGOs interested in Muslim minorities' social conditions in Europe (Amnesty International, George Soros's Open Society Foundation).[51] In 1989 the issue of racism was there but was secondary in the argumentation strategy of those opposed to the ban on headscarves. From 2003 Islamophobia became pivotal as a conceptual tool and explanatory lens through which the causes to defend could be made sense of.[52] The debate now focused less on the boundaries of secularity, and more on its profound changes and the concept's "falsification" to achieve racist, nationalist ends and manipulate forms of identity.[53]

A New Wave?

Since 2003 the struggle against Islamophobia has been borne by a new wave of activists, mainly from ethnic minority backgrounds, within small organizations and collectives, partly trained in the midst of the campaigning around the headscarf affair in the 2003–2004 period. Most of these activists are French citizens with college degrees, who have accrued political and not-for-profit activist experience. They have put into practice the ideas of those seeking to "remove religious specifics" from the struggles linked to Muslims, as identified by Claire de Galembert in regard to the "the headscarf cause." The campaigns against banning the headscarf and against Islamophobia noticeably strengthened one another over the next few years, which saw the emergence of the CCIF in 2003, the Indigènes de la République in 2005, the Indivisibles in 2006, and the Coordination contre le racisme et l'islamophobie (CRI, Coordinating Group against Racism and Islamophobia) in 2008. The idea of "removing the religious specifics" from campaigning here refers to the desire to universalize the cause, based on the concept of commitment "from outside the Muslim community" and renewal of modes of action.[54]

The actions undertaken by the CCIF seem the most diverse. Set up in 2003 by a handful of French Muslims aged between twenty-five and thirty-five, this collective was the result of indignation regarding the increasing normalization of Islamophobia in the post 9–11 context, the headscarf affairs, and the lack of interest in (and even strong resistance to) the struggle against Islamophobia shown by anti-racist movements and the state. Initially relying on volunteers to collect data, perform communications functions, and write annual reports, the CCIF was by 2013 employing three legal specialists funded through subscriptions, donations, and fundraising activities such as annual gala dinners[55] —which completely covered the costs of casework with, and legal assistance to, victims of Islamophobia. CCIF also offers psychological support services and sometimes assistance at school. The CCIF also enjoys a significant international profile: it is recognized as a special consultative member of the ECOSOC (UN) and is regularly invited to contribute by the European Commission against Racism and

Intolerance (ECRI), the Council of Europe, and the Organization for Security and Cooperation in Europe (OSCE). On a different level, the CCIF's statistics and stances have also been used and adopted by Amnesty International, whose 2012 report argues that the treatment of Muslims in French society and by the state is illegal.[56]

From the outset, the CCIF's strategy was based on two modes of action: recording the numbers of Islamophobic acts and the marshalling of antidiscrimination law to defend victims and "produce" case law.[57] On the first point, the CCIF campaigned to top up the data drawn from legal referrals (see chapter 2) by setting up victimization surveys. Regarding the second, its legal strategy has helped establish an acknowledgement of Islamophobia by the courts (criminal, civil, and prud'hommes [labor tribunals]) as well as by the Défenseur des droits (ex-Halde).[58] Bearing in mind that the direction of travel of French law is one of ever-tightening restrictions on the religious freedom of Muslims in France, and that the European Court of Human Rights has refused to slow this movement down—in the name of member states' right to retain some leeway in their own legal systems—the CCIF's legal strategy has weakened. In around 2010 the collective embarked on a diversification of its means of action. As well as its legal strategy, it added a strategy of consciousness-raising aimed at elected politicians (especially in parliament) and (mass) mobilization of the governed via communication campaigns and public events (conferences across the whole country and public protests). Humor is also sometimes deployed, as in the case of the successful distribution of "pains au chocolat" at Paris Saint-Lazare Station as a response to Jean-François Copé's comments (see introduction).

The CRI, founded by Abdelaziz Chaambi and a few activists from Lyon, also carried out actions in support of the victims of Islamophobia. Chaambi, a cofounder of the Union des jeunes musulmans, was a member of various collectives (apart from the CCIF and the Indivisibles) that constitute the space of anti-Islamophobia campaigning. A member of the Islam et laïcité Commission, he was also a member of the CEPT, various social fora and the Mouvement des indigènes de la République. The establishment of the CRI stemmed from criticism that the CCIF was not "radical enough" and the need to take the struggle up to a more political level. Chaambi's path illustrates the movement that characterizes the narrow space of the struggle against Islamophobia. Indeed, it is no coincidence that many activists involved in various collectives against the exclusion of the teenage girls wearing headscarves also contributed to the Appel des indigènes de la République (particularly its architect and spokesperson, Houria Bouteldja) in January 2005.[59]

Since 2005, in addition to its participation in platforms articulating demands and public demonstrations, the movement that resulted from this appeal, the Mouvement des indigènes de la République (MIR), has embodied the intellectual hub of the fight against Islamophobia, through its production and dissemination of activist writing, its building of bridges with U.S. academia, and its participation in public and televised debates, etc. On its website, the MIR—which became the Parti des indigènes de la République (PIR) in February 2010—disseminates information received from other organizations and communicates its activist agenda (public demonstrations and meetings). It also provides its own analyses, particularly of the racial, social, and political bases of Islamophobia. The PIR's commitment to fighting Islamophobia was bolstered by the links it developed to Ramon Grosfoguel, a professor at the University of California-Berkeley, a specialist in Latin American minorities and Caribbean migration. Grosfoguel is particularly interested in the contemporary persistence of modes of governance based on colonial models (chapter 5).[60] The concept of "coloniality of power" has been quite successful in France, especially among movements of Muslim (the Institut international de la pensée islamique, IIIT, International Institute for Islamic Thought) and anticolonial (PIR) intellectuals.[61]

Ramon Grosfoguel organized an international colloquium ("New Post-9/11 Racial/Ethnic Configurations: The Problem and Practical Effects of Islamophobia"), held at the Fondation Maison des sciences de l'homme (FMSH) in Paris in June 2006.[62] This colloquium was held again, in winter 2013, in partnership with the Centre d'analyse et d'intervention sociologiques (CADIS, EHESS), alongside a campaigning event in which the PIR took an active role.[63] The PIR strategy was to develop and disseminate a political framework in the form of a matrix, accounting for the unspoken racial organization of French society. This interpretation aimed to think through and combat Islamophobia by addressing its political and colonial roots. In a core text for the party, Houria Bouteldja states that "Islamophobia is primarily a form of state racism [. . .] whose only goal is to keep a population in a subaltern status." She goes on to say that it represents a symptom of the decline of "white European identity," an "irrational fear" as a response to the desire of the subjugated groups to "live and establish themselves, and to transform the status quo established by racism and colonialism, which means a de facto loss of power and related privileges."[64]

Lastly, in a different tone, the activities carried out by the Indivisibles should also be noted. This not-for-profit organization fights all stereotypes, prejudices, and forms of racism, with no exceptions or hierarchies, by using the weapons of humor and mockery.[65] The group spreads comic visual images illustrating statements deemed racist or that convey types of conflations that help generate racism. Every summer, it holds an event—the "Y a Bon Awards"[66]—modeled on the various cultural award ceremonies, and which ironically reward the perpetrators of the "best" racist statements. This ceremony, active in the condemnation of Islamophobic prejudices, was criticized for giving an award to the journalist Caroline Fourest, who had excoriated a Muslim not-for-profit for having held a women-only basketball tournament, accusing it of being funded by the Palestinian Hamas movement.

The comedy culture that makes the Indivisibles stand out goes together with its more conventional initiatives, like participation in public campaigning and debates in the media. Access to the media and the capacity to mobilize well-known figures in the press, the arts, and the theater are specific resources that this organization holds, as the composition of the jury (renewed annually) for the "Y'a Bon Awards" demonstrates ("Y'a bon" means "it's good" in colonized African slang and was used by colonizers to mock Africans, so the organizers of the awards take this colonial expression to turn it against contemporary racist discourses). The variety of positions held by its founder, Rokhaya Diallo (filmmaker and television producer at Canal+, RTL, Public Sénat, etc.), helps spread the group's ideas and to galvanize a support network in the fields of cultural production and journalism.

These different organizations were all established and are led by French ethnic minority people highly critical of traditional anti-racism—particularly SOS-Racisme and the Licra—and its inability or refusal to effectively fight racism and discrimination, especially Islamophobia. They deploy a variety of modes of action and aspire to be self-funding in the name of a political autonomy understood as the very cornerstone of their activities.

Even though these initiatives, analyses, and some of the activists move back and forth between the various mobilization spaces, it is true that significant differences in approach remain, as illustrated by the debate on the "We Are the Nation" campaign launched by the CCIF in Autumn 2012.[67] Its main message is that French Muslims are French like everyone else, and its principal visual image was an appropriation of the painting by Jacques-Louis David called *Le serment du Jeu de Paume* (The tennis court oath). This campaign drew two kinds of critique. The first came from media "elites" who denied the CCIF's legitimacy in using "our" symbols, like the concept of "nation" and David's painting. The other line of criticism came from ethnic minorities who were critical of using "their" symbols in a sense that "evacuates the question of race" by giving the illusion that the accompanying slogan ("We are [also] the nation") could be made a reality by merely believing in it. According to Bouteldja, "the CCIF has indeed omitted this annoying dimension: the question of racism/colonialism that divides the body of the nation. The slogan 'We are (also) the nation' becomes meaningless once this reality is taken into consideration. The campaign thus has to produce fantasies, illusions, and dreams."[68] What the PIR condemns then is an "integrationist impasse," particularly as the people chosen to front the campaign were the most reassuring and compliant representatives of the Muslim presence in France.[69]

At a time when legislation on public expressions of Islam, the public rhetoric surrounding it, and public opinion regarding Muslims is becoming increasingly harsh, it is difficult to predict the future directions of the new actors in the struggle against Islamophobia. The French national context is obviously inimical to the strategy of universalizing it, even though a growing number of international actors (NGOs, UN, Council of Europe, U.S. State Department, Turkey, etc.) support their grievances on the world stage.

Fragmented Campaigning and Institutional Recognition

The year 2013 was also a turning point in terms of political campaigning. In a context of semantic controversies, amplified in the publishing watershed constituted by the publication and media coverage afforded to several books documenting the reality of Islamophobia (see earlier in this chapter), an international Forum against Islamophobia was held in Paris on 14 December 2013. Established by the 14 December collective, the forum's objective was to "debate the contours of what some prefer to call 'anti-Muslim racism,' and the way to step up the struggle against a rapidly changing racist system, and to do this with the participation of organizations on the ground, political and community activists, and researchers, both French and foreign." This initiative thus marked the convergence toward an "anti-Islamophobia front" comprised of multiple organizations,[70] but included neither the Collectif contre le racisme et l'islamophobie, the Ligue de défense judiciaire des musulmans[71] nor researchers and media such as Oumma.com and Beur FM. Several hundred participants drawn from the whole country attended the forum, which would have been unthinkable just a few years previously. Among the noteworthy aspects of this forum was the presence of organizations such as the LDH, represented by its director, Pierre Tartakowsky, and editor of the LDH journal, Gilles Manceron, some sections of the MRAP, and trade union activists. These organizations were ones in which the struggle against Islamophobia had caused intense divisions for several years, and which had steadily distanced themselves from it. Although their attendance at the forum did not translate into a visible renewal of interest, it was no less significant as a way of relegitimizing the cause.

The forum's organizers also conceived of it as a means of gathering transnational momentum for collaboration, basically with anglophone academia. Indeed, the forum had been announced in April 2013 at the behest of the Parti des indigènes de la République spokesperson, Houria Bouteldja, during a seminar at the University of Berkeley held by the Center for Race and Gender. Some U.S. academics, particularly Ramon Grosfoguel and Hatem Bazian, helped institutionalize academic research on Islamophobia through the launch of the Islamophobia Research and Documentation Project and the biannual *Islamophobia Studies Journal*. Those campaigning against Islamophobia in France thus linked up with specific academics who were specialists in this area and whose academic work was a good fit to their political commitment. This network decided to hold an annual international colloquium in Paris, in partnership with the researchers at the Centre d'analyse et d'intervention sociologique (EHESS), while this book's authors' seminar at the EHESS on the "construction of the Muslim problem" ended in May 2014.

Yet the action of not-for-profit organizations and community activists cannot be reduced to only running conferences. It is worth noting that one of them, the CCIF, engaged in sustained activity in the area of giving legal assistance to victims and lobbying with national and international institutions. On the national level, the CCIF was granted a hearing with the CNCDH, which, in its next report, broke with the political line it had previously followed on the struggle against Islamophobia. However, although the CCIF received a lukewarm reception in France, it actually took part in the work of many international organizations involved in defending human rights, such as the UN, the OSCE, and the European Union (through the Agency for Basic Rights).[72] Its annual report— focused especially on the statistics about victims of Islamophobia—constitutes an informative and considerable resource for many NGOs like Amnesty International. Moreover, it led an innovative project in Europe called "Iman" (Islamophobia Monitoring & Action Network), that brought together actors and partners from eight European countries, implemented with the support of the European Commission and aiming at coordinating local efforts in the fight against Islamophobia. This project plans to establish a methodological apparatus for harmonizing the recording and follow-up of incidents and victims of Islamophobia, as well as the dissemination of legal expertise, in the relevant countries. In September 2014 the project's linchpin, the former CCIF spokesperson, became chief advisor on Islamophobia at the Office for Democratic Institutions and Human Rights (ODIHR), an agency of the OSCE.

However, the central strand of the CCIF's campaigning strategy, marshalling the law in support of, and for the protection of victims, as well as the creation of case law that would be favorable to individual liberties, was undermined by a series of rulings. First, the Supreme Court's final ruling on the "Baby Loup" case on 25 June 2014 further extended the principle of "secular neutrality" to all bodies (whether public or private) providing care and / or education to young children.[73] Moreover, in the case of a French Muslim citizen challenging the 2010 law banning the full veil, the European Court of Human Rights deemed the "preservation of conditions for 'mutually tolerant coexistence' a legitimate aim" of the French government, with member states having a "substantial margin of judgement" in this regard. We cannot address the significant bases for and consequences of these two rulings here, but we would just underscore that after them, the legal strategy of organizations fighting Islamophobia seemed obviously hamstrung: all the more so because the rulings would probably provide the impetus for more campaigns aimed at banning public expressions of Muslim-ness in other arenas.

Actions carried out by not-for-profits engaged in the struggle against Islamophobia thus played a role in raising the awareness of institutions responsible for the fight against racism and discrimination. This is particularly true of the CNCDH, which had repeatedly rejected the use of the concept of Islamophobia. In preparation for its 2013 report, the CNCDH decided to hold an in-house debate on the concept: "The discussions were rich, solidly backed up with evidence, sometimes passionate and always driven by the desire to push the fight against racism forwards."[74] The report contained a long introductory overview that reviewed the various arguments supporting and opposing the use of this concept. The CNCDH concluded that "the debate ended up being less about the legitimacy of the term than its definition"[75] and "it concluded by using the term 'Islamophobia' to refer to this rampant, dangerous phenomenon, which threatened the idea of 'mutually tolerant coexistence' and requires us all to remain vigilant."[76]

The terminology "Islamophobia" has a number of advantages from the perspective of fighting discrimination. The term has a potent suggestive potential, it is incisive and clear. The power of the word makes a serious phenomenon visible. The term "Islamophobia" reveals a latent form of racism, which seeks to remain imperceptible, concealed beneath the acceptable cloak of freedom of speech. In this context, refusing to speak of "Islamophobia" may be perceived as a willingness to deny the reality and scope of a phenomenon which has been particularly sensitive for several years, and which turns people of Muslim faith into a homogenous and socially problematic group. "Islamophobia" has the benefit of designating an ideology hostile to Muslims, and perceptible beyond scattered anti-Muslim acts. If this terminology has steadily and substantially permeated everyday institutional language, it has been to acknowledge the acute nature of this growing and harshly experienced reality, that is constructing a "Muslim problem" in France.[77]

The CNCDH's change of tack is not necessarily an isolated strategy, judging by the positions adopted on this point by the Parti socialiste, which has been divided over this matter. On one side is the stance defended by then-prime minister Manuel Valls, for whom the struggle against Islamophobia is a "Salafist Trojan horse."[78] On the other, PS leaders started to acknowledge the existence of Islamophobia. While in 2004 National Secretary Jean-Christophe Cambadélis doubted that "so-called Islamophobia" existed, he devoted several pages of his 2014 book to Islamophobia, recognizing the concept's reality and even calling for it to be actively combatted.[79] In his terms, Islamophobia is merely a threat from the extreme Right, and much less responsibility for its normalization is attributed to the Left. On 16 January 2015, President François Hollande used the word "Islamophobia" for the first time, in his New Year message to the diplomatic corps. On 29 May the CCIF's annual dinner received a representative of the PS—spokesperson Corine Narassiguin—as a guest for the first time. On 20 June 2015 the PS annual congress in Poitiers passed the "Socialist renewal" motion, which condemned "the anti-Semitic and Islamophobic words and attacks that are increasing in frequency in many countries, as they are in France" and stated its intent to "fight racism, anti-Semitism, Islamophobia, xenophobia, and other forms of discrimination."[80] This motion was signed by all members of the government, including Manuel Valls. This acknowledgement of the struggle against Islamophobia certainly complied with electoral tactics but also with a political conviction that Islamophobia was an active fracture within French society. Whatever the case may be, this ideological shift in the PS provoked indignant responses from certain journalists, at the *Figaro* and elsewhere (Fourest, Mohamed Sifaoui, etc.), who began an intense campaign discrediting the CCIF in the press and on social media.[81]

From 2013 the question of Islamophobia would give rise to contradictory trajectories that make the current context highly volatile. On one hand, the series of attacks since 2013 and the ideological victory and media domination of Islamophobic political projects in France, whether they prioritize patriotic or republican rhetoric, translate electorally into more support for the extreme right bloc embodied by Marine Le Pen. On the other, despite resistance and divisions, the Left has become increasingly open to the warnings of those highlighting the danger of Islamophobia for the balance of French society, and above all, the danger for Muslims.[82] Islamophobia and its recognition as a public issue seem to go hand in hand, even if this form of racism has the benefit of very powerful producers and communicators in the media, politics, and civil service.

The significant "march against Islamophobia" held on Sunday 10 November 2019, which brought between 13,500 and 25,000 people onto the streets (according to the various estimates), would reflect both the widening and fragility of the anti-Islamophobia front. Run by a newly established organization, the Plate-forme L.e.s. Musulmans,[83] the event included the extreme left Nouveau parti anticapitaliste (NPA), the Comité Adama (the main organization campaigning against police violence), the Collectif contre l'islamophobie en France (CCIF), the Union communiste libertaire (UCL), the Union nationale des étudiants de France (Unef), the journalist Taha Bouhafs, and the former deputy mayor of Saint-Denis, Majid Messaoudene. Among the signatories of the appeal and taking part in the march were also long-standing allies, like academics Vincent Geisser, Eric Fassin, Etienne Balibar, and Sylvie Tissot, journalists Dominique Vidal, Rokhaya Diallo, and Alain Gresh, as well as organizations such as the Union juive française pour la paix (UJFP), Attac, the Union syndicale solidaires, and the Front uni des immigrations et des quartiers populaires (FUIQP), etc. Apart from the Parti socialiste, which had been significantly weakened after the 2017 presidential election and its 6.36 percent national vote, the leading figures of the left-wing parties were there. This list included Olivier Besancenot of the NPA, Yannick Jadot MEP and leader of the ecologist party, Europe-Ecologie Les Verts (EE-LV), Philippe Martinez, general secretary of the CGT union, several leading figures from the Parti communiste, the Antifa movement, and especially Jean-Luc Mélenchon. Also present was the entire parliamentary group of La France insoumise, the most popular left-wing party in the recent presidential election, a party that had hitherto stood out both by its refusal to use the word Islamophobia, and its anticlerical ideology. The success of this march, violently attacked by the entire political Right, the government, and the republicanist Left, evidenced the fragile but nevertheless enduring legitimacy of campaigns against Islamophobia in the French context.

Recognition or Denial? The Limits of the Fight against "Radicalization"

However, the line between recognition and denial is a thin one. Racism's existence can be acknowledged without providing the resources to fight it, while concealing the deep roots of structural racism. Indeed, while the French government appears to recognize Islamophobia, its security policy contributes heavily to the widespread suspicion cast over people presumed to be Muslims, via calls to "condemn" acts by ISIS, the available legal arsenal relating to "defending terrorism," the extension of police powers, the implementation of anti-"radicalization" strategies in state schools and social services, and the use of the state of emergency (to sanction raids and house arrests, the majority of which appear unfounded). It is therefore the neosecularist framing that prevails in interpreting political violence: instead of understanding its social and political underpinnings, it is analyzed as the symptom of a "sickness of Islam," to use Abdelwahab Meddeb and Abdenour Bidar's expression, the cure for which lies in the administration of a form of shock therapy comprised of classes in secularity. This neosecularist framing is a particularly powerful form of culturalism, obfuscating the genuine sources of political violence, which are the NATO powers' foreign policy and social and racial inequalities in Western societies.

In fact, the "Muslim community" is perceived as a homogenous group that is a breeding ground for political violence. The steps taken after the murders in 2015 are similar to forms of collective punishment insofar as this set of legal and bureaucratic tools feeds into the process of identifying any form of Muslim religiosity as an "indicator of radicalization." The concept of "radicalization," coined in sociology to account for the polarization and escalation of the level of (symbolic or physical) violence in political conflicts, has been distorted from its original meaning by the purveyors of expertise in Islam and terrorism. For example, the expertise produced by Dounia Bouzar, of the Centre de prévention des dérives sectaires en islam (Centre for the Prevention of Sectarian Excesses Related to Islam) and the private consultancy Bouzar Expertises became the unquestioned administrative norm within several ministries where she worked, in numerous state agencies, and local authorities responsible for protection and regulation of young people. Thus, wearing hijab, a beard, long robes, or headbands, the act of prayer, reading the Quran, being fastidious about food, fasting during Ramadan, etc. are perceived by many state agencies dealing with schools and social services as precursory signs of "radicalization" and political violence. This kind of expertise has contributed to deep religiosity being conflated with security threats.

Using the Anti-Terrorist Act of 13 November 2014, which inserted "defending terrorism" into the criminal code, the state prosecuted dozens of people, the overwhelming majority of whom had no link with armed groups identifying themselves with Islam (chapter 10).[84] We thus find ourselves in a particularly pernicious "double bind," of interdependence between actors who are simultaneously rivals and linked to each other, in a maelstrom from which it will be difficult to escape: imperialism feeds political violence, which fuels Islamophobia, and then itself feeds political violence, which fuels imperialism, etc. Political violence and Islamophobia need one another in order to propagate. ISIS and the Islamophobes share the idea of a clash of civilizations, of the incompatibility between "Islam" and "Republic," between "Muslims" and "Western society." Even without coordination, each one is in some way the political "service provider" of the other. It is therefore a matter of urgency for those who govern to commit themselves to a critical process in order to understand and act on the social and political bases of the violence. Edgar Allan Poe's fisherman in "A Descent into the Maelstrom," who is sucked down to the bottom of deep waters, overcomes his fear, sees how the vortex works, and manages to escape by holding on to floating cylindrical objects. Like Poe's fisherman, French elites should shake off their stunned response, their culturalism, and their Islamophobia to analyze the situation using tools provided by the social sciences and develop a policy that enables us to break out of the cycle of escalating violence.

Compensatory security policy, a genuine headlong rush, can lead only to the *point of no return*. As Norbert Élias stresses,

> There are processes in which the impression of impending danger is so inexorably overwhelming that most men become incapable of detaching themselves and controlling their fear, even if the process itself [. . .] still offers them the chance to take control of it and thus emerge unscathed. But there are also critical processes that are too advanced to allow those implicated in them any chance whatsoever of retaining their physical or psychic integrity, or even just surviving. As great as their detachment and their ability to reflect realistically could be, the process has, as far as they are concerned, reached a point of no return. Whatever they think and do, they cannot escape.[85]

CHAPTER 15

Lawyers in the Fight against Islamophobia

The equality of all human beings is one of the basic tenets of human rights. Article 1 of the Universal Declaration of Human Rights states that "all human beings are born free and equal in dignity and rights. They are endowed with reason and conscience and should act towards one another in a spirit of brotherhood." The struggle against racism and discrimination flows from the fight for human rights. Act no. 72–546 (1 July 1972) on the struggle against racism introduced into French law the principle of the illegality of discrimination on various grounds, one of which is religion. Then, under the impetus of the new European rules set out in the 2000s, French law armed itself with a stronger, more consistent legal arsenal.[1]

Once the legal norms had been established, the basic question was how they are put into practice, that is, their political value. The existence of a principle or protective rule does not mean that the state actually enforces it in practice. Various grounds for racism and discrimination are recognized by the law, but to what extent are they considered by civil society, the state, and the legal system? The rule in question and its legitimacy also have to be distinguished from one another. Political acknowledgement of a social ill influences the behavior of the actors involved in its prevention, manifestation, and repression. However, whether it is the word that describes it, the reality it covers, the symbolic status of its victims or the organizations that defend them, Islamophobia seems considerably discredited in contemporary France.[2]

This legitimacy/equality dialectic has structured the production, use, and application of antidiscrimination law when the presumed victims are Muslim. The production and use of the law always reflect a political power relationship favoring some social groups and disadvantaging others.[3] Inequalities before the law assume different forms, not restricted to the translation of class, gendered, or racialized relationships into criminal law.[4] Alongside the mechanisms of social filtering of those implicated by the legal system, it is essential to clarify the logics of the social filtering of victims, particularly those of racism and discrimination. In regard to the visible Muslim presence in France, we have emphasized that this plays out first and foremost around the definition of the secular norm and its legal contours, which have been constantly shifting since the late 1990s. The stakes of legitimacy deeply impact the way the law develops, the way it is deployed by victims and their defenders, and the way that hearings work. Indeed, for half a century, theorists of sociological jurisprudence have started from the premise that actors in the legal system, especially judges (regardless of their jurisdiction and positions), are driven by opinions and colored by representations and prejudices that influence both their desire to prosecute and the way they judge. In one of our research studies we encountered dozens of lawyers and other members of legal professions driven by legal disputes around Islamophobia in France.[5] They were keen to stress that they were operating in a context of profound mistrust and the undermining of Muslim populations. This political illegitimacy seemed first of all to be a source of restrictions of rights, through what we have described and analyzed as a process of gradual and organic "legal discrimination by a capillary-like process." As lawyer Elsa Bourdier also summarizes it,

> a slippage has thus occurred: starting from a protection for all (in 1905, the state was neutral so that everyone could practice their religion), to an obligation (in which neutrality is then applied to the users of a public service, in particular, schools), and finally to an order (where we have lost the principle of neutrality on the part of the state, which now inserts itself into the private sphere of religious practices, in naturalization procedures, for instance).[6]

The Fight against Islamophobia in the Courts?

The legitimacy of a cause and/or a category of victim are not the only factors that decide whether the criminal or civil law courts would be interested in pursuing a case. Several conditions must be met before a racist or discriminatory action is recognized and addressed as such. First, the victim must be clearly aware that there was a racist dimension to their experience; next, an official complaint is lodged; the complaint is recorded as such by the relevant officer and last, material evidence and testimonies corroborate the complaint. At issue are the choice to take action and the means of following up the complaint. On this point, the nature of the relationship between victim and respondent is decisive in the way these events are likely to be dealt with, given that "the lack of a relationship or a distant relationship seem to work in favor of a prosecution."[7]

In terms of the victims' relationship to legal bodies, the quality and clarity of the laws,[8] legal training, and awareness raising of police officers in relation to dealing with people bringing complaints about racist incidents are decisive in how complaints about racism, and plaintiffs themselves, are processed.[9] Within the criminal law framework, there must be an agreement between the police and the prosecutor about the charges arising from the racist and discriminatory dimension of an incident. As Abdellali Hajjat, Narguesse Keyhani, and Cécile Rodrigues emphasize, racist comments are covered by press freedoms in France, whose technical nature is obviously an obstacle to them being open to prosecution as such.[10] As this team of researchers explains, "Various factors influence this legal process: legal and political aspects, organizational and practical factors, the specific occupational definition of the racist situation, the type of racism, and the profiles of the respondent and the victim. This combination of factors has the effect of creating a hierarchy of more or less 'serious' offenses, but also, of the racisms that it is more or less legitimate to combat."[11]

In their article on how racist incidents are dealt with by the French criminal justice system, Hajjat, Keyhani, and Rodrigues's discussion of the lack of prosecutions shows there are several factors that favor the categorization of an incident as "no action taken" under the pretext that a racist offense is not confirmed as such. This is true for the overall number of cases that a court may hear. The striking observation in French criminal justice is that the volume of racist cases is very low, never exceeding 1 percent of the cases ruled on in the judiciary court (previously known as the criminal court): an area of litigation whose clearly secondary status can be partly explained by the organizational and human (staffing) limits specific to each court. A logic of "hierarchization of offenses deserving prosecution" flows from this. The anticipation of the rulings is another criterion of hierarchization of offenses, when prosecutors make the possibility of prosecution rest on the chances of getting a guilty verdict, which restricts the hearings of the cases in which there is still doubt over racist motivation.

The type of racism is another important factor, more directly tied to the subject of this article. According to Hajjat, Keyhani, and Rodrigues, there is an "implicit hierarchy of racisms and anti-racisms in which anti-Jewish and anti-Muslim racisms are in positions higher than other forms of racism, particularly anti–North African and anti-Black." Their study brings out the fact that cases in which Jews are targeted are thirty-nine times "more likely to be confirmed as racist than those not involving an anti-Jewish incident. Cases entailing anti-Muslim racism are eight times more likely to be confirmed as racist than cases with no anti-Muslim incident."[12]

At an institutional level, these differences can be explained by the raised awareness of successive governments and courts about the struggle against anti-Semitism, to which a number of Jewish and anti-racist organizations have actively contributed. The definition of the anti-racist struggle as a priority may be constructed at the national level, via criminal law policies driven by the government, but also at the local level, via in-house initiatives, or by taking local specifics into account. In the American courts, it has been demonstrated that the more the anti-racist cause is viewed as legitimate and worth investing in by prosecutors, the greater the chances of racism cases being addressed by the courts.[13] The perceived legitimacy of racism against Muslims is clearly weaker than that of anti-Semitism, even though the criminal courts' relative responsiveness to these incidents may be surprising, due to the discrediting of the struggle against Islamophobia in France and the not-for-profit organizations engaged in it. A more detailed analysis comparing the content of the incidents taken to court or categorized under each type of racism could be revealing. But above all we should be in a position to identify the scope of the litigation in cases based on discrimination in the civil courts, particularly those incidents that are dealt with, according to the lawyers we interviewed, via other legal categories of offense.

These stakes of legitimacy bound up with the status of the victims also come to the surface when the subject of observation is the victim's social and racial status. This seems to be "a variable that influences the legal process since, paradoxically, Arab and Black victims get less confirmation that offenses committed against them are racist than do white French victims," just as "crimes in which upper-class people are suspects are less likely to end with charges being brought than those with working or middle-class suspects. The higher up the social ladder the suspect is located, the less likely it is that the crime will result in charges or prosecution, which confirms a long tradition of French research on criminal justice system responses."[14] The notion that there are ideal types of "good victim" and "bad suspect" is far from new. The concept of the "ideal victim" was popularized by Norwegian criminologist Nils Christie, whose systematic analysis of stereotypes identified the normative and moral hierarchies underpinning the allocation of a victim's "quality."[15]

Political Illegitimacy and the Paradoxes of Campaigning via the Law

As Liora Israël reminds us, the law can be a weapon in struggles for equality.[16] However, after thirty years of judicialization and never-ending political debates on the "Muslim problem," the weapon of the law has been partly turned back on Muslims by enshrining a growing number of forms of discrimination.[17] The legitimization of this treatment, as illegal as it is differential, has helped accelerate the process of stripping value away from the strategy of using the law in the struggle against Islamophobia. The growing number of legal norms extending the duty of religious neutrality since the beginning of the twenty-first century has contributed to the increasingly rapid loss of efficiency in the strategy of fighting Islamophobia through the courts. The majority of lawyers in our sample agree that this situation has translated a series of political defeats conceded to marginal elites that advocate for the "extension of the new secularity" into the legal context.[18] How then can we understand the uninterrupted momentum of the use of the law in the struggle against Islamophobia? How do lawyers grasp the risks of a political backlash when they are prioritizing a legal strategy based on jurisprudence?

The lawyers interviewed have to a greater or lesser degree embraced a rather ambivalent discourse, both on the necessity and the dangers of a legal fight against Islamophobia. They consider that deploying the law enables a case to be publicized in order to provoke the broadest possible moral and political support. Through this type of case, "B," a lawyer at the Paris bar, thus wants to make "an impact, because often, in the media-centered society that we have nowadays, there has to be a trial to make the issue worth considering. So, it's already a tool for campaigning that allows a debate to be started [...] And regarding the ruling, that can actually lead to something concrete. That's how I think about my role as a lawyer and then the use of law in such campaigns." Ideally, the trial helps politicize the basic issues (freedom, equality, the position of minorities) and potential favorable rulings create legal anchors for the robust protection of subjugated groups. On a broader scale, they bolster human rights, individual freedoms, and freedom of conscience. However certain lawyers and their clients have seen their strategy of using the law to campaign backfire on them, and by extension, on the visible section of Muslim communities. The increasing number of such situations has altered the strategic vision of some of our interviewees, particularly the more experienced ones:

"B: Anyway, I really don't think the law is the ultimate solution. Or not the only solution, in any case. That seems obvious to me. My perspective on the law really has changed since I became a lawyer. My opinion on the use of the law really has changed. Those two things are not the same thing at all. You have to see what the law is in practice."

For many lawyers involved in the struggle against Islamophobia, the use of the law previously acclaimed is henceforth potentially seen as a kind of deadlock. Indeed, using the law to this end is a risky strategy even when it results in victory at the first level of courts, such is power and tenacity of political campaigns and government majorities—especially those on the right—that feel the reduction of rights and of the visibility of Muslims are prerequisites for state authority and "mutually tolerant coexistence." In fact, the number of referrals and therefore rulings on the restriction or reaffirmation of religious freedoms by the Conseil d'État and the Cour de cassation as well as by the EU courts, has risen noticeably since the turn of this century.

These lawyers have observed and are concerned about a steady erosion of their legal leeway in recent years, which indicates the limits of using the law as a campaigning tool. Bearing in mind the fact that the extension of the duty to remain neutral in public space to the private sector enjoys a strong majority in public opinion, and recalling a political context that makes discourses on inclusion, cosmopolitanism, and the complexity of visible Muslim practices barely comprehensible, most lawyers increasingly wonder about the durable political effects of this process of progressive legal disarmament:

MARWAN MOHAMMED (MM): In terms of analysis, do you think appealing to the Conseil d'État, the Cour de cassation, or the CEDH, etc., is a useful strategy?

"G." (LAWYER AT THE PARIS BAR): Well, it's a double-edged sword because if the law is against you . . . if the Conseil d'État rules against you. Politically, it's an utter catastrophe because they will always be able to use it against you. But in other cases, saying that the law protects me is to say that there are basic texts that govern how society works. They have to be complied with and when they are, you are respected. That is to say that you can't just do whatever you like. There are rules that regulate social relationships. They must be complied with. Therefore, if these rules don't exist anymore, then it's an utter catastrophe. Either you live in a dictatorship, or it's chaos.

MM: I ask because basically, all the cases that have been pushed, like Baby-Loup, via the case about wearing niqab that was ruled on by the CEDH, etc.—have all been defeated. And since 2003, this strategy has ended up in a restriction of freedoms.

"G.": Yes. That's right.

MM: Isn't that something that might lead to the nonprofit organizations and maybe the victims themselves (who often have other cultural or economic obstacles to get round) wondering, "If I go to court it might be disastrous for everyone?"

"G.": That's obvious. Like in the surgeon's case. We talked about it several times: are we doing this, or are we not doing this? It's risky because if the Conseil d'État says that the beard is a little over 5 cm, then it's religious and we've had it! It's clearly a risk that we're taking. But at the same time, we have to fight. We can't stand idly by [...] We've got our arguments and lower courts have not supported us. But the lower courts do not necessarily follow the arguments in texts. It's always a matter of interpretation. It's a battle. That's all.

In the last case referred to, a doctor from an Arab country, on a placement in a hospital in Île-de-France, refused to follow the orders of the director of that establishment, who had asked him to trim his beard, referring to the principle of religious neutrality. In the end, an administrative appeal court dismissed his case, and the doctor was fired by the hospital.[19] On 12 February 2020, the Conseil d'État ultimately ruled in favor of the plaintiff and therefore in favor of the lawyer's strategy. But other similar examples could be used to show how such cases have profoundly changed the law and actually helped undermine the legitimacy of the law and weakened its protective function, particularly in relation to public manifestation of religious affiliations.

Illegitimacy as a Constraint in Victims' Presentation of Self

Lawyers stress that the mechanisms operating in the social and political arenas also function within the legal one, with even higher risks of discrediting them. However, they also emphasize that the pressure bears more heavily upon the victims of discrimination whom they defend. The majority of these lawyers explain the hearings as follows: apart from the exceptional cases where a judge is known for their anti-racist probity, you should build your defense on the assumption that the judges are Islamophobic, or at least that there is a well-entrenched stock of negative opinions and prejudices at play. Faced with this situation various strategies are used depending on the case and the identity of the judge.

Agreeing to deny that Islamophobia is relevant enables some lawyers to defuse the way in which the hearing plays out when they realize that it might stand in the way of winning the case. One lawyer referred to the case of a Muslim woman, illegitimately dismissed for wearing a headscarf at the end of a working day, a case which—against all expectations—was lost in the employment tribunal. On appeal, the lawyer decided to deemphasize the Islamophobic aspect of the dismissal, by pleading that it was instead a wrongful termination of the employment contract. Another lawyer told us about the importance of a strategy of reducing the client's religious visibility before the court (for instance, if a female client wears a headscarf, this lawyer advises them to take it off for the courtroom). In this way, this attitude actually sanctions the prejudice by altering the appearance and attitude of the victim in order to win the case.

Other nonwhite lawyers, with Arab names, mainly from Muslim backgrounds, have to neutralize the implicit accusation of "playing the 'race' card." As one of them told us, "Here, when an Arab takes on an Arab [as a client], there are loads of comments about ethnic divisiveness and I feel like this gets taken out on the client a bit." In response, some try to refute the assumed suspicion of "playing the race card" by deploying such tactics as hiring a white lawyer or getting support from non-Muslim people and / or witnesses. On this point, another interviewee told us about a client for whom their non-Muslim work colleagues all attended an important day of the hearing together, which in that lawyer's mind was influential, as their client won the case. However, he says, "I think if I'd turned up [. . .] with fifteen guys with beards and ten women in headscarves, it wouldn't have had the same result." Therefore, to guarantee the legitimacy of a Muslim victim of discrimination, the presence of what he terms "normal people" was in his opinion the decisive factor. This anticipation of judges' Islamophobia stems from what is called "hearing norms" experienced firsthand, the political climate, and unenlightened opinions about Muslims, as well as the stakes of reputation specific to the legal world.

The climate of suspicion around Muslims has the effect of legitimizing the discrimination they experience. The very deeply entrenched conflation in public discourse between Islam (religious visibility) and Islamism makes hijab and the women wearing it highly suspect. Like several other lawyers, "B." identifies this very widespread link made by judges, between Muslims and Islamists. He explains that they do not see clients as believers but as activists, and that means, he argues "that the result is a different kind of sentencing than there is for other groups. That's clear." For those involved, this means having to explain and clarify their intentions, both in their private lives and in public, as well as in the courtroom. The fact that they are asked such questions, and that the motivations, desires, and intentions of women who wear the headscarf are under scrutiny comprises an invasive incitement for them to speak about their religious life, to justify their practices, and reveal intimate details of their faith.

This prompting to speak about intimate faith, which can be analyzed as orders to remove one's headgear morally, in order to avoid doing so physically, can be found among the clients of lawyers to whom we spoke.[20] One of them told us about how several of his headscarf-wearing clients spontaneously begin their stories by explaining the reasons why they wear hijab, without being asked or even urged to do so either by the judge or their lawyer (the majority of whom are often very embarrassed by this unveiling of intimate details). However, these demands for unveiling the intimate can be considered powerful markers of social illegitimacy, when being oneself has to be filtered through the neutralization of rejection and suspicion.

These "illegitimacy effects" are not always felt but are always feared. This influences the way in which lawyers prepare their clients for the legal process. No lawyer states that prejudice completely dominates the material elements of the case, eclipsing the nature of the exchanges. But most of them have had often-repeated experiences of inequality of treatment that might assume different forms. "B.," for instance, thinks not all judges—in the context of the press—conceptualize the public insults aimed at Islam and Muslims in the same way as they do those involving other groups, particularly Jews, who seem to be the baseline in terms of protection and legitimate victimhood. He feels that "discrimination relative to the fact that someone is Muslim, is located on the same level as the fact that someone is Jewish or a woman. In practice, it isn't so, but legally it's the same thing." Sometimes playing on the fact that he is himself from a Jewish background, he advocates an educational approach and is quick to use rhetorical devices highlighting what he sees, following the example of his colleagues, as unequal treatment. To neutralize the "illegitimacy effects" perceived to characterize certain judges in cases linked to press freedoms, he urges a pedagogical offensive against the judges: "Then come the various rhetorical techniques. The one I use is quite easy. The one I use is to say: 'You say that about Roms or Muslims, but would you say it about Jews? Would it be shocking for you? If it would shock you to hear it about one group, why wouldn't it shock you to hear it about the others?'"

"G." subscribes to a more uncompromising strategy in terms of arguments and support for his plaintiffs. He states that "some forms of discrimination are more unacceptable than others" and feels that "what would be called scandalous if it was used to refer to another community . . . is categorized as overzealous when referring to the Muslim community. Like I said, imagine that an engineer was suspended because they belonged to a Catholic church or not-for-profit, let's say the Secours catholique. They're told: 'You're in the Secours catholique. You go to such and such a priest. You're a threat to domestic security.' Or: 'You're Jewish. You visited such and such a Rabbi. It's over for you.' In my opinion this throws up a problem. We're fighting the zeitgeist, the general trends, the current environment that is quite hostile to Muslims." A lawyer from Strasbourg also thinks "everything covered by discrimination is subject to a type of interpretation that's more political than it is legal."

Lastly, even in cases that are won, where the victims are acknowledged as victims, some lawyers, among the most optimistic about the republican and egalitarian nature of the legal system, think that judges still exhibit clemency toward perpetrators of Islamophobic acts, compared to those targeting other social groups, through racism and various kinds of discrimination:

> LAWYER "M": Yes, when the case is solid of course, it is well received. A good
> reception means listening, and interest being shown. After that, the problem
> is usually in the sentencing. I think the sentences are too light.
> MM: For religious discrimination?
> "M": Yes. For cases involving Muslims.

Getting the perspectives of the lawyers we interviewed enabled us to observe the particular relationships and tensions between the law, its instrumentaliza-tion, and the political legitimacy of a cause. Since the late 1990s the use of legal means in the struggle against Islamophobia, especially discrimination affecting women wearing hijab, has contributed to a shift in the concept of protection. The blossoming of the "new laïcité," together with the political and legal successes accrued by its advocates, contextualizes the passage of a concept of protection that had prioritized protecting religious freedoms to one in which the struggle is now against a perceived underlying Islamist scene said to threaten society, and thus the capacity for "mutually tolerant coexistence," republican institutions, and women's rights. This cognitive and legal slippage, from a version of laïcité that protects individual freedoms, constructed around a neutral state, towards an approach influenced by the political emergency of neutralizing Islamism— regularly conflated with any Muslim religious visibility—has deeply marked national and European law and weakened legal strategies centering the struggle against Islamophobia. From stigmatized groups to the legislature, via the forces of law and order, lawyers and judges, controversies, campaigns, and political power relationships have each had an impact, through their way of addressing social and symbolic status—and thus the incidents reported by Muslims criticiz-ing Islamophobia. Lawyers find themselves and their clients at the intersection of these various levels and actors, and they face crucial choices in terms of strate-gies of using the law. All the lawyers we encountered argue in favor of political action that would enable them to transcend the limits of the legal struggle they encounter, but the practical contours of such strategic uses of the law appear very fluid. How indeed can you take action on behalf of a group constructed as a fifth column within the nation? How can you acknowledge the victim status of women wearing headscarves while the channel through which discrimination against them flows is widely constructed as a symbol of women's oppression and antirepublican conquest?

Against Islamophobic Hegemony

> Just as the Jews ignored completely the growing tension
> between state and society, they were also the last to be
> aware that circumstances had forced them into the center
> of the conflict. They therefore never knew how to evaluate
> antisemitism, or rather never recognized the moment when
> social discrimination changed into a political argument.
> For more than a hundred years, antisemitism had slowly
> and gradually made its way into almost all social strata in
> almost all European countries until it emerged suddenly as
> the one issue upon which an almost unified opinion could
> be achieved.
>
> —Hannah Arendt, *Antisemitism*

As these last lines are being written (March 2021), the radicalization of Islamophobic hegemony among the French "elites" can be illustrated by four
phenomena: an ideological overlap / proximity between the mainstream Right
and the Far Right, unprecedented since the Second World War; the extension
of the logic of suspicion regarding (those assumed to be) Muslims, via the "anti-
separatism" bill introduced by the government on 9 December 2020; the criminalization of anti-racist nonprofit organizations, culminating in the government
decree on the disbanding of the Collectif contre l'islamophobie en France, on
2 December 2020; and the opening up of a new Islamophobic field of struggle in
academia, around the fake debate on "Islamo-leftism," which is part of the project of challenging academic freedom.

Islamophobic Hegemony

The cross-party political nature of Islamophobia has been bolstered and is now articulated in every controversy relating to the Muslim presence in public space, just like the one sparked by an elected representative of the Far Right. On 11 October 2019, during a plenary session of the Bourgogne-Franche-Comté regional council (in the east of France), Julien Odoul, head of group and member of the national executive committee of Rassemblement national (formerly the Front national)—humiliated a woman in a headscarf who accompanied her teenage son on a school trip, whose theme was "My Republic and I." Despite her dignified attitude, the picture of this mother consoling her tearful son circulated in the media and triggered a delayed, ambiguous, and indignant pushback, a reminder that even when the Far Right commits the initial act of aggression, solidarity with women wearing headscarves cannot be expected. To explain his attitude, Julien Odoul used no explicitly xenophobic terms but justified what he had done in the name of "secular principle," and "the country's laws," before he and his colleagues published a press release condemning the "Islamist provocation" of women wearing hijab.[1]

Two days later, Minister of Education Jean-Michel Blanquer stated that although there was no law prohibiting this mother from being on the trip, and immediately added, "the headscarf itself is undesirable in our society, it's not something to be encouraged. What it says about the status of women does not match our values." Julien Odoul took the opportunity to affirm, "that's exactly what I said."[2] The minister also received support from former Socialist prime minister Manuel Valls, who said he was "totally" in agreement.[3] The Right also got its teeth into the matter, particularly through Nadine Morano, a member of the European Parliament for the right-wing Les Républicains party and former minister in the Nicolas Sarkozy administration, who said she was "in favor of banning hijab in the public sphere." Viewers also had the chance to hear the deputy editor of the right-wing daily paper *Le Figaro* state on news channel LCI that he "hated the Muslim religion" and that he refuses to stay on any bus if there is a woman wearing a headscarf on it. Moreover, LCI presenter Olivier Galzi compared the Islamic headscarf to an SS uniform.[4] On 22 October 2019, Éric Ciotti, a member of parliament for Les Républicains, submitted a bill aiming to ban parents accompanying their children on school trips from wearing conspicuous religious signs. The government refused to do so, although several MPs in the majority group, such as Aurore Bergé, said they would lend support to such a bill if the opportunity arose.[5] According to the account offered by the newspaper *Libération*, this issue was debated on television at least eighty-five times between 11 and 17 October 2019. Of the 286 people invited to participate, none was a hijab-wearing woman.[6]

Throughout this politico-media sequence, the Far Right, the mainstream Right, and various elements of the Left shared the same frameworks of understanding and vocabulary about Islam and Muslims. This was framed not as a confrontation between unchanging, white Catholic France and its unassimilable nonwhite, non-European populations but as the defense of an embattled "Republic" beset by "Islamism." As well as sharing vocabulary, political actors shared media and ideological staging posts.[7] It was thus not surprising to see the ubiquitous political scientist Laurent Bouvet agree to be interviewed on the far-right conspiracy theory website "Novopress"[8] or Patrick Kessel, honorary president of the Comité laïcité république (a spin-off from the fringes of the Grand Orient de France, one of the French freemasons' federations) responding to an invitation to appear on the far-right website Riposte laïque,[9] various presenters and contributors to which have several times been found guilty of incitement to racial and religious hatred as well as of glorifying terrorism. What can be said about the attitude of head of state Emmanuel Macron (and several of his ministers) who agreed to promote the far-right magazine *Valeurs actuelles*, created in 1966 by the fascist Raymond Bougrine,[10] by granting it a long interview during which he stated—referring to the humiliated mother incident—that "Julien Odoul got caught out. Apparently, this woman was closer to political Islam circles than was thought."[11] The president thus cast himself in the role of accusing a suspicious and duplicitous culture, characteristics that can be considered significant markers of contemporary Islamophobia.

Beyond the fact that the head of state here blames the victim and inverts the roles, he also validates the allegations of the regional elected members of the Rassemblement national that Julien Odoul had been the victim of "Islamist" manipulation. The president could have at least been expected to provide some evidence for these accusations, especially in the columns of a press outlet spearheading the dissemination of racist ideas and opinions in France. The "Islamist" manipulation theory was later patiently contradicted by an investigation by the newspaper *Libération*,[12] in which the head of the local branch of the FCPE (Parents' Association) stipulated that "it was exactly because we had so few volunteers that Fatima E. ended up going on the school trip in Dijon. She was not originally supposed to take part." She had been moving homes and could not find childcare for her daughter, but managed to do a favor for the teacher who had organized the trip. The reality is far from the numerous accusations of "Islamism" and duplicity, encouraged by the president, voices from the Left and Far Right, and numerous journalists and polemicists who criminalized and demonized this

mother on television and radio programs and social media, identifying the hijab
as a marker of commitment to "Political Islam" and "Islamism."

Extending the Logic of Suspicion

Although the solutions proposed for the "Muslim problem" differ according
to the various strands of the Islamophobic bloc (the Far Right seeks to exclude
Muslims from France, the "Republicans" keep promulgating exclusionary laws
within society and advocate cultural assimilation), the notable convergence of
their discursive and political strategies manifests itself in shared discourses and
struggles, coalitions to pass legislation, and sometimes electoral alliances, but
above all, by extending the logic of suspicion. There is thus a consensus over
the idea that visible Muslims are dangerous "Islamists" and "fundamentalists"
accused of fueling terrorism by promoting a "discourse of victimhood." The
use of shaming categories also targets those who pose questions about the role
of racial dynamics in French society or organize on the basis of their minority
positioning. Free from the constraints of having to refer to actual social realities, a system of equivalence and the use of fluid and blurred categories enables
the entrepreneurs of Islamophobia to present themselves as "universalists" protecting French society from "ethnic divisiveness" and to claim that their fight
was not with Muslims but with "Islamism," the "Salafists," the "Muslim brotherhood" or, to use a fashionable expression, with "political Islam." Thanks to
solid media and political messengers (such as former Socialist prime minister
Manuel Valls and current ministers Jean-Michel Blanquer, Gérald Darmanin,
and Marlène Schiappa), they have successfully planted the idea that behind every headscarf-wearing woman, every nonprofit volunteer, every activist fighting
Islamophobia, and every public statement of Muslim-ness is a hidden masculine
backstage world whose aim is to Islamize French society. Lastly, given that these
categories serve to evoke an enemy within, this boils down to considering any
form of Muslim affirmation in public space as an attack on Frenchness, democracy, and republicanism. This highly potent suspicion-casting, criminalizing,
and excluding machine is based on a form of Islamophobic conspiracy theory
that is not grasped as such.[13]

It is therefore unsurprising that it has become so easy to confuse visible signs
of religiosity with signs of radicalization, or that this is done at the highest levels
of state. Just to give one example, after the 2019 murders of four officials in the
state intelligence department by a colleague who had converted to Islam, the
debate on ways to identify violent "radicalization" took off again. Since 2015 so-
called experts and public authorities had developed strategies for identification

and warning, whose criteria were regularly criticized for their academic frailties and their normativity, which sometimes turned out to be discriminatory and damaging to civil liberties.[14] When he gave a statement to the National Assembly's commission on laws after these dreadful killings, which had also been humiliating for the state, Minister of the Interior Christophe Castaner sought to adopt a stance embodying a state on the offensive, stating that a "hardline religious practice, particularly exacerbated in relation to Ramadan, is a sign that should enable a warning about such people to be triggered." He also emphasized that a "change in behavior, or in the group someone spends time with, wearing a beard," whether someone "used to greet others with kisses, and no longer does so," or "a regular or conspicuous practice of ritual prayer" could all be considered signs of "radicalization."[15]

This understanding of what "radicalization" means often goes hand in hand with the use of the notion of "Islamization," which is part of the Far Right's repertoire. It is frequently referred to by academics close to power like political scientists Gilles Kepel and Bernard Rougier,[16] who are the main promoters, in the political and media spheres, of the ideas of "conquest," "domination," and "Islamist ecosystem" in the working-class suburbs.[17] They propagate the idea of an underground continuum that allegedly comprises terrorism claiming justification in Islam, the plurality of the existing forms of Islamism in France, anti-Islamophobia activism, as well as any institutionalized presence of Islam (e.g., sandwich bars, halal butchers, religious bookshops, sports clubs and organizations, or those dedicated to humanitarian objectives or those including equality at school, etc.) or of dress codes connected with it. As Laurent Bonnefoy emphasizes, regarding Bernard Rougier, "the general approach is to ignore interactions between these Islamist movements on one hand, and general society and its institutions on the other. The situation in which Muslims find themselves in French society, and the difficulties they have inherited from colonial history are never included in the analysis. That some of them turn their backs on society can thus only ever be the outcome of Islamist ideologies at work behind the scenes. Discrimination and obvious Islamophobia in both media representations and state policies figure only in this scenario as epiphenomena, of secondary importance vis-à-vis 'conquering' Islamist agit-prop."[18] It is far from surprising that these two academics took part in the drafting of the law "reinforcing Republican principles" passed in the National Assembly on Tuesday 17 February 2021, before being introduced into the Senate on 30 March.

Following a logic unconnected to reality, this law posited a weak Republic facing down a powerful "Islamism." This had entailed "divisive infiltration, insidious yet powerful," which "has gradually corrupted the foundations of our society in some areas [. . .] It is the manifestation of a deliberate, theorized and politico-religious project, whose objective is to have religious norms prevail over the common law ones that we freely gave ourselves." In the wake of "studies" by Kepel and Rougier, "Islamism" is presumed to be at play everywhere that Muslims are visible, maintaining its "efforts to undermine that extend to many spheres; neighborhoods, public services, particularly schools, the voluntary sector, and the structures governing worship."[19] By authorizing—via metonymy—the targeting of visible and organized Muslims under the pretext of targeting "Political Islam" or "Islamist separatism," the wide-ranging extension of the logic of suspicion has bolstered an Islamophobic consensus that paradoxically plays directly into the hands of the "jihadist" ideologues and groups that really do hate France, while obscuring the chances of genuinely scientific knowledge about Islamist phenomena.

This law is unprecedented in terms of the changes it will entail and the variety of areas of personal and public life that come under its remit. It continues to extend the duty of religious neutrality to private organizations, and state powers are strengthened by the allocation of public grants and authorizations, including when they emanate from local authorities. Préfets also have the right to monitor and censor the legal organization of not-for-profit organizations linked to religion and, more broadly, across the entire voluntary sector that will be subject to a "Republican contract" setting out criteria for access to specific resources.[20] Beyond these attacks on freedom of worship and association, and on the principle of separating church and state, which will firstly impact Muslim nonprofit organizations, family education is also targeted with significant restrictions added to home schooling since it now has to be authorized by local authorities, whereas previously, it had only to be declared. Besides, the conditions for disbanding nonprofits have been made much more flexible, opening up the path to criminalizing a greater number of nonprofit organizations and activist groups whose aims displease whoever holds power.

Criminalizing Anti-Racist Organizations: The Case of the CCIF

Another phenomenon illustrating Islamophobic radicalization is the criminalization of anti-racist not-for-profits fighting Islamophobia, particularly the CCIF, which was disbanded on 2 December 2020. This was the first time since the Vichy régime, which targeted Jewish organizations, that the French government had disbanded an anti-racist not-for-profit. This type of exceptional measure is generally used against far-right or jihadist groups that—through their actions or their publications—incite racial hatred or organize themselves into private violent militia. CCIF members were therefore stupefied to hear Minister of the Interior Gérald Darmanin (of the governing La République en marche party) announce the plan to disband their organization the day after the murder of history teacher Samuel Paty by the jihadist Abdoullakh Anzorov in Conflans-Sainte-Honorine (northwest of Paris) on 16 October 2020. The CCIF had allegedly become an "enemy of the Republic." In fact, it was in no way responsible for or complicit in this murder, but the fact that the CCIF had been mentioned during the case was the pretext that the government used to finally disband the organization.

Indeed, since the CCIF was set up, in 2003, it had been subjected to repeated campaigns of vilification by certain public actors (journalists, politicians, academics, etc.) who most often deny the existence of Islamophobia and have even been key propagators of Islamophobia in the public realm. Insofar as the CCIF was the main anti-Islamophobia organization in France, it is hardly surprising to find Islamophobia-deniers attempting to discredit it. Casting aspersions on the CCIF's reputation and the work it carried out, and turning the organization itself into a political issue, is a way to deny Islamophobia. The CCIF had thus been in a paradoxical situation for a long time: on one hand it was lambasted by Islamophobic public figures, and on the other, it enjoyed forms of national and international recognition, particularly due to its collaborations with French Muslim and non-Muslim not-for-profit organizations, the Commission nationale consultative sur les droits de l'homme, (CNCDH), the United Nations, and several European Union institutions.

This tension between being politically undermined and institutionally recognized had been tested since the 2015 terrorist attacks and the multiple legal battles it had fought. The CCIF had first been unfairly criticized for its supposed links with the Muslim Brotherhood, without these ever being clearly specified or the nature of the relationship being established. CCIF statistics on Islamophobia were challenged by journalists such as Caroline Fourest and Isabelle Kersimon, who had no qualms about lying to convince the public.[21] The most well-known Islamophobes, like racist polemicist Éric Zemmour and the far-right leader Marine Le Pen, were taken to court by the CCIF and, sometimes, convicted by French courts. The right-wing and far-right press then labeled these prosecutions "legal jihad," establishing an imaginary link between the CCIF's *cause-lawyering* and the terrorist acts carried out in France.

However, the CCIF categorically condemned all the attacks committed on French soil that claimed Islamic justification. It is definitely because the CCIF demarcated itself very clearly from jihadist elements that the vilifying discourse rarely led to the idea that it should be disbanded. Yet this is what happened in October 2020, following Abdoullakh Anzorov's murder of Samuel Paty. Anzorov had targeted the teacher because Brahim Chnina, the father of one of Paty's pupils, had accused him, in a Facebook video, of having shown obscene cartoons of the Prophet Muhammad in class. When he accused Paty, Chnina had mentioned the CCIF as an organization to contact in order to condemn what he saw as Islamophobia. The CCIF was contacted by Chnina and had asked him to take down the video from social media so that a resolution could be sought via mediation. But Chnina did not take this advice and the video ended up in the hands of Anzorov, who thus found the target for his murderous tendencies.

Following the publication of the decree disbanding the CCIF, one might have expected a significant outcry from not-for-profits and political organizations advocating civil liberties. But the responses were very timid. A few newspaper articles in *Libération*, *Le Monde* and *Mediapart* set out the facts exonerating the CCIF, but these stories were not picked up and did not circulate within the other mass media. In the political field, only a few far-left parties reacted (Nouveau parti anticapitaliste and La France Insoumise), while the mainstream right-wing parties warmly greeted the news. In the voluntary sector, a few human rights organizations, such as the Ligue des droits de l'homme, l'Union juive française pour la paix, the GISTI (Groupe d'information et de soutien des immigrés, Immigrant Information and Support Group), the Syndicat des avocats de France (French Lawyer's Union), and European Network against Racism, etc., criticized an attack on the freedom of association and the establishment of the offense of "holding opinions." The weakness and tentativeness of the criticisms of the disbanding of the CCIF thus reveal the state of the basic freedoms in France in the 2020s, where a government is capable of producing a deliberately misleading discourse about an anti-racist organization without it triggering a political or media outcry.

Threats to Academic Freedoms: Censorship in the Name of Free Speech

While Islamophobic hegemony has led to a challenge to the freedoms of association and opinion, it has also affected academic freedoms. When Islamophobia became an ideology widely shared by French political and media elites at the turn of the twenty-first century, any alternative anti-Islamophobia discourse has since been subjected to a racist reprimand. Since anti-Islamophobia activists are constantly discredited, it is not surprising that this discrediting has been extended to academics who have formulated a critical analysis of Islamophobia.

Thus, the accusation of "Islamo-leftism," hitherto reserved for Muslim activists and their non-Muslim allies, is increasingly leveled at academics, perceived as "accomplices" and "useful idiots" of political violence linked to Islam.

This concept was minted in the early 2000s by far-right intellectual Pierre-André Taguieff.[22] It was supposed to give a name to the alliance between European far-left activists and Islamist activists in the context of the anti-Zionist cause within which, according to Taguieff, the "new Judeophobia" is concealed. Anti-Zionism and anti-Semitism are thus understood as synonyms. While that analysis does not correspond to the facts,[23] this concept became increasingly successful in the French public domain, to the point that after the Paris attacks of 2015, academics working on Islamophobia were labeled "Islamo-leftists" and accused of justifying the massacre of *Charlie Hebdo* journalists. The concept of "Islamo-leftist" also entails a racist dimension because it is an aspect of the racialization of academics (assumed to be) Muslims, like the authors of this book, whose research is allegedly then not "objective" and pursues a hidden "activist agenda" from the very heart of academia.

This is how the theory of the Muslim plot, which had hitherto been reserved for political and activist spaces, reached the academy. From autumn 2016, press outlets such as *Le Point*, *L'Express*, *L'Obs*, *Marianne*, *Valeurs actuelles*, *Le Figaro*, *Charlie Hebdo*, etc., published increasingly frequent headlines about Islamo-leftism and, more broadly, on critical race theories and gender studies. Basing themselves on the examples of "Free Speech" campaigns carried out in the USA since the 1980s,[24] the whole raft of anti-racist and feminist critical thinking, developed and taught in universities and research centers, was characterized as the "enemy of the Republic." This vilification campaign aimed at critical thinking in universities gained allies in academia, particularly those involved in the tiny neosecular far-right Le Printemps républicain (Republican Spring) and the Vigilance Universités network, which drew up lists of academics and research projects deemed "deviant" and "anti-republican."

This militant activism by journalists and reactionary academics had not managed to get any political foothold until the day after Samuel Paty's murder, when Minister of Education Jean-Michel Blanquer adopted the conspiracy theory discourse about Islamo-leftism, and right-wing deputies Julien Aubert and Damien Abad (Les Républicains) called (in vain) for a parliamentary enquiry to be set up to investigate "ideological intellectual excesses in academic circles." A few months later, in February 2021, it was the turn of Minister for Higher Education and Research Frédérique Vidal, to pick up the baton on this conspiracy theory by asking Alliance Athéna a social science research body, to carry out a study of "Islamo-leftism in universities."

In other words, an alliance between journalists, academics, and reactionary political actors has brought about a genuine attack on academic freedoms. This desire for power and control over social science research is similar to the practices of the most authoritarian contemporary political regimes (Viktor Orbán in Hungary, Jair Bolsonaro in Brazil, Shinzō Abe in Japan, Recep Tayyip Erdoğan in Turkey, etc.). In response, thousands of academics, professional social science associations, and important institutions, such as the Conférence des présidents d'université (the group representing the heads of French universities) and the Centre national de la recherche scientifique (national academic research body), protested in the strongest terms against this constraint on research, even if they tended to underestimate the racist dimension of the concept of Islamo-leftism. However, if the mechanisms of Islamophobia analyzed in this book are not thwarted by a huge social and political campaign in favor of basic freedoms and the maintenance of the rule of law, there is an ominous possibility that the wind of reaction blowing through French society will end very badly, as the history of the twentieth century unfortunately demonstrates.

Breaking with Essentialism

Our critical analysis of the modalities and effects of the construction of the "Muslim problem" obviously does not mean that sociopolitical phenomena linked to "Islam" should not be studied. For example, political violence claiming justification through Islam and the activism of movements advocating a radical rupture with the rest of society are, of course, topics to be analyzed. However, unlike the strategy of ideologues, so-called experts, and certain politicians promoting racializing interpretations of Muslim agency, we believe the numerous stakes bound up with Muslim identity require a "profane" strategy of enquiry, that is, an analysis that, as in the canonical expression of sociologist Émile Durkheim, explains a social fact by reference to a social fact (historical, economic, social, and political factors). This approach, as exemplified by the work of Fabien Truong (on Amédy Coulibaly),[25] Laurent Bonelli and Fabien Carrié (on "radicalized" young people),[26] and Montassir Sakhi (on French jihadists in ISIS),[27] means rejecting the assumed religious "essence" of the action observed and thinking hard about how the term "Muslim" is deployed by social actors. This perspective breaks with the trend of the "political analyst" and security expertise that has legitimized the dominant political alarmism about Islam, by reducing Muslim populations, their desires, and their individual and collective practices to a purely "religious" motivation for action. In other words, it seems to us a necessary and urgent matter to reject the processes by which the plurality and complexity of social identities borne by Muslims is crushed, with the "Muslim" shrunk into a (one-dimensional) difference perceived as definitively dangerous. This essentialization of the "Muslim"—as in previous periods when the "immigrant" and the "beur" were essentialized—is one of the keystones of Islamophobia.

If we are referring here to phenomena as extreme as the use of terrorism, and we cite the names of researchers who have taken the care to distinguish themselves from essentialist readings, it is in order to more effectively encourage all observers to adopt similar strategies when they address social practices that appear to be "religious," such as the wearing of the kippa, of the hijab, of the crucifix, or the beard. These social facts should not be automatically envisaged as "problems." In most cases they are merely mundane manifestations of cultural and religious pluralism in a democratic society. The extent of the "Muslim problem" is above all a matter of perception: the more hostile and restrictive one's perception of the Other, the more serious the "Muslim problem" appears. Yet the problem is probably less "Muslim" than we imagine.

NOTES

INTRODUCTION

1. One of the particularities of Islamophobia in France is that much of it emanates from those identifying with the Left. See T. Peace, "Islamophobia and the Left in France," in I. Zempi and I. Awan (eds.), *The Routledge International Handbook of Islamophobia* (Abingdon: Routledge, 2019), 110–122.

2. F. Gil, *Traité de l'évidence* (Grenoble: J. Millon, 1993).

3. For the philosopher Spinoza, "sad" passions like hatred, anger, violence, and fear led mankind into a state of servitude and mental passivity.

4. M-A. Valfort, *Discriminations religieuses à l'embauche: Une réalité* (Paris: Institut Montaigne, 2015).

5. R. Liogier, *Le mythe de l'islamisation: Essai sur une obsession collective* (Paris: Seuil, 2012).

6. The reader should refer to the opinion polls carried out for the Commission nationale consultative des droits de l'homme (CNCDH—National Consultative Commission on Human Rights, a government agency).

7. J. Dakhlia and B. Vincent (eds.), *Les musulmans dans l'histoire de l'Europe* (Paris: Albin Michel, 2011).

8. A. Hajjat, *Les frontières de l'"identité nationale": L'injonction à l'assimilation en France métropolitaine et coloniale* (Paris: La Découverte, 2012).

9. J. Maclure and C. Taylor, *Laïcité et liberté de conscience* (Paris: La Découverte, 2010).

10. J. Bauberot, *Laïcité 1905–2005, entre passion et raison* (Paris: Le Seuil, 2004).

11. A. Barb, "La laïcité en France et aux États-Unis: Perspectives historiques et enjeux contemporains," *Questions internationales* 76 (November–December 2015): 90.

12. Barb, "La laïcité en France," 90.

13. Jacques Chirac, 19 June 1991, quoted by M. Peyrot, "La plainte du MRAP contre M. Chirac: Le procès des 'odeurs,'" *Le Monde*, 31 January 1992.

14. On radio station France Inter in 1997, quoted by Pierre Tevanian and Sylvie Tissot, *Mots à maux: Dictionnaire de la lepénisation des esprits* (Paris: Dagorno, 1998), 114.

15. D. Sénécal, "Entretien avec Michel Houellebecq," *Lire*, 1 September 2001 (accessible at http://www.lexpress.fr).

16. M. Houellebecq, *Plateforme* (Paris: Flammarion, 2001), 260.

17. O. Fallaci, *La rage et l'orgueil* (Paris: Plon, 2002), 137–138.

18. Fallaci, *La rage et l'orgueil*, 140 and 146.

19. A. Finkielkraut, "Fallaci tente de regarder la réalité en face," *Le Point*, 24 May 2002 (accessible at www.lepoint.fr).

20. P-A. Taguieff, *Actualité juive*, 20 June 2002.

21. R. Misrahi, *Charlie Hebdo*, November 2002 issue.

22. R. Millet, *Langue fantôme suivi de Éloge littéraire d'Anders Breivik* (Paris: P.-G. de Roux, 2012).

23. *Ce soir ou jamais!* France 3, 7 February 2012.

24. *Frances Infos*, 26 March 2012.

25. J-F. Copé, *Manifeste pour une droite décomplexée* (Paris: Fayard, 2012), 41.

26. O. Fallaci, *La rage et l'orgueil*; A. Del Valle, *Le totalitarisme islamiste à l'assaut des démocraties* (Geneva: Éditions des Syrtes, 2002); T. M. Savage, "Europe and Islam: Crescent Waxing, Cultures Clashing," *Washington Quarterly* 27, no. 3 (2004): 25–50; B. Ye'or, *Eurabia: The Euro-Arab Axis* (Madison, N.J.: Farleigh Dickinson University Press, 2005); M. Phillips, *Londonistan: How Britain Is Creating a Terror State Within* (London: Encounter Books, 2006); C. Caldwell, *Reflections on the Revolution in Europe: Immigration, Islam, and the West* (London: Penguin, 2009); R. S. Leiken, *Europe's Angry Muslims: The Revolt of the Second Generation* (Oxford: Oxford University Press, 2011); R. S. Leiken, "Europe's Immigration Problem, and Ours," *Mediterranean Quarterly* 15, no. 4 (2004): 203–18.

27. See I. Jablonka, "La peur de l'islam: Bat Ye'or et le spectre de l'"Eurabie,'" *La Vie des idées*, 1 May 2006, available at www.laviedesidees.fr; Liogier, *Le mythe de l'islamisation*.

28. M. Tribalat, "Islam et immigration face au déclin démographique européen: Derrière les fantasmes, la vérité des chiffres," *Atlantico*, 17 October 2012, available at www.atlantico.fr.

29. M. Vianès, *Les Islamistes en manoeuvre: Silence, on manipule* (Paris: Hors commerce, 2004), 21.

30. Vianès, *Les islamistes en manœuvre*, 60.

31. C. Tasin, "Que faire des musulmans une fois le Coran interdit?," *Boulevard Voltaire*, 1 March 2013, available at www.bvoltaire.fr.

32. See V. Amiraux, "Islamophobie," in A. Bihr and R. Pfefferkorn (eds.), *Dictionnaire des inégalités* (Paris: Armand Colin, 2013).

33. M. Mauss, "Essai sur le don: Forme et raison de l'échange dans les sociétés archaïques," in *Sociologie et anthropologie* (1923; Paris: PUF, 1966), 274.

34. E. Terray, "La question du voile: Une hystérie politique," *Mouvements*, no. 32 (2004): 96–104.

35. See J. Marelli, "Usages et maléfices du thème de l'antisémitisme en France," in N. Guénif-Souilamas (ed.), *La République mise à nu par son immigration* (Paris: La Fabrique, 2006), 133–159.

36. N. Elias, "Notes sur les juifs en tant que participant à une relation entre établis-marginaux," in *Norbert Elias par lui-même* (Paris: Fayard, 1991), 152. Our emphasis.

37. Elias, "Notes sur les juifs," 31.

38. P. Bourdieu, "Un problème peut en cacher un autre," in *Interventions 1961–2001: Science sociale & action politique* (Marseille: Agone, 2002), 305.

39. A. Sayad, "'Coûts' et 'profits' de l'immigration," *Actes de la recherche en sciences sociales*, no. 61 (1986): 79–82.

40. See R. Castel, *La discrimination négative: Citoyens ou indigènes?* (Paris: Seuil, 2007).

41. L. Mathieu, *L'espace des mouvements sociaux* (Bellecombe-en-Bauges: Éditions du Croquant, 2012).

CHAPTER 1. Islamophobia as a Social Ordeal

1. CCIF, reports for 2003–2012, available at https://web.archive.org/web /20201126184431/http://www.islamophobie.net/rapports-ccif/.

2. H. Asal, "Islamophobie: La fabrique d'un nouveau concept. État des lieux de la recherche," *Sociologie* 5, no. 1 (2014): 13–29.

3. V. Amiraux, "Existe-t-il une discrimination religieuse des musulmans en France?," *Maghreb/Machrek*, no. 183 (2005): 67–81.

4. For a relatively exhaustive list, consult the CCIF reports, available at https://web .archive.org/web/20201126184431/http://www.islamophobie.net/rapports-ccif/, and those by the CNCDH, available at www.cncdh.fr.

5. F. Fregosi, "Mosquées et salles de prière en France," in M. Flores-Lonjou, and F. Messner (eds.), *Les lieux de culte en France et en Europe: Statuts, pratiques, fonctions* (Louvain: Peeters, 2007), 243–268.

6. As evidenced by attacks on Sikhs.

7. We currently know little about the social, economic, and psychological effects of this steady and continuous restriction of the individual freedoms of French Muslim women who wear hijab.

8. All the following examples are drawn from the CCIF reports, the only ones to try and obtain an overview of Islamophobic acts in France.

9. See the Maman toutes égales collective's website, www.mamanstoutes-egales.com.

10. A. Hajjat, *Les frontières de l'identité nationale: L'injonction à l'assimilation en France métropolitaine et coloniale* (Paris: La Découverte, 2012).

11. N. Keyhani, C. Rodrigues, A. Celestine, S. Delarre, S. Laplanche-Servigne, and A. Hajjat, "Des paroles et des actes: La justice face aux infractions racistes," 2018, http:/ /www.gip-recherche-justice.fr/publication/des-paroles-et-des-actes-la-justice-face-aux -infractions-racistes/.

12. On the most routine forms of Islamophobia, see the book by journalist N. Henni-Moulaï, *Petit précis de l'islamophobie ordinaire* (Paris: Les Points sur les I, 2012).

13. R. Castel, *La discrimination négative: Citoyens ou indigènes?* (Paris: Seuil, 2007).

14. I. Chouder, M. Latrèche, and P. Tevanian, *Les filles voilées parlent (Paris: La Fabrique, 2008).

15. M. L. Fernando, *The Republic Unsettled: Muslim French and the Contradictions of Secularism* (Durham: Duke University Press, 2014).

16. F. Dubet, O. Cousin, E. Macé, and S. Rui, *Pourquoi moi? L'expérience des discriminations* (Paris: Seuil, 2013).

17. K. Zebiri, "The Redeployment of Orientalist Themes in Contemporary Islamophobia," *Studies in Contemporary Islam*, no. 10 (2008): 4–44; M. Franks, "Crossing the Borders of Whiteness? White Muslim Women Who Wear the Hijab in Britain Today," *Ethnic and Racial Studies* 23, no. 5 (2000): 917–929; E. Özyürek, *Being German, Becoming Muslim:*

Race, Religion, and Conversion in the New Europe (Princeton, N.J.: Princeton University Press, 2015); P. Kuppinger, *Faithfully Urban: Pious Muslims in a German City* (New York: Berghahn Books, 2015); M. H. Rogozen-Soltar, *Spain Unmoored: Migration, Conversion, and the Politics of Islam* (Bloomington: Indiana University Press, 2017).

18. See Zebiri, "Redeployment of Orientalist Themes," 34.

19. Dubet et al., *Pourquoi moi?*, 11.

20. C. Beauchemin, C. Hamel, M. Lesné, P. Simon, et al., "Les discriminations: Une question de minorités visibles," *Population et sociétés*, no. 466 (2010); EU-Midis, *Enquête de l'Union européenne sur les minorités et la discrimination: Données en bref—les musulmans*, 2010 (accessible at http://fra.europa.eu/eu-midis).

21. Which enables us to distinguish or articulate what is due to personal dispositions (psychological, social, cultural and even religious) from what is more specifically due to resources (economic, legal), the relationship to institutions and more pressingly, from what is due to the assessment of facts (serious or not, material elements available for mobilization, etc.). It is also likely that the defiance emerging from the public pronouncements of high-level political figures acts as an effective brake: public acknowledgement of harm suffered is a powerful basis for legitimization and commitment for the victims.

22. Dubet et al., *Pourquoi moi?*, 13.

23. P. Cuturello, "Discrimination: Faire face ou faire avec? Le(s)sens du mot discrimination chez les jeunes d'origine maghrébine," *Agora Débats/Jeunesse*, no. 57 (2011): 63–78.

24. We are thinking here of the Muslim "Fils de France" (Sons of France) movement, which engages in the promotion of patriotism that is so far rare in the public vocabulary and debate. For the leaders of this movement, the fight against Islamophobia shows a victim mentality.

25. Dubet et al., *Pourquoi moi?*, 16.

26. This theory is worth taking seriously, whether it is in relation to immigrants or French people of immigrant origin, whose "double exile," expatriation, and the "hejira" toward Muslim or other Western countries (especially Great Britain) is thought to be motivated by the experience of Islamophobia.

27. Dubet et al., *Pourquoi moi?*, 93.

28. A. Sen, *Identité et violence* (Paris: Odile Jacob, 2007).

29. F. Fanon, *Peau noire, masques blancs* (Paris: Seuil, 1952).

30. Dubet et al., *Pourquoi moi?*, 82.

31. A. T. Ahmed, S. A. Mohammed, and D. R. Williams, "Racial Discrimination and Health: Pathways and Evidence," *Indian Journal of Medical Research*, no. 126 (2007): 318–327.

32. Dubet et al., *Pourquoi moi?*, 85.

33. Fanon, *Peau noire, masques blancs*; A. Memmi, *Portrait du colonisé, précédé de portrait du colonisateur* (Paris: Éditions Corréa, 1957). This has been translated as *The Colonized and the Colonizer.*

CHAPTER 2. Measuring Islamophobia

1. V. Amiraux and M. Leghmizi, *Monitoring Minority Protection in EU Member States, Focus on France* (Open Society Institute, 2004), available at www.opensocietyfoundations .org; C. Allen and J. Nielsen, *Summary Report on Islamophobia in the EU after 11 September 2001* (EUMC, 2002), available at http://fra.europa.eu.

2. Observatoire européen des phénomènes racistes et xénophobes, "Les musulmans au sein de l'Union européenne: Discrimination et islamophobie," 2006.

3. For an insight into these surveys and a synthesis of work on the measurement of origins, see O. Masclet, *Sociologie de la diversité et des discriminations* (Paris: Armand Colin, 2012), 35–57.

4. For an example of how this data is used, see E. Bleich, "Where Do Muslims Stand on Ethno-Racial Hierarchies in Britain and France? Evidence from Public Opinion Surveys, 1988–2008?," *Patterns of Prejudice* 43, no. 3–4 (2009): 379–400; M. Helbling, *Islamophobia in Western Europe and North America* (London: Routledge, 2011); M. Helbling, "Islamophobia in Switzerland: A New Phenomenon or a New Name for Xenophobia," in S. Hug and H. Kriesi (eds.), *Value Change in Switzerland* (Lanham: Lexington Press, 2010), 65–80.

5. Although these same assumptions are also spread within the discipline of sociology and especially political science.

6. H. Dekker and J. Van Der Noll, "Islamophobia and Its Explanation," in Helbling, *Islamophobia*, 113.

7. A theory based on the idea that frequent contact between groups fosters the spread of positive emotions and the emergence of more empathetic stances. For an overview of intergroup theories, see T. Pettigrew, "Intergroup Contact Theory," *Annual Review of Psychology* 49 (1993): 65–85.

8. Dekker and Van Der Noll, "Islamophobia and Its Explanation."

9. The most radical critiques were made by Alain Morice and Véronique De Rudder. According to them, the CNCDH polls should be stopped as "the responses are induced by the questions (their content, but also the choice of words, and how the sentences are constructed)" and because "the questionnaire does not measure racism but [...] produces it, and is itself impregnated with this ideology." A. Morice, "Du seuil de tolérance au racisme banal, ou les avatars de l'opinion fabriquée," *Journal des anthropologues*, nos. 110–111 (2007): 382.

10. Patrick Champagne states that the scientific robustness of opinion polls is very poor and considers them merely beliefs whose social and political effects are very real. P. Champagne, *Faire l'opinion: Le nouveau jeu politique* (Paris: Minuit, 1990). A foucauldian strand of criticism sees opinion polling as instruments of control and power, seeking to impose a reconstructed opinion on a real one, with some scholars calling it a disciplinary mechanism. L. Peer, "The Practice of Opinion Polling as a Disciplinary Mechanism: A Foucauldian Perspective," *International Journal of Public Opinion Research* 4, no. 3 (1992): 230–242.

11. Beyond this poll, the partiality and politicized nature of the CNCDH shows itself particularly in the weight it accords to the various anti-racism actors and community representatives, their agendas, priorities, choice of categories, and how its analysts interpret the data. Its refusal to use the term "Islamophobia" is a political decision.

12. Morice, "Du seuil de tolérance," 387.

13. P. Bourdieu, "L'opinion publique n'existe pas," *Les Temps modernes* (1972), 1292–1309.

14. The questionnaires are included as appendices in the annual reports.

15. N. Heinich, "La sociologie à l'épreuve des valeurs," *Cahiers internationaux de sociologie*, no. 121 (2010): 287–315.

16. C. Dargent, *Sociologie des opinions* (Paris: Armand Colin, 2011).

17. Morice, "Du seuil de tolérance." In response to the criticism aimed at the questionnaire's capacity to perform its role effectively, the pollsters maintain that prejudices—like

radio waves—are already there and that their tools—like a radio receiver—merely pick them up. The durability of the opinions is thus summoned to prove the preexistence of the "waves" in question. However, the durability in question is based on the "barometer" that is itself being critiqued, which leads Morice to comment, not without reason, that this argument enables an "endless, circular process of approval."

18. For a critique of the academic use of opinion polls, see Jouanneau and Laurens's review of S. Brouard and V. Tiberj, «Français comme les autres?, Sociétés politiques comparées» in *Revue européenne d'analyse des sociétés politiques*, no. 7 (September 2008).

19. In total, three clustering exercises were carried out. First, categories based on very different criteria (nationality, culture, religion, race, origin, etc.) are linked in several questions. Second, the responses given to different questions are grouped together to construct scales of "ethnocentrism" and indices of "tolerance." Lastly, the respondents are clustered into new groups. This series of exercises, like all questionnaire-based surveys, contains a number of biaises and implicit assumptions.

20. For a critique of the concept of tolerance, see P. Tevanian, *La mécanique raciste* (Paris: Éditions Dilecta, 2008).

21. For a detailed presentation, see N. Mayer, G. Michelat, and V. Tiberj, *Montée de l'intolérance et polarisation anti-islam*, CNCDH report (2012), 29.

22. N. Mayer, G. Michelat, and V. Tiberj, *Racisme et xénophobie en hausse: Retournement historique ou effet de contexte?*, CNCDH report (2011), 37.

23. Mayer, Michelat, and Tiberj, *Racisme et xénophobie en hausse*, 40.

24. Speech by President Nicolas Sarkozy, in Grenoble, on 30 July 2010, marking a hardening of his position on the issues of security, religion, and immigration.

25. Mayer, Michelat, and Tiberj, *Racisme et xénophobie en hausse*, 44.

26. J. Baubérot, *La laïcité falsifiée* (Paris: La Découverte, 2012).

27. CNCDH, "2016 Report on the Fight against Racism, Anti-Semitism and Xenophobia," 286.

28. See M. Malik (ed.), *Anti-Muslim Prejudice: Past and Present* (London: Routledge, 2012).

29. Helbling, "Islamophobia in Switzerland."

30. K. O. Kalkan, G. C. Layman, and E. M. Uslaner, "'Bands of Others'? Attitudes toward Muslims in Contemporary American Society," *Journal of Politics* 71, no. 3 (2009): 1–16.

31. "When aversion to Islam is correlated with ethnocentrism, the majority of the sample (68 percent) either score low on both scales (i.e., neither ethnocentric nor hostile to Islam) or score high on both (ethnocentric Islamophobic)." Mayer, Michelat, and Tiberj, *Racisme et xénophobie en hausse, 2011*, 48.

32. Mayer, G. Michelat, and Tiberj, *Montée de l'intolérance*, 45.

CHAPTER 3. From Negative Opinions to
Discriminatory Acts

1. W. Doise, "Attitudes et représentations sociales," in D. Jodelet (ed.), *Les Représentations sociales* (Paris: PUF, 1994), 220–238.

2. L. Mucchielli, "Les techniques et les enjeux de la mesure de la délinquance," *Sasee/Agir*, no. 93 (2010), available at www.laurent-mucchielli.org.

3. The data regularly presented by the Conseil français du culte musulman's (CFCM) Islamophobia Observatory, which are widely covered in the press, come from the Ministry of the Interior. The observatory in question records no data and simply communicates those received from the ministry.

4. The CCIF was never recognized by the Ministry of the Interior, despite repeated requests. However, although no formal partnership was established, a slight change in the government's stance should be noted. While congratulating itself for having "created the Observatoire national de islamophobie within the CFCM, in June 2011, responsible for aggregating anti-Muslim incidents recorded by regional bodies at the national level," an operation that we have seen had been achieved by the ministry, the government acknowledged the "collaboration with the Collectif contre islamophobie en France (CCIF) initiated by the CFCM" because of "its local reach and its expertise in the field of statistics."

5. In this chapter, all information on the development of strategies for recording incidents in the criminal justice system is taken from the CNCDH's annual reports, in which guidance from the ministries and the commission's critiques and recommendations are compiled.

6. The HALDE was an official institution fighting against all forms of discrimination. Victims of discrimination could file a complaint that was reviewed by legal officers. The HALDE was not a court, but it could both contact perpetrators of discrimination so as to find a solution and publish public reports and recommendations.

7. B. Godard, "La convention cadre sur la recension des actes antimusulmans entre l'État et le CFCM: Compensation d'une islamophobie d'État ou prise en compte d'une nouvelle sorte de xénophobie?," research paper, seminar on Islamophobia, EHESS, 2012.

8. These are cases that, in terms of both the law and evidence, make criminal prosecutions possible.

9. The Ministry of Justice listed fewer than ten incidents "that can officially be labelled anti-Muslim" between January and November 2003. On the other hand, it underlined that desecrations of tombs are first aimed at Catholic tombs and are often linked to "Satanist" rituals.

10. The extent to which the CCIF's strategy runs counter to the weakness of the contributions made by other non-profits must be stressed. The syntheses and reports published by traditional anti-racist organizations rarely include statistical data on religious-based exclusion. It should be noted anyway that, under the guidance of the MRAP's former director Mouloud Aounit, Islamophobia had steadily been incorporated into that organization's repertoire of defensible causes (as early as 2003 in the movement's annual report). The MRAP's contribution to the CNCDH's 2009 report has provided some indicative figures on anti-Islamophobia activities. Out of twenty-seven legal cases initiated by the MRAP in 2009, fourteen were related to racism based on origins or skin color (one of which was in the context of sport), six were about Islamophobia, four about anti-Semitism, and the last three related to comments directed at Rom and Travelers. The MRAP also publicized the results of Internet vigils carried out on "over 2,000 URLs (more than 1,000 of which were blogs)." A quick analysis of the content of almost fifteen hundred of these revealed references to various themes, with Islamophobia at the top of the list (75 percent), ahead of anti-Semitism (44 percent) and "various" forms of racism (23 percent). This approach was neither extended nor followed up in the years after, which goes against the selective nature of the guidance notes

on Internet racism—focused on anti-Semitism—given by the CNCDH to Marc Knobel (deputy director of Licra and researcher at the Conseil représentatif des institutions juives de France, CRIF).

11. This 12 February 2019 article from *Le Monde* specifies the methods used in counting these incidents: https://www.lemonde.fr/les-decodeurs/article/2019/02/12/actes-antisemites-et-islamophobes-un-decompte-hasardeux_5422565_4355770.html.

12. P. Simon and J. Stavodebauge, "Les politiques anti-discrimination et les statistiques: Paramètres d'une incohérence," *Sociétés contemporaines*, no. 53 (2004): 62. See also M. Lesné and P. Simon, "La mesure des discriminations dans l'enquête 'Trajectoires et origines,'" Ined, Document de travail, no. 184 (2012), Paris.

13. The more abstract, overall question, less anchored in experience than the "situated" questions, produces fewer statements (of discrimination). These gaps are only relevant to the overall numbers rather than the risk of discrimination facing each group.

14. C. Beauchemin, C. Hamel, M. Lesné, and P. Simon, "Les discriminations: Une question de minorités visibles," *Population & sociétés*, no. 466 (2010): 1–4.

15. D. Fassin, "L'invention française de la discrimination," *Revue française de science politique* 52, no. 4 (2002): 403–423.

16. For a presentation and a detailed analysis, refer to Y. Brinbaum, M. Safi, and P. Simon, "Les discriminations en France: Entre perception et expérience," Ined, Document de travail, no. 183 (2012).

17. As regards the small proportion of people linking discrimination with religion, our statistical analysis relates to the population aged eighteen to sixty, which means a slightly different outcome from the scores presented by the TeO "discrimination" team (whose field is often limited to the eighteen to fifty age group).

18. Between 16 percent of Jews (in the eighteen to sixty age group) and 20 percent of eighteen- to fifty-year-olds.

19. Among those who state they are Jewish or Muslim, "three quarters [. . .] say they are very religious, whereas less than a quarter of Catholics state this." C. Fouteau, "Immigrés, musulmans: Enquête sur leurs pratiques religieuses," *Médiapart*, 14 January 2013; based on data from the TeO survey.

20. An analysis we carried out on the part of the TeO sample aged eighteen to sixty.

21. Around two-thirds of men say they wear "religious clothing," and for 37 percent of them this means jewelry.

22. F. Dubet, O. Cousin, E. Macé, and S. Rui, *Pourquoi moi? L'expérience des discriminations* (Paris: Seuil, 2013).

23. P. Ndiaye, *La condition noire* (Paris: Calmann-Lévy, 2008).

24. P. Simon and V. Tiberj, "Les registres de l'identité: Les immigrés et leurs descendants," Ined, Document de travail, no. 176 (2012): 10.

25. A. Tausch, C. Bischof, T. Kastrum, and K. Mueller, *Against Islamophobia: Muslim Communities, Social-Exclusion and the Lisbon Process in Europe* (New York: Nova Science Publishers, 2007).

26. V. Amiraux, *La discrimination religieuse dans l'éducation: Ethnicisation et/ou racialisation du religieux dans les contextes multiculturaliste britannique et républicain français*, report produced for DREES/MiRe, 2008. For "minority logic" see Ndiaye, *La condition noire*, 368.

27. Brinbaum, Safi, and Simon, "Les discriminations en France," 8.

28. Brinbaum, Safi, and Simon, 16.

29. O. Masclet, *Sociologie de la diversité et des discriminations* (Paris: Armand Colin, 2012), 48–57.

30. Brinbaum, Safi, and Simon, "Les discriminations en France," 21.

31. Lesné and Simon, "La mesure des discriminations," 59.

32. V. Amiraux, "Existe-t-il une discrimination religieuse des musulmans en France?," *Maghreb/Machrek*, no. 183 (2005): 74.

33. P. Simon and J. Stavodebauge, "Les politiques anti-discrimination et les statistiques: Paramètres d'une incohérence," *Sociétés contemporaines*, no. 53 (2004): 67.

34. Agence des droits fondamentaux de la commission européenne (Fundamental Rights Agency—FRA), *European Union Minorities and Discrimination Survey*, 2008, http://fra.europa.eu.

35. The surveys of the general population usually aim to measure crime and feelings of lack of safety by asking individuals direct questions and thus enabling the many deficiencies of official record-keeping to be bypassed. Despite the numerous and regular surveys of this type carried out in France and Europe, none of them, until relatively recently, included racist and discriminatory incidents as offenses worth measuring.

36. J. Goodey, "Racist Violence in Europe: Challenges for Official Data Collection," *Ethnic and Racial Studies* 30, no. 4 (2007): 570–589.

37. Many critiques could and have been made about the way this survey's samples were devised and structured. To find out the details of the method used, see "EU-Midis: European Union Minorities and Discrimination Survey," at http://fra.europa.eu.

38. C. Adida, D. Laitin, and M. A. Valfort, *Les Français musulmans sont-ils discriminés dans leur propre pays? Une étude expérimentale sur le marché du travail*, French American Foundation Report (2010), available at http://equality.frenchamerican.org.

39. M. A. Valfort, *Discriminations religieuses à l'embauche: Une réalité* (Institut Montaigne, 2015), 27; see also M. A. Valfort, "La religion, facteur de discrimination à l'embauche en France?," *Revue economique* 68, no. 5(2017): 895–907.

40. M. Bertrand and S. Mullainathan (2004), "Are Emily and Greg More Employable Than Lakisha and Jamal? A Field Experiment on Labor Market Discrimination," *American Economic Review* 94, no. 4 (2004): 991–1013.

41. C. Adida, D. Laitin, and M. A. Valfort, "Mesurer la discrimination: Apports de l'économie expérimentale," www.laviedesidees.fr, 3 May 2013.

42. Adida, Laitin, and Valfort, "Mesurer la discrimination."

43. See V. De Rudder, "'Seuil de tolérance' et cohabitation pluriethnique," in P-A. Taguieff (ed.), *Face au racisme*, vol. 2 (Paris: La Découverte, 1991), 154–166; M. Marié, "Quelques réflexions sur le concept de seuil de tolérance," *Sociologie du Sud-Est*, nos. 5–6 (1975): 39–50; A. Morice, "Du seuil de tolérance au racisme banal, ou les avatars de l'opinion fabriquée," *Journal des anthropologues*, nos. 110–111 (2007): 379–408.

CHAPTER 4. From Anti-Orientalism to the Runnymede Trust

1. C. Fourest and F. Venner, "Islamophobie?," *ProChoix*, nos. 26–27 (2003), available at www.prochoix.org.

2. P. Bruckner, "L'invention de l'"islamophobie"," *Libération*, 23 (November 2010).

3. We thank Farhad Khosrokhavar for this information.

4. We thank Yves Gonzalez-Quijano for this information.

5. On Lopez: F. Bravo López, "Towards a Definition of Islamophobia: Approximations of the Early Twentieth Century," *Ethnic and Racial Studies* 34, no. 4 (2011): 556–573. On administrator-ethnologists: Grandhomme, "Connaissance de l'islam et pouvoir colonial: L'exemple de la France au Sénégal, 1936–1957," *French Colonial History* 10 (2009): 171–188. On Delafosse: J-L. Amselle and E. Sibeud (eds.), *Maurice Delafosse: Entre orientalisme et ethnographie: L'itinéraire d'un africaniste (1870–1926)* (Paris: Maisonneuve & Larose, 1998). These administrator-ethnologists were working in a context where the word "phobia" met with a degree of success following the breakthrough of psychology and psychoanalysis. According to the Robert dictionary (the French equivalent of the OED or the OAD), the French equivalents of "phobia" and "phobic" first appeared in 1880 and 1910 respectively. "Xenophobia" was first used in 1906, and its use continues until the present day, whereas "Islamophobia" only appears in that dictionary in 2006.

6. Maurice Delafosse (1870–1926) began his career in the colonial administration as junior clerk in indigenous affairs, 3rd class in Côte d'Ivoire then, after having been consul in Liberia and teaching at the École spéciale des langues orientales and the École coloniale, was appointed as head of civil affairs for the government of French West Africa in Dakar. Alain Quellien had a PhD in law, held a degree from the École coloniale and the École spéciale des langues orientales vivantes, and was an editor in the Ministry of the Colonies. Paul Marty (1882–1938) was born in Algeria and was director of indigenous affairs in Rabat (Morocco), from 1912 to 1921.

7. M. Delafosse, "L'état actuel de l'Islam dans l'Afrique occidentale française," *Revue du monde musulman* 11, no. 5 (1910):57. Our italics.

8. P. Marty, "L'islam en Guinée," *Revue du monde musulman* 36 (1918–1919): 174: "It should be acknowledged however that in the Touba region, from 1908 to 1911, there were some genuine reasons for concern in the colonial administration, and which were more objective than ambient Islamophobia."

9. M. Delafosse, "L'âme d'un peuple africain: Les Bambara" (review of Joseph Henry, *L'Âme d'un peuple africain: Les Bambara; leur vie psychique, éthique, sociale, religieuse* (Münster, 1910), *Revue des études ethnographiques et sociologiques* 2, nos. 1–2: 10.

10. A. Quellien, *La politique musulmane dans l'Afrique occidentale française* (Paris: Émile Larose, 1910), 133. Based on a thesis presented to the University of Paris Faculty of Law of the on 25 May 1910. Our italics.

11. Ibid., 135.

12. On Overweg and Barth: J. Von Richardson, A. Overweg, H. Barth, and E. Eduard Vogel, *Die Entdeckungsreisen in Nord-und Mittel-Afrika* [The Discovery of North and Central Africa] (Leipzig: Carl B. Lorck, 1857); H. Barth, *Voyages et découvertes dans l'Afrique septentrionale et centrale pendant les années 1849 à 1855* (Paris: A. Bohné, 1860). On Binger: L-G. Binger, *Du Niger au Golfe de Guinée* (Paris: Hachette & Cie, 1891) and Quellien, *La politique musulmane*, 136.

13. Quoted in Quellien, *La politique musulmane*, 137.

14. O. Lenz, *Timbouctou: Voyage au Maroc, au Sahara et au Soudan*, vol. 1 (Paris: Hachette & Cie, 1886), 460.

15. Quellien, *La politique musulmane*, 154.

16. Ibid., 154.

17. See the biographies of Dinet: F. Arnaudiès, *Étienne Dinet et El Hadj Sliman Ben Ibrahim* (Alger: P. & G. Soubiron, 1933); J. Dinet-Rollince, *La vie de E. Dinet* (Paris: Maisonneuve, 1938; D. Brahimi, *La vie et l'oeuvre d'Étienne Dinet* (Paris: A.C.R, 1984); F. Pouillon, *Les deux vies d'Étienne Dinet, peintre en Islam: l'Algérie et l'héritage colonial* (Paris: Balland, 1997).

18. One of his paintings was reproduced in the famous book by G. Hanoteaux, (ed.), *Histoire des colonies françaises*, vol. 2: *Algérie* (Paris: Plon, 1929), 384.

19. E. Dinet and S. Ben Ibrahim, *La vie de Mohammed, Prophète d'Allah* (Paris: L'Édition d'Art H. Piazza, 1918), vii.

20. Letter from Dinet to his sister, 7 January 1929, quoted in Dinet-Rollince, *La vie de E. Dinet*, 196.

21. Letter from Dinet to his sister, 8 March 1929, quoted in ibid., 197.

22. Nacir Ed Din Étienne Dinet and S. Ben Ibrahim Baâmer, *Le pèlerinage à la maison sacrée d'allah* (Paris: Hachette, 1930), 167.

23. Ibid., 173.

24. Ibid., 174–175.

25. "pseudoscientific Islamophobia": Ibid., 176; "religious": ibid., 183.

26. S. Zwemer, *L'Islam, son passé, son présent et son avenir* (1907; reprint, Paris: Fédération française des associations chrétiennes d'étudiants, 1922), 295: "The offensive should be mounted tactfully, and wisely, but vigorously. From the East to the West and the North to the South, the Church must mobilize all its forces and enlist them beneath the banner of its leader [. . .] The bloody fields of Africa and Asia await new martyrs!"

27. Dinet and Ben Ibrahim Baâmer, *Le Pèlerinage*, 173.

28. Ibid., 174.

29. Ibid., 183.

30. E. Dinet and S. Ben Ibrahim Baâmer, *L'Orient vu de l'Occident, essai critique* (Paris: H. Piazza, 1925).

31. E. Dinet and S. Ben Ibrahim Baâmer, *The Life of Mohammed, the Prophet of Allah* (Paris: Paris Book Club, 1918).

32. S. A. Cook, "Chronicle: The History of Religions," *Journal of Theological Studies*, no. 25 (1924): 101–109. See F. Bravo López, "Islamofobia y antisemitismo: La construcción discursiva de las amenazas islámica y judía," (PhD diss. in Arabic and Islamic studies, Autonomous University of Madrid, 2009), 62. This thesis was published as *En casa ajena: Bases intelectuales del antisemitismo y la islamofobia* [In someone else's home: The intellectual bases of anti-Semitism and Islamophobia] (Barceona: Edicions Bellaterra, 2012).

33. G. C. Anawati, "Dialogue with Gustave E. von Grynebaum," *International Journal of Middle East Studies* 7, no. 1 (1976): 124. See A-K. Vakil, "Is the Islam in Islamophobia the Same as the Islam in Anti-Islam; or, When Is It Islamophobia Time?," in S. Sayyid and A. Vakil (eds.), *Thinking through Islamophobia: Global Perspectives* (New York: Columbia University Press, 2010), 41.

34. C-V. Aubrun, "Jules Horrent, Roncesvalles: Étude sur le fragment de cantar de gesta conservé à l'Archivo de Navarra (Pamplona)," *Bulletin Hispanique* 53 (1951): 429.

35. B. Loupias, "Góngora et la Mamora, II," *Bulletin Hispanique* 90, nos. 3–4 (1988): 346.

36. A-M. Duperray, "Les Yarse du royaume de Ouagadougou: L'écrit et l'oral," *Cahiers d'études africaines* 25, no. 98 (1985): 188.

37. H. Djaït, *L'Europe et l'Islam* (Paris: Seuil, 1978), 60–64.

38. E. Said, "Orientalism Reconsidered," *Cultural Critique*, no. 1 (1985): 89–107.

39. P. Goble, "Islamic 'Explosion' Possible in Central Asia," *Report on the USSR* 2, no. 7 (16 February 1990): 22–23. This information is republished in M. Rosenblum, "Islam Resurgent Vibrant Faith of Koran Surviving Dying Faith of Communism," Associated Press, 23 July 1990, and H. Jenkins Jr., "A Dance on Shevardnadze's Grave," *Insight*, 4 February 1991.

40. C. Allen, *Islamophobia* (Farnham: Ashgate, 2010).

41. B. Parekh, "Europe, Liberalism and the 'Muslim Question,'" in T. Modood, A. Triandafyllidou, and R. Zapata-Barrero (eds.), *Multiculturalism, Muslims and Citizenship* (London: Routledge, 2006), 179–203.

42. N. Meer, *Citizenship, Identity and the Politics of Multiculturalism: The Rise of Muslim Consciousness* (Basingstoke: Palgrave, 2010).

43. J. Solomos, *Race and Racism in Britain* (Basingstoke: Palgrave, 2003).

44. R. Miles and A. Phizacklea, *Labour and Racism* (London: Routledge, 1980).

45. M. Barker, *The New Racism* (London: Junction Books, 1981).

46. K. Siddiqui, *The Muslim Manifesto: A Strategy for Survival* (Muslim Institute, 1990).

47. Runnymede Commission on Antisemitism, *A Very Light Sleeper: the Persistence and Dangers of Anti-Semitism* (London: Runnymede Trust, 1994).

48. Runnymede Trust, Commission on British Muslims and Islamophobia, *Islamophobia: A Challenge for Us All* (London: Runnymede Trust, 1997).

CHAPTER 5. Academic Research

1. Runnymede Trust Commission on British Muslims, *Islamophobia: Its Features and Dangers—A Consultation Paper* (London: Runnymede Trust, 1997).

2. See C. Allen, *Islamophobia* (Farnham/Burlington: Ashgate, 2010), 65–80.

3. Allen, *Islamophobia*, 67.

4. M. Rokeach, *The Open and Closed Mind* (New York: Basic Books, 1960), 7–9. For A. Shryock, "Introduction: Islam as an Object of Fear and Affection," in A. Shryock (ed.), *Islamophobia/Islamophilia: Beyond the Politics of Enemy and Friend* (Bloomington: Indiana University Press, 2010), 1–25, Islamophobia and Islamophilia share the same tendency to essentialize Islam and Muslims. Both blur both the significant differences within the group of Muslims, and the similarities between Muslims and non-Muslims. This is why he calls for Islam to be analyzed as an object of fear or affection.

5. M. Banton, "Islamophobia: A Critical Analysis," *Dialogue* (December 1998): 3.

6. It is difficult to explain why some scholars continue to use the Runnymede Trust's definition. There must be academic and historical reasons, such as a fit between the analytical frameworks of social psychology and political science, which rely on opinion polls, and an ignorance about the conditions under which the definition was generated.

7. See Allen, *Islamophobia*. Three articles offer a synthesis of recent work on Islamophobia: B. Klug, "Islamophobia: A Concept Comes of Age," *Ethnicities* 12, no. 5 (2012): 665–681; T. Kayaoglu, "Three Takes on Islamophobia," *International Sociology* 27, no. 5 (2012):

609–615; H. Asal, "Islamophobie: La fabrique d'un nouveau concept: État des lieux de la recherche," *Sociologie* (2013): 13–29. Kayaoglu is much more critical of the existing corpus.

8. On Halliday, see F. Halliday, "Anti-Muslimism in Contemporary Politics," in *Islam and the Myth of Confrontation* (London: I. B. Tauris, 1996); F. Halliday, "'Islamophobia' Reconsidered," *Ethnic and Racial Studies* 22, no. 5 (1999): 892–902; F. Halliday, *Two Hours That Shook the World: September 11, 2001—Causes and Consequences* (London: Saqi, 2002). Mohammad Tamdgigi suggests rewriting the Runnymede Trust definition of Islamophobia based on this critique: M. Tamdgigi, "Beyond Islamophobia and Islamophilia as Western Epistemic Racisms: Revisiting Runnymede Trust's Definition in a World History Context," *Islamophobia Studies Journal* 1, no. 1 (2012): 54–81.

9. S. Sayyid, "Out of the Devil's Dictionary," in S. Sayyid and A. Vakil. (eds.), *Thinking through Islamophobia: Global Perspectives* (New York: Columbia University Press, 2010), 16.

10. C. Allen, "Undoing Proximity: The Impact of the Local-Global Nexus on Perceptions of Muslims in Britain," presented at "The Globalisation and Localisation of Religion" EASR Congress, University of Bergen, Norway, 11 May 2003.

11. E. Özyürek, "The Politics of Cultural Unification," *American Ethnologist* 32, no. 4 (2005): 509–512.

12. J. Cesari, "Islamophobia in the West: A Comparison between Europe and the United States," in J. L. Esposito and I. Kalin (eds.), *Islamophobia: The Challenge of Pluralism in the 21st Century* (New York: Oxford University Press, 2011), 21; M. Maussen, *Anti-Muslim Sentiments and Mobilization in the Netherlands: Discourse, Policies and Violence, Challenge* (Paris, n.p., 2006), 100.

13. Cesari, "Islamophobia in the West," 24.

14. R. Miles and M. Brown, *Racism* (1989; reprint, New York: Routledge, 2003), 166.

15. Werbner: P. Werbner, "Islamophobia: Incitement to Religious Hatred. Legislating for a New Fear?," *Anthropology Today* 21, no. 1 (2005): 5–9; Werbner shares this perspective with S. Salaita, expressed in "Beyond Orientalism and Islamophobia: 9/11, Anti-Arab racism, and the Mythos of National Pride," *New Centennial Review* 6, no. 2 (2006): 245–266. For the alternative perspective, see R. Antonius, "Un racisme respectable," in J. Renaud, L. Pietrantonio, and G. Bourgeault (eds.), *Les Relations ethniques en question: Ce qui a changé depuis le 11 septembre 2001* (Montréal: Les Presses de l'Université de Montréal, 2002), 253–271, and S. Bouamama, *L'affaire du foulard islamique: La production d'un racisme respectable* (Roubaix: Éditions du Geai bleu, 2004).

16. Allen, *Islamophobia*, 138.

17. B. Bunzl, "Rejoinder," *American Ethnologist* 32, no. 4 (2005): 534.

18. In Great Britain, six PhD dissertations with the term Islamophobia in their title were defended between 1997 and 2011: Y. Fox-Howard, "Conflict Resolution: A Study of Identity, Social/Economic Exclusion, Islamophobia and Racism" (University of Wales, Lampeter, 1997); D. Tyrer, "Institutionalised Islamophobia in British Universities" (University of Salford, 2003); C. Allen, "Islamophobia: Contested Concept in the Public Space" (University of Birmingham, 2005); V. Marten, "Accounting for Islamophobia as a British Muslim: The Centrality of the 'Extra-Discursive' in the Discursive Practices of Islamophobia" (Manchester Metropolitan University, 2010); L. Moosavi, "Defying Gravity: Islamophobia, Belonging and 'Race' in the Experiences of Muslim Converts in Britain" (Lancaster University, 2011);

S-R. Nabi, "How Is Islamophobia Institutionalised? Racialised Governmentality and the Case of Muslim Students in British Universities" (University of Manchester, 2011).

19. Cesari, "Islamophobia in the West," 24.

20. Miles and Brown, *Racism*.

21. Allen, *Islamophobia*, 190.

22. S. Sheehi, *Islamophobia: The Ideological Campaign against Muslims* (Atlanta: Clarity Press, 2011).

23. Z. Sardar, "Racism, Identity and Muslims in the West," in S. Z. Abedin and Z. Sardar, (eds.), *Muslim Minorities in the West* (London: Grey Seal, 1995), 1–17. Cited in Allen, *Islamophobia*, 14.

24. D. Hussain, "The Impact of 9/11 on British Muslim Identity," in R. Geaves, R. et al. (eds.), *Islam and the West: A Post September 11th Perspective* (Aldershot: Ashgate, 2004), 115–129, quoted by Allen, *Islamophobia*, 14.

25. V. Geisser, *La nouvelle islamophobie* (Paris: La Découverte, 2003), 21.

26. Ibid., 11 and 95. Following the publication of *La nouvelle islamophobie*, Geisser published two entries on Islamophobia in dictionaries. In one, Islamophobia "refers basically to a culturalist, essentialist mode of thought which amalgamates real or imagined belonging to Islam with a globalizing and totalizing entity, and often hides behind an anti-racist, universalist line of argument in order to effectively underscore the (so-called) 'cultural deficit' of Islam and Muslims." See *Dictionnaire des racismes, de l'exclusion et des discriminations* (Paris: Larousse, 2010), 419–420. In the other, Islamophobia is a form of "anti-Muslim neo-racism" and the "product of a heterophobic imaginary that understands it as a more or less legitimate response to some "initial violence," whether committed by Muslim individuals or groups, whose secret endgame is allegedly to topple our value system." *Dictionnaire de la violence* (Paris: PUF, 2011), 742–747.

27. Kayaoglu, "Three Takes on Islamophobia."

28. C. Guillaumin, *L'idéologie raciste: Genèse et langage actuel* (1972; reprint, Paris: Gallimard, 2002).

29. R. Miles, *Racism and Migrant Labour* (London: Kegan Paul, 1982), 170.

30. A. Rattansi, *Racism: A Very Short Introduction* (Oxford: Oxford University Press, 2007), 107.

31. N. Meer and T. Modood, "The Racialisation of Muslims," in Sayyid and Vakil, *Thinking through Islamophobia*, 83.

32. Meer and Modood, "Racialisation of Muslims," 79.

33. The phrase used by G. Spivak, "The Rani of Sirmur: An Essay in Reading the Archives," *History and Theory* 24, no. 3 (1985), 247–272.

34. S. Garner and S. Selod, "The Racialization of Muslims: Empirical Studies of Islamophobia," *Critical Sociology* 41, no. 1 (2015), 9–19.

35. R. Grosfoguel and E. Mielants, "The Long-Durée Entanglement between Islamophobia and Racism in the Modern/Colonial Capitalist/Patriarchal World-System," *Human Architecture: Journal of the Sociology of Self-Knowledge* 5, no. 1 (2006): 1–12. See also M. Mestiri, R. Grosfoguel, and E. Y. Soum (eds.), *Islamophobie dans le monde moderne* (Saint-Ouen: IIIT France, 2008). This book was developed out of the first international colloquium on Islamophobia organized in France, by the University of Berkeley and the Institut interna-

tional de la pensée islamique (International Institute for Islamic Thought, at the Fondation de la Maison des sciences de l'homme (Paris, 2–3 June 2006).

36. W. D. Mignolo, "Islamophobia/Hispanophobia: The (Re)Configuration of the Racial Imperial/Colonial Matrix," *Human Architecture: Journal of the Sociology of Self-Knowledge* 5, no. 1 (2006): 13–28.

37. S. Sayyid, "Out of the Devil's Dictionary," in Sayyid and Vakil, *Thinking through Islamophobia*, 17.

38. Tyrer, "Institutionalised Islamophobia in British Universities"; D. Tyrer, "'Flooding the embankments': Race, Biopolitics, and Sovereignty," in Sayyid and Vakil, *Thinking through Islamophobia*, 93–115; D. Tyrer, *The Politics of Islamophobia: Race, Power and Fantasy* (London: Pluto Press, 2013).

39. S. Sayyid, "Thinking through Islamophobia," in Sayyid and Vakil, *Thinking Through Islamophobia*, 3.

40. S. Cohen, *Folk Devils and Moral Panics* (London: Mac Gibbon and Kee, 1972), 9.

41. G. Morgan and S. Poynting, "Introduction: The Transnational Folk Devil," in *Global Islamophobia: Muslims and Moral Panic in the West* (Farnham: Ashgate, 2012), 1–14.

42. J. K. Puar, *Terrorist Assemblages: Homonationalism in Queer Times* (Durham: Duke University Press, 2007), 20–21.

43. See the contributions to the colloquium "Sexual Nationalisms: Gender, Sexuality, and the Politics of Belonging in the New Europe," University of Amsterdam, 27–28 January 2011; also G. Bhattacharyya, *Dangerous Brown Men: Exploiting Sex, Violence and Feminism in the War on Terror* (London, Zed Books, 2008).

44. See, inter alia, L. Deeb, "Gendering Islamophobia and Islamophilia: The Case of Shi'I Muslim Women in Lebanon," in Shryock, *Islamophobia/Islamophilia*, 94–110; H. S. Mirza, "Embodying the Veil: Muslim Women and Gendered Islamophobia in 'New Times,'" in Z. Gross, L. Davies, and A. Diab (eds.), *Gender, Religion and Education in a Chaotic Postmodern World* (New York/London: Springer, 2013), 303–316.

45. M. Mohammed, "Un nouveau champ de recherche," *Sociologie* 5, no. 1 (2014): 1–11.

46. I. Bouzelmat, "Le sous-champ de la question raciale dans les sciences sociales françaises," in *Mouvements* (2019), available at http://mouvements.info/le-sous-champ-de -la-question-raciale-dans-les-sciences-sociales-francaises/.

47. This seminar was organized by us between 2011 and 2014.

48. A. Hajjat and M. Mohammed (eds.), special issue, «Sociologie de l'Islamophobia,» *Sociologie* 5, no. 1 (2014).

49. For French researchers : "L'islamophobie en questions," Sciences Po Paris, 20 April 2013; "Le religieux au prisme de l'ethnicisation et de la racisation," Université Paris Nanterre, 17–18 September 2014; "Religion et discrimination," Université Paris Diderot, 3 October 2016; "Lutter contre l'islamophobie, un enjeu d'égalité?," Université Lyon 2, 14 October 2017 (canceled). British and/or American academics: "Les représentations médiatiques de l'islam et des musulmans," Université Saint-Quentin-en-Yvelines, 19–20 June 2018, organized by Simon Dawes. Ramon Grosfoguel and Hatem Bazian (University of California, Berkeley) organized six conferences hosted either in academic or activist venues between 2013 and 2019.

50. In 2019 there were only five French PhD dissertations containing "Islamophobia" in

their title in various disciplines: English, management sciences (Saadani, 2021), public law, psychology and foreign languages and literatures (source: www.theses.fr).

51. H. Karimi, "Assignation à l'altérité radicale et chemins d'émancipation: étude de l'agency de femmes musulmanes françaises" (sociology thesis, Université de Strasbourg, 2018); L. Odasso "La mixité conjugale : Une expérience de migration : Approche comparée des effets de la stigmatisation sur les natifs et leurs partenaires 'arabes' en Vénétie et en Alsace" (sociology thesis, Université de Strasbourg, 2013); M-C. Willems, "Musulman-e-s : Socio-sémantique historique des usages du terme musulman et enjeux contemporains de l'ethnicisation, racisation et confessionnalisation" (sociology thesis, Université Paris Nanterre, 2016). Available at http://www.theses.fr/2016PA100152.

52. A. Celestine, A. Hajjat, and L. Zevounou, "Rôle des intellectuel.les, universitaires 'minoritaires,' et des porte-parole des minorités," *Mouvements* (2019), available at http://mouvements.info/role-des-intellectuel%c2%b7les-minoritaires/.

53. A. Hajjat, "Islamophobia and French Academia," *Current Sociology* 69, no. 5 (2021): 621–640.

54. See the reviews by M. Doytcheva, "Liogier (Raphaël), le mythe de l'islamisation: Essai sur une obsession collective," *Revue française de sociologie* 56, no. 1 (2005): 174–177; F. Dubet, "Galland (Olivier), Muxel (Anne) (ed.), La tentation radicale. Enquête auprès des lycéens," *Revue française de sociologie* 59, no. 4 (2018): 740–745; M. Madoui, of Mohammed Hajjat, "Islamophobie: Comment les élites françaises fabriquent le 'problème musulman,'" *Revue française de sociologie* 56, no. 4 (2015): 804–807.

55. G. Mauger, "Islamophobie (1)," *Savoir/Agir* 36 (2016): 113–121; G. Mauger, "Islamophobie (2) Sur la 'radicalisation islamiste,'" *Savoir/Agir* 37 (2016): 91–99; G. Mauger, "Islamophobie (3) Burkini et laïcité," *Savoir/Agir* 38 (2016): 97–104.

56. Mauger, "Islamophobie (1)," 116.

57. Ibid.

58. J. Favret-Saada, *Comment produire une crise mondiale avec douze petits dessins* (Paris: Fayard, 2015).

59. P. Hervik, *The Annoying Difference: The Emergence of Danish Neonationalism, Neoracism, and Populism in the Post-1989 World* (London: Berghahn, 2011).

CHAPTER 6. The Postcolonial Immigration "Problem"

1. See F. Fregosi, A. Boubeker, and H. Paris, *L'exercice du culte musulman en France: Lieux de prière et d'inhumation* (Paris: La Documentation française, 2006). On Salafism: S. Amghar, *Le salafisme d'aujourd'hui: Mouvements sectaires en Occident* (Paris: Michalon, 2011).

2. S. Fath, *Du ghetto au réseau: Le protestantisme évangélique en France, 1800–2005* (Genève: Labor et Fides, 2005).

3. According to Europol's annual reports for 2007–2012, the number of "successful, planned or failed attacks" has wavered between a maximum of 583 (in 2007) and a minimum of 174 (in 2011). Each year, the proportion of "Islamist" attacks has varied from 0 percent (2008 and 2011) to 1.2 percent (2010) while the proportion of regionalist and "separatist" attacks has fallen from 91 percent (2007) to 63 percent (2011). Between 2006 and 2011, the proportion of "Islamist" attacks was 0.4 percent (nine in total) compared to 83 percent for

separatist (1,860) and 10 percent "far left" attacks (226). Over the same period, 95.8 percent of attacks carried out in France (931 out of 972) were attributed to "separatists."

4. J. Gusfield, *La culture des problèmes publics: L'alcool au volant: La production d'un ordre symbolique* (1984; reprint, Paris: Economica, 2009).

5. V. Dubois, "L'action publique," in A. Cohen, B. Lacroix, and P. Riutort (eds.), *Nouveau manuel de science politique* (Paris: La Découverte, 2009), 311–325.

6. Hannah Arendt, *Antisemitism: Part 1 of Origins of Totalitarianism* (1951; reprint, New York: Harvest, 1985), 56.

7. This link is relevant to national situations where there is a relatively high level of working-class immigration from majority Muslim countries (Great Britain, Germany, Netherlands, Italy, etc.). In these cases, the "Muslim problem" connects the immigrant/Muslim presence in Europe (an enemy within) with political violence justified by reference to Islam (an external enemy). Even if this connection also exists in the USA, Canada, and Australia, it is less relevant: the social issues that the construction of the "Muslim problem" derives from are basically to do with foreign policy. According to former Black Panther Party activist Mumia Abu Jamal, the situation of U.S. Muslims is closer to that of Japanese Americans than that of African Americans. S. Sheehi, *Islamophobia: The Ideological Campaign against Muslims* (Atlanta: Clarity Press, 2011), 14.

8. A. Spire, *Étrangers à la carte* (Paris: Grasset, 2005); G. Noiriel, *Immigration, racisme et antisémitisme* (Paris: Fayard, 2007); S. Laurens, *Une politisation feutrée* (Paris: Belin, 2009).

9. See Laurens, *Une politisation feutrée*, 216–220.

10. See for example J. Bowen, *Why the French Don't Like Headscarves: Islam, the State and Public Space* (Princeton: Princeton University Press, 2007), 66–67.

11. G. Kepel, *Les banlieues de l'islam* (Paris: Seuil, 1987).

12. See N. Hatzfeld and J-L. Loubet, "Les conflits Talbot: Du printemps syndical au tournant de la rigueur (1982–1984)," *Vingtième siècle*, no. 84 (October-December 2004): 151–160.

13. Withol C. De Wenden and R. Mouriaux, "Syndicalisme français et islam," *Revue française de science politique* 37, no. 6 (1987), 804.

14. North African union leaders used religious references such as "God is with us," "We'll win with God's help," etc., which shows they were seeking to build a union struggle by resonating with a vocabulary that the workers were already familiar with, rather than propagating a fundamentalist Muslim discourse.

15. V. Gay, "De la dignité à l'invisibilité: Les OS immigrés dans les grèves de Citroën et Talbot 1982–1984" (master 2 de sociologie, EHESS, 2011), 147–151; "Ouvriers ou musulmans? L'altérisation des ouvriers immigrés dans les grèves du début des années 1980," Presentation at the seminar "Islamophobie: La construction du 'problème musulman,'" EHESS. See also J. Barou, "Les immigrés maghrébins et l'islam en France," *Hommes et migrations*, no. 1097 (November 1986); J. Barou, M. Diop, and S. Toma, "Des musulmans dans l'usine," in R. Sainsaulieu and A. Zehraoui (eds.), *Ouvriers spécialisés à Billancourt: Les derniers témoins* (Paris: L'Harmattan, 1995).

16. C. Harmel, *La CGT à la conquête du pouvoir* (Paris: Bibliothèque d'histoire sociale, 1983); Kepel, *Les banlieues de l'islam*.

17. Internal PSA memo, "Le problème musulman dans les événements Citroën et Talbot de mai-juin 1982," quoted by Gay, "De la dignité à l'invisibilité," 224.

18. Gay, "De la dignité à l'invisibilité," 224.

19. This is what happened to the immigrant workers occupying the Talbot-Poissy factory, who were attacked by members of a right-wing trade union who were supported by its leadership, and removed by force. This was cheered by nonstriking workers who chanted racist slogans such as "Arabs to the gas chambers!," and "Drown the Blacks in the Sea!" "Les douze heures de la violence," *Libération*, 6 January 1984.

20. T. Deltombe, *L'Islam imaginaire: La construction médiatique de l'islamophobie en France, 1975–2005* (Paris: La Découverte, 2005), 49–52.

21. Between the two rounds of the Local Government elections in March 1983, the RPR (center-right) slate in the North-Eastern Paris suburb of Aulnay-sous-Bois put out a pamphlet called "La faucille et le Coran" (The Sickle and the Quran).

22. Europe 1, 26 January 1983.

23. *Le Monde*, 11 February 1983.

24. *Ibid.*

25. Quoted in Gay, "Ouvriers ou musulmans?," 150.

26. The construction of the "Islamic peril" by the communications department was part of the internal conflict in the field of antiterrorism. The collapse of the Soviet Union generated an imbalance of power between the Direction de la surveillance du territoire (DST, Homeland Surveillance Unit) the Renseignements généraux (RG, Government Communications Department), and the Direction nationale de l'antiterrorisme (DNAT, National Antiterrorism Unit) that ended up with the DST emerging as the most powerful of the three. Islam had begun to pose a threat when, according to the police's analytical frameworks, it became transnational, and was supported by strong, primarily working-class and ideologically hostile immigrant communities (L. Bonelli, "Un ennemi anonyme et sans visage: Renseignement, exception et suspicion après le 11 septembre 2001", *Cultures et conflits*, no. 58 [2005]: 101–129.)

27. S. Halimi, *Quand la gauche essayait: Les leçons de l'exercice du pouvoir, 1924, 1936, 1944, 1981* (Paris: Arléa, 2000).

28. See A. Hajjat, *La marche pour l'égalité et contre le racisme* (Paris: Éditions Amsterdam, 2013).

29. This principle had been established by the 1889 Nationality Act. It stated that when a child became an adult, a French-born child of foreign parents would automatically access French nationality. The principle of "demonstrating a desire to be French" was adopted into law between 1993 and 1998.

30. D. Memmi, "Savants et maîtres à penser: La fabrication d'une morale de la procréation artificielle," *Actes de la recherche en sciences sociales*, no. 76 (1989): 82–103. See also M. Bachir-Benlahsen, "Faire de sagesse vertu: La réforme du code de la nationalité," *Politix* 4, no. 16 (1991): 33–40; M. Feldblum, *Reconstructing Citizenship: The Politics of Nationality Reform and Immigration in Contemporary France* (Albany: State University of New York Press, 1999).

31. E. Said, *Covering Islam: How the Media and the Experts Determine How We See the Rest of the World* (1981; reprint, London: Vintage Books, 1997), 9.

32. M. Long, *Être français aujourd'hui et demain: Rapport remis au Premier ministre par Marceau Long, président de la Commission de la Nationalité* (Paris: La Documentation française, 1988), 1:135.

33. Long, *Être français*, 1:368–369.

34. E. Said, *L'Orientalisme: L'Orient créé par l'Occident* (1979; reprint, Paris: Seuil, 1980); A. Filaliansary, "Islam, laïcité, démocratie," *Pouvoirs*, no. 104 (2003), 5–19.

35. One example, inter alia, is that of India, where some medieval Muslim sultans "came to the conclusion that religious affairs should be separated from those of the state" and where "it was acknowledged [in the sixteenth century] that the state ought not to discriminate between Muslims and non-Muslims, and should instead adopt the principle of 'peace for everyone'" (N. Hassan, "État et laïcité: L'expérience islamique," in Mohammed Arkoun [ed.], *L'Islam: Morale et politique* [UNESCO/Desclée de Brouwer: Paris, 1986,] 221).

36. J-F. Bayart, *L'Islam républicain* (Paris: Albin Michel, 2010).

37. Long, *Être français*, 1:26.

38. *Ibid.*, 1:27.

39. Long, *Être français*, 2:48–49.

40. B. Étienne, in Long, *Être français*, 1:131.

41. Long, *Être français*, 1:26–27. Our emphasis.

42. See S. Laacher, "L'intégration comme objet de croyance," *Confluences méditer-ranée*, no. 1 (Autumn 1991): 53–63; N. Guénif-Souilamas, "Immigration/intégration: Le grand découplage," *Ville-École-Intégration Enjeux*, no. 131 (December 2002): 232–239; A. Boubeker, "Ethnicité, relations interethniques ou ethnicisation des relations sociales: Les champs de la recherche en France," *Ville-École-Intégration Enjeux*, no. 135 (December 2003): 40–50; A. Hajjat, *Les frontières de l'"identité nationale": L'injonction à l'assimilation en France métropolitaine et coloniale* (Paris: La Découverte, 2012).

43. H. Tincq, "Les musulmans de France et l'affaire Rushdie: Islam et libertés," *Le Monde*, 19 March 1989.

44. Hajjat, *Les frontières de l'"identité nationale."*

45. Deltombe, *L'Islam imaginaire.*

46. *Le Nouvel Observateur*, 2–8 November 1989.

47. See J. Baubérot, *La laïcité falsifiée* (Paris: La Découverte, 2011).

48. Between 1980 and 1989, 157 North Africans were killed, and 187 attacked in racially motivated incidents. Vincent Gay, "Ouvriers ou musulmans? L'altérisation des ouvriers immigrés dans les grèves du début des années 1980," 21 December 2012, http://islamophobie .hypotheses.org).

49. R. Antonius, "Un racisme respectable," in J. Renaud, L. Pietrantonio, and G. Bourgeault (eds.), *Les relations ethniques en question: Ce qui a changé depuis le 11 septembre 2001* (Montréal: Les Presses de l'Université de Montréal, 2002), 253–71; N. Guénif-Souilamas, "La Française voilée, la beurette, le garçon arabe et le musulman laïc: Les figures assignées du racisme vertueux," in N. Guénif-Souilamas (ed.), *La République mise à nu par son immigration* (Paris: La Fabrique, 2006), 109–132.

CHAPTER 7. (Lack of) Knowledge about Islam

1. See, inter alia, E. Said, *Covering Islam: How the Media and the Experts Determine How We See the Rest of the World* (1981; reprint, London: Vintage Books, 1997); work by J. G. Shaheen, including *The TV Arab* (n.p.: Popular Press, 1984), *Arab and Muslim Stereotyping in American Popular Culture* (Washington, D.C.: Georgetown University Center for

Muslim-Christian Understanding, 1997), *Reel Bad Arabs: How Hollywood Vilifies a People* (Northampton, Mass.: Olive Branch Press, 2001), and *Guilty: Hollywood's Verdict on Arabs after 9/11* (Northampton, Mass.: Olive Branch Press, 2008); T. M'hamsadji, "L'Image de l'Orient arabe dans les médias américains" (PhD thesis in anglophone studies, université Paris-VII, 1987); K. Hafez (ed.), *Islam and the West in the Mass Media: Fragmented Images in a Globalizing World* (Cresshill, N.J.: Hampton Press, 1999); E. Poole, *Reporting Islam: Media Representations of British Muslims* (London: I. B. Tauris, 2002); E. Poole and J. Richardson (eds.), *Muslims and the News Media* (London: I. B. Tauris, 2006); M. D. Brown, "Comparative Analysis of Mainstream Discourses, Media Narratives and Representations of Islam in Britain and France Prior to 9/11," *Journal of Muslim Minority Affairs* 26, no. 3 (2006): 297–312; P. Gottschalk and G. Greenberg, *Islamophobia: Making Muslims the Enemy* (Lanham: Rowman and Littlefield, 2007); S. Joseph and B. D'Harlingue, with Alvin Ka Hin Wong, "Arab Americans and Muslim Americans in the New York Times, Before and After 9/11," in J. Amaney and N. Naber (eds.), *Race and Arab Americans before and after 9/11: From Invisible Citizens to Visible Subjects* (Syracuse: Syracuse University Press, 2008), 229–275; L. Lindekilde, P. Mouritsen, and R. Zapata-Barrero, "The Muhammad Cartoons Controversy in Comparative Perspective," *Ethnicities* 9, (no. 3): 291–313 (introduction to special issue); C. Allen, *Islamophobia* (London: Ashgate, 2010); P. Morey and A. Yaqin, *Framing Muslims: Stereotyping and Representation since 9/11* (Cambridge, Mass: Harvard University Press, 2011); J. Petley and R. Richardson, *Pointing the Finger: Islam and Muslims in the British Media* (Oxford: Oneworld Publications, 2011); K. Culcasi and M. Colsen, "The Face of Danger: Beards in the U.S. Media's Representations of Arabs, Muslims, and Middle Easterners," *Aether: The Journal of Media Geography* 8, no. b (September 2011): 82–96; S. Joseph and B. D'Harlingue, "The Wall Street Journal's Muslims: Representing Islam in American Print News Media," *Islamophobia Studies Journal* 1, no. 1 (2012): 131–162; H. Ansari and F. Hafez (eds.), *From the Far Right to the Mainstream: Islamophobia in Party Politics and the Media* (Frankfurt: Campus Verlag, 2012); R. Antonius, "A Mediated Relationship: Media Representations of Muslims and Arabs as a Political Process," in J. Hennebry and B. Momani (eds.), *Targeted Transnationals: The State, the Media, and Arab Canadians* (Vancouver: University of British Columbia Press, 2013). On France, see S. Rabah, *L'Islam dans le discours médiatique: Comment les médias se représentent l'Islam en France?* (Beirut: Al-Bouraq, 1998); T. Deltombe, *L'Islam imaginaire: La construction médiatique de l'islamophobie en France, 1975–2005* (Paris: La Découverte, 2005); P. Tevanian, *Le voile médiatique: Un faux débat: "L'affaire du foulard islamique"* (Paris: Raisons d'agir, 2005); Commission Islam et laïcité, *Islam, médias and opinions publiques: Déconstruire le choc des civilisations* (Paris: L'Harmattan, 2006); J. Gaertner, "L'Islam dans le cinéma français," *Cahiers de la Méditerranée*, no. 76 (2008); J. Ouaidat, *La représentation du monde arabo-musulman à la télévision française* (Paris: L'Harmattan, 2012).

2. Among the most well-documented internal media analyses are Deltombe, *L'Islam imaginaire*; C. A. Bail, "The Fringe Effect: Civil Society Organizations and the Evolution of Media Discourse about Islam since the September 11th Attacks," *American Sociological Review* 77, no. 6 (2012): 855–879.

3. For a critique of media-centrism, see S. Hall, C. Critcher, T. Jefferson, J. Clarke, and B. Roberts, *Policing the Crisis: Mugging, the State, and Law and Order* (London: Macmillan,

1978); B. Le Grignou, *Du côté des publics: Usages et réceptions de la télévision* (Paris: Economica, 2003).

4. J. Berthaut, E. Darras, and S. Laurens, "Pourquoi les faits divers stigmatisent-ils? L'hypothèse de la discrimination indirecte," *Réseaux*, no. 157–158 (2009): 90–124.

5. For a quantification before and after 11 September 2001 in France, see Deltombe, *L'Islam imaginaire*; in Great Britain, B. Whitaker, "Islam and the British Press after September 11," www.al-bab.com, 19 October 2005; M. Bromley, and S. Cushion, "Media Fundamentalism: The Immediate Response of the UK National Press to September 11th," in B. Zelizer and S. Allan, *Journalism after September 11th* (London: Routledge, 2003), 160–177; in the USA, Bail, "Fringe Effect."

6. Nasar Meer and Tariq Modood seek to understand why the dominant British discourse rebuts the idea that Islamophobia might be a type of racism. They carried out an internal analysis of media discourse, through a critical evaluation of the arguments mobilized, and four interviews with journalists holding powerful positions in the media field, which makes generalizing the findings difficult. "Refutations of Racism in the 'Muslim Question,'" *Patterns of Prejudice* 43, nos. 3 & 4 (2009): 332–351.

7. See J. Sedel, *Les médias et la banlieue* (Latresne: Le Bord de l'eau, 2009); L. Mucchielli, *Violences et insécurité: Fantasmes et réalités dans le débat français* (Paris: La Découverte, 2001).

8. This exclusion partially explains the creation of alternative Muslim media, such as the Internet sites www.oumma.com, www.saphirnews.com, www.al-kanz.org, etc. Since the early 2010s, this exclusion has usually been less powerful thanks to the success of the journalist's training offered by the online newspaper *Bondy Blog*, from which several Muslim-background journalists have found permanent jobs in some outlets, particularly the online newspaper *Mediapart*.

9. This is the figure of the "repentant sinner," identified by Noam Chomsky and Edward S. Herman as a feature of the anti-communist U.S. media system. *La fabrique du consentement: De la propagande médiatique en démocratie* (Marseille: Agone, 2008). It is represented by Muslim intellectuals referred to as "moderates," who fuel common sense about Islam, particularly in relation to the ban on wearing hijab in state schools in France, (e.g., Abdenour Bidar, Malek Chebel, Abdelwahab Meddeb, Mohamed Sifaoui, Kamel Daoud, Boualam Sansal, Zineb El Rhazoui, etc.) and justify the visceral Islamophobia of Oriana Fallaci in Italy (Magdi Allam). In some media, individual opposition to the Act of 15 March 2004 seems unspeakable even for non-Muslim journalists, like "this journalist at the end of their career who produced two pages of writing on wearing headscarves that was highly supportive of the 2004 Act on secularity but said in an interview that they were hostile to the law." Berthaut, Darras, and Laurens, "Pourquoi," 120. Nevertheless there do happen to be Muslim journalists integrated into the media world who challenge and even shut down some Islamophobic discourses, like when Aziz Zemmouri (*Le Figaro*, then *Le Point*) criticized Éric Zemmour's racism ("Aziz Zemouri Takes Down Éric Zemmour," www.oumma.com, 29 March 2010) or talked some sense into lawyer Gilbert Collard (a future Front national deputy) by texting him (thus demonstrating how interconnected people are in this milieu) who had stated that Muslims observing Ramadan did not swallow their saliva and spat it out, "which is dangerous in the middle of a period when the H1N1 flu virus is being spread" (RMC, 25 August 2009).

10. Berthaut, Darras, and Laurens, "Pourquoi," 9910.

11. We could hypothesize that the differences in media coverage of countries, cities, and regions and between different outlets are partly linked to marketing taking or not taking into account changes in the social composition of Muslim immigration, particularly the emergence of middle and upper classes within it.

12. See G. Noiriel, *Immigration, racisme et antisémitisme XIXe–XXe siècle: Discours publics, humiliations privées* (Paris: Fayard, 2007).

13. See P. Bourdieu, *Sur la télévision* (Paris: Liber, 1996).

14. See J. Salingue, "Les obsessions islamiques de la presse magazine," www.acrimed.org, 6 novembre 2012; I. Hanne, "Le Point et L'Express sans gêne avec l'Islam," www.ecrans.fr, 31 October 2012.

15. "Charlie Hebdo a triplé ses ventes avec les caricatures," www.leparisien.fr, 3 October 2012. The reaction of the French media to the publication of the Jyllands-Posten cartoons was not unanimous. For a discursive analysis of the French debates on this global affair, see C. Boe, J. Berthaut, C. Hmed, S. Jouanneau, and S. Laurens, "Should Voltaire Be a Prophet in His Own Country? An Analysis of the Media's Treatment of the Cartoon Crisis," in R. Kunelius, E. Eide, O. Hahn, and R. Schroeder (eds.), *Reading the Mohammed Cartoons Controversy: An International Analysis of Press Discourses on Free Speech and Political Spin* (Bochum: Projekt Verlag, 2007), 43–65.

16. Berthaut, Darras, and Laurens, "Pourquoi," 106.

17. To use Pierre Bourdieu's phrase in *Sur la télévision*.

18. On opinion polls, see A. Garrigou, *L'ivresse des sondages* (Paris: La Découverte, 2006); P. Lehingue, *Subunda: Coups de sonde dans l'océan des sondages* (Bellecombe-en-Bauges: Éditions du Croquant, 2007).

19. P. Bourdieu, "L'opinion publique n'existe pas," in *Questions de sociologie* (Paris: Minuit, 1984), 222–235.

20. See P. Tevanian, "Pour 100 % des musulmans, les sondages sont plutôt une menace: Réflexions sur la construction médiatique de l'islamophobie," http://lmsi.net, 24 October 2012; B. Magnin and H. Maler, "Sondage Ifop-Le Figaro sur les musulmans: Une incitation biaisée à la stigmatisation," www.acrimed.org, 12 November 2012.

21. J. Fourquet quoted in J-M. Guénois, "L'image de l'islam se dégrade fortement en France," *Le Figaro*, 24 October 2012.

22. See A. Hajjat, "L'emprise de Valeurs actuelles," *Carnet de recherche Racismes*, 13 November 2020, https://racismes.hypotheses.org/222.

23. In Italy, the most representative example is media intellectual Oriana Fallaci, whose massive, storming success—with sales in the millions of her trilogy (*The Rage and the Pride*, *The Force of Reason*, and *Interview with Myself: Apocalypse*)—has been studied by Bruno Cousin and Tommaso Vitale. Their survey of Italian intellectuals claiming to be Islamophobic is original in that it is a genuine sociology of the Italian intellectual field, which analyzes at the same time the intellectuals' trajectories, social characteristics, and positioning between the intellectual field and the domain of power. Fallaci's success can thus be explained both by the consolidation of a political legitimacy based on a strategy of progressive and charismatic construction (from the seasoned reporter to the privileged witness to the "Islamic threat") and by her long-lasting multiple positioning across various social fields (journalistic, intellectual, etc.). Fallaci in fact leant heavily on the system of mutual guarantees between the media field (RCS press group, Médiaset group, etc.) and the political domain (the Berlusconi

Right), which greatly facilitated the dissemination and commercial success of her writing. See B. Cousin and T. Vitale, "Les intellectuels italiens et islamophobie," *ContreTemps*, no. 12 (2011): 91–105; "Italian Intellectuals and the Promotion of Islamophobia after 9/11," in G. Morgan and S. Poynting (eds.), *Global Islamophobia: Muslims and Moral Panic in the West* (Farnham: Ashgate, 2012), 47–65. See also A. Testa and Gary Armstrong, *"We Are Against Islam!": The Lega Nord and the Islamic Folk Devil*, Sage Open, 2012, 1–14, https://journals.sagepub.com/doi/10.1177/2158244012467023.

24. For a review of the academic knowledge on the "Muslim problem" in France, see F. Dasseto, "L'Islam transplanté: Bilan des recherches européennes," *Revue européenne des migrations internationales* 10, no. 2 (1994): 201–211; S. Tersigni, "Jalons pour une lecture imbriquée du genre et du religieux dans le champ des migrations et des relations interethniques en France," *Cahiers du Cedref*, no. 16 (2008): 251–273; V. Geisser, "La 'question musulmane' en France au prisme des sciences sociales: Le savant, l'expert et le politique," *Cahiers d'études africaines*, no. 206–207 (2012): 351–366.

25. J. Leca, "L'islam, l'État et la société en France: De la difficulté de construire un objet de recherche et d'argumentation," *Annuaire de l'Afrique du Nord* 27 (1988): 41–72.

26. M. Weber, *La science, profession et vocation* (Marseille: Agone, 2005); N. Elias, *Engagement et distanciation: Contributions à la sociologie de la connaissance* (Paris: Fayard, 1993).

27. Geisser, "La 'question musulmane.'"

28. For a Europe-focused review, see V. Amiraux, "État de la littérature: L'islam et les musulmans en Europe: Un objet périphérique converti en incontournable des sciences sociales," *Critique internationale* 3, no. 56 (2012): 141–157.

29. Geisser, "La 'question musulmane,'" 351–352.

30. See V. Amiraux, "Expertises, savoirs et politique: La constitution de l'islam comme problème public," in B. Zimmermann (ed.), *Les sciences sociales à l'épreuve de l'action* (Paris: EHESS, 2004), 209–245.

31. C. Hamès, "L'éveil des écrits sur l'islam contemporain en Europe," *Archives des sciences sociales des religions* 68, no. 2 (1989): 147.

32. G. Kepel, *Le Prophète et Pharaon: Les mouvements islamistes dans l'Égypte contemporaine* (Paris: La Découverte, 1984).

33. G. Achcar, "L'orientalisme à rebours: de certaines tendances de l'orientalisme français après 1979," *Mouvements* 2, no. 54 (2008): 136. Achcar's assessment is challenged by Geisser, "La 'question musulmane,'" 357: "This critique seems greatly exaggerated as Kepel's work is always solidly based on rigorous methodological foundations, in no way likely to fuel a slippage into the vulgarization of philosophy."

34. F. Khosrokhavar, "Du néoorientalisme de Badie: Enjeux et méthodes," *Peuples méditerranéens*, no. 50 (1990): 121–148.

35. Said, *Covering Islam*, 100.

36. Amiraux, "Expertises, savoirs et politique," 213.

37. See A. Gresh, "Bernard Lewis et le gène de l'islam," *Le Monde diplomatique*, August 2005, 28; C. Bottici and B. Challand, "Rethinking Political Myth: The Clash of Civilizations as a Self-Fulfilling Prophecy," *European Journal of Social Theory* 9, no. 3 (2006): 315–336; and idem., *The Myth of the Clash of Civilizations* (London: Routledge, 2010).

38. E. Said, "Impossible Histories: Why the Many Islams Cannot Be Simplified," *Harper's*, July 2002, quoted in Gresh, "Bernard Lewis."

39. See L. Dakhli, "L'islamologie est un sport de combat: De Gilles Kepel à Olivier Roy, l'univers impitoyable des experts de Islam," *Revue du Crieur* 1, no. 3 (2016): 4–17; F. Carrié, *Radicalisation: Fantasmes et réalités* (Paris: Éditions Amsterdam, 2022).

40. B. Rougier (ed.), *Les territoires conquis de l'islamisme* (Paris: Presses universitaires de France, 2020). For an academic approach to the link between jihadism and prison, see C. de Galembert, *Islam et prison* (Paris: Éditions Amsterdam, 2020).

41. L. Bonnefoy, "Idées toutes faites sur *Les territoires conquis de Islamisme*," *Orient XXI*, 10 February 2020, https://orientxxi.info/lu-vu-entendu/idees-toutes-faites-sur-les -territoires-conquis-de-l-islamisme,3618.

42. See T. Deltombe, "Armer les esprits: Le business des 'experts' à la télévision française," in D. Bigo, L. Bonelli, and T. Deltombe (eds.), *Au nom du 11 Septembre: Les démocraties à l'épreuve de l'antiterrorisme* (Paris: La Découverte, 2008), 302–319; Geisser, "La 'question musulmane.'"

43. The myth of "Islamization" is particularly developed by O. Fallaci, *La rabbia e l'orgo-glio* (Milan: Rizzoli, 2001); A. Del Valle, *Le totalitarisme islamiste à l'assaut des démocraties* (Paris: Éditions des Syrtes, 2002); T. M. Savage, "Europe and Islam: Crescent Waxing, Cul-tures Clashing," *Washington Quarterly* 27, no. 3 (2004): 25–50; B. Ye'or, *Eurabia: L'axe euro-arabe* (2005; reprint, Paris: Jean-Cyrille Godefroy Éditions, 2006); M. Phillips, *Londonistan: How Britain Is Creating a Terror State Within* (London: Encounter Books, 2006); C. Cald-well, *Une révolution sous nos yeux: Comment l'islam va transformer la France et l'Europe* (2009; reprint, Paris: Les Éditions du Toucan, 2011); R. S. Leiken, *Europe's Angry Muslims: The Revolt of the Second Generation* (Oxford: Oxford University Press, 2011), and "Europe's Immigra-tion Problem, and Ours," *Mediterranean Quarterly* 15, no. 4 (2004): 203–218.

44. See I. Jablonka, "La peur de l'islam: Bat Ye'or et le spectre de l''Eurabie,'" *La Vie des idées*, 1 May 2006, available at www.laviedesidees.fr; R. Liogier, *Le mythe de l'islamisation: Essai sur une obsession collective* (Paris: Seuil, 2012).

45. Caldwell, *Une révolution sous nos yeux*.

46. R. K. Merton, *Éléments de théorie et de méthode* (Paris: Plon, 1965), 143.

47. See "De l'islamophobie dans Science et Vie junior," www.alkanz.org, 15 May 2013.

48. See L. Abu-Lughod, *Do Muslim Women Need Saving?* (Cambridge, Mass: Harvard University Press, 2013); A. Hajjat, "La 'femme musulmane opprimée': Genèse d'un nouveau genre littéraire à succès (1988–2003)," *French Cultural Studies* (2021): 251–268, https://doi .org/10.1177%2F09571558211002438.

49. See A. G. Hargreaves, "Testimony, Co-Authorship and Dispossession among Women of Maghrebi Origin in France," *Research in African Literatures* 37, no. 1 (2006): 42–54.

50. P. Bourdieu, "Une révolution conservatrice dans l'édition," *Actes de la recherche en sciences sociales*, nos. 126–127 (1999): 3–28.

51. S. Hall, "Codage/Décodage," *Réseaux* 12, no. 68 (1994): 27–39.

52. Le Grignou, B. *Du côté des publics*.

CHAPTER 8. The Islamophobic Political Cause

1. On the concept of the "exception," see G. Agamben, *State of Exception* (Chicago: University of Chicago Press, 2003); S. M. Barkat, *Le corps d'exception: Les artifices du pouvoir colonial et la destruction de la vie* (Paris: Éditions Amsterdam, 2005).

2. See R. Lefebvre and F. Sawicki, *La société des socialistes: Le PS aujourd'hui* (Bellecombe-en-Bauges: Éditions du Croquant, 2006); D. Éribon, *D'une révolution conservatrice et de ses effets sur la gauche française* (Paris: Éditions Leo Scheer, 2007).

3. "Revolving doors" refers to the practice whereby senior civil servants who are graduates of the prestigious grandes écoles decide to leave the service of the state for the private sector.

4. C. Braconnier and J-Y. Dormagen, *La démocratie de l'abstention: Aux origines de la démobilisation électorale en milieu populaire* (Paris: Gallimard, 2007).

5. Collectif Cette France-là, *Cette France-là 01/07/2008–30/06/2009*, vol. 2 (Paris: La Découverte, 2010).

6. Broadcast on Antenne 2, 5 September 1984.

7. A. Collovald, *Le "populisme du FN": Un dangereux contresens* (Bellecombe-en-Bauges: Éditions du Croquant, 2004), 154.

8. For a sociological analysis of Front national voters, see Collovald, *Le "populisme du FN."*

9. C. Allen, *Islamophobia* (London: Ashgate, 2010).

10. P. John, H. Margetts, D. Rowland, and S. Weir, *The BNP: The Roots of Its Appeal* (Colchester: Democratic Audit, Human Rights Centre, University of Essex, 2006), 17.

11. See P. Lehingue, *Le vote: Approches sociologiques de l'institution et des comportements électoraux* (Paris: La Découverte, 2011).

12. C. Braconnier, "Comprendre les comportements électoraux par les approches environnementales" (thesis in political science, Université de Cergy-Pontoise, 2009).

13. Racist ideology is no longer usually based on the concept of race but on that of culture; instead of referring to the principle of racial inequality, it deploys cultural difference and shifts from heterophobia (the negation of the dominated culture) to heterophily (the positive assessment of foreign culture as long as it stays at home). See P-A. Taguieff, *La force du préjugé: Essai sur le racisme et ses doubles* (Paris: La Découverte, 1988).

14. The title of chapter 12 of Pierre-André Taguieff's edited collection (*Face au racisme*, vol. 1, *Les moyens d'agir* [Paris: La Découverte, 1991]). Basing their work in the social sciences, the authors of this chapter (Anne-Marie Delcambre and Jean Weydert, a reinterpretation of political scientist Jean Leca and sociologist Jacqueline Costa-Lascoux) deconstruct the negative representations of Islam: "conquering Islam," "Is France a future Islamic republic?," "fundamentalism of disoriented youth," "Islam as a threat to French identity," "Islam resistant to secular values," "Islam as an obstacle to assimilation." The quality of this book is in stark contrast to Taguieff's later adoption of Islamophobic stances, which embody exactly what he began by critiquing.

15. F. Lebaron, "La droite française, l'Europe et l'effet phobie,'" *Mémoires des luttes*, 13 February 2013, www.medelu.org.

16. P. De Villiers, *Les mosquées de Roissy* (Paris: Albin Michel, 2006).

17. "Marine Le Pen lance une nouvelle offensive contre la viande halal," Agence France Presse, 18 February 2012.

18. See L. Chambon, *Marine ne perd pas le Nord* (Paris: Le Muscadier, 2012); I. Van der Valk, *Islamophobie aux Pays-Bas* (Amsterdam: Amsterdam University Press, 2012).

19. L. Chambon, "Le FN ressuscite la droite," *Minorités*, no. 129 (13 May 2012), www.minorites.org.

20. See A. Mondon and A. Winter, *Reactionary Democracy: How Racism and the Populist Far Right Became the Mainstream* (London: Verso, 2020).

21. See L. Lévy, *"La Gauche," les Noirs et les Arabes* (Paris: La Fabrique, 2010), 13–14.

22. In the United States, Barack Obama was the subject of persistent rumors, propagated by political opponents during the presidential campaigns of 2008 and 2012, suggesting that he was actually a Muslim. Insofar as these rumors are perceived as forms of political undermining, he had to state that "[he had] never been a Muslim." See S. Sheehi, *Islamophobia: The Ideological Campaign against Muslims* (Atlanta: Clarity Press, 2011); N. Lean, *The Islamophobia Industry: How the Right Manufactures Fear of Muslims* (London: Pluto Press, 2012); D. Kumar, *Islamophobia and the Politics of Empire* (Chicago: Haymarket Book, 2012). In Australia, the conservative Liberal Party pursued a similar tactic against the Labor Party in 2007, distributing a false pamphlet supporting the latter, produced by a fictitious Islamist group. K. M. Dunn and A. Kamp, "A Failed Political Attempt to Use Global Islamophobia in Western Sydney: The 'Lindsay Leaflet Scandal,'" in G. Morgan and S. Poynting (eds.), *Global Islamophobia: Muslims and Moral Panic in the West* (Farnham: Ashgate, 2012), 143–160.

23. "Appels de Ramadan et des 700 mosquées à voter Hollande, l'intox," www.liberation.fr, 26 April 2012.

24. See the section in the *Revue française de science politique*, no. 60 (August 2010), "Représentants et représentés: Élus de la diversité et minorités visibles"; and the findings of M. Avanza, "Qui représentent les élus de la 'diversité'? Croyances partisanes et points de vue de 'divers,'" *Revue française de science politique*, no. 60 (2010): 754–767; "Manières d'être divers. Les stratégies partisanes de la 'diversité' aux élections municipales de 2008," in D. Fassin (ed.), *Les nouvelles frontières de la société française* (Paris: La Découverte, 2010), 403–425.

25. On this concept, see L. Mathieu, *L'espace des mouvements sociaux* (Bellecombe-en-Bauges: Éditions du Croquant, 2012).

26. For an overview of the European extreme Right, see D. Vidal, *Le ventre est encore fécond: Les nouvelles extrêmes droites européennes* (Paris: Libertalia, 2012); R. Taras, *Xenophobia and Islamophobia in Europe* (Edinburgh: Edinburgh University Press, 2012). For a synthetic map: "Anatomy of Islamophobia," *World Policy Journal*, no. 28 (2011): 14.

27. "Les 'Assises internationales contre l'islamisation de l'Europe,' un dîner de (néo)cons pour le Bloc Identitaire et Riposte Laïque," *REFLEXes*, 20 December 2012, http://reflexes.samizdat.net.

28. In the USA, this loose network is composed of conservative evangelists and other Christians (Jerry Falwell, Pat Robertson, John Hagee, etc.), factions of the Tea Party, pro-Israel movements, influential bloggers such as Robert Spencer (Jihad Watch and the Freedom Center, by neoconservative David Horowitz) and Pamela Geller (founder of Stop Islamization of America in 2010, which merged in 2011 with Stop Islamization of Europe to form Stop Islamization of Nations), liberal intellectuals, etc. It is actively supported by media outlets such as Fox News and figures in the Republican Party (Newt Gingrich, Sarah Palin, etc.).

29. The Tribunal was organized by the following movements and information sites: Résistance républicaine, Actions Sita, Free World Academy, Institut européen de socialisation et d'éducation, L'élan nouveau des citoyens, Bloc identitaire, Comité Lépante, Ligue du droit des femmes, Riposte laïque, Vérité, valeurs et démocratie, Novopress, L'Ordre républicain, Liberty Vox, Rebelles.info, Le Gaulois, Puteaux-libre, Union gaulliste, Drzz.info, SDF, L'Observatoire de l'islamisation, Parti de l'innocence, Ligue de défense française, Cared, le Cercle

Aristote, le Blog des gaullistes populaires, Laïcité et République sociale, Bivouac-ID, Union des jeunes pour le progrès (UJP), Force et initiative républicaine de coalisés (IRC).

30. See M. Zancarini-Fournel, "Études de cas: Des féministes islamophobes," seminar on Islamophobia, EHESS, 15 February 2013.

31. On 23 March 2012, the Seventeenth chamber of the tribunal correctionnel at the Palais de Justice in Paris found Pierre Cassen and Pascal Hilout guilty of incitement to racial hatred toward Muslims, following a suit filed by the Ligue des droits de l'homme (LDH). In an editorial written under the pseudonym Cyrano (11 October 2010), Cassen had wondered: "Can we count on 'moderate' Muslims when we have to fight the heart of Islam?"

32. Former teacher and activist in the women's liberation movement.

33. Former nursery schoolteacher and ex-member of the Parti socialiste, she was elected as a local councilwoman on a UMP list in Caluire, a middle-class area of Greater Lyon, and appointed as a delegate to l'Égalité hommes-femmes. She then joined Nicolas Dupont-Aignan's Debout la République! party and ran unsuccessfully for them in the 2009 European elections. She was a founding member and patron of the Ni putes ni soumises (NPNS) Greater Lyon and the Rhône regional branch—decorated with the Légion d'honneur by Fadela Amara in October 2009—and is still invited to event by NPNS despite her alliance with the extreme Right. See the program for the "États généraux de la laïcité" in Lyon, on 14 September 2011 on the www.npns.fr site. She was also secretary and then vice-president of the Coordination française du lobby européen des femmes de Bruxelles, before her dismissal because of her political positions.

34. Richard Millet is the author of a "Literary Eulogy" of the Norwegian extreme-right terrorist Anders Breivik. See *Langue fantôme suivi de Éloge littéraire d'Anders Breivik* (Paris: P.-G. de Roux, Paris, 2012).

35. "Les 'Assises internationales.'"

36. For example, journalist Caroline Fourest criticized the exclusion of a woman wearing a headscarf from a private space (the case of Fanny Truchelut's rural gîte in 2006), the banning of minarets in Switzerland, the Tribunal against Islamization, etc.

37. F. Lorcerie (ed.), *La politisation du voile en France, en Europe et dans le monde arabe* (Paris: L'Harmattan, 2005).

38. P. Bourdieu and L. Boltanski, "La production de l'idéologie dominante," *Actes de la recherche en sciences sociales*, no. 2 (1976): 3–73.

CHAPTER 9. Legal Discrimination by a Capillary-
Like Process

1. For more details, see J. Beaugé and A. Hajjat, "Élites françaises et construction du 'problème musulman': Le cas du Haut Conseil à l'intégration (1989–2012)," *Sociologie* 5, no. 1 (2014): 31–59. See also P. Baehr and D. Gordon, "From the Headscarf to the Burqa: The Role of Social Theorists in Shaping Laws against the Veil," *Economy and Society* 42, no. 2 (2013): 249–280.

2. P. Bourdieu and L. Boltanski, "La production de l'idéologie dominante," *Actes de la recherche en sciences sociales*, no. 2 (1976): 3–73.

3. F. Baroin, *Pour une nouvelle laïcité*, Club Dialogue & Initiative (2003), available at www.dialogue-initiative.com.

4. E. Poulat, *Notre laïcité publique: "La France est une République laïque"* (Paris: Berg International, 2003).

5. See A. Hajjat, *Les frontières de l'"identité nationale": L'injonction à l'assimilation en France métropolitaine et coloniale* (Paris: La Découverte, Sciences humaines, 2012).

6. J. Baubérot, "L'acteur et le sociologue: La commission Stasi," in D. Naudier and M. Simonet (eds.), *Des sociologues sans qualités? Pratiques de recherche et engagements* (Paris: La Découverte, 2011), 101–116.

7. F. Lorcerie, "À l'assaut de l'agenda public: La politisation du voile islamique en 2003–2004," in F. Lorcerie (ed.), *La politisation du voile en France, en Europe et dans le monde arabe* (Paris: L'Harmattan, 2005), 11–36.

8. P. Bernard, "Membre de la commission Stasi, Alain Touraine raconte sa conversion au principe d'une loi," *Le Monde*, 18 December 2003.

9. In relation to the charter project, the commission was composed of Blandine Kriegel, Michel Sappin, Jacqueline Costa-Lacoux, Carole Da Silva, Gaye Petek, Myriam Salah-Eddine, Jean-Philippe Wirth, Benoît Normand, and Richard Senghor (rapporteur). Alain Seksig was then appointed head of the Mission laïcité at the HCI. The recommendations on religious neutrality in private companies were established by a working group from the Observatoire de la laïcité that had been meeting since 2007. Apart from certain (former or current) HCI members (Alain Seksig, Gaye Petek, Malika Sorel), well-known advocates of the "new laïcité" are: Françoise Hostalier (UMP deputy), Élisabeth Badinter (philosopher), Ghaleb Bencheikh (theologian), Abdennour Bidar (philosopher), Yolène Dilas-Rocherieux (sociology lecturer at the Université Paris-Ouest-Nanterre and author of an article against wearing hijab in the university), Sihem Habchi (Ni putes ni soumises), Patrick Kessel (journalist and chair of the Comité laïcité républicain), Catherine Kintzler (professor of philosophy at Université Lille-III), and Barbara Lefebvre (professor of history and geography and coauthor of "Les territoires perdus de la République"). The composition of the Observatory changed on 5 April 2013 (see www.gouvernement.fr/gouvernement/observatoire-de-la-laicite).

10. L. Boltanski, "L'espace positionnel: Multiplicité des positions institutionnelles et habitus de classe," *Revue française de sociologie* 14, no. 1 (1973): 25.

11. HCI, *Études et intégration: Faire connaître les valeurs de la République. Les élus issus de l'immigration dans les conseils municipaux, 2001–2008* (Paris: La Documentation française, 2009), 40.

12. HCI, *Les défis de l'intégration à l'école: Recommandations relatives à l'expression religieuse dans les espaces publics de la République* (Paris: La Documentation française, 2011), 1.

13. HCI, *La laïcité dans la fonction publique: De la définition du principe à son application* (Paris: La Documentation française, 2012), 15.

14. In addition to the Observatoire de la laïcité, we can note Minister of Education Vincent Peillon's establishment of a committee on teaching "secular morals" on 12 October 2012. This committee was composed of Rémy Schwartz (former member of the HCI and rapporteur of the Stasi Commission), Alain Bergougnioux (historian), and Laurence Loeffel (lecturer in education science) ("Un trio d'experts pour faire la leçon de 'morale laïque,'" *Le Monde*, 11 October 2012). On 8 January 2018, the minister of education set up an advisory board on secularity, which adopted a strongly neo-secular orientation.

15. Certain newspapers have established special issues or specialist sections. One example

among others is the blog "Digne de foi: Éclairage sur le fait religieux et la laïcité" by *Le Monde* journalist Stéphanie Le Bars, http://religion.blog.lemonde.fr.

16. The idea of a code was first put forward by the Ligue de l'enseignement in its evidence to the Stasi Commission: Jean-Michel Ducomte, lecturer in public law at Sciences-Po Toulouse and chair of the Ligue de l'enseignement, outlined a version of it on the association's website, https://laicite.lalingue.org/, which was then taken up by the minister of the interior, Claude Guéant (DJO, 2011). See C. Hoyeau, "Un code de la laïcité pour garantir la neutralité du service public," *La Croix*, 23 October 2011.

17. Examples of master's programs: "Religions et laïcité dans la vie professionnelle et associative" (Institut européen en sciences des religions, a secular, state-funded institute in Paris); "Laïcité, droit des cultes et des associations religieuses" (Université Aix-Marseille); "Sciences du religieux et de la laïcité" (Université Lyon 2).

18. These specialist magazines include the following: *Vive la République!*, newsletter of the not-for-profit République et laïcité (1999); *Laïcité et territoires* (Secularity and Territories) by the Ligue de l'enseignement; *Les Essentiels QCL Collectivités territoriales et laïcité* (QCLs (The Essential on Local and Regional Authorities and Secularity) by Question croyance(s) & laïcité (a training and advisory service for people managing religious pluralism in public settings), of which twenty-two issues were published between 2008 and 2010; *Laïcité info* and *Prix de la laïcité* from the influential Comité laïcité république (founded by Pierre Bergé and chaired by Patrick Kessel); and lastly, the establishment of the "Certificat diversité et laïcité" issued by the Licra to public and private-sector organizations (2013) etc.

19. Cabinet "Cultes et cultures consulting" or Observatoire du fait religieux dans le monde du travail de Dounia Bouzar (www.cultesetcultures-consulting.com).

20. Here we could point to sociologist Jean Baubérot (specialist in secularity and the only member of the Stasi Commission to abstain); the Islam et laïcité Commission (www.isla-mlaicite.org) within the Ligue de l'enseignement (which was thus split over "nouvelle laïcité"); the Les mots sont importants (LMSI) collective; the Une école pour tou-te-s collective, etc. (see chapter 5). Jean Baubérot's concept of "falsified secularity" is part of the struggle for the definition of secularity and sets up an opposition between the "fake" "new secularity" and the "authentic" old-style secularity. J. Baubérot, *La laïcité falsifiée* (Paris: La Découverte, 2012).

21. HCI, *20 ans au service de l'intégration, 1990–2010* (Paris: La Documentation française, 2010), 11–12.

22. HCI, *La laïcité dans la fonction publique*, 10.

23. HCI, *Les défis*, ii. Our emphasis.

24. HCI, *La laïcité dans la fonction publique*, 15.

25. F. Lorcerie, "Les professionnels de l'école et l'affaire du voile: Des personnels très partagés sur l'incrimination du voile," in Lorcerie, *La politisation*, 73–94; P. Tevanian, *Le voile médiatique: Un faux débat: "L'affaire du foulard islamique"* (Paris: Raisons d'agir, 2005), 19–26.

26. J-P. Obin, *Les signes et manifestations d'appartenance religieuse dans les établissements scolaires* (Paris: Ministère de l'Éducation nationale, 2004).

27. The Ministry of Education was represented by the minister (Luc Chatel), the director-general of schools (Jean-Michel Blanquer, future minister of education), the head of the Inspectorate in Life and Earth sciences (Dominique Rojat), and the dean of the Vie

scolaire group (Claude Bisson-Vaivre). The Ministry of Higher Education was represented by the head of strategy in the General Directorate for Higher Education and Employment (Alain Coulon) and the dean of the University of Strasbourg Law School and writer of the "Laïcité et enseignement supérieur" (Higher Education and Secularity' guide for the Conference of University Provosts) (Christian Mestre).

28. HCI, *La laïcité dans la fonction publique*, 12.

29. Ibid., 9.

30. Ibid., 15.

31. Around three thousand signs were recorded in state education establishments in 1994–1995; 1,465 in 2003–2004; and 639 in 2004–2005. H. Chérifi, *Application de la loi du 15 March 2004 sur le port des signes religieux ostensibles dans les établissements d'enseignement publics* (Paris: La Documentation française, 2005), 41–44.

32. HCI, *La laïcité dans la fonction publique*, 37. Our emphasis.

33. HCI, *Les défis*, 95.

34. Ibid., 101. Our emphasis.

35. Ibid. Our emphasis.

36. G. Noiriel, *État, nation et immigration: Vers une histoire du pouvoir* (Paris: Belin, 2001).

37. P. Bourdieu, *Langage et pouvoir symbolique* (Paris: Seuil, 2001), 73–74.

38. Dominique Rojat, inspecteur général de l'Éducation nationale en sciences de la vie et de la Terre, in HCI, *La laïcité dans la fonction publique*, 35.

39. HCI, *La laïcité dans la fonction publique*, 38.

40. HCI, *Les défis*, 95.

41. Since the early 2000s, there has been a proliferation of journalistic reports, inside stories, and university research, funded through government competitive tendering, on "Muslims in prison," "Muslims in the army," "Islam in hospitals," "Islam in private-sector companies," etc.

42. A. Sayad, "Immigration et 'pensée d'État,'" *Actes de la recherche en sciences sociales*, no. 129 (1999): 5–14.

43. HCI, *Charte de la laïcité dans les services publics et autres avis* (Paris: La Documentation française, 2007), 27–32.

44. HCI, *Les défis*, p. 94.

45. HCI, *La laïcité dans la fonction publique*, 33.

46. HCI, *Charte de la laïcité*, 32–35.

47. Direction des Journaux Officiels, *Laïcité et liberté religieuse: Recueil de textes et de jurisprudence* (Paris: La Documentation française, 2011).

48. HCI, *Charte de la laïcité*, p. 43.

49. HCI, *De la neutralité religieuse en entreprise*, Avis au Premier ministre, 2011, 7.

50. Ibid., 6.

51. *Entreprise et religion: État des lieux, problématiques et acteurs* (Religious expression and secularity in the company setting), produced in December 2010 and updated in April 2011, by Anne Lamour. It is also cited by journalist Cécilia Gabizon, another member of the HCI in "Voile islamique: Malaise dans les entreprises," *Le Figaro*, 7 February 2011.

52. HCI, *De la neutralité religieuse en entreprise*, 9.

53. AFP news release. The ruling by the Conseil has not to our knowledge been made public.

54. See S. Hennette-Vauchez and V. Valentin, *L'affaire Baby Loup ou la nouvelle laïcité* (Issy-les-Moulineaux: LGDJ–Lextenso éditions, 2015).

55. E. Dockès, "Liberté, laïcité, Baby Loup: De la très modeste et très contestée résistance de la Cour de cassation face à la xénophobie montante," *Droit social*, no. 5 (May 2013): 388.

56. See L. Mozère, "Les difficultés des assistantes maternelles étrangères face au chômage: Quelques indications concernant leur usage de la langue," *Les Cahiers du CEDREF*, no. 8–9 (2000), available at http://cedref.revues.org.

57. S. Slama, "Le privilège du national: Étude historique de la condition civique des étrangers en France" (PhD diss. in public law, université Paris-X-Nanterre, 2003), 252.

58. Dockès, "Liberté, laïcité, Baby Loup."

CHAPTER 10. The Depoliticization of Violence and the Politics of Compensation

1. This section is based on A. Hajjat, "A Double-Bind Situation? The Depoliticization of Violence and the Politics of Compensation," in G. Titley, D. Freedman, G. Khiabany, et al. (eds.), *After Charlie Hebdo: Terror, Racism and Free Speech* (London: Zed Books, 2017), 79–96.

2. W. E. B. Du Bois, *The Souls of Black Folk* (Chicago: A. C. McClurg, 1903).

3. F. Aubenas, "Magnanville: Les fractures françaises au grand jour," *Le Monde*, 20 June 2016.

4. "À Nice, plus d'un tiers des victimes de confession musulmane," *Mediapart*, 19 July 2016.

5. P. Val, *Malaise dans l'inculture* (Paris: Grasset, 2015), 83. See C. De Montlibert, "Philippe Val et la haine de la sociologie," *Le Monde*, 21 April 2015.

6. C. Fourest, *Éloge du blasphème* (Paris: Grasset, 2015); BFM TV, 8 January 2015. See les Indivisibles, "Non-coupables," 1 February 2015, http://www.lesindivisibles.fr/non-coupables/.

7. D. Sieffert, *Israël-Palestine, une passion française: La France dans le miroir du conflit israélo-palestinien* (Paris: La Découverte, 2004).

8. CNCDH (Commission nationale consultative des droits de l'homme), *La lutte contre le racisme, l'antisémitisme et la xénophobie: Année 2015* (Paris: La Documentation française, 2016).

9. "Incitations à la haine, racisme, intox: Des élus et cadres du FN se lâchent," *Bastamag*, 23 January 2015.

10. "Meurtre de M. El Makouli: L'irresponsabilité pénale requise," *La Provence*, 16 June 2016.

11. CNCDH, *La lutte contre le racisme, l'antisémitisme et la xénophobie*).

12. "Terrorisme: La crainte d'une réplique de l'ultradroite," *Libération*, 13 July 2016.

13. "Coup de fil au sein d'une cellule clandestine de l'ultra-droite," *Mediapart*, 24 June 2018; "Révélations sur des 'patriotes' qui projetaient des attentats islamophobes," *Mediapart*, 1 April 2019.

14. The founder of the National Front, Jean-Marie Le Pen, was dismissed from the party by its actual leader, his daughter Marine Le Pen, when he repeated that gas chambers were a "detail" of Second World War history.

15. *France Inter*, 6 January 2016. Badinter stated, "We mustn't be afraid to be labeled as Islamophobes."

16. "Attentat: Rioufol ouvre le bal des 'dérapages,'" *Politis*, 8 January 2015.

17. A national association of judges.

18. Syndicat de la magistrature, "Apologie du terrorisme: Résister à l'injonction de la répression immédiate!," 20 January 2015, http://www.syndicat-magistrature.org/Apologie -du-terrorisme-Resister-a.html.

19. "Apologie du terrorisme: La justice face à l'urgence," *Le Monde*, 22 January 2015.

20. Amedy Coulibaly (1982–2005) was involved in the January 2015 terror attacks in Paris, claiming to be a member of the Islamic State. On 8 January 2015, he killed the police-woman Clarissa Jean-Philippe in Montrouge and seriously wounded a highway patrolman. The next day, he committed a hostage-taking in a kosher convenience store located at Porte de Vincennes, murdering four people of the Jewish faith, and was later killed by the SWAT team.

21. Chérif and Saïd Kouachi carried out the attack on the *Charlie Hebdo* offices in Paris on 7 January 2015, which killed twelve people. They were killed by police on 9 January.

22. "Nice: Le petit garçon, entendu par la police pour apologie du terrorisme, témoigne," *La Dépêche*, 5 February 2015.

23. "Un enfant de 9 ans entendu pour 'apologie de terrorisme,' son père porte plainte," *Le Parisien*, 30 January 2015.

24. "Dans le tourbillon médiatique," *La Nouvelle République*, 3 January 2016.

25. "Bombardier Crespin: Menacé de licenciement parce qu'il n'est pas 'Charlie'?," *La Voix du Nord*, 29 January 2015.

26. "Deux mois de prison ferme pour apologie d'acte terroriste," *Rue89 Bordeaux*, 16 December 2015.

27. L. Bonelli and F. Carrié, *La fabrique de la radicalité: Une sociologie des jeunes djihad-istes français* (Paris: Seuil, 2018).

28. "Etat d'urgence: Les perquisitions en chute libre," *Le Monde*, 14 January 2016.

29. See A. Hajjat, *Les frontières de l'identité nationale': L'injonction à l'assimilation en France métropolitaine et coloniale* (Paris: La Découverte, 2012).

30. "Les missions locales et la PJJ mobilisées pour la prévention de la radicalisation," Directions.fr, 19 May 2015.

31. "Radicalisation religieuse: L'Education nationale dérape," *Mediapart*, 21 November 2014.

32. Interview with a CAF director, 20 July 2016.

CHAPTER 11. Construction and Circulations of
European Representations of Islam and Muslims

1. For an overview, see M. Rodinson, *La Fascination de l'Islam* (1980; reprint, Paris: La Découverte, 2003); F. Quinn, *The Sum of All Heresies: The Image of Islam in Western Thought* (New York: Oxford University Press, 2008).

2. The "anti-Semitic archive" is Enzo Traverso's phrase. This idea is defined as being in the sense of an early Foucault, not like a library, or a body of documents and texts, but rather as the regulatory mode of a discursive practice, as Traverso puts it, "the law on what can be said, and the system governing the appearance of statements as individual/unique events,"

by allowing them to 'subsist and change regularly.'" E. Traverso, *La fin de la modernité juive: Histoire d'un tournant conservateur* (Paris: La Découverte, 2013), 126.

3. See the classic work by N. Daniel, *Islam et l'Occident* (Paris: Éditions du Cerf., 1993); J. Dakhlia and B. Vincent (eds.), *Les musulmans dans l'histoire de l'Europe*, 2 vols. (Paris: Albin Michel, 2011–2013).

4. J. Tolan, *Les Sarrasins* (2000; reprint, Paris: Flammarion, 2003), 21.

5. Daniel, *Islam et l'Occident*, 14.

6. Tolan, *Les Sarrasins*, 20 and 363 respectively.

7. It is a shame to observe that to our knowledge there is no historical work on representations of the Prophet in European discourse from the Middle Ages to the present.

8. Daniel, *Islam et l'Occident*, 16.

9. Tolan, *Les Sarrasins*, 366. See below.

10. J. Cohen, "The Muslim Connection, or the Changing Role of the Jew in High Medieval Theology," in Jeremy Cohen (ed.), *From Witness to Witchcraft: Jews and Judaism in Medieval Christian Thought* (Wiesbaden: Harrassowitz, 1996), 141–162.

11. Tolan, *Les Sarrasins*, 363.

12. Ibid., 364.

13. See Daniel, *Islam et l'Occident*, 360–84; A. Thomson, "L'Europe des Lumières et le monde musulman: Une alterité ambiguë," *Cromohs*, no. 10 (2005): 1–11, www.cromohs .unifi.it.

14. Thomson, "L'Europe des Lumières."

15. Ibid.

16. Ibid. A comparable change can be identified in the British vision of India. In the middle of the nineteenth century the positive vision of Indian civilization gives way to a negative view stressing its "inferiority," given that there is a difference in the representations of Hindus and Muslims in India. J. Pitts, *Naissance de la bonne conscience coloniale: Les libéraux français et britanniques et la question impériale, 1770–1870* (Ivry-sur-Seine: Éditions de l'Atelier, 2008).

17. See H. Laurens, *Orientales* (Paris: CNRS Éditions, 2007); H. Laurens, J. Tolan, and G. Veinstein, *L'Europe et Islam, quinze siècles d'histoire* (Paris: Odile Jacob, 2009).

18. See J. Waardenburg, "Mustashrikun," *The Encyclopaedia of Islam*, 2nd ed. (Leiden: Brill, 1993): 7:735–753.

19. See H. Laurens, *L'Expédition d'Égypte 1798–1801* (Paris: Seuil, 1997).

20. On the "race war" see M. Foucault, *"Il faut défendre la société": Cours au Collège de France, 1975–1976* (Paris: Gallimard/Seuil, 1997); on pseudoscientific racial anthropology see C. Reynaud-Paligot, *La République raciale: Paradigme racial et idéologie républicaine (1860–1930)* (Paris: Presses universitaires de France, 2006).

21. P. Weil, "Histoire et mémoire des discriminations en matière de nationalité française," *Vingtième siècle, Revue d'histoire*, no. 84 (2004): 522; E. Saada, *Les enfants de la colonie: Les métis de l'empire français entre sujétion et citoyenneté* (Paris: La Découverte, 2007); Y. Urban, *L'indigène dans le droit colonial français (1865–1955)* (Paris: LGDJ, 2010); A. Hajjat, *Les frontières de l'identité nationale': L'injonction à l'assimilation en France métropolitaine et coloniale* (Paris: La Découverte, 2012).

22. Court of Algiers, 5 November 1903, *Revue algérienne et tunisienne de législation et de jurisprudence*, 1904, 2, 25, quoted in Weil, "Histoire et mémoire," 8.

23. See N. Bancel, P. Blanchard, and L. Gervereau, (eds.), *Images et colonies: Monographie et propagande coloniale sur l'Afrique française de 1880 à 1962* (Nanterre/Paris; BDIC/Achac, 1993); B. De L'estoile, *Le goût des autres: De l'Exposition coloniale aux arts premiers* (Paris:-Flammarion, 2007).

24. See A. Ruscio, *Que la France était belle au temps des colonies . . . Anthologie de chansons coloniales et exotiques françaises* (Paris: Maisonneuve & Larose, 2001); U. Mathis-Moser, "L'image de 'l'Arabe' dans la chanson française contemporaine," 2, no. 2 (2003): 129–143.

25. See A. Arondekar, "Without a Trace: Sexuality and the Colonial Archive," *Journal of the History of Sexuality*, no. 14 (2005): 10–27.

26. On the sensual "Arab woman," see J. Clancy-Smith, "Islam, Gender, and Identities in the Making of French Algeria, 1830–1962," in J. Clancy-Smith and F. Gouda (eds.), *Domesticating the Empire: Race, Gender and Family Life in French and Dutch Colonialism* (Charlottesville: University Press of Virginia, 1998), 154–174; W. Woodhull, "Unveiling Algeria," *Genders*, no. 10 (1991): 112–131. On the same woman as "oppressed," see, inter alia, L. Ahmed, "Western Ethnocentrism and Perceptions of the Harem," *Feminist Studies* 8, no. 3 (1985): 521–534; F. Mernissi, *Le harem politique: Le Prophète et les femmes* (Paris: Albin Michel, 1987).

27. See E. Dorlin, *La matrice de la race: Généalogie sexuelle et coloniale de la nation française* (Paris: La Découverte, 2006).

28. For a general overview, see J. Waardenburg, "Mustashrikun."

29. E. Said, *Covering Islam: How the Media and the Experts Determine How We See the Rest of the World* (1981; reprint, London: Vintage Books, 1997), 93.

30. See R. Allison, *The Crescent Obscured: The United States and the Muslim World 1776–1815* (New York: Oxford University Press, 1995); C. Sears, "A Different Kind of Slavery. American Captives in Barbary, 1776–1830" (PhD diss., University of Delaware, 2007); P. Miranda, "Captive in Barbary: The Stereotyping of Arabs, Turks and Islam in Early American Society, 1785–1850" (B.A. thesis, University of Delaware, 2012). See also J. Rana, "The Story of Islamophobia," *Souls: A Critical Journal of Black Politics, Culture, and Society* 9, no. 2 (2007): 148–161.

31. From the 1950s, Black Islam was constructed as a "domestic threat" by the FBI. E. Curtis, *Islam in Black America: Identity, Liberation, and Difference in African-American Islamic Thought* (Albany: State University of New York Press, 2002); S. Daulatzai, *Black Star, Crescent Moon: The Muslim International and Black Freedom beyond America* (Minneapolis: University of Minnesota Press, 2012).

32. Said, *Covering Islam*, 80–133.

33. Ibid., 52.

34. P. Bourdieu and L. Boltanski, "La production de l'idéologie dominante," *Actes de la recherche en sciences sociales*, no. 2 (1976): 3–73.

35. T. Deltombe, *Islam imaginaire: La construction médiatique de l'islamophobie en France, 1975–2005* (Paris: La Découverte, 2005).

36. E. Said, *L'Orientalisme: L'Orient créé par l'Occident* (1979; reprint, Paris: Seuil, 1980), 262.

37. T. Shepard, "'Something Notably Erotic': Politics, 'Arab Men,' and Sexual Revolution in Post-Decolonization France, 1962–1974," *Journal of Modern History* 84, no. 1 (2012): 82.

38. Mathis-Moser, "L'image de 'l'Arabe.'"

39. N. Guénif-Souilamas and E. Macé, *Les féministes et le garçon arabe* (La Tour d'Aigues: L'Aube, 2006); *Nouvelles questions féministes*, dossier "Sexisme et racisme: Le cas français," 25, no. 1.

40. M. D. Brown, "Comparative Analysis of Mainstream Discourses, Media Narratives and Representations of Islam in Britain and France Prior to 9/11," *Journal of Muslim Minority Affairs* 26, no. 3 (2006): 297–298.

41. E. Fassin, "La démocratie sexuelle et le conflit des civilisations," *Multitudes*, no. 26 (2006): 130.

42. See the highly pedagogical A. Gresh and D. Vidal, *Les 100 clés du Proche-Orient* (Paris: Pluriel, 2011).

CHAPTER 12. Anti-Semitism and Islamophobia

1. G. Anidjar, *The Jew, the Arab: A History of the Enemy* (Stanford: Stanford University Press, 2003); F. Bravo López, "Islamofobia y antisemitismo: La construcción discursiva de las amenazas islámica y judía" (PhD diss. in Arabic and Islamic studies, Autonomous University of Madrid, 2009).

2. See also J. Renton and B. Gidley, eds., *Antisemitism and Islamophobia in Europe: A Shared Story?* (London: Palgrave Macmillan, 2017); Idem., "Genealogies of 'Jews' and 'Muslims': Social Imaginaries in the Race–Religion Nexus," *Patterns of Prejudice* 54, nos. 1–2 (2020).

3. N. Meer and T. Noorani, "A Sociological Comparison of Anti-Semitism and Anti-Muslim Sentiment," *Sociological Review* 56, no. 2 (2008): 196.

4. See G. I. Langmuir, *Toward a Definition of Antisemitism* (Berkeley: University of California Press, 1990).

5. L. Poliakov, *Histoire de l'antisémitisme: Du Christ aux juifs de Cour* (Paris: Calmann Lévy, 1955), 20.

6. L. Poliakov, *Histoire de l'antisémitisme*, vol. 1, *L'Âge de la foi* (Paris: Seuil, 1991), 7.

7. Poliakov, *Histoire de l'antisémitisme*, 1:13. The following quotes are drawn from the same page.

8. See J. Pasto, "Islam's 'Strange Secret Sharer': Orientalism, Judaism, and the Jewish Question," *Comparative Studies in Society and History* 40, no. 3 (1998): 437–474.

9. M-A. Matard-Bonucci, "L'Antisémitisme(s): Un éternel retour?," *Revue d'histoire moderne & contemporaine* 62, nos. 2–3 (2015): 7–14. Quote from p. 10.

10. J-F. Schaub, *Pour une histoire politique de la race* (Paris: Seuil, 2015).

11. Langmuir, *Toward a Definition*, 328.

12. Bravo López, "Islamofobia y antisemitismo," 24, our translation.

13. R. Zia-Ebrahimi, "When the Elders of Zion Relocated to Eurabia: Conspiratorial Racialization in Antisemitism and Islamophobia," *Patterns of Prejudice* 52, no. 4 (2018): 314–337. See also *Anti-sémitisme et islamophobie: Une histoire croisée* (Paris: Éditions Amsterdam, 2021).

14. Langmuir, *Toward a Definition*, 338.

15. A. Davis, "Rape, Racism and the Myth of the Black Rapist," chapter 11 in *Femmes, race et classe* (Paris: Éditions des femmes, 1983), 217–253.

16. See G. Bechtel, *La sorcière et l'Occident: La destruction de la sorcellerie en Europe des origines aux grands bûchers* (Paris: Plon, 1997).

17. P. Annichino and N. Marzouki, "Mosque Controversies in the United States: Emotions, Politics and the Right to Religious Freedom," *Annuaire Droit et Religions* 6 (2012–2013), accessible at http://papers.ssrn.com.

18. See I. Jablonka, "La peur de l'islam: Bat Ye'or et le spectre de l'"Eurabie,'" *La Vie des idées*, 1 May 2006, available at www.laviedesidees.fr; R. Liogier, *Le mythe de l'islamisation: Essai sur une obsession collective* (Paris: Seuil, 2012).

19. On "race war" see M. Foucault, *"Il faut défendre la société": Cours au Collège de France, 1975–1976* (Paris: Gallimard/Seuil, 1997); on racial anthropology, see C. Reynaud-Paligot, *La République raciale: Paradigme racial et idéologie républicaine (1860–1930)* (Paris: Presses universitaires de France, 2006); on conspiracies, see E. Kreis, "Quis ut Deus? Antijudéo-maçonnisme et occultisme en France sous la IIIe République" (history thesis, École pratique des hautes études, 2011).

20. H. Arendt, *Antisemitism: Part 1 of Origins of Totalitarianism* (1951; reprint, New York: Harvest, 1985), 157.

21. Ibid., 157.

22. E. Said, *L'Orientalisme: L'Orient créé par l'Occident* (1979; reprint, Paris: Seuil, 1980), 319.

23. E. Traverso, *La fin de la modernité juive: Histoire d'un tournant conservateur* (Paris: La Découverte, 2013), 126.

24. Ibid., 126.

25. N. Meer and T. Noorani, "A Sociological Comparison of Anti-Semitism and Anti-Muslim Sentiment," *Sociological Review* 56, no. 2 (2008): 203–206.

26. See A. Hajjat, *Les frontières de l'identité nationale': L'injonction à l'assimilation en France métropolitaine et coloniale* (Paris: La Découverte, 2012).

27. Traverso, *La fin*, p. 126.

28. C. Torrekens, "Islamo-gauchisme," *La Revue Nouvelle* 75, no. 5 (2020): 54–58.

29. S. Schiffer and C. Wagner, "Anti-Semitism and Islamophobia—New Enemies, Old Patterns," *Race and Class* 52, no. 3 (2011): 77–84.

30. E. Benbassa (ed.), *Dictionnaire des racismes, de l'exclusion et des discriminations* (Paris: Larousse, 2010), 437 and passim.

31. On the other hand, the image of the "beautiful Jewish girl," an incarnation of beauty, sensuality, and carnal temptation, is also similar to the figure of the "beurette." E. Fournier, *La "Belle Juive": D'"Ivanhoé" à la Shoah* (Paris: Champ Vallon, 2012).

32. E. Said, "Orientalism Reconsidered," *Cultural Critique*, no. 1 (1985): 99.

33. Ibid., 99.

34. Ibid., 99.

35. Pasto, "Islam's 'Strange Secret Sharer'"; J. M. Hess, "Johann David Michaelis and the Colonial Imaginary: Orientalism and the Emergence of Racial Antisemitism in Eighteenth-Century Germany," *Jewish Social Studies* 6, no. 2 (2000): 56–101.

36. Anidjar, *The Jew, the Arab*, xi.

37. Anidjar, *Ibid.*, 33.

38. R. Southern, *Western Views of Islam in the Middle Ages* (Cambridge, Mass.: Harvard University Press, 1962), 5.

39. S. H. Griffith, "Jews and Muslims in Christian Syriac and Arabic Texts of the Ninth Century," *Jewish History* 3, no. 1 (1988): 65.

40. See, in particular, T. Mastnak, *Crusading Peace: Christendom, the Muslim World and Western Political Order* (Berkeley: University of California Press, 2002); J. Cohen, *Living Letters: Ideas of the Jew in Medieval Christianity* (Berkeley: University of California Press, 1999) [Cohen analyses the texts of Saint Augustine and Thomas Aquinas]; B. Blumenkranz, *Juifs et chrétiens dans le monde occidental* (Paris: Imprimerie nationale, 1960), 430–1096; J. Trachtenberg, *The Devil and the Jews: The Medieval Conception of the Jew and Its Relation to Modern Antisemitism* (New Haven: Yale University Press, 1944).

41. A. H. Cutler and H. Elmquist Cutler, *The Jew as Ally of the Muslim: Medieval Roots of Anti-Semitism* (Notre Dame, Ind.: University of Notre Dame Press, 1986). By citing their neologism, we do not share the Cutlers' point of view expressed in their book, which has been strongly (and rightly) criticized by Medievalist historians for its lack of academic rigor.

42. Blumenkranz, *Juifs et chrétiens*, 380–384.

43. *Ibid.*, 381.

44. Ibid., 380.

45. *Ibid.*, 383.

46. *Ibid.*, 384.

47. Cutler and Cutler, *The Jew*, 7.

48. C. Ginzburg, *Le Sabbat des sorcières* (Paris: Gallimard, 1992), 46. (See the chapter "Lépreux, juifs, musulmans," 43–69.)

49. See Pasto, "Islam's 'Strange Secret Sharer.'"

50. G. Anidjar, *Semites* (Stanford: Stanford University Press, 2008), 18.

51. See M. Olender, *Les langues du paradis: Aryens et Sémites: Un couple providentiel* (Paris: Gallimard/Le Seuil, 1989).

52. Said, *L'Orientalisme*, 396n26.

53. E. Renan, *Histoire générale et système comparé des langues sémitiques* (Paris: Imprimerie nationale, 1855), 4. Our translation.

54. See Pasto, "Islam's 'Strange Secret Sharer.'"

55. This decree did not include the Jews of M'zab, whose land was only annexed in 1882. The senatus-consult was not extended to them due to their supposed lack of "civilization." See L. Blévis, "Sociologie d'un droit colonial: Citoyenneté et nationalité en Algérie (1865–1947): Une exception républicaine?" (PhD diss. in sociology, Université Paul-Cézanne [Aix-Marseille], 2004); E. Saada, "Une nationalité par degré: Civilité et citoyenneté en situation coloniale," in P. Weil and S. Dufoix (eds.), *L'esclavage, la colonisation et après* (Paris: PUF, 2005), 193–227.

56. See Reynaud-Paligot, *La République raciale*.

57. G. Agamben, *Ce qui reste d'Auschwitz* (Paris: Payot, 1999), 49–111. See also Anidjar, *The Jew, the Arab*, 138–146.

58. P. Levi, *If This Is a Man*, trans. Stuart Woolf (New York: Orion Press, 1959), 101–102.

59. Ibid., 22.

60. Agamben, *Ce qui reste d'Auschwitz*, 105.

61. P-J. Le Foll-Luciani, *Les juifs algériens dans la lutte anticoloniale: Trajectoires dissidentes, 1934–1965* (Rennes: Presses universitaires de Rennes, 2015).

62. See R. Zia-Ebrahimi, *Antisémitisme et islamophobie: Histoire croisée* (Paris: Éditions Amsterdam, 2021o).

63. A. Léon, *La conception matérialiste de la question juive* (1942; reprint, Paris: Études et Documentation Internationales, 1968); J. Parkes, *An Enemy of the People: Antisemitism* (Harmondsworth: Penguin Books, 1945); J. Isaac, *Genèse de l'antisémitisme: Essai historique* (Paris: Calmann-Lévy, 1956); Arendt, *Antisemitism*. See also Langmuir, *Toward a Definition*.

64. Léon, *La Conception*, 26–39.

65. Ibid., 9.

66. Arendt, *Antisemitism*, 62.

67. Ibid., 62.

68. Léon, *La Conception*, 53.

69. Ibid., 9.

70. Arendt, *Antisemitism*, 21.

71. M. Dreyfus, *L'Antisémitisme à gauche: Histoire d'un paradoxe, de 1830 à nos jours* (Paris: La Découverte, 2009).

72. Arendt, *Antisemitism*, 69.

73. Ibid., 56.

74. Ibid., 184–185.

75. See Z. Sternhell, *Naissance de l'idéologie fasciste* (Paris: Fayard, 1989).

76. A. Gingrich, "Anthropological Analyses of Islamophobia and Anti-Semitism in Europe," *American Ethnologist* 32, no. 4 (2005): 514.

77. M. Bunzl, "Between Anti-Semitism and Islamophobia: Some Thoughts on the New Europe," *American Ethnologist* 32, no. 4 (2005): 506. In the same journal issue and in another work, *Anti-Semitism and Islamophobia: Hatreds Old and New in Europe* (Chicago: Prickly Paradigm Press, 2007), Bunzl's text is debated by several anthropologists and historians of Europe.

78. S. Sand, "From Judaeophobia to Islamophobia," *Jewish Quarterly*, 23 July 2010, available at http://jewishquarterly.org.

79. Arendt, *Antisemitism*, 79.

80. Ibid., 80.

81. W. Benz, *Comparing Concepts of the "Other as Enemy" Scientific Imperative—Political Irritant* (Berlin: Center for Research on Antisemitism, 2008). This text was a response to the criticisms provoked by running the colloquium "The Muslim as Enemy, the Jew as Enemy" (8 December 2008). See Schiffer and Wagner, "Anti-Semitism and Islamophobia"; and A. Bötticher, "Islamophobia? The German Discussion about Islamophobia," *Central European Political Studies Review* 11, nos. 2–3 (2009): 210–229.

CHAPTER 13. The Denial of Islamophobia

1. L. Mucchielli, "L'islamophobie: Une myopie intellectuelle?," *Mouvements*, no. 31 (2004): 90–96.

2. This division is especially valid in mainland France, as in its colonies, particularly Algeria, the French Republic refused to apply the principle of laïcité (secularity) and allowed the indigenous population a system of exception for managing religious practice. J. Baubérot, *Histoire de la laïcité en France* (2000; reprint, Paris: PUF, 2010), "Que sais-je?"

3. G. Calvès, "Les discriminations fondées sur la religion: Quelques remarques sceptiques," in E. Lambert-Abdelgawad and T. Rambaud (eds.), *Analyse comparée des discriminations religieuses en Europe* (Paris: Société de la législation comparée, 2011), 9–23; J-P. Delannoy, *Les religions au parlement français: Du général de Gaulle (1958) à Giscard d'Estaing (1975)* (Paris: Éditions du Cerf, 2005), 95.

4. It is indeed the visibility of Muslim religious observance that "causes a problem," as the speech of the then-minister of the interior Manuel Valls shows. He complimented the wearing of the kippa while at the same time stigmatizing the choice of the hijab. "Manuel Valls: Les juifs de France 'peuvent porter avec fierté leur kippa'!," www.lepoint.fr, 24 September 2012.

5. V. Amiraux, "Existe-t-il une discrimination religieuse des musulmans en France?," *Maghreb/Machrek*, no. 183 (2005): 77.

6. Ibid.

7. V. Amiraux, "Le port de la burqa en Europe: comment la 'religion' des uns est devenue l'affaire publique des autres," in David Koussens and Olivier Roy (eds.), *Quand la burqa passe à l'Ouest: Enjeux éthiques, politiques et juridiques* (Rennes: PUR, 2014).

8. Even in the UK, this does not prevent liberal political elites rejecting the requests by British Muslims to be recognized as a "racial group" in the same way as Jews and Sikhs. This refusal denies Muslims the protection of the 1976 Race Relations Act against exclusion and discrimination. N. Meer and T. Modood, "Refutation of Racism in the 'Muslim Question,'" *Patterns of Prejudice* 3/4, no. 43 (2009): 332–351.

9. J-M. Woehrling, "Le droit français de la lutte contre les discriminations à la lumière du droit comparé," *Informations sociales*, no. 148 (2008): 58–71.

10. Calvès, "Les discriminations," 12.

11. The principle of the "buffer zone" might act as a self-fulfilling prophecy, as the banishment from social and political life to which it leads may be a driver for the "ethnically divisive" behavior that was criticized in the first place.

12. F. Parvez, "Debating the Burqa in France: The Antipolitics of Islamic Revival," *Qualitative Sociology* 34, no. 2 (2011): 287–312.

13. On the French reception of Ramadan's speech, see A. Zemouri, *Faut-il faire taire Tarik Ramadan?* (Paris: L'Archipel, 2005); S. Khiari, *Sainte Caroline contre Tariq Ramadan: Le livre qui met un point final à Caroline Fourest* (Paris: Éditions la Revanche, 2011).

14. D. Schneidermann, "La liste de Patrick Cohen," *Libération*, 17 March 2013.

15. C. Fourest and F. Venner, *Marine Le Pen* (Paris: Grasset, 2011), 276. Caroline Fourest also accused the CCIF of being the "friend of the Islamists" (France Culture, 20 December 2010).

16. J-M. Guénois, "Le CCIF, une association qui milite pour le port du voile," *Le Figaro*, 14 November 2012.

17. G. Kepel, *Quatre-vingt-treize* (Paris: Gallimard, 2012), 228.

18. The Ligue des droits de l'homme (LDH, Human Rights League) was established at the end of the nineteenth century, in the aftermath of the Dreyfus Affair; the Ligue internationale contre le racisme et l'antisémitisme (Licra, ex-LICA, International League against Racism and Anti-Semitism) in a context of the rise of fascism in 1930s Europe. The Mouvement contre le racisme et pour l'amitié entre les peuples (MRAP, Movement against Racism and for Friendship between Peoples) was set up in 1949 by members of the former

French resistance (mainly Jews and communists) and has remained close to the radical Left. SOS-Racisme was established in 1984 by the Socialist Party, in the context of the rise in popularity of the Far Right and the mobilization of the children of postcolonial immigrants in working-class areas and has stayed close to several Jewish community organizations, particularly the Union des étudiants juifs de France (UEJF, Union of Jewish Students of France) and the Conseil représentatif des institutions juives de France (CRIF, Representative Council for Jewish Institutions in France).

19. On anti-racism and Palestine, see S. Kassir and F. Mardam-Bey, *Itinéraires de Paris à Jérusalem: La France et le conflit judéo-arabe*, vol. 2, *1958–1991* (Paris: Minuit, 1993); D. Sieffert, *Israël-Palestine, une passion française* (Paris: La Découverte, 2004); E. Debono, *Aux origines de l'antiracisme: La LICRA, 1927–1940* (Paris: CNRS Éditions, 2012); T. Peace, "The French Antiracist Movement and the 'Muslim Question,'" in *Political and Cultural Representations of Muslims: Islam in the Plural* (Leiden: Brill, 2012), 131–146.

20. P.-A. Taguieff, *La nouvelle judéophobie* (Paris: Mille et une nuits, 2002).

21. V. Geisser, *La nouvelle islamophobie* (Paris: La Découverte, 2003).

22. "Indeed, it is often forgotten that the decision to appoint the Stasi Commission was not simply a response to Muslim girls wearing headscarves, but also a reaction to wider concerns about the banlieues [. . .], such as violence against women and anti-Semitism." Peace, "French Antiracist Movement," 134.

23. Geisser, *La nouvelle islamophobie*; SOS-RACISME and UEJF), *Les Antifeujs: Le Livre Blanc des violences antisémites en France* (Paris: Calmann-Lévy, 2002).

24. C. Coroller, "Une manif qui divise les antiracistes," *Libération*, 6 November 2004.

25. The rule of "pariah status" ("infréquentabilité" in French) does not apply to racist and violent groups such as the Ligue de défense juive (LDJ, Jewish Defense League) or the BETAR, alongside which SOS-Racisme has demonstrated against anti-Semitism several times.

26. These terms are not only used to describe movements aiming to impose Muslim rules and institutions on the whole of society, or even the most rigorous and marginal versions of Islam, but refer to anything to do with practiced and visible Islam. Peace, "French Antiracist Movement," 136.

27. D. Sopo, *SOS antiracisme* (Paris: Denoël, 2005), 26.

28. H. Goldman, *Le rejet français de l'islam* (Paris: PUF, 2012), 16.

29. Peace, "French Antiracist Movement"; See also H. Asal, "'Au nom de l'égalité!' Mobilisations contre l'islamophobie en France: La campagne contre l'exclusion des mères voilées des sorties scolaires," in J. Talpin, J. O'Miel, and F. Frégosi (eds.), *L'islam et la cité: Engagements musulmans dans les quartiers populaires* (Villeneuve d'Ascq: Presses universitaires du Septentrion, 2017).

30. During the first headscarf affair, in Creil in 1989, Harlem Désir, the then-director of SOS-Racisme, was fiercely opposed to a ban on religious signs in school, arguing that it might even be a form of racism.

31. "Me Francis Terquem quitte SOS Racisme pour le Mrap," *Libération*, 20 January 2004.

32. Colloque du MRAP, "Du racisme à l'islamophobie," Assemblée nationale, 20 September 2003.

33. LCI, 24 October 2003.

34. P. Bruckner, "Le chantage à l'islamophobie," *Le Figaro*, 5 November 2003; C. Fourest and F. Venner, "Ne pas confondre islamophobes et laïques," *Libération*, 17 November 2003.

35. "The problem with the term Islamophobia is that it has been used especially by the Iranians, who criticized women who refused to wear headscarves before it became compulsory in Iran. It was then started up again after the Rushdie affair. [. . .] It originates with the Islamists, and in general, you shouldn't use your enemy's vocabulary, in this case when you're working in the area of anti-racism, because the Islamists are incompatible with anti-racism." "Interview with Dominique Sopo (SOS-Racisme) by 'Enquête & Débat,'" 27 October 2010, accessible at www.dailymotion.com.

36. Thinking through the significant resistance to measuring Islamophobia in Ireland, James Carr, using the Foucauldian theory of "technologies of power," argues that the government's refusal to name and measure the acts targeting Islam and Muslims can be understood as "institutional racism," i.e., discrimination through neglect aimed at perpetuating a social order and hiding political strategies whose management necessitates denying the reality of such a situation. J. Carr, "Regulating Islamophobia. The need for collecting disaggregated data on racism in Ireland," *Journal of Muslim Minority Affairs* 31, no. 4 (2011), 574–593.

37. S. Zappi, "La lutte contre l'islamophobie divise les militants du MRAP, en congrès à Bobigny," *Le Monde*, 5 December 2004.

38. For Pierre Mairat, director elect of and lawyer for the MRAP, "this ethnically divisive framework should be avoided. We're not here to defend religion." Zappi, "La lutte contre l'islamophobie."

39. These quotations are drawn from the MRAP newsletter, *Différences*, no. 253 (January–March 2005).

40. During these debates, another parallel with anti-Semitism was performed as a response to the oft-expressed fear of losing members because of adopting the term "Islamophobia." The annual ethical report stressed that "in 1930, during the rise of anti-Semitism, it would have been untenable to say "we're not going to fight anti-Semitism because we might lose members.""

41. C. Porin and A. Spire, "Pourquoi nous quittons la LDH," *Le Monde*, 23 November 2006.

42. Firstly, the Union juive française pour la paix (UJFP, French Jewish Union for Peace) and the Une autre voix juive collective (Another Jewish Voice Collective.) See Dominique Vidal, *Le Mal-Être juif: Entre repli, assimilation et manipulation* (Paris: Agone, 2003).

43. V. Geisser, "Les institutions juives en France et le foulard: L'emblème d'un 'nouvel antisémitisme' musulman?," in F. Lorcerie (ed.), *La politisation du voile en France, en Europe et dans le monde arabe* (Paris: L'Harmattan, 2005), 96.

44. Geisser, "Les institutions juives," 97. See also V. Geisser, "Les institutions juives face au spectre de l'"islamisation' de la cause palestinienne en France," in E. Benbassa (ed.), *Israël-Palestine: Les enjeux d'un conflit* (Paris: CNRS Éditions, 2010), 223–243.

45. An institution set up to administer Jewish worship and congregations in France by Napoleon I, through an imperial Decree in 1808.

46. R. Prasquier, "Réflexions sur l'islamophobie," www.crif.org, 9 November 2012.

47. The state legal ombudsman (otherwise translated as Defender of Rights) is a public institution dedicated to the protection of rights and the promotion of equality.

48. "Le Défenseur des droits reçoit le crif," Crif, 16 April 2013, http://www.crif.org/fr /lecrifenaction/le-défenseur-des-droits-reçoit-le-crif/36369.

49. P. Boniface, Est-il permis de critiquer Israël? (Paris: Robert Laffont, 2003); A. Badiou and E. Hazan, L'Antisémitisme partout: Aujourd'hui en France (Paris: La Fabrique, 2011).

50. N. Zomersztajn, "Une proposition belge inacceptable de résolution contre l'islamophobie," http://www.cclj.be, 21 April 2013.

51. Vidal, Le Mal-Être juif; E. Benbassa and J-C. Attias, Les Juifs ont-ils un avenir? (Paris: Jean-Claude Lattès, 2001).

52. Geisser, "Les institutions juives," 99.

53. Geisser, La nouvelle islamophobie.

54. P-A. Taguieff, La judéophobie des Modernes: Des Lumières au Jihad mondial (Paris: Odile Jacob, 2008), 37.

55. Ibid.

56. Ibid., 420.

57. "For twelve years, politically correct opinion has been practicing denial of reality due to the idea that it is not possible for there to be pockets of racists and anti-Semites in the groups of those who are victims of racism. That is what has prevented a serious confrontation with anti-Semitism in all that time. Worse still, the concept of Islamophobia was coined deliberately to ban people from thinking about the facts and defusing the application of the category of 'anti-Semite' to these circles." S. Trigano, "Un tournant dans le rapport à l'antisémitisme," http://jssnews.com, 12 October 2012.

58. Taguieff, La judéophobie des Modernes, 38.

59. P-A. Taguieff, "Propalestinisme, endoctrinement islamiste et judéophobie en France (suite et fin)," http://www.crif.org, 15 January 2013.

60. For example, Anders Breivik's "2083. A European Declaration of Independence" (2011), available online, copiously cites Bat Ye'Or, Oriana Fallaci three times, and Alain Finkielkraut twice.

61. Their activity in this area is limited to a handful of commitments in high-profile trials around discrimination (the Houria Demiati case) or the publication of racist pamphlets, particularly against the publisher of the French translation of Oriana Fallaci's The Rage and the Pride. This business plan of Islamophobia denial also reached the international arena, since the Licra ran a campaign against the UN's recognition of the specific nature of Islamophobia. In 2007, two years before the Durban Review Conference—following on from the World Conference Against Racism- organised by UNESCO in Geneva ("Durban II"), the Licra published a report critical of the UNHCR, especially over its recognition of Islamophobia driven by Special Rapporteur Doudou Diene.

62. CNCDH, La lutte contre le racisme et la xénophobie: Rapport d'activité (Paris: La Documentation française, 2003), 184, available at www.ladocumentationfrancaise.fr.

63. Ibid., 261.

64. Ibid., 233.

65. Ibid., 187.

66. Ibid., 181.

67. Ibid., 183.

68. CNCDH, *La lutte contre le racisme et la xénophobie: Rapport d'activité* (Paris: La Documentation française, 2011), 30, available at www.ladocumentationfrancaise.fr.

69. CNCDH, *La Lutte contre le racisme* (2003).

70. Ibid., 15.

71. G. Michelat and N. Mayer, "L'image de l'islam et des musulmans en France," CNCDH, *La Lutte contre le racisme* (2003), 223.

72. Alain Morice has already put his finger on this habit of diluting racism into "softer" ideas of "ethnocentrism" or "intolerance." He argues that "racism as a manifestation of a power relationship is left drowning in a relativist current of relative behavior and utterances that vary in seriousness." A. Morice, "Du seuil de tolérance au racisme banal, ou les avatars de l'opinion fabriquée," *Journal des anthropologues*, nos. 110–111 (2007): 379–408. The idea of ethnocentrism actually refers less to the rejection and domination of the Other, and a more or less conscious trend of prioritizing and overestimating the group to which you belong. Unlike racism which is defined first by the rejection of the Other, there is a priori nothing to condemn in preferring yours and loving yourself.

73. Geisser, *La nouvelle islamophobie*.

74. CNCDH, *Rapport 2010*, Note du ministère de l'Intérieur, 136.

75. Ibid., 136.

76. Ibid., 137.

77. "Islamophobia exists. You know this. Alas, you do not have friends only" (Paris, 28 September 2006); "In France as in Algeria, we must fight all forms of racism, all forms of Islamophobia, all forms of anti-Semitism, with unfailing determination. There is nothing more like an anti-Semite than an Islamophobe" (Algiers, 3 December 2007).

78. France Inter, 28 August 2012.

79. "Quelles perspectives pour les relations euro-méditerranéennes?," www.parti-socialiste.fr, 28 August 2010.

80. "Les grandes dates de la guerre contre la laïcité," www.partisocialiste.fr, 18 February 2009.

81. The groups cited were the Indigènes de la République and Ouma.com [*sic*]) which did not even participate in this action (see: "Le mensonge indigne de Raquel Garrido, porte-parole du Parti de gauche": "Oumma attaque Fourest," www.oumma.com, 16 September 2012; and "Le Parti de gauche et le déni de l'islamophobie," www.indigenes-republique.fr, 21 September 2012).

82. "Appel de militant-e-s et sympathisant-e-s du Front de Gauche. Contre l'offensive islamophobe, pour un front large et massif des exploité-e-s et opprimé-e-s," http://fdg contreislamophobie.e-monsite.com, 20 April 2012.

83. "Libertaires et sans-concessions contre l'islamophobie!" www.bboykonsian.com, 27 September 2012.

84. "Refuser la confusion et la xénophobie," http://lafederation.org, 2 April 2013.

85. "Mouloud Aounit, ancien président du MRAP, est mort," www.lemonde.fr, 10 August 2012.

86. This section draws partly on our article, A. Hajjat and M. Mohammed, "Du déni à la reconnaissance: La plasticité de l'idéologie dominante," *JefKlak*, 1 October 2014, www.jefklak.org/?p=1001.

87. Commission nationale consultative des droits de l'homme (2014), *La lutte contre le racisme*.

88. The data are drawn from the Factiva database, which publishes a major proportion of the Western press, and the online archives of the *Le Monde* newspaper.

89. C. Fourest and F. Venner, "Islamophobia?," *ProChoix*, nos. 26–27 (2003), available at www.prochoix.org; P. Bruckner, "Le chantage à l'Islamophobia," *Le Figaro*, 5 November 2003.

90. The AFP journalists who used the term most often were new recruits: Charlotte Plantive (June 2008), Annick Benoist (June 2009), Pauline Froissart (July 2009), and Benoît Fauchet (June 2014).

91. In August 2013 the press revealed the content of an unpublished report to the Haut Conseil à l'intégration, an official body disbanded in 2012, advocating a ban on wearing the headscarf at universities.

92. Quoted by C. Fouteau, "Femmes voilées: À Argenteuil, les musulmans ne veulent plus 'se laisser endormir'," www.mediapart.fr, 22 June 2013.

93. Nevertheless, the préfet admitted fault in interview given to *Libération* (21 September 2013). He explained he had used the word Islamophobia because there had been a "demand for recognition from the section of the population that also experiences the impacts of the choice of words." However, he went on to tell the journalist from *Libération*, he would no longer be using the term as: "I realized it could also be manipulated."

94. The ACLEFEU collective was formed the day after the rebellions of November 2005 triggered by the tragic deaths of seventeen-year-old Zyed Benna and fifteen-year-old Bouna Traoré. Its mission was to act as a means of channeling the voices of the working-class districts into big institutions.

95. "Rencontre avec des représentants d'associations des banlieues, en présence de M. François Lamy," Élysée press release (www.elysee.fr), 24 June 2013.

96. English versions of these titles: "Our Unloved"; "The Coming Populism"; "The Myth of Islamization"; "Dictionary of Islamophobia."

97. C. Askolovitch, *Nos mal-aimés: Ces musulmans dont la France ne veut pas* (Paris: Grasset, 2013), 24.

98. J. Scott, *La domination et les arts de la résistance: Fragments du discours subalterne* (1992; reprint, Paris: Éditions Amsterdam, 2008), 81–82.

99. J. Clarini, "Rentrée des idées: Une vue d'ensemble des essais à paraître cet automne," *Le Monde des livres*, 28 August 2013.

100. A semi-exhaustive list: France Culture, France Inter, Radio Zinzine, Mediapart, *Le Monde*, *Libération*, *L'Humanité*, AFP, *Le Parisien*, *Les Inrocks*, *La Croix*, *La Vie*, BastaMag, Saphir News, *Courrier de l'Atlas*, Oumma.com, Rue 89, *Politis*, ContreTemps, LMSI, etc. Outside France, it drew attention especially from the Algerian press (*El Watan*, *Le Courrier d'Algérie*, *Le Temps d'Algérie*, Algérie Presse Service) and Al Jazeera.

101. We were invited to speak by the following organizations: CCIF, CRI, Uni'T, Forum international contre l'islamophobie, NPA, Association des Muslims de Metz, Rectorat de Paris, Club des retraités de la MGEN, etc.

102. Sales figures: 2,200 copies were sold between September 2013 and June 2014. This figure is not commensurate with the sales of Askolovitch's book (3,500–4,000) and especially not with those of Alain Finkielkraut's, *L'identité malheureuse* (around 100,000).

103. Show on France Culture, 15 December 2014; I. Kersimon and J-C. Moreau, *Islamophobie: La contre-enquête* [Islamophobia: The counterinvestigation] (Paris: Plein jour, 2014). For a deconstruction of their "counterinvestigation," see "Statistiques de l'Islamophobia: Misère du journalisme mensonger," *Mediapart* blog, 21 February 2015, https://blogs.mediapart.fr/abdellali-hajjat/blog/260215/statistiques-de-lIslamophobia-misere-du-journalisme-mensonger. See also C. Fourest, *Éloge du blasphème* [Elogy to blasphemy] (Paris: Grasset, 2015).

104. C. Fourest, "Peut-on combattre le racisme avec le mot 'Islamophobie'?," *Huffington Post*, 1 October 2013.

105. See "Islamophobie: Quand Caroline Fourest supprime des mots dans son texte de 2003," Al-Kanz.org, 1 October 2013.

106. The CCIF is an NGO funded basically through subscriptions and donations (collected via its annual dinners), and not by the government of Qatar. Open Society, a think tank set up by Soros, did fund just one part of the campaign "Nous sommes (aussi) la nation" in 2012. The CCIF regularly invite Tariq Ramadan to its public events.

107. A. Gresh, "L'islamophobie, '*Le Monde*' et une (petite) censure," *Nouvelles d'Orient*, 5 November 2013.

108. G. Kepel, "Une posture victimaire," *Le Monde*, 1 November 2013.

109. P-A. Taguieff, "Islamophobie chimérique, christianophobie réelle, anti-Islamophobie criminelle," *Sur le ring*, Summer 2009.

110. P-A. Taguieff, "Les équivoques de la lutte contre l'extrémisme: Extrême droite, islamisme, islamophobie," *Huffington Post*, 2 October 2013.

111. P-A. Taguieff, "Petites leçons pour éviter tout amalgame," *Le Monde*, 1 November 2013.

CHAPTER 14. The Struggle for the Recognition of Islamophobia

1. V. Amiraux, "L''affaire du foulard' en France: Retour sur une affaire qui n'en est pas encore une," *Sociologie et sociétés* 41, no. 2 (2009): 296.

2. C. De Galembert, "Cause du voile et lutte pour la parole légitime," *Sociétés contemporaines*, no. 74 (2009): 19–47.

3. Ibid., 20.

4. Ibid., 22.

5. As we have seen, this observatory depends on a single person (Abdallah Zekri) and has no capacity to record or provide legal help, restricting itself to communicating information on the basis of data provided by the Ministry of the Interior.

6. The only exception is the Comité 15 mars et liberté, set up in 2004, run by Abdallah Thomas Milcent, and supported by the Ligue française de la femme musulmane (LFFM), the UOIF, and the Fonds de défense des musulmans en justice (FDMJ). For some time, the UOIF conveyed events initiated by other organizations such as the CCIF, whose website was directly linked to from the UOIF's homepage.

7. De Galembert, "Cause du voile," 23.

8. Ibid., 40.

9. Ibid., 19.

10. The physical and social basis on which anti-Islamophobia campaigning would theoretically be likely to be built. On the generational discrepancies in the way discrimination is
experienced and processed, see chapter 1.

11. See F. Khosrokhavar, *L'Islam des jeunes* (Paris: Flammarion, 1997); J. Cesari, *Musulmans et républicains, les jeunes, l'islam et la France* (Paris: Complexe, 1998); J. Cesari, "Aux
origines du mouvement des jeunes musulmans: L'Union des jeunes musulmans. Entretien
avec Yamin Makri," in A. Boubeker and A. Hajjat (eds.), *Histoire politique des immigrations
(post) coloniales: France 1920–2008* (Paris: Éditions Amsterdam, 2008), 217–224.

12. De Galembert, "Cause du voile," 38.

13. Established in 1866 by Jean Macé, the Ligue de l'enseignement is France's largest
confederation of secular NGOs and movements.

14. For example, only three appearances of the term can be found prior to 11 September 2001 in *Le Monde* (J-P. Peroncel-Hugoz, "La vraie vie des musulmans," 1 January 1988;
E. Mallet, "Culture ou barbarie," 10 December 1994; M. Samson, "L'Europe face à l'intolérance ethnique," 24 February 2001).

15. M. Morineau, "Laïcité et Islam: Histoire d'une Commission et itinéraire d'une réflexion," *Confluences méditerranée*, no. 57 (2006), 142.

16. Michel Morineau says that a series of seminars on the topic of "Islam and secularity"
were supported or initiated by the Ligue in the 1985–1990 period. In late 1990, "the Grand
Orient had organized a seminar on secularity at rue Cadet [the organization's headquarters],
without inviting the Ligue to take part! That sums up the gulf between the two big secular
institutions of civil society . . . the headscarf affair had struck!"

17. "The commission brought together Muslims, Catholics, Protestants, Jews, Agnostics
and Atheists with Muslim representation of at least a third, or even half of the membership. Finally, some balance. We wanted the whole 'family of Muslim not-for-profits' to be
in it, but not as representatives of their home organizations (UOIF, FNMF, Paris Mosque,
COJEP for Turkish Islam, CAM for Islam in the Comoros and the Indian Ocean, Présence
musulmane, EMF, JMF). Men and women, with and without headgear, young people, older
people, and in relation to all the socio-occupational categories, staff of both secular and
faith-based organizations, teachers, journalists, researchers (CNRS, EHESS, EPHE), local
authority employees, civil servants, French and European high-level civil servants." Morineau, "Laïcité et Islam," 147.

18. Ibid., 148.

19. Ibid., 148.

20. C. Fourest, *Frère Tariq: Discours, stratégie et méthode de Tariq Ramadan* (Paris: Grasset, 2004). For a response, see T. Ramadan, "Mensonges et dérobades de Caroline Fourest et
quelques autres réflexions," http://www.tariqramadan.com, 28 October 2004.

21. Fourest, *Frère Tariq*.

22. Therefore during the first ESF, Fouad Imarraine, a member of the Collectif des
musulmans de France (CMF), took part in a seminar called "The Place of Islam and Islamophobia in Europe," organized by the LDH and the Fédération internationale des droits de
l'homme (FIDH). At the second forum, held in Île-de-France in 2003, some members of
the CMF and the MIB participated in the French organizing committee and the organizing
secretariat, a role with input into the program, and responsibility for three plenary sessions
and twelve seminars.

23. T. Peace, "L'impact de la 'participation musulmane' sur le mouvement altermondial-iste en Grande-Bretagne et en France," *Cultures & Conflits*, 2008, available at http://conflits.revues.org.

24. José Bové, leader of the Confédération paysanne (Peasant Confederation), for example, visited Jordan in 2001 to show solidarity as part of a delegation including MIB members.

25. Peace, "L'impact."

26. Ibid.

27. De Galembert, "Cause du voile," 43.

28. Ibid.

29. The Une école pour tous-tes collective, the Collectif féministes pour l'égalité (CFPE) collective, the Centre d'études et d'initiatives de solidarité internationale (Cedetim), the Les mots sont importants (LMSI, Words Are Important) collective, and the CCIF, CMF, and NPA (ex-LCR) were joined by EFIGIES (feminist academics), Homosexuel-les musulman-es de France (HM2F), the Parti des indigènes de la République (PIR), the Union juive française pour la paix (UJFP), les Blédardes, and *Contretemps* magazine.

30. N. Guénif-Souilamas and E. Macé, *Les féministes et le garçon arabe* (La Tour d'Aigues: L'Aube, 2006).

31. N. Dot-Pouillard, "Les recompositions politiques du mouvement féministe français au regard du hijab," *Sociologies* (2007), available at http://sociologies.revues.org.

32. Ibid.

33. Ibid.

34. Ibid.

35. P. Tevanian, *Le voile médiatique: Un faux débat: "L'affaire du foulard islamique"* (Paris: Raisons d'agir, 2005).

36. J. Scott, *The Politics of the Veil* (Princeton, N.J.: Princeton University Press, 2007).

37. Dot-Pouillard, "Les recompositions politiques."

38. Ibid.

39. A sign of the political legitimacy of this strand is that portraits of Ni putes ni soumises activists hang on the gates of the National Assembly.

40. M. Zancarini-Fournel, "Étude de cas: Des féministes islamophobes," paper presented at the "Islamophobie: La construction du problème musulman" seminar, EHESS, 15 February 2013.

41. Dot-Pouillard, "Les recompositions politiques."

42. A convergence that played a decisive role in the emergence of Muslim feminism in France. As researcher Zahra Ali points out, "Christine Delphy's famous: 'Why not?' in response to the possibility of a Muslim feminism, in a CEPT rally at the Trianon Hotel (4 February 2004, available at www.lmsi.net), stayed in the minds of both feminists and committed Muslims." Z. Ali, "Des féministes musulmanes en France: Enjeux, conflits et pratiques" (masters' thesis in sociology, EHESS, 2009), 114.

43. Our focus on these groups should not however blind us to the existence and dyna-mism of local bodies with lower media profiles, whose campaigns against Islamophobia are their main or secondary objective. Here we are thinking of Enfants de la Patrie (www.enfantsdelapatrie.net), a not-for-profit in the Greater Lyon area, which aims to record "racist, discriminatory and / or Islamophobic acts, [. . .] sensitize the public to the dangers

of such acts, and promote the values of living together, [...] fighting all forms of racism, discrimination based on identity and religion, and [...] supporting victims of this discrimination."

44. In popular speech, the Arabic word "bled" means "country of origin." The "blédard-es" are people from the "bled," and in a pejorative use of the term, this means "backward."

45. Dot-Pouillard, "Les recompositions politiques."

46. E. Dorlin (ed.), *Black Feminism: Anthologie du féminisme africain-américain, 1975–2000* (Paris: L'Harmattan, 2008).

47. Z. Ali (ed.), *Féminismes islamiques* (Paris: La Fabrique, 2012).

48. C. Mohanty, *Feminism without Borders: Decolonizing Theory, Practicing Solidarity* (Durham: Duke University Press, 2003).

49. Dot-Pouillard, "Les recompositions politiques."

50. De Galembert, "Cause du voile," 44.

51. Particularly the reports by the Open Society Institute (since 2001), Amnesty International (*Choice and Prejudice: Discrimination against Muslims in Europe*, http://www.amnesty.org, April 2012), and the comments by the European Commission ("Fearmongering, xenophobia and austerity budgets threaten the protection of human rights," in T. Hammarberg, "Human Rights in the European Democracies," Council of Europe–Commissioner for Human Rights, 9 December 2010, available at https://wcd.coe.int.)

52. See the campaign launched on 18 May 2013 by the Collectif mamans toutes égales (www.mamanstoutes-egales.com).

53. J. Baubérot, *La laïcité falsifiée* (Paris: La Découverte, 2011).

54. Enfants de la Patrie (see note 43 above) and other smaller campaigning groups are also relevant in this regard.

55. For the year 2012, the CCIF's budget stood at 215,000 Euros.

56. Amnesty International, *Choice and Prejudice*.

57. L. Israel, *L'arme du droit* (Paris: Presses de Sciences Po, 2009).

58. Demonstrated in the appendices to the CCIF's annual reports in which their main activities in the legal field have been listed.

59. In an interview with Jérémy Robine, Bouteldja explains that the shift from anti-Arab racism to Islamophobia in the form of "stigmatizing, essentializing discourses on Islam, Muslims, Islamism" was one of the most pressing motivations for the launch of the MIR. "Les 'indigènes de la République': Nation et question postcoloniale. Territoires des enfants de l'immigration et rivalité de pouvoir," *Hérodote* 120, no. 1 (2006): 118–148, quote from 125. This appeal was made by a coalition of activists and leading figures on the political left, and from the campaigns that had developed around working-class neighborhoods and about immigration, all of whom condemned a legacy of ideas that saturate the treatment of the banlieues and postcolonial minorities.

60. The University of Berkeley is home to the first research unit and first journal devoted to Islamophobia and holds an annual international conference on Islamophobia. Bouteldja regularly takes part, and at the fourth annual international conference (spring 2013), contributed to securing the passage of a resolution of solidarity with French Muslims and against Islamophobic discourses in France.

61. He ran a training session on colonial domination at the PIR premises in autumn 2011.

62. M. Mestiri, R. Grosfoguel, and E. Soum, *Islamophobie dans le monde moderne* (Paris: Institut international de la pensée islamique, 2008).

63. Particularly as part of the Politics & Islam group that met regularly in Paris, a space for political thinking made up of activists and intellectuals from various campaigning spaces that we have outlined in this chapter (i.e., activists from the feminist movement, the Far Left, Muslims, the anti-globalization movement, etc.).

64. H. Bouteldja, "Islamophobie: Quand les Blancs perdent leur triple A," www.indigenes-republique.fr, 28 November 2012.

65. In a similar register, we point the reader to the book by journalist Nadia Henni-Moulaï, *Petit précis de l'Islamophobia ordinaire* [A short summary of ordinary Islamophobia], and the contribution of comedians such as Samy Amara and Samia Orosemane.

66. In 1915, during the First World War, the powdered chocolate brand "Banania" chose a supposedly hilarious image of a Senegalese soldier for its marketing and attached the slogan "Y'a bon," referring to a type of spoken French associated with Senegalese soldiers. The poster, bringing together a raft of racist stereotypes, has been condemned for decades in France.

67. See www.noussommeslanation.fr.

68. H. Bouteldja, "À propos de la campagne contre l'islamophobie du CCIF: Être ou ne pas être le colonel Bendaoued," www.indigenes-republique.fr, 17 December 2012.

69. Other critiques focused on the appropriation of the idea of the nation (Yamin Makri on the Globislam website, http://globislam.over-blog.com). Another criticism, this time a cross-cutting one from literalist Muslim circles to the far-right nationalist ones, targeted the contribution made to the campaign by the Open Society Institute, a foundation belonging to U.S. financier George Soros. More broadly, the links cultivated between activists or high-profile figures from ethnic minority backgrounds or the banlieues with the state and U.S. foundations are regularly condemned by Youssef Boussoumah of the PIR.

70. Présence et spiritualité musulmanes, Collectif des féministes pour l'égalité, CCIF, Maman toutes égales, Islam et laïcité Commission, Parti des indigènes de la République, UJFP, Solidaires, CMF, MRAP, LDH, ATTAC, etc.

71. This exclusion seems to be explained by political and ideological differences.

72. Organization for Security and Cooperation in Europe.

73. In this ruling, the Supreme Court validated a community crèche's sacking of an employee wearing a headscarf to work.

74. CNCDH, *La lutte contre le racisme, l'antisémitisme et la xénophobie: Année 2013* (Paris: La Documentation française, 2014), 13.

75. Ibid., 19.

76. Ibid., 20.

77. Ibid., 20.

78. Interview with Manuel Valls, then-minister of the interior, in *Le Nouvel Observateur*, 31 July 2013.

79. J-C. Cambadelis, *L'Europe sous la menace national-populiste* (Paris: Éditions de l'Archipel, 2014).

80. Motion A "Le renouveau socialiste," http://congres.parti-socialiste.fr/motions/motion-a-le-renouveau-socialiste.

81. An example is the article "Islam: Cambadélis interpellé sur la présence du PS au dîner d'un collectif controversé," *Le Figaro*, 9 June 2015.

82. "Pourquoi la manifestation organisée aujourd'hui contre l'islamophobie divise-t-elle la gauche?," *Franceinfo*, 7 November 2019, https://www.francetvinfo.fr/societe/religion /religion-laicite/pourquoi-la-manifestation-contre-l-Islamophobia-prevue-le-10-November -divise-t-elle-la-gauche_3691323.html.

83. A campaign cofounded by the former director of the Collectif contre l'islamophobie en France and bringing together various individual, faith-based, and not-for-profit components of Muslims in France. It seeks particularly to represent the descendants of immigrants, converted Muslims and more widely, the French Muslim middle classes, who see no place for themselves in the traditional faith-based institutions and want to keep their independence in relation to the state.

84. This section reproduces parts of A. Hajjat, "Reflections on the January 2015 Killings and Their Consequences," *Migration and Citizenship Newsletter of the American Political Science Association* 3, no. 2 (2015): 7–14.

85. N. Élias, *Engagement et distanciation: Contributions à la sociologie de la connaissance* (Paris: Fayard, 1993), 77.

CHAPTER 15. Lawyers in the Fight against Islamophobia

1. On the idea of discrimination, and a reminder of changes in anti-discrimination law, see L. Bereni and V-A. Chappe, "La discrimination, de la qualification juridique à l'outil sociologique," *Politix* 94, no. 2 (2011): 7–34.

2. Part 2 of this book contains a section focusing specifically on the history and development of the term "Islamophobia."

3. On criminal law, refer to G. Rusche and O. Kirchheimer, *Punishment and Social Structure* (New York: Columbia University Press 1939), or K. Beckett and B. Western, "Governing Social Marginality: Welfare, Incarceration, and the Transformation of State Policy," *Punishment and Society* 3, no. 1 (2001): 43–59.

4. S. Raoult and A. Derbey, "La justice de classe, la nouvelle punitivité et le faux mystère de l'inflation carcérale," *Revue de science criminelle et de droit pénal comparé* 11 (2018): 255–265; F. Jobard and S. Nevanen, "La couleur du jugement: Discriminations dans les décisions judiciaires en matière d'infractions à agents de la force publique (1965–2005)," *Revue française de sociologie* 48, no. 2 (2007): 243–272.

5. The lawyers in the sample were selected with reference to their accumulated experience of having been involved in dozens of Islamophobia cases, whether they were to do with violence, discrimination, desecrations, disputed police profiling, etc. These lawyers have mostly had access to these cases and clients through human rights and public freedom not-for-profits and anti-racist organizations, the Ligue des droits de l'homme (LDH) and the Collectif contre l'islamophobie en France (CCIF). For a more detailed analysis of the motivations and career trajectories of these lawyers, see M. Mohammed, "Défendre un groupe social illégitime: Les lawyers dans la lutte contre l'Islamophobie," *Communications* 107 (2020), 251–271.

6. E. Bourdier, "Des libertés à la répression: Un renversement à peine voilé de la laïcité," *La Revue des droits de l'homme*, no. 11 (2017), https://journals.openedition.org /revdh/2751.

7. A. Hajjat, N. Keyhani, and C. Rodrigues, "Infraction raciste (non) confirmée: Sociol-

ogie du traitement judiciaire des infractions racistes dans trois tribunaux correctionnels," *Revue française de science politique* 69, no. 3 (2019): 407–438, 419.

8. N. Hall, "Policing Hate Crime in London and New York City: Some Reflections on the Factors Influencing Effective Law Enforcement, Service Provision and Public Trust and Confidence," *International Review of Victimology* 18, no. 1 (2012): 73–87.

9. E. Boyd, R. Berk, and K. Hamner, "Motivated by Hatred or Prejudice: Categorization of Hate-Motivated Crimes in Two Police Divisions," *Law & Society Review* 30, no. 4 (1996): 819–850.

10. Hajjat, Keyhani, and Rodrigues, "Infraction raciste (non) confirmée."

11. Ibid., 411.

12. Ibid., 422–423.

13. D. Haider-Markel, "Regulating Hate: State and Local Influences on Hate Crime Law Enforcement," *State Politics & Policy Quarterly* 2, no. 2 (2002): 126–160.

14. Hajjat, Keyhani, and Rodrigues, "Infraction raciste (non) confirmée," 427.

15. N. Christie, "The Ideal Victim," in E. Fattah (ed.), *From Crime Policy to Victim Policy: Reorienting the Justice System* (London: Palgrave Macmillan, 1986), 17–30.

16. L. Israël, *L'Arme du droit* (Paris: Presses de Sciences Po, 2009).

17. For more detail on this, see chapter 9 on legal discrimination by capillary-like action.

18. S. Hennette-Vauchez and V. Valentin, *L'affaire Baby Loup ou la nouvelle laïcité* (Issy-les-Moulineaux: LGDJ-Lextenso éditions, 2015).

19. "Conseil d'État, 5ème–6ème chambres réunies, 12/02/2020, 418299," République Française, https://www.legifrance.gouv.fr/affichJuriAdmin.do?idTexte =CETATEXT000041569373.

20. On this point, see M. Fernando, *The Republic Unsettled: Muslim French and the Contradictions of Secularism* (London: Duke University Press, 2014).

CONCLUSION. Against Islamophobic Hegemony

1. Facebook page for le Rassemblement national de Bourgogne France-Comté, https://m.facebook.com/RassemblementNationalBFC/photos/a.725052681227884 /904960996570384?type=3&sfns=mo.

2. "La droite salue le 'courage' de Blanquer sur le voile," *L'Obs*, 14 October 2019, https://www.nouvelobs.com/politique/20191014.OBS19743/la-droite-salue-le-courage-de -blanquer-sur-le-voile.html.

3. "Cette folle semaine où un élu RN, Julien Odoul, a relancé la chasse au voile," *L'Obs*, 18 October 2019, https://www.nouvelobs.com/politique/20191018.OBS20000/cette-folle -semaine-ou-un-elu-rn-julien-odoul-a-relance-la-chasse-au-voile.html.

4. "Le journaliste Olivier Galzi compare le voile aux 'uniformes SS' sur LCI," *L'Obs*, 17 October 2019, https://www.nouvelobs.com/societe/20191017.OBS19931/le-journaliste -olivier-galzi-compare-le-voile-aux-uniformes-ss-sur-lci.html.

5. "Cette folle semaine."

6. Robin Andraca, "Une semaine sur les chaînes d'info: 85 débats sur le voile, 286 invitations et 0 femme voilée," *Libération*, 17 October 2019, https://www.liberation.fr/checknews /2019/10/17/une-semaine-sur-les-chaines-d-info-85-debats-sur-le-voile-286-invitations-et-0 -femme-voilee_1758162.

7. In terms of the national print press, *Le Figaro*, *Causeur*, *Valeurs actuelles*, *Le Point*, or *Marianne* play crucial roles in broadcasting and popularizing Isamophobic theories, as do 24/7 tv news channels *LCI*, *C'NEWS*, and *BFM TV*.

8. "'La Gauche doit reconquérir les valeurs de la Nation et de la République' entretien avec Laurent Bouvet, professeur à Sciences-po Paris," *Novo Press*, 16 December 2011, https://fr.novopress.info/104790/la-gauche-doit-reconquerir-les-valeurs-de-la-nation-et-de-la-republique-entretien-avec-laurent-bouvet-professeur-a-sciences-po-paris-audio/.

9. "Patrick Kessel, président d'honneur du Comité Laïcité République," *Riposte Laïque*, 19 January 2009, https://ripostelaique.com/Patrick-Kessel-president-d-honneur.html.

10. See A. Hajjat, "L'emprise de *Valeurs actuelles*," *Carnet de recherche Racismes*, 13 November 2020, https://racismes.hypotheses.org/222.

11. Geoffroy Lejeune, Louis de Raguenel, Tugdual Denis, "Communautarisme: 'C'est un énorme problème pour nous,' reconnaît Emmanuel Macron," *Valeurs*, 30 October 2019, https://www.valeursactuelles.com/clubvaleurs/politique/communautarisme-cest-un-enorme-probleme-pour-nous-reconnait-emmanuel-macron-112307.

12. Pauline Moullot and Anaïs Condomines, "L'élu RN Julien Odoul a-t-il été piégé par Fatima E., comme l'a affirmé Macron dans 'Valeurs actuelles'?," *Libération*, 5 November 2019, https://www.liberation.fr/checknews/2019/11/05/l-elu-rn-julien-odoul-a-t-il-ete-piege-par-fatima-e-comme-l-a-affirme-macron-dans-valeurs-actuelles_1761427.

13. Alain Bertho, "L'État a-t-il le monopole du complotisme légitime," *Regards.fr*, 4 December 2020, http://www.regards.fr/idees-culture/article/l-etat-a-t-il-le-monopole-du-complotisme-legitime.

14. C. Donnet, "Les signalements pour 'risque de radicalization' dans les établissements scolaires en France, nouvel outil de régulation de l'islam," *Déviance et Société* 3, no. 3 (2020), 420–452.

15. "Christophe Castaner liste les signes de radicalisation? 'Vous avez une barbe vous-même,' lui répond un député," *Europe1*, 9 October 2019, https://www.europe1.fr/politique/christophe-castaner-liste-les-signes-de-radicalisation-religieuse-vous-avez-une-barbe-vous-meme-lui-repond-un-depute-3924324.

16. Kepel uses the term Islamization without inverted commas, uncritically and without contextualization in his 2012 essay *Quatre-vingt-treize* (Paris: Gallimard). For a critique of his obsessions, the reader should refer to V. Geisser (G. Kepel, "Gilles Kepel hanté par l'islamisation de la France," *Orient XXI* [2016], https://orientxxi.info/lu-vu-entendu/gilles-kepel-hante-par-l-islamisation-de-la-france,1149).

17. H. Esmili, "Les nouveaux faussaires: Le Maître, l'Établi et l'Aspirant," *Contretemps*, 6 June 2020, https://www.contretemps.eu/nouveaux-faussaires-maitre-etabli-aspirant/.

18. "Idées toutes faites sur 'les territoires conquis de l'islamisme,'" *Orient XXI*, 10 February 2020, https://orientxxi.info/lu-vu-entendu/idees-toutes-faites-sur-les-territoires-conquis-de-l-islamisme,3618.

19. "Projet de loi no. 3649 confortant le respect des principes de la République," Assemblée Nationale, 4 October 1958, https://www.assemblee-nationale.fr/dyn/15/textes/l15b3649_projet-loi.

20. A préfet is a state representative in a department or region, responsible to the minister of the interior.

21. See A. Hajjat, "Statistiques de l'islamophobie: Misère du journalisme mensonger," *Club de Mediapart*, 26 February 2015, https://blogs.mediapart.fr/abdellali-hajjat/blog/260215/statistiques-de-lIslamophobia-misere-du-journalisme-mensonger.

22. C. Torrekens, "Islamo-gauchisme," *La Revue Nouvelle*, no. 5 (22 November 2020), 54–58.

23. T. Peace, *European Social Movements and Muslim Activism: Another World but with Whom?* (Basingstoke: Palgrave Macmillan, 2015).

24. "Université: Censurer au nom de la liberté d'expression," *Carnet de recherche Racismes*, 4 November 2020, https://racismes.hypotheses.org/209.

25. F. Truong, *Loyautés radicales: L'islam et les "mauvais garçons" de la Nation* (Paris: La Découverte, 2017).

26. L. Bonelli and F. Carrié, *La fabrique de la radicalité: Une sociologie des jeunes djihadistes français* (Paris: Seuil, 2018).

27. S. Montassir, *L'Etat et la révolution: Discours et contre-discours du jihad : Irak, Syrie, France* (Saint-Denis: Université Paris 8, 2020).